安乐哲比较儒学哲学关键词

温海明 路则权 主编

华夏出版社
HUAXIA PUBLISHING HOUSE

图书在版编目（CIP）数据

安乐哲比较儒学哲学关键词 / 温海明，路则权主编．－－北京：华夏出版社有限公司，2021.10
ISBN 978-7-5222-0160-3

Ⅰ．①安… Ⅱ．①温… ②路… Ⅲ．①安乐哲－儒学－思想评论 ②安乐哲－比较哲学－研究 Ⅳ．① B222.05 ② B712.6

中国版本图书馆 CIP 数据核字（2021）第 155296 号

安乐哲比较儒学哲学关键词

主　　编	温海明　路则权
责任编辑	董秀娟
装帧设计	中文天地
责任印制	周　然

出版发行	华夏出版社有限公司
经　　销	新华书店
印　　装	三河市少明印务有限公司
版　　次	2021 年 10 月北京第 1 版　　2021 年 10 月北京第 1 次印刷
开　　本	720×1030　1/16
印　　张	22
字　　数	360 千字
定　　价	88.00 元

华夏出版社有限公司
地址：北京市东直门外香河园北里 4 号　　邮编：100028
网址：www.hxph.com.cn　　电话：（010）64663331（转）
若发现本版图书有印装质量问题，请与我社营销中心联系调换。

"儒学大家、泰山学者工程专项经费资助"

主　编　温海明　路则权
副主编　关　欣　韩　盟

编写说明

安乐哲先生是当代中西比较哲学大家,长期致力于推进中西哲学对话,翻译过《论语》《中庸》《孝经》《孙子兵法》等中国传统哲学的重要经典,并有一系列相关著作对中国哲学问题展开深入研究。他强调,要用一套有特色的英文词汇来分析和理解中国哲学思想,尤其是先秦儒家哲学。近年来,他特别提倡"儒家角色伦理学",致力于向西方世界推介中国哲学、思想和文化,并作出了重要贡献,获聘山东省"儒学大家",并获得"孔子文化奖"、国家"友谊奖"等重要荣誉称号。

安先生对中国哲学的重要概念都有他独特的理解和翻译,所以他的关键术语词汇表相比之前的译文可以说非常有特色。作为一本儒学比较哲学关键术语词典,本书选取了20世纪80年代以来安先生十本有代表性的哲学著作中的关键词汇,将英文原著与中译本中对应内容一并摘录。本书的编辑初衷是帮助学习儒学和中国哲学与文化的学生和研究者们,来系统了解安乐哲先生的初衷和策略,并期待能够为有意了解安乐哲先生哲学研究工作的读者提供索引,同时亦为对中西哲学感兴趣的普通读者提供方便。

本书的编辑工作始于2019年春夏之交,在安乐哲先生亲自指导下,由"泰山学者"、尼山世界儒学中心孔子研究院特聘专家、中国人民大学温海明教授和尼山世界儒学中心孔子研究院副研究员、"尼山学者"、孔子研究院海外儒学研究与传播中心副主任路则权召集,安乐哲"儒学大家"团队在中国人民大学哲学院会议室筹备了第一次会议,基本敲定了本书的编辑体例、摘录词条范围。随后由孔子研究院路则权、张海涛、黄星、刘文剑,以及中国人民大学哲学院硕士生关欣、尹海洋、陈迪芳等共同参与完成了初步的词条摘录和初稿编辑工作。2020年夏，疫情初缓之际，温海明教授带领中国人民大学哲学院学生关欣、尹海洋、秦凯丽、赵晨、黄天夷、李占科、韩盟、郑鹤杨、钱玉玺、寇哲明（Benjamin Coles）、任寒山（Carson Ramsdell）以及孔子研究院黄星等人在曲阜慎修书院集中完成对初稿的编辑和校对工作。在此过程中，温海明教授对词典编定工作做了总体安排，关欣负责整体的修订工作。

本书从筹备到出版，前后历时两年之久，关欣从中国人民大学哲学院的硕士生，成为北京大学哲学系的博士生。师生们在编辑过程中，也遇到了一些问题，如安乐哲先生对个别关键词（比如"仁"）的翻译在不同时期有所变化，有些中译本和对应英文原著内容有所不同，原文脚注保留与否等。总体上，师生们秉持着不增减原文内容的基本原则，在摘录时尽量保证摘录内容的连贯性；另考虑到词典编辑的整体性，在编校时对少部分摘录内容的格式、语法等做了细微调整；同时，考虑到阅读时中英文对照的排版要求，隐去了原文脚注，对此读者如有需要可根据标注的原书页码自行查阅，亦不失便利。

从关键词选取、确定体例到文本校对，安乐哲先生对本书的编辑工作提供了具体的指导和帮助。因为有安先生的支持，本书的编辑和出版才得以展开。虽然所选内容可能存在部分未尽善之处，但是我们由衷地希望本书能够不负期许，为有心的读者指出一条了解安乐哲先生比较哲学思想、深入学习中西比较哲学，以及从事思想和文化比较研究的入门路径。我们也希望更多的人能够通过本书关注到儒学在当今时代所具有的世界性的重要意义，关注到新时代中国哲学在与西方哲学对话过程中的创新和发展。

编者
2021年6月

目 录
CONTENTS

编写说明

主 题 词

    人   Human Becomings ··· 1

    天   *Tian* ··· 2

    天人合一   The Continuity and Interdependence Between *Tian* and the Human Being (*tianren heyi*) ······································· 10

形 上 学

    道   *Dao* ··· 17

    本   Root (*Ben*) ··· 28

    理   *Li* ··· 32

    帝   *Di* ··· 36

    天命   *Tianming* ··· 42

    诚   Creativity (*Cheng*) ·· 57

    气   *Qi* ··· 64

    阴阳   *Yin & Yang* ·· 65

    神   Spirits/Gods ··· 69

    几   *Ji* ··· 70

    变通 / 易   The Perpetual Interface Between Flux and Persistence (*Biantong/Yi*) ·· 73

| 混沌 | Hundun | 76 |
| 自然 | Spontaneously so | 78 |

伦理学

德	De	84
性	Xing	92
仁	Authoritative Person & Consummate Person / Conduct (Ren)	95
义	Appropriate (Yi)	101
利	Profit (Li)	118
礼	Observing Ritual Propriety	120
乐	Enjoyment/Music	123
耻	Shame (ch'ih)	128
信	Living Up to One's Word (hsin*)	135
教	Education	140
孝	Family Reverence (Xiao)	145
谏	Remonstrance (Jian)	147
伦	Lun	153
直	True Person	154
家	Family	157
爱	Loving (Ai)	164
四端	Four Inklings (siduan)	165
忠	Doing One's Best (Chung)	173
恕	Shu	176
善	Felicity/Efficacy	194
友	Friendship	195

认识论

| 智/知 | To Realize (Zhi) | 207 |

物	Things	216
名	*Ming*	217
象	Image (*Xiang*)	219
心	Heart-and-mind (*Xin*)	221
精神	Spirit (*Jingshen*)	224
身/体	Body	226

政 治 哲 学

政	Effecting Sociopolitical Order (*Cheng*)	229
正名	The Ordering of Names (*Cheng Ming*)	231
民	*Min*	248
无为	*Wu-wei*	253
法	Laws (*Fa*)	259
势	*Shih*	262

修 养 论

小人	Small Person	267
君子	Exemplary Person	269
圣/圣人	Sage/Sagacity	283
学	Learning	297
中/中庸	Centering / Equilibrium / Focus / Balance	299
和	Harmony	305
无欲	Objectless Desire	307
物化	Transformation of Things (*Wu Hua*)	318
真人	*Chen Jen*	326

参 考 书 目 ·································· 339

主题词

人

此世界的"人"(human being)不可避免是一"〔生〕成〔着的〕人"(human becoming)。

(《生民之本:〈孝经〉的哲学诠释及英译》,第83页)

个性在西方社会中是作为创造性和独创力的标志而受到珍视的;在中国,个性发展的目标则关涉通过实现个体之间共享的整体情感获得彼此信赖。

(《通过孔子而思》,第25页)

从人类作为独立、分离的自我无限扩展的意义之中心的角度思考,人就是"自我"与"他者"、"我"与"我们"、"主体"与"客体"、"此刻"与"彼时"之间不可分割的连续统一体。

(《通过孔子而思》,第140页)

Human Becomings

Indeed, a human being in this world is irreducibly a "human becoming."
(*The Chinese Classic of Family Reverence: A Philosophical Translation of the Xiaojing*, p. 65)

Difference is prized in Western societies as a mark of creativity and originality, while in China the goal of personality development involves the achievement of interdependence through the actualization of integrative emotions held in common among individuals.
(*Thinking Through Confucius*, p. 23)

Reflecting on the human being as a focus of meaning unbounded by a notion of discrete and discontinuous selfhood, person is then an indivisible continuum between "self" and "other," between "I" and "we," between "subject" and "object," between "now" and "then."
(*Thinking Through Confucius*, p. 119)

每个（儒）人都是独一无二的，而通过那些使其独特突出的诸重要关系的培养，他们当然会逐渐更个人化。但这些人是角色人（roles-bearers）而非权利人（rights-bearers）；他们的自由并非在独立（being independent）的意义上，因为他们的生活无法避免与许多其他人的生活密切交织着。他们也并非自主，因为他们所做或能做的事情极少与其他人的生活没有关系。换句话说，儒家是关系性自我（relational selves）。我们是孩子、姊妹、父母、邻居、朋友、学生、同事、爱人等等。当我们生活（live）——而非扮演（play）——的所有这些特定角色全部表达出来，其相互链接也很清楚时，我们每个人就都会独一无二被确定为一个人，则无法再去拼凑出一个纯然自主个体自我的人。

（《生民之本：〈孝经〉的哲学诠释及英译》，第 38 页）

Each Confucian person is unique, and of course becomes increasingly individuated through the cultivation of significant relations that make him or her distinctive and distinguished. But such persons are roles bearers rather than rights bearers; they are not free in the sense of being independent, for their lives are intimately and inextricably bound up with the lives of many others. And they are not autonomous, for there is little that they do, or can do, that does not have significance for the lives of those others. Confucian persons, in other words, are relational selves. We are children, siblings, parents, neighbors, friends, students, colleagues, lovers, and much more. When all of the specific roles we live—not "play"—have been inventoried, and their interconnections made clear, then each of us has been uniquely specified as a person with precious little left over to piece together a bare, autonomous, individual self.

(*The Chinese Classic of Family Reverence: A Philosophical Translation of the Xiaojing*, pp. 31-32)

天

Tian

对于"天"这个词，我们打算采用音译。这在很大程度上是因为，

Tian is a term that we have chosen not to translate, largely because we believe

通常所用的英文译法"Heaven"，为之强加了若干中国文化没有的，源自耶稣—基督传统的意象；而"Nature"也同样不可取。在很多语境中，单独使用的"天"字实际上是在指代"天地"——它暗示"天"并不是独立于世的。《圣经》中的上帝常常被转喻为创世之"Heaven"，而文言文中的"天"即是世界。

"天"既包含有世界是什么之意，又隐喻了世界如何为之的反思。"万物"是中国人指代所有客观事物的成语。但是，万物并不是独立于秩序世界之外的"天"的创造物；恰恰相反，万物构成了"天"。"天"既是造物者，又是滋养创造物的沃土。在秩序本身及其规定性之间并不存在严格的界限。正是因为超秩序的缺失，道家之"道"和佛教的 dharma 这两个概念才颇具相似性；而且二者都曾经提及具体现象和从中总结出来的规律。

因此，"天"应该是一种从其自身组成成分中抽绎出来的、自在自现的秩序。但是，"天"并不仅仅是"事物"；它是一种活生生的文化——发生、流传，直至成为人类社会中不可替代的元素。"天"是

its normal English rendering as "Heaven" cannot but conjure up images derived from the Judeo-Christian tradition that are not to be found in China; and "Nature" will not work either. In the first place, *tian* is often used alone to render *tiandi* 天地 —"the heavens and the earth"—suggesting that *tian* is not independent of this world. The God of the Bible, often referred to as metonymically "Heaven," *created* the world, but *tian* in classical Chinese *is* the world.

Tian is both *what* our world is and *how* it is. The "ten thousand things (*wanwu* 萬物)," an expression for "everything," are not the creatures of a *tian* which is independent of what is ordered; rather, they are constitutive of it. *Tian* is both the creator and the field of creatures. There is no apparent distinction between the order itself, and what orders it. This absence of superordination is a condition made familiar in related notions of the Daoist *dao* and the Buddhist *dharma* which at once reference concrete phenomena and the order that obtains among them.

On this basis, *tian* can be described as an inhering, emergent order negotiated out of the dispositioning of the particulars that are constitutive of it. But *tian* is not just "things"; it is a living culture—crafted, transmitted, and now resident in a human community. *Tian* is anthropomorphic, suggesting its intimate relationship with the process of euhemerization—historical human beings

一个神、人同形同性的概念。这种性质揭示出它与"神话即历史"的观念的密切联系——历史人物被尊崇为神灵——此即中国人祖先崇拜的渊源。很可能,正是祖先崇拜这个共同基础,使得商代的人文化的"帝",与盘踞于黄河谷地的如罗马人一般嗜血好战的周人所拜的"天"相融合。……由于并不存在什么超然的造物主作为真、善、美的源泉,"天"似乎是一种聚焦于前人精神的,经年叠累而成就的文化遗产。因而,当我们发现在这种文化中,神话、理性和历史的纷繁关系与西方传统迥然不同时,并不感到丝毫诧异。诸如周公和孔子这样的重要文化人物常常被神化为"天";而"天"本身也在与人合一的过程中具体化为上述人物。

不言不语的"天"通过神谕、反常的气候现象和自然条件的改变等方式与人类进行有效的、但意图并不总是那么明确的交流。"天"由此进入人类社会的话语系统——并且成为其中最为重要的元素。儒家世界中的各种秩序相互依存,相互影响、一荣俱荣、一损俱损。人文社会的衰败紊乱将会波及自然环境。

becoming gods—that grounds Chinese ancestor reverence. It is probably this common foundation in ancestor reverence that allowed for the conflation of the culturally sophisticated Shang dynasty's *di* 帝 (ancestral spirits) with the notion of *tian* associated with the Zhou tribes, militant and Romanesque, who conquered the Yellow River valley….In the absence of some transcendent creator deity as the repository of truth, beauty and goodness, *tian* would seem to stand for a cumulative and continuing cultural legacy focused in the spirits of those who have come before. It is not surprising, then, that the relationship between *mythos*, *logos*, and *historia* is radically different from the Western tradition. Culturally significant human beings—persons such as the Duke of Zhou and Confucius—are "theomorphized" to become *tian*, and *tian* is itself made anthropomorphic and determinate in their persons.

Finally, *tian* does not speak, but communicates effectively although not always clearly through oracles, through perturbations in the climate, and through alterations in the natural conditions of the human world. *Tian* participates in a discourse shared by the human community—at least by the most worthy among them. Given the interrelatedness and interdependency of the orders defining the Confucian world, what affects one, affects all. A failure of order in the human world will symbiotically be reflected in the natural environment. Although *tian*

尽管"天"不是耶稣—基督文化传统中的那种回应个人需要的人格神，但是作为祖先的集合体，"天"毫不偏颇地护佑其子嗣尽可能地在所有方面实现和谐圆满。也就是说，"天"不是先验的，而是尽心尽责地服务于子孙后代。对此，《尚书》早已明言曰："天聪明，自我民聪明。"

（《〈论语〉的哲学诠释》，第47—48页）

"天"是一个我们不打算翻译的术语。作为其惯常的英文翻译，"Heaven"只是变幻出了我们犹太—基督教传统的令人误解的联想而已。那些神学的联想多半与中国的经验无关，却常常给中国文化的各种实践附加书写了一些与其自身相异的预设（presuppositions）。无论如何，如果我们能够发展一种对于"天"的理解的话，我们必须将这个术语从那些不幸的联想中解救出来。

首先，"天"常常被用作"天地"的简称，这一点说明，"天"与这个世界不是彼此独立的。"天"指示着我们周遭运行着的世界，它无穷无尽、不断进展、始终处在更新

is not the "personal" deity responsive to individual needs as found in the Judeo-Christian worldview, as aggregate ancestor it would seem that *tian* functions impartially on behalf of its progeny to maximize the possibilities of emergent harmony at all levels. That *tian* is not transcendental, but indeed functions on behalf of its progeny, is seen clearly in the *Book of Documents*: "*Tian* hears and sees as the people hear and see."

(*The Analects of Confucius: A Philosophical Translation,* pp. 46-48)

Tian is a term we choose not to translate. Its conventional English rendering as "Heaven" cannot but conjure up misleading associations drawn from our Judeo-Christian tradition. These theological associations are largely irrelevant to the Chinese experience but, nonetheless, have often overwritten Chinese cultural practices with presuppositions that are alien to them. In any case, we must extricate the term from these unfortunate associations if we are to develop an understanding of *tian*.

In the first place, *tian* is often used as an abbreviation for *tiandi* 天地 —"the heavens and the earth"—suggesting that *tian* is not independent of this world. Denoting the world as it turns around us, it is bottomless, ever advancing, and always novel. As

之中。正如《中庸》第二十六章所描述的：

> 天地之道，可一言而尽也："其为物不贰，则其生物不测。"
>
> 天地之道，博也，厚也，高也，明也，悠也，久也。

《圣经》中的"God"（上帝），通常转喻为"Heaven"。"God"或"Heaven"创造了（created）世界。但是，古代中国的"天"，却不是世界的创造者，而就是（is）世界。"天"既是我们的世界之所是（*what* our world is），同时又是我们的世界之如何是（*how* our world is）。万事万物不是独立于其所制序（ordering）之外的一个"天"的受造物（creatures）。"天"既是"一"也是"多"。它既是各种过程和事件从中产生的单一的根源，又是由这些过程和事物构成的多种价值的场域（multivalent field）。

在此基础上，"天"可以被描述为由各个特定个体的各种倾向协调而出的必然发生的秩序（emergent order）。此外，"天"不只是自然世

described in *Zhongyong* 26:

> The way of heaven and earth can be captured in one phrase: Since events are never duplicated, their production is unfathomable.
>
> The way of heaven and earth is broad, is thick, is high, is brilliant, is far-reaching, is enduring.

The God of the Bible, often referred to metonymically as "Heaven," *created* the world, but *tian* in classical Chinese *is* the world. *Tian* is both *what* our world is and *how* it is. The "ten thousand processes and events (*wanwu* 萬物)" are not the creatures of a *tian* that is independent of what is ordered; rather, they are constitutive of it. *Tian* is both one and many. It is both the single source from which processes and events emerge, and the multivalent field constituted by them.

On this basis, *tian* can be described as the emergent orders negotiated out of the dispositions of the many particulars that are presently constitutive of it. Moreover, *tian* is not just the natural world, independent of human artifice. Rather, *tian* is a living, cumulative artifact, inclusive of nature and nurture that is not only inseparable from the human experience but is in an important degree expressive of it. It is created and

界,独立于人工。毋宁说,"天"是活生生的、累积性的人工产物。既包括自然,也包括人对它的养育。那种养育不但与人类经验不可分离,同时也在相当程度上恰恰是人类经验的表达。它是在一个特定的人类社群内部得以创造和传播的。

"天"常常是被人化的,这一点提示着它与一种独特的中国的神话即历史观(euhemerization)的密切关系。这种神话即历史观是基于祖先崇拜的。或许正是这种基于祖先崇拜的共同基础,说明了具有文化复杂性的商代的"帝"观念与周人"天"观念的合并。大约在公元前的第一个千年周人的部落征服了黄河流域。有很多很好的理由假定,对于中国"神灵"大体上都是已逝的祖先这样一种主张来说,"天"也并非例外。在缺乏某种超越的创造者(transcendent creator)的情况下,"天"可以被认为是代表着一种累积和持续的文化遗产,这种文化遗产由那些先人的神灵所聚焦。

"天"不说话,但是,通过人制的甲骨、气候的紊乱以及使人类世界境域化的自然条件的改变等,它却能够有效地与人进行沟通和交流。

transmitted within a particular human community.

Tian is often anthropomorphized, suggesting its intimate relationship with a distinctly Chinese version of euhemerization that grounds ancestor reverence. It is probably this common foundation in ancestor reverence that allowed for the conflation of the culturally sophisticated Shang dynasty's *di* 帝 (ancestral spirits) with the notion of *tian* associated with the Zhou federation of tribes who conquered the Yellow River valley at the turn of the first millennium BCE. There are good reasons to assume that *tian* is not an exception to the claim that Chinese gods are, by and large, dead people. In the absence of some transcendent creator, *tian* would seem to stand for a cumulative and continuing cultural legacy focused by the spirits of those who have come before.

Tian does not speak but communicates effectively, although not always clearly, through human-generated oracles, through perturbations in the climate, and through alterations in the natural conditions that contextualize the human world. *Tian* participates in a discourse shared by the most worthy persons in the human community. Given the interrelatedness and interdependency of the orders defining the Confucian world,

"天"参与着为人类社群中最为贤德的人们所共享的话语。鉴于界定儒学世界的各种秩序的关联性和相互依赖性，影响一件事物的东西同时也影响着所有的事物。有这样一种假定：人类世界的秩序的失败也会在自然世界中得到反映。

（《切中伦常：〈中庸〉的新诠与新译》，第97—99页）

古典中国传统总体上表现出借助内在和自然概念解释存在的浓厚兴趣。这类概念不会发展那些打算解释宇宙本身发生的理论。现象就是"so of themselves"——自然。即便偶然有对起源理论的指涉也暗蔽在对转化更为突出的探讨中。上面所引《论语·阳货》（天何言哉？四时行焉，百物生焉）即是明证。就此，"天"就不是一个生成了独立于自己的世界的先在创造性原理。它更确切地说是一个自然产生的现象世界的总称。"天"完全是内在的，所有建构它的成分都不会独立于它而存在。说现象"创造""天"和"天"创造现象都同样正确。因此，"天"和现象的关系是一种彼此依存的关系。"天"的意义和价值是

what affects one affects all. It is assumed that a failure of order in the human world will be reflected in the natural environment.

(*Focusing the Familiar: A Translation and Philosophical Interpretation of the Zhongyong,* pp. 79-80)

The classical Chinese tradition generally evidences a strong interest in explaining existence by reference to immanental and naturalistic concepts. Such concepts preclude the development of theories that propose to explain the origin and birth of the cosmos per se. Phenomena are *tzu-jan* 自然: "so of themselves." The only occasional references to theories of genesis are eclipsed by the far more prominent discussions of transformation. The passage from the *Analects* (17.19) cited above ("What does *t'ien* have to say? And yet the four seasons turn and the myriad things are born and grow within it.") is a case in point. In this context, *t'ien* is not a preexisting creative principle which gives birth to and nurtures a world independent of itself. *T'ien* is rather a general designation for the phenomenal world as it emerges of its own accord. *T'ien* is wholly immanent, having no existence independent of the calculus of phenomena that constitute it. There is as much validity in asserting that phenomena "create" *t'ien* as in saying that

其种种现象意义和价值的一个功能。"天"的秩序由彼此相关的成分之间获得的和谐来表达。

中国古代封建结构使之成为最终主宰化身的"天"的形象与我们将之解释为宇宙论整体的"天"并非不一致。"天"作为其代理人——"天子"的始祖与其子孙后代有着内在的关系。生身之父活着是儿子的楷模，死后亦对其眷顾和保护。而子辈则成为祖先精神的化身和延续。他们彼此关联，彼此诠释。"天"作为统治者与他的"帝国"有种比拟关系，统治者就是他的"帝国"（或其"命"），而"帝国"也正是统治者。

（《通过孔子而思》，第255—256页）

"天"作为规定中国人的精神性的核心观念，不能解释为一个超越的范畴，……〔这一观念的〕英文翻译，如"Heaven"、"Providence"（意为天意、天命、天公、上帝），或"God"（意为上帝）显然会造成误解。现在我们要进而讨论"道"，它对于理解中国人的感悟方式同样极其重要。我们将会发现，它与

t'ien creates phenomena; the relationship between *t'ien* and phenomena, therefore, is one of interdependence. The meaning and value of *t'ien* is a function of the meaning and value of its many phenomena, and the order of *t'ien* is expressed in the harmony that obtains among its correlative parts.

The projection of the classical Chinese feudal structure on to *t'ien*, making it the ultimate ruler, is not inconsistent with our explanation of *t'ien* as the cosmological whole. *T'ien* as primitive ancestor of his deputy, the "son of *t'ien*," has an intrinsic relationship with his progeny. The father is the source and model of the son in life, and his counsel and guardian in death. The offspring, for his part, is the psychophysical embodiment and continuation of his progenitor. They are correlatives, requiring each other for explanation. *T'ien* as ruler has an analogous relationship with his empire. The ruler *is* his "empire" (or "command"), and the "empire" *is* the ruler.

(*Thinking Through Confucius*, pp. 206-207)

Tian, a central notion in defining Chinese spirituality, is not to be interpreted as a transcendent category.... English translations such as "Heaven," "Providence," or "God" are decidedly misleading. We shall now proceed to a discussion of *dao* 道, an equally fundamental notion for the understanding

"天"一样,也必须解释为明显非超越的观念。此外,在西方寻找与中国的精神性相当的东西将引导我们聚焦于西方的神秘主义传统,虽然我们对这一点将不加详述。这是因为,就像我们在前面所说,有很好的理由相信,神秘体验本身从根本上说是非超越的。

(《汉哲学思维的文化探源》,第252页)

天人合一

伏羲、神农所实践的是一种"域境化"做法,即有效地实现、将人类经验与自然运行过程视作同一域境,且使其相合,努力将宇宙的可用性创造潜能,利用到最好程度——伏羲、神农在对《易经》一套深邃卦象的建构之中,耕种出一种"文化"与"自然"之间厚重的不分性。这是一种被体悟到的人的经验与自然促使文化间相互对接的和谐性,这种和谐状态显明地表达于对这一关系特点的描述性用语中,

of the Chinese sensibility. We shall find that this notion, as well as *tian*, must be interpreted as distinctly nontranscendent. Further, though we shall not elaborate this point in any great detail, a search for Western counterparts to Chinese spirituality would lead to a focus upon the tradition of mysticism in the West. For, as we discussed above, there is good reason to believe that mystical experience is itself fundamentally nontranscendent.

(*Thinking from the Han*, p. 244)

The Continuity and Interdependence Between *Tian* and the Human Being (*tianren heyi*)

By their efforts at *ars contextualis*— the art of effectively contextualizing and coordinating the experience of the human being within the processes of nature in an effort to optimize the creative possibilities of the cosmos— Fu Xi and Shen Nong cultivated a thick continuity between "nurture" and "nature" expressed in the evocative images that constitute the *Yijing*. This perceived resonance between the human experience and the natural and cultural forum in which it occurs is made explicit in expressions that have come to characterize the relationship, such as "the

如"天人合一"(宗教性、自然、文化的域境与人经验的不分性)、"天人相应"或"天人感应"(精神领域与人经验的相互照应——不分)。值得注意,这种用语所表示的,是人类经验方面延续不分的共生相互性,而不是世界中两个原本分立不连的方面后有的结合性。人类的修养不是把世界与人类经验作为两件分立的事物而使它们结合在一起,而是让同属经验的两个本身不可分的部分,由于生态连续性(也即"我与我的世界")而更深度、紧密地相合。

(《儒家角色伦理学:一套特色伦理学词汇》,第 64 页)

其实,在这样的儒家传统之中,有一种从"为仁"向着一种以人为中心"宗教感"的直接通道,可作为对人格修养最高的表述。儒家"宗教感",也即获得价值感和人格归属感的那种强烈意义,在充满意义的人与人关系交融成长之中,油然而生;当家庭与社会成员都诚心诚意渴望在其与他人关系之上奉献自己之时,它是那种"精神",是人们为一种被激发的灵感而活着。

continuity between the religious, natural, and cultural context, and the human experience" (*tianren heyi* 天人合一), and the "mutual responsiveness of the numinous context and the human experience" (*tianren xiangying* 天人相應 or *tianren ganying* 天人感應). It is important to note that such expressions report on the continuing symbiotic mutuality of these dimensions of experience rather than on the reconciliation of two originally separate aspects of the world after the fact. Personal cultivation is not the bringing together and the "uniting" of the world and human experience, but is rather the deepening and intensifying of the productive continuities that conjoin two inseparable aspects of experience, that is, oneself and one's world.

(*Confucian Role Ethics: A Vocabulary*. pp. 53-54)

Indeed, in this Confucian tradition, there is a direct corridor from the achieved consummate life to a human-centered religiousness as the highest expression of personal cultivation. Confucian religiousness—the powerful sense of achieved worth and personal belonging that arises from the concerted growth of meaningful relations—is the *spirituality* achieved when members of family and community *aspire* to contribute themselves utterly in their relations with others, and thus live *inspired* lives. Such religiousness is itself

这种"宗教感"本身,是家庭兴旺、社会繁荣的源泉,也是它的效果。具有这样"宗教感"的生活也是社会生活品质的直接效果。换句话说,人倾向聚群的"宗教性"不仅是社会幸福生活之"本"和幸福社会发达成长的"种子",而且最重要的,它是成熟果实、光彩四射的花朵。人的修身与人的精神性,二者的共生协同,生动地蕴含在常用语言之中。这种语言也常是研究"中国宗教感"的学者,将儒家传统的家国忠孝,与亚布拉罕传统的崇拜上帝,进行区分而启用的。也就是说,"天人合一"即儒家传统的"宗教感"的特质。

(《儒家角色伦理学:一套特色伦理学词汇》,第104—105页)

"天人合一"(自然与文化域境,同人的经验之间互系不分)——这个流行成语的基本意义是阐述儒家宗教感的意识,讲的也是与"潜能"同一的道理。人是受文化的陶冶才成仁的,成仁的生活才可成为文化资源,才能使人成仁具有可能。"潜能"是在这样孜孜追求的人与富于灵感的世界协同合力中萌发的。

the source and product of the flourishing family and community, and the quality of this religious life is a direct consequence of the quality of communal living. Said another way, religiosity is not only the root of the flourishing community and the seed from which it grows, but is most importantly its mature fruit, its radiant flower. The synergy between personal cultivation and the numinous is captured in the familiar mantra that is often appealed to by students of Chinese religiousness in distinguishing Confucian familial and communal reverence from Abrahamic God-inspired worship: That is, Confucian religiousness is characterized by "the symbiotic continuity between the natural and cultural context and the human experience" (*tianren heyi* 天人合一).

(*Confucian Role Ethics: A Vocabulary*, p. 92)

The basic significance of the mantra, "the continuity between the natural and cultural context, and the human experience" (*tianren heyi* 天人合一) that is invoked to describe the Confucian religious sensibility is making this same point about potential. It is the person nourished by culture who becomes consummately human, and it is the life of the consummate human who contributes to the cultural resources that make a consummate humanity possible. Potentiality emerges in these collaborations between aspiring persons and an inspired world.

(*Confucian Role Ethics: A Vocabulary*, p. 156)

（《儒家角色伦理学：一套特色伦理学词汇》，第174页）

简而言之，自古至今的中国哲学家只认可一种人类经验与自然文化环境之间的不断融合，即所谓"天人合一"。不过，这种融合经常被误解为对自然学科的削弱。它不是被理解为多少主观性东西与客观性东西的相互融合，因而尊重人类社会集体对其所在环境进行有效改造的能力"以及"自然世界对这种人类改造的抵制，而是受到一种信仰的支配，道德的主观性对一个可无限塑造的自然世界具有几乎绝对的改造力量。这样的信仰阻碍我们正确对待一种潜能——自然科学坚持改善人类条件。正是这个原因，"唯意志论"变成了一种简单主观主义，它对需求科学和技术集体努力的真正原因打了折扣，认为是对自然进行"人化"，以建立主观与客观之间的生产力关系。李泽厚认为，这种关系是人类自由的先决条件。

（《儒家角色伦理学：一套特色伦理学词汇》，第293页）

儒家的宗教性产生于这样一个

The argument, simply put, is that Confucian philosophers from classical times have recognized a continuity between the human experience and their natural and cultural context that is captured in the mantra *tianren heyi* 天人合一. The nature of this continuity, however, has often been misunderstood. Instead of being a continuity between what is more or less subjective and more or less objective, respecting both the ability of the collective human community to transform its environment productively and the resistance of the natural world to this human transformation, it has been dominated by the belief that the moral subject holds almost absolute transformative powers over an infinitely malleable natural world. Such a belief has retarded an appreciation of the potential that the natural sciences hold to improve the human condition. As such, this voluntarism has become a kind of raw subjectivism that discounts the real need for collective efforts in science and technology to "humanize" nature in order to establish a productive relationship between subject and object, a relationship that Li Zehou takes to be a precondition for human freedom.

(*Confucian Role Ethics: A Vocabulary*, p. 264)

Confucian religiousness begins from the assumption that there is a continuity and interdependence between *tian* 天,

基本假定：即天人一体，相互依赖。天与特殊的个人之间的关联，经常用"天人合一"的术语加以表达，这一术语被用来概括这一时期的宗教感悟方式。因此，孟子说：

尽其心者，知其性也。知其性，则知天矣。（《孟子·尽心上》）

在儒家经典中，天与道即使不被用以相互替代，也是经常相互联系的。孔子始终认为："人能弘道，非道弘人。"

天人一体、相互依赖表现于源于孟子的、人们熟悉的哲学路线："万物皆备于我。"我们可以对这一主张作以下解释。人作为环境中人（persons-in-context）总是完全处于一定的境况之中，在一个由特定的社会、文化和自然的条件所规定的世界中继承了传统。个人既形成了又形成于他所处的区域，这区域是由事情和事件构成的。在一个特定的情境中，他或她总是开放的，按照母亲、姐妹等等身份以许多不同的方式，被重新规定，从这个意义上说，一个人是易变的，是多值的（multivalent）。通过任何一个这类

conventionally translated as "Heaven," and the human being (ren 人). This correlativity between tian and the particular person is often captured in the claim that tianren heyi 天人合一 (literally, "tian and human beings are continuous")used to summarize religious sensibilities during this period. Hence, the *Mencius* observes:

For a person to realize fully one's heart-and-mind is to realize fully one's nature and character, and in so doing, one realizes *tian*.

Tian and "the way" (*dao* 道) are often associated if not used interchangeably in the classical Confucian corpus. And Confucius insists that "it is the human being who broadens the way, not the way that broadens the human being."

The continuity and interdependence between *tian* and the human being is reflected in the familiar line from the *Mencius*: "All of the myriad things are here in me." We can explain this claim in the following way. Persons are radically situated as persons-in-context, inhering as they do in a world defined by specific social, cultural, and natural conditions. Persons shape and are shaped by the field of things and events in which they reside. A person is fluid and multivalent in the sense that, in any particular situation, he or she is open to redefinition in

身份，个人被置于整体、系统中，并成为诸关系的核心，他既是从扩大了的关系区域内的焦点角度，又是从这种区域内的局部角度，来体现社群。

在这里讲一个类似情况可能是有用的。一部音乐作品中任何一个音符的全部价值，只有通过了解此音符在这个被演奏的整个作品中的地位，才能加以确定。这样，任何一个音符在它当中蕴涵了整个乐谱。这个音符可以说是对种种关系的整个区域的聚焦，这些关系是由诸音乐成分构成的。这里重要的是种种关系的区域不受限制，相反，它是特殊细节的无限的蓄积，并且是始终开放的，能够更多地包容。与此特殊的音符相关的细节的区域可以扩展到包括同一作曲家另一部作品的一个乐章，或他的所有作品，或一个时代的音乐作品，等等。

"环境中的人"像音乐演奏中的特殊音符，是多值的，他从其特殊的角度对人的社会及其自然环境加以聚焦。因此，他们或多或少是重要的，或多或少与整体相联接，或多或少地代表了他们的社群的价值和在文化上的重要性。

many different ways by appeal to the roles of mother, sister, and so on. Articulated and brought into focus in any one of these roles, a person expresses the community from both a focal and a local perspective within the extended field of relationships.

An analogy might help here. The full value of any one note in a musical composition can only be assayed by understanding its place in the entire piece of music as performed. Any one note thus has implicate within it the entire score. That note may be said to focus the entire field of relationships constituted by the compositions. Important here is that the field of relationships is not circumscribed, but an unbounded reservoir of particular detail that remains open and available for further inclusion. The field of relevant detail for the particular note can be extended to include a movement in another piece by the same composer, or his entire corpus, or the musical product of a particular era, and so on.

"Persons-in-context," like the particular note in the musical performance, are multivalent, bringing the human community and its natural surrounds into focus from their particular perspective. As such, they are more or less distinguished, more or less articulated, more or less representative of the values and cultural importances of their communities.

This language of focus and field provides us with a way of talking about the continuity and interdependence of the human being

这种焦点与区域的用语给我们提供了一种方法，据以论述中国人的世界观所规定的天人一体、相互依赖的关系。天是区域，是社会的、文化的和自然的环境，因而从某种意义上说，大于特殊的个人（"天生德于予"），同时又蕴涵和聚焦于特殊的个人（"万物皆备于我"）。正像我们在前面指出的，天经常以拟人的方法被加以描绘。但是这种关系是双向的，反之亦然。人也是似神的。这就是说，当一个人成功地以榜样的方式将文化及其制度聚集于己，当他作为一个他的社群及效法他的后代的典范出现之时，他就通过他们仿效的模式而扩展了自己，从而成为尊崇的对象。因此，按照儒家的语汇，修身扩大了一个人（"大人"），他因而是名副其实地"超尘拔俗"。

（《汉哲学思维的文化探源》，第 271—272 页）

and *tian* presupposed in the Confucian worldview. *Tian* is the field, the social, cultural, and natural context, and is in some sense greater than the particular person ("*Tian* has given life to and nourished excellence in me"), as well as being implicate within and brought into focus by the particular person ("all of the myriad things are here in me"). As we have noted above, *tian* is frequently described in anthropomorphic terms. But the relationship is bidirectional, and works the other way as well. The human being is also theomorphic. That is, when a person is successful in focusing culture and its institutions in a manner that is exemplary, and emerges as a model for his community and future generations to which they defer, he has extended himself through their patterns of deference, and has become the object of reverence. Hence, in the Confucian vocabulary, cultivation enlarges one's person (*da ren* 大人), so that one becomes literally "larger than life."

(*Thinking from the Han,* pp. 263-265)

形上学

道

"道"字由两个部分组成:"辶"意为行走;"首"是指包括头发和眼睛在内的头部,也有最前方之意。"道"字通常通"导"(与"道"同语根)。"导"意为"领导"。"道"字是一个具有动词性、过程性和动态性的重要词语。它最早见于《尚书》开凿沟渠,"疏导"河水,以防决堤的叙述之中。"首"这个元素的存在赋予"道"字"领导",或"引导"之意。

如果我们将"道"首先理解为动词的话,它其他几个引申意义就会自然浮现出来:传导;道路、方法、技术、办法;解释、说、道理。但是,就其本质而言,"道"似乎是指修整道路的工程规划;略作引申,即是修葺平整的通途大路。也正是这一引申,使得"道"常常在翻译中被名词化为"路",但是,

Dao

The character has two elements: *chuo* 辶 "to pass over, " "to go over," "to lead through" (on foot), and *show* 首 , itself a compound literally meaning "head"—hair and eye together—and therefore "foremost." *Dao* is used often as a loan character for its cognate, *dao* 導 , "to lead." Thus the character is significantly verbal, processional, and dynamic. The earliest appearance of *dao* in the *Book of Documents* is in the context of cutting a channel and "leading" a river to prevent the overflowing of its banks. Even the *shou* "head" component has the suggestion of "to lead," or "to give a heading."

Taking the verbal *dao* as primary, its several derived meanings emerge rather naturally: to lead through, and hence, road, path, way, method, art, teachings; to explain, to tell, doctrines. At its most fundamental level, *dao* seems to denote the active project of "road building," and by extension, to connote a road that has been made, and hence can be traveled. It is by this connotation that

我们必须将简单地在道路上旅行和开拓自己的路径这二者明确地区分开来。按照我们的理解,实现"道"的过程,就是用源自某个文化先驱的特定方式去体验、诠释和影响世界,并且同时将这种处世之道发扬光大。上述处世之道恰恰可以为文化承继者们指点迷津。

孔子认为,"道"的最基本的含义是人道,即"为人之道"。诚如《论语》第十五篇第二十九章所言:"人能弘道,非道弘人。"

(《〈论语〉的哲学诠释》,第45—46页)

在"仅仅在路上旅行"以及"开辟自己的旅程"之间,我们必须做出区分。实现"道"就是去经验、去诠释、去影响我们所在的世界,所采取的方式是强化并拓展从我们的文化先驱那里继承而来的生活方式。"道"必然要求对那些来者呈现出真实,以能够被那些来者所信任的方式生活在这个世界之中,在这种意义上,"道"是"真理"。正是由于这个原因,我们通常将"道"翻译为"the proper way"。

对孔子而言,在传统的早期,

dao is so often nominalized in translation ("the Way"), but we must distinguish between simply traveling on a road, and making the journey one's own. In our interpretation, to realize the *dao* is to experience, to interpret, and to influence the world in such a way as to reinforce and extend the way of life inherited from one's cultural predecessors. This way of living in the world then provides a road map and direction for one's cultural successors.

For Confucius, *dao* is primarily *rendao* 人道, that is, "a way of becoming consummately and authoritatively human." As 15.29 tells us: "It is the person who is able to broaden the way, not the way that broadens the person."

(*The Analects of Confucius: A Philosophical Translation,* pp. 45-46)

We must distinguish between simply traveling on a road, and making the journey one's own. To realize *dao* is to experience, to interpret, and to influence the world in such a way as to reinforce and extend a way of life inherited from one's cultural precursors. *Dao* is "truth" in the sense that it entails *being true* to those who have come before, and living in the world in a way that *can be trusted* by those yet to come. It is for this reason that we translate *dao* usually as "the proper way."

For Confucius, early on in the tradition, *dao* is primarily *rendao* 人道, that is, "a way of becoming consummately and authoritatively

"道"基本上即"人道",也就是"成为一个圆满而有权威的人的方法"(成人之道)。《中庸》多次提到《论语》,将其作为经典的权威,也多次提到孔子本人,将其作为一个值得效法的典范。通过这种方式,《中庸》阐明了这种儒家的成人之道。不过,或许是受到道家的影响,当然肯定还受到孟子的影响,《中庸》强调圣人对于其周遭世界的深远的转化效果。

通过创造性地参与转化和滋养世界的各种活动,诸如孔子那样的圣人获得了一种真正的宇宙性的地位,成为天地完全的伙伴。界定繁荣社群的那些既经修养了的道德的、审美的和宗教的感受性,受到自然环境韵律的启发并有机地整合到自然环境的韵律之中。那些感受性具有一种升华灵性的效果,那种升华灵性的效果给世界增添了意义和价值。

如同许多经典文献一样,《中庸》一书,对"天之道"和"人之道"进行了区分。这两个范畴远不是将自身融化到那种排斥性的"自然/培养"(nature/nurture)的两分法之中,而是共生(symbiotic)和彼

human." The *Zhongyong* elaborates upon this Confucian way of becoming authoritatively human with many allusions to the *Analects* as canonical authority and to Confucius himself as a model worthy of emulation. But, perhaps influenced by Daoistic and certainly Mencian sensibilities, the *Zhongyong* emphasizes the profoundly transformative effect that consummate human beings have on the world around them.

Sages such as Confucius, through their creative participation in the transforming and nourishing activities of the world, achieve a truly cosmic stature, becoming full partners with heaven and earth. The cultivated moral, aesthetic, and religious sensibilities that define the flourishing community, inspired by and fully integrated into the rhythms of the natural environment, have an elevating spiritual effect that adds significance and value to the world.

In the *Zhongyong*, as in much of the classical corpus, a distinction is made between "the way of *tian* (*tian zhi dao* 天之道)" and "the proper way of human beings (*ren zhi dao* 人之道)." These categories, far from resolving themselves into an exclusive "nature/nurture" dichotomy, are symbiotic and mutually entailing, converging most productively in "the proper way of the exemplary person (*junzi zhi dao* 君子之道)," and ultimately, "the proper way of the sage (*sheng ren zhi dao* 聖人之道)." The project, then, is not to integrate two aspects of our experience that are

此蕴涵的（mutually entailing），并且富有成果地聚合在"君子之道"之中并最终汇聚在"圣人之道"之中。这样一来，这种汇聚的工程就不是将本来彼此独立的我们的生活经验的两个方面整合到一起，而是使他们彼此关联和相互依赖的各种可能性达到最优化的状态。

（《切中伦常：〈中庸〉的新诠与新译》，第82—83页）

简言之，孔子确信，文化——作为社会的精华，其首要的发展是鼓励和表达固有的道德感情——是积累和常规的进步。上古之人虽然有能力发展他们的道德天性，然而他们亦缺乏为增强这一能力所必需的文化制度和规范性指导。尧舜虽说能够以其个人行为和治国业绩为楷模来培养这一道德本性，虽然能够对中国早期文明作出独一无二的持久贡献，但是他们之所以能够做到这一切，主要并非是有适宜的环境，而更多的是归功于他们个人的杰出才能。然而，在西周时期，中国文化的发展就社会交往形式而言已达到了相当成熟的水平——富裕的生活环境有益于体认人类的道德

originally independent of each other, but rather to optimize the possibilities of their correlativity and interdependence.

(*Focusing the Familiar: A Translation and Philosophical Interpretation of the Zhongyong,* pp. 63-64)

In short, Confucius believes that culture—the social refinements developed primarily to encourage and articulate proper moral feelings—is cumulative and generally progressive. Whereas people living in high antiquity had the capacity for developing their moral nature, they were lacking in the cultural institutions and formal guidance necessary to maximize this capacity. That Yao and Shun were able to nurture this moral nature in their conduct and administration and, in doing so, were able to make a signal and lasting contribution to China's emerging civilization, was due more to their own personal excellence than to the congeniality of their environment. By the early Chou period, however, the development of Chinese culture had culminated in a sophisticated pattern for social intercourse—fertile ground indeed in which to encourage human kind's moral nature. The cultural institutions and conventions established by the earlier sages who themselves had "lived" the Way were adapted to structure society and guide contemporaries toward a comparable level of humanity. For Confucius, the early Western Chou period marks a high point in the

本性。由古代有道之圣人建立起来的文化制度和习俗与社会结构相适应，并且引导当时人们向着较高的人文水准迈进。对孔子来说，西周早期实是代表了中国社会进化所达到的一个高峰。然而遗憾的是，这一高峰好景不长。西周早期建设了一个黄金时代后，随着政治斗争的滋长，人们逐渐偏离了"道"。到了西周末年，政治制度已名存实亡，周天子成为野心勃勃的封建诸侯所操纵的傀儡。在这一没落的过程中，建立在道德内容之上的西周文化的声望一落千丈，只有名称和礼仪的空壳被完整地保留下来。与此螺旋式的衰退过程相回应，孔子鼓吹返归周的道统，复兴培育了这一黄金时代的丰富而充实的文化。

（《中国古代的统治艺术：〈淮南子·主术〉研究》，第21—22页）

虽然一些学者在分析《老子》中"道"的意思时，已经指出了这个词具有许多层含义，不过我自己在这里只讨论它的三种含义：常道、天之道和至人之道。

"常道"是道家对全部实在的总称。它被描述为终极的形上学实

evolution of Chinese society. Unfortunately, however, this high point was short-lived. Having achieved the golden age of early Chou, people were gradually deflected from the Way by growing political strife. By the end of Western Chou, the political institutions had been drained of substance and the Chou kings had become puppets manipulated by ambitious feudal lords. In the process of degeneration, the glory that had been the early Chou culture was divested of its underlying moral content; only the name and the ceremonial shell remained intact. In response to this process of spiraling decline, Confucius advocated a return to the Way of Chou and a revival of the fertile and substantial culture which had fostered this golden age.

(*The Art of Rulership: A Study of Ancient Chinese Political Thought,* pp. 5-6)

Although scholars have identified many levels of this term in analyzing its place in the *Lao Tzu*, I shall limit myself to a discussion of only three: the constant *tao*, the natural *tao*, and the *tao* of the consummate person.

The constant *tao* is the Taoist epithet for the sum total of reality. It can be described as the ultimate metaphysical reality, the absolute, the unconditioned, the undifferentiated and holistic, the uncreated, the all-pervading, the ineffable. It is the process of becoming. It is the "source" of the phenomenal world in an

在，是绝对的、无条件的、无差别的、神圣的、自存的、无所不在的和不可言说的。它是一个发生的过程：作为某种意识，它是现象世界的"根源"，然而与其说它是超越的，不如说它是内在的；与其说它是过程的，不如说它是本体的。说"道"是超越的，是就它超越了任何个别而言；然而它又并不是超越的，因为它不是一个孤立的实在。说它是变化的，是由于它是所有现象变化的发动处；然而又是寂然不变的，因此在这个意义上它既不会增加，也不会减少。这个永恒的"道"是超象与现象的对立面的统一。"道"的超象方面是从它作为一个无限的和无差别的存在之总体来理解的。《老子》中的许多地方都将"道"描述为空虚、无形、不可名状、恒常等，以强调它的有机的普遍性。"道"无所不在。"道"的现象方面即指其具备了现象界的特殊性、复杂性、多样性和事实性或"客观实在性"。这一方面又往往有关于"德"、充盈、万物、形、名以及变化之类的描述，具有强调现象界之实在的意义。为了说明"道"具有现象的含义，就必须从整体中

immanent rather than transcendent sense and in an ontological rather than chronological sense. The *tao* is transcendent in that it "goes beyond" any particular; yet it is not transcendent in that it is not a separate reality. It is changing in that it is the locus of all phenomenal change; yet it is unchanging in the sense that it suffers neither increase nor diminution. There are two polar aspects of the constant *tao*: the metaphenomenal and the phenomenal. The metaphenomenal *tao* is the *tao* apprehended in its indeterminate and undifferentiated totality as existence. It is described variously in the text as vacuous, empty, formless, the nameless, the constant, and so on as a means of underscoring its organismic pervasiveness. There is nothing which is not *tao*. Its phenomenal aspect is the *tao* apprehended as the phenomenal world in its particularity, plurality, diversity, and facticity or "thingness." It is described variously as *te*, fullness, the myriad things, form, the named, the changing, and so on as a means of emphasizing the reality of the phenomenal world. In order to apprehend the *tao* as phenomena it is necessary to differentiate the particular from the whole and yet fully understand the same particular with reference to the whole—hence the generative idea of "origin," of "returning," of "mother," the notion of the "uncarved block" and "the dispensation of names." These two polar aspects of the constant *tao*, the

区分出个别，而且也必须依据整体对这同一个个别作出完整的理解，因此就产生了有关"始""返""动"等思想，以及"朴"和"常名"等概念。基于"常道"具有超象与现象这两个对立的方面，所有相关的反义词都可以用来描述它（如恒常与变动，大与小，无形与有形，绝对与相对，等等）。

"道"的观念之成立，基于两个先决的思想条件，它们并非总是为人们所认识。这第一个思想主题是关于某种有机的和神圣的实在概念，它构成了道家相对主义的基础，并解释了"道"的现象与超象这两个方面的关系。这种有机主义的学说反对从根本上消除差异，坚持认为，事物处于各种关系的中心，而这些关系则表明了它在整体中的前后联系。这个事物某种意义上是个别的和相对的，因此它可以从整体中被区分出来；但是它又与每一个其他的事物相"同一"，并且某种意义上是绝对的，因此可以完全推论或确定：任何条件下的个别（这就是说，所有符合于它的条件）就是无条件的整体。这种有机的学说肯定合个别与整体、现象与超象的本体实在，

metaphenomenal and the phenomenal, are the basis on which all dichotomous predications used to describe it can be reconciled (constant/changing, big/small, formless/formal, absolute/relative, and so on).

There are two presuppositions underlying this notion of *tao* which are not always taken into consideration. The first is an organismic and holistic conception of reality which forms the basis for Taoist relativism and explains the relationship between the phenomenal and metaphenomenal aspects of the *tao*. This doctrine of organism denies the essentialistic finality of distinctions, insisting that a thing is a *focus* of relationships determined by its context in the whole. The thing is particular and relative in the sense that it can be differentiated from the whole, but it is "identical" with every other thing and absolute in the sense that the full consequence or definition of any conditioned particular (that is, the full set of its conditions) *is* the unconditioned whole. This doctrine of organism affirms the ontological reality of both the particular and the whole, the phenomenal and the metaphenomenal, but denies any notion of final autonomy, discreteness, or discontinuity in reality. It insists that particulars are mutually determining, mutually defining, and mutually conditioned—and, as such, each particular is a window on the whole. To understand any particular in its fullness is to understand the whole.

(*The Art of Rulership: A Study of Ancient Chinese Political Thought,* pp. 34-35)

但否定任何实在意义上的终极的自主性、孤立性或非连续性。它坚持认为，个别是相互确定、相互限定和互为条件的，而且正因为如此，每一个个别都是一个观察整体的窗户。完整地理解了个别，也就是理解了整体。

（《中国古代的统治艺术：〈淮南子·主术〉研究》，第 63—65 页）

《老子》理解的"天之道"是指自然变化的秩序与规律：复归原则，自然均衡，内在的对立统一，公正无私，等等。因为"天之道"是"常道"的一个方面，所以，这一规律也可以说是"常道"所特有的，但是，这一规律又并非是它的特有属性，因为人类生存往往明显背离这一永恒之道，所以它又必须能够解决人类的这一迷失。这就是说，为了调节人类的行为，"常道"与"天之道"的差别是必然的。人类的行为与天之道不相一致，但却并不脱离常道的范围。

道家学者主张效法天之道，以此作为达到与常道齐一的途径：

人法地，地法天，天

This natural *tao* reflects what the *Lao Tzu* perceives to be the order and regularity of natural change: the reversion principle, natural equilibrium, implicit opposites, impartiality, and so on. Now, this regularity is also characteristic of the constant *tao* inasmuch as the natural *tao* is an aspect of it, but it is not characteristic of it inasmuch as the constant *tao* must also account for the human maverick who is very capable of living at variance with the natural *tao*. That is to say, the "constant *tao*" and "natural *tao*" distinction is necessary in order to accommodate human conduct which is inconsistent with the natural *tao* but does not go beyond the parameters of the constant *tao*.

The Taoist takes as his project the emulation of the natural *tao* as a vehicle for achieving identity with the constant *tao*:

The human being emulates earth;
Earth emulates heaven;
Heaven emulates the *tao*;
And the *tao* emulates that which is natural to it.[*Lao Tzu* 25]

Although it is beyond our concerns here to speculate on what it might mean to achieve identity with the constant *tao*, passages in the *Lao Tzu* and *Chuang Tzu* suggest that this involves an awareness of the unity of all existence in which the self/other dichotomy is reconciled. That both texts do describe human

法道，道法自然。(《老子》二十五章)

尽管对"达致与常道齐一可能意味着什么"这样的问题的思索，已经超出了我们这里所讨论的范围，然而《老子》和《庄子》的这几段话已经包含了某种关于所有的存在物具有统一性，因此自我与他人（他物）也是虽分别却又统一的认识。在这两部著作中，对于人类的完美境界即达致同常道的齐一这一点，都说得十分清楚：

圣人抱一为天下式。(《老子》二十二章)

岂唯形骸有聋盲哉？夫知亦有之。……之人也，之德也，将旁（磅）礴万物以为一。(《庄子·逍遥游》)

故为是举莛与楹，厉与西施，恢恑憰怪，道通为一。其分也，成也；其成也，毁也。凡物无成与毁，复通为一。唯达者知通为一。(《庄子·齐物论》)

这向我们揭示了"道"的第三

consummation as consisting in identity with the constant *tao* is clear:

Therefore the sage embraces the One to become the model of the world. [*Lao Tzu* 22]

Do you think blindness and deafness are limited to just the physical body? One's understanding can also suffer from them…. This person and this kind of inner potency will extend things in all directions to make one. [*Chuang Tzu* 1.2]

Because of this, while we distinguish between a stalk and a bean, a leper and the classic beauty Hsi Shih, the tao unifies every weird and wonderful, strange and extraordinary thing as one. The discrimination of a thing is its actualization, and its actualization is its destruction. Where things are free of actualization and destruction, they are reunified as one. Only the enlightened person understands this principle of unifying as one. [*Chuang Tzu* 2.4]

This leads us to the third level of *tao*. As an exception to nature one can either strive to be in accord with the environment, achieving realization in a way consonant with the underlying principles of nature, or

层含义。作为自然的某种例外，人们既可以经过奋斗以适应环境，在不断顺应自然的根本法则的过程中完善自己，也可能以某种与自然状况不谐调的方式去追求生活。总之存在着两种可能性。至人之道是以天之道为模式并与之相和谐的。下面这段话提到了这个"道"：

> 故失道而后德，失德而后仁，失仁而后义，失义而后礼。（《老子》三十八章）

只有当人与人之间的自然关系遭到破坏，非自然的行为普遍存在时，才需要统一人类行为的各种准则。在道家哲学里，显然至人的道即天之道，而至人则是常道的化身。……

（《中国古代的统治艺术：〈淮南子·主术〉研究》，第67—69页）

值得注意的是，"我知道"是一种及物语法，但"道"并不是这种语法的"谓语"，而是包含实实在在的"主语"意义。这种情况就像"生活""历史"或"经验"，不能以二元论意义去对待。"道"表

one can pursue life in a way inconsistent with the natural condition. These are the two possibilities. The *tao* of the consummate human being is a mode of living patterned on and in concert with the natural *tao*. This is the *tao* referred to in the following passage:

> Therefore when we neglect the *tao*,
> Then *te* arises;
> When we neglect *te*,
> Then benevolence arises;
> When we neglect benevolence,
> Then rightness arises;
> When we neglect rightness,
> Then social norms and rites arise. [*Lao Tzu* 38]

Only when the *natural* expression of interpersonal relationships breaks down and unnatural activity becomes commonplace is it necessary to articulate standards for human conduct. In Taoist philosophy, it would appear that the *tao* of the consummating person is an analog to the natural *tao* and the consummating person is an analog to the constant *tao*....

(*The Art of Rulership: A Study of Ancient Chinese Political Thought,* pp. 37-38)

Importantly, in the transitive "I know the way" (*wo zhidao*), "the way" (*dao*) is not the "object" of knowledge as such, but has a real subjective dimension. It is a term

示指导在世间生活的一种质量道路（qualitative way），它既包含主观性，也包含客观性，是不可分的。"主语"的属性及其做出的行为形式同样是不可分的。"道"不承认亚里士多德的"范畴"，而是同时与主语、谓语条件保持联系性，同时也与"知"的质量以及所知世界的条件保持相关性。"知"既给予其主体"仁"的质量，也给予我们其所知之物，既给予我们采取行为的具体情势，也给予我们采取行为的本身形式。

（《儒家角色伦理学：一套特色伦理学词汇》，第212—213页）

"道"常被一种宇宙"本原"语言描述为我们所知的这一世界的"本原"。但是我在上面已经指出，这个宇宙论意义的"道"，远非那个高高在上形而上学的起始原则，它独立于它的造物，实际上是把它们都包括在内持续不已的生命过程。这种世界本身自生和永远偶然性的血脉展开，是我们的经验场域。正如我们所见到的，如果秩序真是内在和新兴的，而不作为独立原则存在，那么阐述这个"世界形成"的

like "life" or "history" or "experience" that does not resolve into dualisms. *Dao* is a qualitative way of conducting one's life in the world that entails both subject and object, and the attributes of the subject as well as the modality of the actions being carried out. *Dao* defies Aristotle's categories, having as much to do with the conditions of the subject as with the object, and having as much to do with the quality of understanding as it does with the conditions of the world as understood. Knowing tells us as much about the *ren* quality of the person who "knows" as it does about something known, as much about a particular disposition to act as it does about the modality of acting itself.

(*Confucian Role Ethics: A Vocabulary,* pp. 192-193)

Often *dao* 道 is described in the language of a cosmological "source," the "origins" of the world as we know it. But as I have argued above, this cosmological *dao* far from being a superordinated metaphysical principle that stands independent of its creatures is in fact the ongoing living processes that include them all. It is the generative and always contingent genealogical unfolding of the world itself as our field of experience. As we have seen, if order is truly inherent and emergent rather than existing as an independent principle, then the language that describes all aspects of this "world-ing" must be historicized as a

一切语言,一定是历史的,临时的,有时是诗一般的,有时是比喻性语汇,它表述"如我们所知"的这个世界秩序。

(《儒家角色伦理学:一套特色伦理学词汇》,第250页)

本

《牛津英语辞典》告诉我们,"起源"(beginning)指"造成存在的活动或过程","事物通过这一活动或过程得以萌生"。这一萌生的根源即为混沌(χάος)——"基质"、"太初"、"深渊"。另外,"本原"(principle)(arche ἀρχή)这个词直接与archon(ἄρχων古雅典的执政官),即发布命令的权势者有关。本原是思想与活动的起点。不过"起源"这个自身富含诗意的词,经由原先与古英语 *gínan* 这个词的联系,也带有"大豁口",或混沌的"空空洞洞"的意思。本原和起源若究其根本,乃任意多变,纷披淆乱而莫可名状。

因此,始基、本原、起源都和太初、宇宙的第一状态——也即混沌有关。……

provisional, sometimes poetic and sometimes metaphorical vocabulary for the world order *as we know it.*

(*Confucian Role Ethics: A Vocabulary,* p. 227)

Root (*Ben*)

The *Oxford English Dictionary* tells us that "beginning" refers to "the action or process of entering upon existence," "that out of which anything has its rise." The source of this arising is chaos (χάος)—"the elemental," "the first state of the universe," "the great deep or abyss." Further, "principle" (*arche* ἀρχή) is directly related to *archon* (ἄρχων), one authorized to *give orders*. Principles are beginning points of thought and action. But "beginning" itself is a richly poetic term carrying, through primary associations with the Old English *gínan*, the meaning of "the yawning gap," or "gaping void" of chaos. Principles and beginnings dissolve, at their roots, into arbitrariness and confusion.

Thus, *arche, principium,* beginning, all refer to the *origin,* "the first state of the universe"—namely, chaos....

(*Anticipating China: Thinking through*

(《期望中国：对中西文化的哲学思考》，第4页)

亚里士多德已经在非神学的背景下采用了"本原"（άρχή）这个观念，从而去掉了起源观念的神话色彩。亚里士多德所属的那一传统，已经开始忽略直接呈现在非神话语言外观下的混沌状态的存在。

然而，宇宙演化的传说仍具有强大的影响力。雅格指出以下这点也无疑是正确的：对闪族人的空虚混沌的观念的解读已渗入了希腊人混沌的意义。但不光是闪族人，奥菲士教和柏拉图有关混沌的看法同样在强化着这个词的消极意义。

正如"混沌"的词源学表明的，按arche或本原（"本原"原文为Principle，这个英文词也有"原则""原理"的意义——译者）解释的理性有赖虚构的模型。亚里士多德避开神话创作的语言，他并不设定任何最初的创造行为，但这并不妨碍他成为我们把本原理解为秩序的决定性起因的主要来源。

亚里士多德认为，本原是"使事物成为可知的东西，是使事物第一次成其所是的东西，或者说，靠

the Narratives of Chinese and the Western Culture, p. 3)

Already Aristotle has demythologized the concept of beginnings by employing the notion of "principle" (*ἀρχή*) in a nontheological context. Aristotle is part of a tradition that has begun to forget the presence of the chaotic that lies directly beneath the surface of a no-longer-mythologized language.

The effect of the cosmogonic tradition, nonetheless, remains powerful. Jaeger is doubtless correct, as well, when he notes that the Semitic *tohu wa bohu* has been read into the Greek meanings of chaos. But it was not only the Semitic, but the Orphic and Platonic versions of chaos as well, that have reinforced the negative sense of the term.

As the etymology of "chaos" suggests, the construal of reason in terms of *arche or principium* is dependent upon mythical sources. Aristotle's avoidance of mythopoetic language and his rejection of the need to posit any initial creative act did not prevent him from serving as the primary source of our understanding of principles as determining sources of order.

According to Aristotle, a principle, is "that from which a thing can be known, that from which a thing first comes to be, or that at whose will that which is moved is moved and that which

着它，运动的东西运动起来，变化的东西发生变化"。这样，知识的本原和存在的本原就成了思想的来源和创始的原因本身。正如在政治领域，执政官或元首是发布命令者。

（《期望中国：对中西文化的哲学思考》，第13页）

在古代中国，未必会找到柏拉图和亚里士多德博大传统的任何真正的对应物。这就是说，我们不仅要提防寻找柏拉图和亚里士多德的中国翻版的诱惑，而且无论我们抽取的是这两种见解中何者的主要理论范畴，我们在用它对中国的思想家进行解释时，都应当敏锐地意识到其中存在的难点。柏拉图和亚里士多德凭借他们不同的系统（线喻和四因说，以及灵魂的三重模式）对知识加以组织的方式与中国人的组织方式并不一致。况且，在中国的思想家中，也不存在和柏拉图的eidos（种、形式或理念）或亚里士多德ousia（实体、本体或本质）这类概念真正相当的东西。……

（《期望中国：对中西文化的哲学思考》，第98页）

changes changes." As such, principles of knowledge and of being are the origins of thought and sources of origination per se. In the political realm, an *archon* or *princeps* is one who gives orders.

(*Anticipating China: Thinking through the Narratives of Chinese and the Western Culture,* p. 9)

The broad traditions of Plato and Aristotle are unlikely to have any true counterparts in classical China. This means that not only should we avoid the temptation to look for Chinese versions of Plato and Aristotle, but we should be sensitive to the difficulties of employing the major theoretical categories drawn from either of these visions in interpreting Chinese thinkers. The Platonic and Aristotelian modes of organizing knowledge by recourse to their alternative schemes (the Divided Line and the Four Causes, along with the tripartite model of the *psyche*) are inconsistent with the Chinese modes of organization. Further, concepts such as Plato's *eidos* (εἶδος) and Aristotle's *ousia* (οὐσία) have no real equivalents among Chinese thinkers....

(*Anticipating China: Thinking through the Narratives of Chinese and the Western Culture,* pp. 81-82)

在《孟子》及其他儒家经典中，人们熟悉的运用园艺和畜牧比喻，例如知"本"，经常被理解为强调具体的植物和动物的成长，变为它们"本"来应是什么：它们简单地达到内在潜能的实现（实在化）。事实上，恰是农业和养畜具有的对人为环境和大量人为努力的极大依赖性，使得园艺性和畜牧性成为关系构成"成人"的贴切类比。如果没有持续的干预，大多数种子将远不会变成它们本该是的什么，而是变成任何本该不是的东西。如果不是因为我们认为它们会"自然"变化，而对它强度干预培养条件，大多数种子，不仅根本变不成它们本应"自然"的是什么，还会变成任何它们本应"自然"的不是什么。如果没有出于我们认为的它们会"自然"地变为"什么"的大量干预和护理修正的帮助，大部分橡子会变成松鼠，玉米大多会变成奶牛，鸡蛋大多会变成炒鸡蛋。任何种类的"本"或"子"及它将会变成的"什么"，既在于环境的偶然作用，也在于其"开始"的最初条件。

（《儒家角色伦理学：一套特色伦理学词汇》，第172页）

In the *Mencius* and other canonical Confucian texts, the familiar appeal to the horticultural and husbanding metaphors—knowing the "root," for example—is often construed as reinforcing the idea that specific plants and animals grow to become what they essentially are: They simply actualize their inherent potential. But in fact what makes horticulture and husbanding apposite analogies for relationally constituted "human becomings" is the acute dependence that farming and raising animals has upon a contrived environment and upon concentrated human effort. Without sustained intervention, most seeds, far from becoming what they "are," become anything and everything else. Without the benefit of intensive intervention and cultivation on behalf of what we think they will "naturally" become, most acorns become squirrels, most corn becomes cows, and most eggs become omelets. The "root" or "seed" of anything and what it will become is as much a function of the contingencies of circumstances as it is of the initial conditions from which it "begins."

(*Confucian Role Ethics: A Vocabulary*, p. 154)

理

"理",最通常地被英译为"推理"(to reason)或"原理"(principle)。

我们想说明一下,将理不论译为"reason"或译为"principle"这种做法,在突出我们自己的哲学意义的同时,也造成不能接受的损失,因为这样就掩盖了对于鉴别与它的差别的那些最主要的意义。然后,我们的考虑是,通过对这组术语的重建,将那些在我们对文本的阅读和解释中有消失危险的古代中国思想的特点提升到表面来。

"理"在其最初出现时,有名词和动词两种功能,用作"秩序"、"条理",或"纹理",及"治理"、"修饰"或"作记号"。实际上,在其初现时,"理"使人联想出这样一幅景象,即"我疆我理"。它归属于这样一条小路,它是一条通向在耕种的田地的路。

也许受到"理"的部首是玉这个事实的启发,汉代的《说文解字》提出"雕玉或磨玉"及"玉中的纹理或线条"是理的最根本之意义。有意思的是,雕玉要求工匠们的创

Li

Li, most frequently rendered into English as "to reason" or "principle".

We want to give an account of how the conventional translations of *li* as either "reason" or "principle," while foregrounding our own philosophical importances, pay the unacceptable penalty of concealing precisely those meanings which are most essential to an appreciation of its differences. Our concern then, is, through a reconstruction of this cluster of terms, to lift to the surface those peculiar features of classical Chinese thinking that are in danger of receding in our reading and interpretation of texts.

In its earliest occurrences, *li* has both a nominal and verbal function as "order," "pattern," or "markings," and "to order," "to pattern," or "to mark." Actually, in its earliest occurrence, *li* conjures up the image of "dividing up land into cultivated fields *in a way consistent with the natural topography*." It refers to the pathways that permit access to the fields under cultivation.

The *Shuowen*, a Han dynasty Chinese lexicon, inspired perhaps by the fact that *li* is classified under *yu* 玉, the "jade" signific, suggests that "dressing or polishing jade" and the "veins or striations within the jade" are its most fundamental meanings. Significantly, the dressing of

造性的表达要与玉石上自然条纹的固有的可能性保持一致。事实上，最好的宝石是最大限度地将石头本身的丰富的可能性呈现出来。

古代文献中"理"的最常见用法是指事物和事件中固有的形式的和结构的样式，及它们的可理解性。在"自然的"连贯性（天理或道理）与"文化的"连贯性（文理或道理）之间没有严格的区别，正像自然和文化都包含在"道"的概念之中，所以各方都统一于"理"。

（《期望中国：对中西文化的哲学思考》，第257—258页）

与古代西方思想主导趋向截然相反，中国人在描述"万物"的时候没有将静止和永恒性置于优先地位。在认为变化和过程优先于静止的世界里，几乎没有外在的力量来推动外在动因的概念的发展。在这样一个万物变化的世界里，最通常的假设是事物自己在变化。

这种物力论（dynamism）有另外一个重要涵义：既然假定了变化与生成的首要性，那么连贯性就具有非常不同的意义。过程包含了独特性，并使任何严格的同一性概念

jade requires craftsmen to conform their creative expression to those possibilities resident in the natural striations of the stone. In fact, the best lapidary is the one whose art maximizes the richest possibilities of the stone itself.

The most familiar use of *li* in the classical literature is to indicate the inherent formal and structural patterns in things and events, and their intelligibility. In expressing this notion of coherence and intelligibility, no severe distinction is made between "natural" coherence (*tianli* 天理 or *daoli* 道理) and "cultural" coherence (*wenli* 文理 or *daoli* 道理). Just as nature and culture are embraced within the notion of *dao*, so each is integral to *li*.

(*Anticipating China: Thinking through the Narratives of Chinese and Western Culture*, pp. 212-213)

Contrary to the dominant strains of classical Western thoughts, the Chinese did not give priority to rest and permanence in their characterizations of the "ten thousand things." There is little impetus toward the development of notions of external agency in a world where change and process is deemed prior to rest. In such a world of changing things the most normal assumption is that things change themselves.

There is another important implication of this dynamism: Given the assumption

都成问题,这样,连贯的统一性便按照独特个体中的相对的连续性加以描述,而这种连续性是无限开放的而不是系统的;是偶然的而不是必然的;是相互关联的而不是因果关系的。这样,它能够涵盖看上去不一致甚或是矛盾的方面,如这些方面同时被加以思考,而且在过程中被思考,它就能很好地处于连续性的范围之中。

合理,现代汉语译作"合乎理性的"(to be rational)或"合情合理的"(reasonable),这种表达方式包含了对以下这些基本的关系的一种意识:它们决定每种事物,通过各种关联形式使其世界具有意义并可理解。所有的事物在它们具有独特性和复杂性时,以及在它们与其世界的其余部分相联系时,都显现出了一定程度的连贯性。

"理"起源于任何一个特殊事物的独特性,这是个体化的条件,并且同时是经由给定的个体与其他个体之间多种合作形成连续性的基础,由于相似性、生成性或连续性,理同这些特殊事物相关联。从上述意义上看,理构成了一种审美的连贯性。正是这种合作为多种模式的类

of the primacy of change and becoming, coherence takes on quite a different meaning. Process entails uniqueness, and makes any notion of strict identity problematic. As such, coherent unities are characterized in terms of a relative continuity among unique particulars. And such continuity is open ended rather than systematic; it is contingent rather than necessary; it is correlative rather than causal. Thus, it can include aspects which, if entertained simultaneously, would seem inconsistent or even contradictory, yet when entertained in process, are well within the boundaries of continuity.

To be in accord with *li* (*he li* 合理), an expression which in modern Chinese translates "to be rational" or "reasonable," entails an awareness of those constitutive relationships which condition each thing and which, through patterns of correlation, make its world meaningful and intelligible. All things evidence a degree of coherence as their claim to uniqueness and complexity, as well as their claim to continuity with the rest of the world.

Li constitutes an aesthetic coherence in the sense that it begins from the uniqueness of any particular as a condition of individuation, and is at the same time a basis for continuity through various forms of collaboration between the given particular and other particulars with which, by virtues of similarity or productivity or contiguity, it can

比关系提供了基础，这些类比关系模式在这个传统中最有可能接近于"推理"。

作为揭示本质的过程的推理，将特殊视为这种本质的例证，与这种推理相反，理需要探索构成事物与事件的关系模式的关联细节。儒学思维的一个目的是，对相互依赖的条件及其隐性的、模糊的可能性有一种广泛的和畅通无阻的意识，那里每个成分的意义和价值都取决于所构成它的特殊关系之网。

这种"推理"使得不用（逻辑的）推论来弄清具体细节和细微差别成为可能。例如，人们可以诉诸相互关联的类范畴来安排和表述世界上的事项。人们在一堆混乱的具体细节中寻找关联性突出了这些细节中的相似性，包含于任何特殊的"类"之中，或排除了任何特殊的类之外，这都取决于类比活动，而不是依赖于靠同一律或矛盾律的概念的逻辑运作。这种相互关联性意味着提供关于世界的连续性和规则性意识，并且，某些并列（juxtaposition）倾向于最大限度地利用差异、多样性和机会，因而比其他因素更富有和谐性。就此而言，

be correlated. It is this collaboration which provides a ground for the various modes of analogical relationship that are the closest approximation to "reasoning" available in this tradition.

In contrast to reasoning as the process of uncovering essences of which particulars are instances, *li* involves tracing out correlated details forming the pattern of relationships which obtain among things and events. Confucian thinking has as its goal a comprehensive and unobstructed awareness of interdependent conditions and their latent, vague possibilities, where the meaning and value of each element is a function of the particular network of relationships that constitute it.

Such "reasoning" permits noninferential access to concrete detail and nuance. For example, one may appeal to the categories of correlative "kinds"(*lei* 類) to organize and explain items in the world. The correlations one pursues among the welter of concrete details foregrounds similarities among them. Inclusion or exclusion in any particular "kind" is a function of analogical activities rather than logical operations dependent upon notions of identity or contradiction. Such correlations are meant to provide a sense of continuity and regularity in the world, and are more or less effective as coherent orders to the extent that some juxtapositions tend to maximize difference, diversity, and

这种关联性或多或少同连贯的秩序一样发挥作用。

理既是描述的又是规范的,它指出事物应当成为怎样。然而,理的这种规定性方面,除了适合用历史上的模式作类比外,它并不诉诸任何别的秩序。理想寓于历史之中,在这个意义上,理不是"形而上学的",而且必须与某种先验构造或超越目的的论断区分开来。

（《期望中国：对中西文化的哲学思考》，第 260—262 页）

opportunity, and hence are more productive of harmony than others.

Li is both descriptive and normative. It suggests how things ought to be. This prescriptive aspect of *li*, however, does not appeal to any order beyond that which is available by analogy to historical models. Ideals reside in history. In this sense, *li* is not "metaphysical" and must be distinguished from assertions about some a priori structure or transcendent aim.

(*Anticipating China: Thinking through the Narratives of Chinese and Western Culture*, pp. 215-216)

帝

现在来看"帝"这个词。"帝"的来历一般被认为与商代宗教有关。甲骨文字形是"果",青铜铭文是"囧",帛书与竹简是"帝"。中国古文字学者王国维解释"帝"源自"蒂"——花或瓜果跟枝茎相连的部分。文献学者徐中舒将它释读为祭天仪式点燃的火堆,而且延伸为大祭之原始字形"禘"。从《论语》中我们得知孔子对禘祭极为重视:

或问禘之说。子曰："不知

Di

Turning to the term *di* 帝 that is usually associated with the earlier Shang dynasty religiousness, it occurs on the oracle bones as 果, on the bronzes as 囧, and on the silk and bamboo manuscripts as 帝. The literary theorist Wang Guowei 王國維 interprets this character as an early depiction of the stem of a flower or fruit (*di* 蒂). The philologist Xu Zhongshu 徐中舒 reads it as a ceremonial pyre on which to make sacrifices to *tian*, and by extension, as the earlier graphic form for what came to be designated as the grand *di* sacrifice 禘. We learn in the *Analects* that Confucius

也。知其说者之于天下也，其如示诸斯乎！"指其掌。(《论语·八佾》)

虽然较早学者提供的"帝"的解释颇有揣测，并不确切，但我们确知"帝"也用作商王逝后谥号，这又是一个给模糊指涉的神圣对象加上人格形象的例子。

约翰·梅尔（John Major）在对中国经典做英语翻译的时候，为了找到对"帝"这一说法的合适对应词，也曾暗示这种人和神两个空间之间的流变性：

> 我把"帝"译为"thearch"——一个巧妙用词，我认为爱德华·莎伐是第一个用者；用它来指一些特殊人神之物，如上帝（Supreme Thearch）、黄帝（the Yellow Thearch）或被理想化的人君（皇帝）。"Thearch"能很好抓到中国古代思想的特点；它的特点是"神明"（同时地并毫无内在冲突地）或众高神、神话/神性君主以及神化的王室祖先：横跨神、人两边的，影响极重要的人、神之物。

had great reverence for this *di* sacrifice:

> Someone asked the Master for an explanation of the *di* imperial ancestral sacrifice, and he replied: "I don't have one. Anyone who did know how to explain it could rule the empire as easily as having it here." And he pointed to the palm of his hand.

Although such definitions of *di* 帝 offered by earlier scholars are speculative and uncertain, we do know that this term was also used as a posthumous title for the Shang-dynasty kings, again putting a human face on an otherwise rather obscure designator for the numinous.

John Major alludes to this fluidity between the human space and that of the divine in his attempt to provide an appropriate equivalent for this term *di* in his translations of the Chinese canons into the English language:

> I translate *di* [帝] as "thearch"—a felicitous word first used, I believe, by Edward Schafer—when it refers to specific personage such as the Supreme Thearch (*shangdi* [上帝]) or the Yellow Thearch (*huangdi* [黄帝]), or to idealized rulers ("emperors"). Thearch captures well the character of ancient Chinese thought wherein

（《儒家角色伦理学：一套特色伦理学词汇》，第 245—246 页）

有充足的文献资料一致表明，随着周取代商，文化上比较落后的周代统治者将他们原初"天"的观念与文化上较为先进的臣属的商代更为人格化的神进行了同一。"天"和"上帝"在《尚书》和《诗经》中常是互换使用的。在此，我们或许可以推测，周人模仿"帝"与商王室的人际关系，也主张一种类似的与"天"的家庭关系。这反映在周朝统治者所谓"天子"的称呼上——受命于掌管的天"父"。没有理由认为，在将"天"等同于"帝"之前，"天"曾像"帝"那样被视为人类的祖先。不管周代"天"的最初轮廓是什么样子，它无疑在西周时已具备了拟人化的特征。它在文献中被描述为奖惩随意，感觉就像人类统治者那样行事。尽管周似乎确实将宗祖神（"上帝"）提升到某种原始宇宙力量的更高层面，但无疑商却对"天"的人格化是有贡献的。然而对我们这儿的分析意义重大的是，尽管该时期有一个明白无误的神的拟人化解释，但"天"和

divinities might be (simultaneously and without internal contradiction) high gods, mythical/divine rulers, or deified royal ancestors: beings of enormous import, straddling the numinous and the mundane.

(*Confucian Role Ethics: A Vocabulary*, p. 223)

With the Chou domination of the Shang, there is ample documentation of a concerted effort on the part of the culturally inferior Chou rulers to identify their indigenous notion of *t'ien* with the more personal deity of their sophisticated Shang subjects. *T'ien* and *shang-ti* are used interchangeably in parts of the *Book of Documents* and the *Book of Songs*. In this context, we might speculate that the Chou people imitated the personal relationship of *ti* to the royal house of Shang by claiming a similar familial relationship to *t'ien*. This assertion is reflected in the description of the Chou ruler as "son of *t'ien*" (*t'ien tzu* 天子) mandated to power by his ruling "father." There is no reason to believe that prior to this identification of *t'ien* with *ti* that *t'ien*, like *ti*, was perceived as a dimension populated by human ancestors. Whatever the original contours of the Chou *t'ien* might have been, it assumed indisputable anthropomorphic characteristics during the Western Chou period, being described in the literature as rewarding and punishing at will, and exercising itself

"帝"二者谁都不曾表现出是某种超验的神。正是中西文化传统形成的这一区分,必然决定着描述它们的范畴和概念结构的差异。

(《通过孔子而思》,第252页)

虽然古希腊哲学的主题指向普遍主义,这种普遍主义冲动却伴随着希腊化世界和罗马帝国对帝权和人性这类观念的应用,以及奥古斯丁对上帝的超越性的认识,得到了实际表达。奥古斯丁发展了他的上帝意象的学说,他对三重性的灵魂和三位一体论之间的类比关系所作的表述,将人的意义绝对化和普遍化了。此外,奥古斯丁对"意志的发现",使上帝之使然作用的观念最终成形;他将历史的意义表达为一种罪和赎罪的相互激荡,从而为希腊文化综合体添加了独具特色的元素。

中国文化的形成,并不通过诉诸那些规定人的本性,并确立"人类的统一"的普遍范畴;中国人毋宁更愿意用类如"中部之国的人"或"汉人"等方域性语言谈论他们自己。这样,在他们对人之为人的意义的表述中,对文化和历史的理

generally in ways associable with a human ruler. Whereras the impact of the Chou would seem to have had the effect of elevating the status of the ancestor spirit deity, *shang-ti*, to a higher level as a primeval cosmic force, there is little doubt that the influence of Shang seems to have been to contribute to the personalization of *t'ien*. Significant for our analysis here, however, is that although there is an unmistakable anthropomorphic interpretation of deity in this period, neither *ti* nor *t'ien* is ever presented as a transcendent deity. It is this distinction in the emergence and development of the Chinese and Western traditions that has had inestimable weight in determining the categories and conceptual structures that have served to define them.

(*Thinking Through Confucius,* pp. 203-204)

Though the thematics of Greek philosophy pointed toward universalism, the effective expression of this universalist impulse emerged in the Hellenistic and Roman Empires with the employment of notions such as *imperium* and *humanitas*, and of the Augustinian understanding of Divine transcendence. Augustine's articulation of the analogies between the tripartite *psyche* and the trinity in the development of his doctrine of the *imago dei* absolutized and universalized the meaning of the human being. Further, Augustine's "invention" of the will, modeled finally upon the notion of

解中，古代中国思想家都不会援引超越的原则来为他们的见解寻因作证。往昔年代中可供效仿的样板和文化上半神半人的英杰，例如三皇五帝和孔子，行使着诸如理性原则、三位一体的上帝等超越构造的功能，为人提供着对何以为人的认识。另外，在中国人看来，历史并不是由神学或哲学原则预先决定的一种叙事的展开。历史运动是内在的，可通过个人用最具效果的方式应付特殊环境所获得的相对的成功或失败加以说明。

（《期望中国：对中西文化的哲学思考》，第109—110页）

现在我们可以把这个对人的关系性认识用来观照我所命名的"儒家思想'人为中心'的宗教感"。在西方所熟悉的质性本体语言中，"上帝"被理解为不可察觉的人类"灵魂"的放大写照，是作为主宰的"世界灵魂"。可类比于灵魂的，使得我们人类拥有一切的"本体"（beings），看不见、不可改变的本质，造物者"上帝"是那个在这一切"本体存在"（beings）背后的质性的大写字母"Being"（本体存

Divine Agency, and his articulation of the meaning of history as an interplay of sin and redemption added distinctive elements to the Greek cultural synthesis.

　　Chinese culture is not shaped by any appeal to universal categories defining human nature and establishing "the unity of mankind"; rather, the Chinese refer to themselves in more provincial locutions such as "the people of the central states" or "the people of the Han." Thus, neither in their articulations of the meaning of being human, nor in their understandings of culture and history, do classical Chinese thinkers appeal to transcendent principles as the origin or certification of their visions. Exemplary models and cultural heroes from the past, such as the Sage Kings or Confucius, function in the place of transcendent structures such as the principle of Reason, or the trinitarian God, to provide the understanding of what it means to be human. Further, for the Chinese, history isn't seen as the unfolding of a narrative determined in advance by theological or philosophical principles. Historical movements are immanent, explicable by appeal to the relative success or failure of individuals to negotiate their particular circumstances in the most successful manner.

(*Anticipating China: Thinking through the Narratives of Chinese and the Western Culture,* pp. 90-91)

　　We can now carry this relational

在）——唯一的一个贯穿性、看不见的设计，隐藏在背后主宰着我们这个"universe"（同一体）"宇宙"——我们这个"单一秩序"的宇宙。威廉·詹姆斯对这种习已成癖的人类雕虫小技，把名称转为"东西"十分担忧——我们这里做的等于是，把"灵魂"这个理念作为一个本质，给出一个自立性"主体"，不是加于人类，就是加于"上帝"：

> 一组属性，是我们通过它们所认识的一个质的情况，对人的实在经验而言，这些属性就是此处唯一的"现金价值"……于是我们所使用的名字，是作为对这组属性现象的主宰方式……可是"东西"的这些现象特征……肯定不是原属存在名字中的，如果不是因为名字，它们是哪儿都不属的。它们是"adhere"（依附），或者说"cohere"（黏合），更是"彼此相互地"；而且这个"一个质"概念，是我们近不得身的，对于它，我们是想，表明这个凝聚力，质的概念是它的根据，就像水泥能黏合一片片

understanding of person over to shed some light on what I would call a Confucian understanding of human-centered religiousness. In the familiar language of substance ontology, "God" is to be understood as the imperceptible human "soul" writ large as a subsisting "world soul." Analogous to the soul as the invisible, immutable essence that makes us human "beings," the creator God is the essential Being behind these beings—the one coherent invisible design standing behind and sustaining our "*uni*-verse," our "single-ordered cosmos." William James worries over this "inveterate human trick of turning names into things"—what we do here when we attribute this notion of "soul" as a substance that provides discrete agency to either human beings or to God:

> A group of attributes is what each substance here is known-as, they form its sole cash-value for our actual experience.... The name we then treat as in a way supporting the group of phenomena.... But the phenomenal properties of things... surely do not inhere in names, and if not in names then they do not inhere in anything. They *ad*here, or *co*here, rather, *with each other*, and the notion of a substance inaccessible to us, which we think accounts for such cohesion by supporting it, as cement

马赛克，是必得要放弃的。

（《儒家角色伦理学：一套特色伦理学词汇》，第234—235页）

might support pieces of mosaic, must be abandoned.

(*Confucian Role Ethics: A Vocabulary,* pp. 213-214)

天命

古文典为揭示"命"的各种不同意义提供了帮助。《说文》从词源上将该字分为"令"（to command）和"口"两部分，并将其定义为"使"（to command, to cause）。古代文本有无数"令"和"命"换用的例子。这样，显然"命"所表示的一个根本意思就是"下令、使执行"（to command, to cause to happen）。

"命"在与语言和沟通的关系上，似乎与其他几个构成孔子思想基架的核心概念都一样，突出了"口"的重要性。"命"在其他几种古词典中的定义也都强化了"口"在"命"作为某种用言辞表达和传达的命令这一意义上的限定作用。《尔雅》将之释为"告"（to inform），《广雅》释为"呼"（to call, to speak）。或许，最值得注意的是，

Tianming

The classical lexicons are of some assistance in unfolding the various dimensions of meaning conveyed by *ming*. Etymologically, the *Shuo-wen* analyzes the character into its two components, *ling* 令 , "to command," and *k'ou* 口 , "mouth," and defines it as *shih* 使 , "to command," "to cause." There are numerous examples in the early texts of *ling* and *ming* being used interchangeably. It is clear then that the fundamental idea represented by *ming* is "to command," "to cause to happen."

In its association with language and communication, *ming* seems to share a significant characteristic with several of the other core concepts that constitute the infrastructure of Confucius' thought. The importance of the *k'ou* 口 "mouth" to qualify *ming* as a verbalized and communicated command is reinforced by the several definitions of *ming* found in other early lexicons. The *Erh-ya* has *kao* 告 "to inform," *Kuang-ya* has *hu* 呼 "to call," and "to speak." Perhaps most significantly, *ming* not only means "to name," like *ming** 名 , but on

"命"不仅同"名"一样意味着"命名"(to name),而且,有时也确实与"名"换用。

"命"后来逐渐用来指称限定社会存在的某些特定情况:寿夭、禄位、福寿——不仅是一时之"命运",而且是"生命"本身。至少早在周克商时,"天命"(the command of t'ien)就用来作为君主能否继续在位的一个条件。古代文献中,"天命"常被描述为跟治国威望有关,而且与之彼此牵动。

唐君毅在概述古代哲学文献时总结道:

> "命"这个字代表天和人的相互关系……我们可以说,它既不是仅外在地存于天,也不仅内在地存于人;而是存在于天人的相互关系中,即存在于它们的相互影响和回应,彼此取予之中。

唐君毅的这一解释反映了《左传》对"命"的定义:"民受天地之中以生,所谓命也。"《孟子》所谓:"莫非命也……"《孟子》解释了"命"的普遍存在且试图将之与

occasion is actually used interchangeably with this character.

At some point which is not entirely clear, *ming* came to designate certain specific conditions that define existence in the world: lifespan, social and economic status, physical health—not only one's "lot" in life, but one's "life" itself. At least as early as the Chou conquest of Shang, the concept *t'ien ming* 天命, "the command of *t'ien*," emerged as a condition for the ruler's political continuance in office. In the early corpus, this "command" of *t'ien* is frequently described as contingent upon and responsive to the particular character of the ruling authority.

T'ang Chün-i, in a survey of the early philosophical literature, concludes that:

> The term "*ming*" represents the interrelationship or mutual relatedness of Heaven and man….We can say that it exists neither externally in Heaven only, nor internally in man only; it exists, rather, in the mutuality of Heaven and man, i.e., in their mutual influence and response, their mutual giving and receiving.

In this analysis, T'ang reflects the *Tso-chuan* definition of *ming* which states: "That the people receive the context of the heavens and earth in being born and growing is what is called *ming*." The *Mencius* observes, "There is

"天"区别开来："莫之为而为者，天也；莫之致而至者，命也。"（《孟子·万章上》）该章似乎在说，"天"指的是自然和人类世界自然生发的过程本身，而"命"则表示为它的生发提供语境的特定现象产生的条件和可能性。"天"不是"他者"的产物。

"命"作为决定个别现象产生的因果条件，既是其诸种可能性又同时是其局限性。"命"是所处境遇种种局限性协调出的可能性未来。同样，"天"本身也可根据限定它的条件来表征。《中庸》引《诗》曰："维天之命，於穆不已"，随即评论道："盖曰天之所以为天也。"这并不意味着"天"是由"他物"所生，而是由特定因果条件以某种特定方式决定的。

如果"天"确实指称某一特定视角对整个存在过程的认识，那么，唐君毅将"命"定义为"天和人的相互关系"就没有错。这就是说，"命"可比于像"势"（conditions or circumstances）这样的概念，因为二者都可描述构成既定事件基体的现有种种条件——身体、心理或环境——的结合体。但也正如唐君毅的定义所表明的那样，由于"命"

nothing which is not *ming*...." Mencius clarifies the ubiquity of *ming* and attempts to distinguish it from *t'ien*: "Those things that are done (*wei* 爲) without anything doing them are *t'ien*; those things that occur without anything causing them (*ch'ih* 致) are *ming*." From this passage, it would appear that while *t'ien* designates the process itself of the natural and human worlds arising spontaneously, *ming* represents those conditions and possibilities of a particular phenomenon which provide the context for its arising. There is not something "other" that makes *t'ien*.

As the causal conditions defining a particular event, *ming* is both its possibilities and its limitations. *Ming* is a possible future negotiated within the limitations of the sponsoring circumstances. As such, *t'ien* itself can be described in terms of its defining conditions. The *Chung-yung* cites the *Book of Songs*: "Ah! The *ming* of *t'ien*—so profound and unceasing," and then provides the following commentary: "This (that is, *ming*) then describes what makes *t'ien* what it is." This does not mean that *t'ien* is made by something "other", but that there are certain causal conditions that define it in a certain way.

If *t'ien* is indeed a designation for a particular perspective on the whole process of existence, T'ang Chün-i is not wrong in defining *ming* as "the interrelatedness or mutual relatedness of Heaven and man." That is, *ming* might be compared to a notion such as *shih* 勢,

总似乎涉及人类视角,这两个概念还是有着重要的不同。

如果"命"被理解为决定世界特定人类视角的种种条件和可能性,那它必然涉及对现象因果渊源的解释。另外,因为不涉意义和价值超验根源的宇宙发生论意义上的概念,那它准确地说就是对创造个体世界的条件性环境的解释。因此,"命"完全是个体"创造的世界"。这说明了"名"和"命"之间显而易见的关系:"命"就是"命名"世界。叶山(Robin Yates)的墨家研究也给出了同样的结论:

> 在我看来,事实不应该是:中国曾经有精致的创世神话,后来流失在传承过程中。中国人的创世实际是通过命名对关系和界限的划分——无论地理、政治、宗教还是社会——它被描述得就像一个历史事件。

"命"以一种散点的方式体现了对存在过程的观察。区分个别事物既是对它的"命名",也是意识到它所出现的语境。而该语境被理解为"自我"语境还是"他者"语

"conditions or circumstances," in that both can describe a calculus of existing conditions—physical, moral, environmental—that constitute the matrix for a given event. As T'ang Chün-i's definition would also indicate, the two notions have important differences, however, in that *ming* always seems to involve the human perspective.

If *ming* is to be understood as the conditions and possibilities that define a particular human perspective in the world, this is but to say that it involves an interpretation of the causal matrix for each particular phenomenon that arises in it. Moreover, without the concept of a cosmogonic act on the part of some transcendent source of meaning and value, it is precisely the interpretation of one's conditioning environs that is the creation of one's world. Thus *ming* is nothing less than one's *created world*. This explains the apparent relationship between "naming" (*ming**) and *ming*: to *ming* is to "articulate" the world. Robin Yates, in his work on the Mohists, arrives at a similar conclusion:

> It is not the case, in my opinion, that the Chinese once had elaborate creation myths that were lost in the course of transmission. The demarcation of boundaries and relationships, geographical, political, religious and social, by naming, described as though it was an historical event, *was* the creation of the Chinese world.

境取决于命名行为达致的特定焦点（particular focus）。如果一个人根本趋向被动存在，其个人的秩序和意义是从其实际的文化语境中衍生出的，那么，他大体上是外在权威的产物。而如果一个人将自我秩序和意义播撒于世界，那么，他就是其环境的实际文化构成富有意义的创造因素。当然，这一"创造世界"的过程是一种互相创造，是由"天"所代表的可能性范围与个人理解、选择和实现其中某些可能性的能力共同塑造的。

"命"与关系性概念"礼"有重要相似之处。"命"的宇宙论维度使其成为"因果条件"（causal conditions），它似乎一直都有个从统治者中心的社会作为"命令"之"命"的历史发展线索。这一发展轨迹与"礼"（rites）的拓展类似，"礼"也是从早期仅限于表达统治者与神的关系，发展成泛指整个社会结构的一般概念。"命"包含"礼"是因为文化一致本身就是一套首要的因果条件；而"命"又超出了"礼"的概念，是因为它包括所有的条件——生物学、社会、经济、地理、历史等等。

Ming entails viewing the process of existence in a discursive way. The discrimination of the particular entails both a "naming" of it and a perception of it as emerging out of a certain context. And the extent to which this context is construable as "self" and as "other" is a function of the particular focus achieved in the act of naming. Where a person leads a fundamentally passive existence, deriving his order and meaning from his physical and cultural context, he is largely a product of external authority. Where a person diffuses his order and meaning throughout the world, he can be a significant factor in authoring the physical and cultural constitution of his environment. Such "world making" is, of course, a co-authored interpretation that emerges out of the range of possibilities represented by *t'ien* with the individual's ability to understand, select and effect certain of these possibilities.

There is an important analog to *ming* in the relational concept, *li*, "ritual action." The cosmological dimension of *ming* as "causal conditions" seems to have been a historical development from the *ming* of "command" in a ruler-centered world. This development parallels the extension of *li*, "rites," from its early restricted usage as a relationship obtaining between ruler and deity to the generalized notion of pervasive social structures. The concept *ming* embraces

"命"和"礼"的另一个相似之处在于它们都是可以改变的。既然人是意义和价值的最终根源，因此文化一致性就随时可以重组和再诠释。事实上，尽管"命"为未来设了某些限制，但没有哪一种既定因素在任何意义上都是颠扑不破的。每一要素就其相关于人类社会而言，都有一个人类的意义。因为人类是给出命名的根源，他可以通过改变"名"的意义来改变世界。从历史上看，基本类似的环境却形成人类经验如此不同的文化结构，这一事实正表明了受诠释行为影响的条件的可变性。

在我们转入《论语》中"命"的具体例子之前，我们将首先看一下孔子的许多注者在"命"的认识上的一些共同看法。其中刘殿爵所译《论语》一书导论中提出的观点最为清晰和系统。他说：

> 无论早期著作中"命"是否作为"天命"的缩写来使用，但毫无疑问，到了孔子的时代，它已发展为具有不同的独立意义的术语。

li inasmuch as cultural consensus itself is a premier set of causal conditions. It extends beyond *li* in that *ming* includes all conditions—biological, social economic, geographical, historical, and so forth.

Another parallel between *ming* and *li* is that they are both alterable. Since the human being is the ultimate source of meaning and value, cultural consensus is always open to reformulation and reinterpretation. In fact, although *ming* sets certain limitations on possible futures, none of the given factors are in any sense incontrovertible. Each of the factors, insofar as it has bearing on the human world, has a human meaning. Since the human being is the source of discursive naming, he can alter his world by altering its meaning. The fact that, historically, a basically similar environment has sponsored such a vast range of cultural structures for the human experience is evidence of the flexibility of conditions as influenced by acts of interpretation.

Before turning to specific examples of *ming* as it appears in the *Analects*, we shall first qualify several assertions concerning *ming* that are shared by many commentators on Confucius, but which are perhaps most clearly and systematically advanced by D.C. Lau in the introduction to his translation of this text. Lau states:

> Whether *ming* was simply used

刘殿爵为这一区分做了进一步解释，指出"命"就是"Destiny"："不是人类作用的产物"，"人类对此无能为力"。这样，"命"就成了我们最好随任之的某种神秘事物。将孔子归于宿命论的说法，历史上最早可追溯到《墨子》，《墨子·非儒》中对孔子有言辞激烈的批评：

> 有强执有命以说议曰："寿夭贫富，安危治乱，固有天命，不可损益。"

刘殿爵认为，"天命"同"命"相比，前者是一种道德诫令，指示"人该如何行事"。这样，人应当理解和遵从"天命"。刘殿爵基本上认定孔子是个"温和的命定论者"，按照事实和价值来划分"取决者"和"被决者"：

> 一个人富贵寿终与否均取决于"命"。无论他做出多大努力结果都不会变。这样，就他的运势来说，"命"就是他抽到的签。

刘殿爵认为，只有认识到人类

as an abbreviation for *t'ien ming* in early texts, there is no doubt that by Confucius' time, it had developed into a term with a different and independent meaning.

Lau goes on to clarify this distinction, venturing that *ming* is "Destiny": "things which are brought, about, not by human agency," things "over which human endeavour has no effect." As such, *ming* is a mystery which we do best to leave alone. This attribution of fatalism to Confucius has historical precedent as far back as the *Mo Tzu*, which criticizes him with verve:

> The Confucians think that there is an ultimate determination of men's long life or premature death, poverty or wealth, order or disorder [in the world] by *ming*, which can neither be decreased nor increased.

For Lau, *t'ien ming*, in contrast to *ming*, is a moral imperative "concerned with what man ought to do." As such, it can be understood and obeyed. Lau's argument here is basically that Confucius is a "soft determinist," separating determined and determinable along the lines of fact and value:

> Whether or not a man is going to end up with wealth, honour and long life is due to Destiny. No amount of effort on

存在那些先定因而无法逃脱的"实在"本质,才会使人相信反对命运是徒劳的,也才会反而激起他"专心追求道德的完善"。人尽管不能操纵他的存在,他却可以掌握自己屈从或违背这些前定的道德诫命,这些道德诫命体现在作为"义"的"天命"中,在刘殿爵看来,"天命"就是"义"(rightness)既定的原则。

刘殿爵宣称《论语》中"天命"和"命"的根本区别是"理解孔子思想倾向的关键",这很可能是站不住脚的。正如他本人承认的那样,早期著作中"命"常被用作"天命"的缩写。《孟子》及其后来的一些著作中"命"也是这种用法。《论语》似乎不可能是这种情况的唯一例外。尽管古代文献中显然有把"天命"专门用作朝代延续更替的政治理由的传统,但正如我们上文所论,在孔子的时代,该因果条件的概念已从君主及其朝廷扩展为用到一般人身上了。

《论语》中"天命"和"命"都在这一宽泛的意义上使用。如果说它们之间有某种区别的话,那就在于"命"可同时在狭义和广义上使用。"天命"特指从特定视角建构的

his part will make any difference to the outcome. Thus, in the context of the fortunes of an individual, *ming* is his lot.

Lau contends that it is only an understanding of the predetermined and hence inescapable nature of the "factual" aspects of human existence that will persuade man of the futility of opposing them and will instead encourage him to "bend his efforts to the pursuit of morality." Although man does not control the facticity of his existence, he does have control over his own compliance or noncompliance with those predetermined moral imperatives which are embedded in *t'ien ming* as *yi* 義, which are (for Lau) given principles of rightness.

Lau's claim that a radical distinction between *t'ien ming* and *ming* in the *Analects* is "vital to the understanding of Confucius' position" may be unwarranted. As Lau himself allows, *ming* is frequently used as an abbreviation for *t'ien ming* in the early texts. It is also used in this way in the *Mencius* and later texts. It would seem rather improbable that the *Analects* would be the sole exception to this usage. Although there is a clear tradition of *t'ien ming* being used specifically in the early literature as a political justification for dynastic succession and continuity, as we have observed above, by the time of Confucius this notion of causal conditions had been extended from the ruler and his court to be applied to human beings generally.

存在整体的诸因果条件，"命"却不仅指涉整体，还可专指个别现象构成的因果关系。

其次，将"命"译为"Fate"或"Destiny"，且将"天命"解释为某种道德诫命，都带有强烈的超验意味。"to destine"（注定）这个动词在盎格鲁—欧洲传统中的意思是"打结、牢固"（to make fast or firm）、"预先固定"（to fix beforehand）、"先定"（to predetermine）。"Fate"有着类似的意思"已给出"——神的判决。这些术语的专有名词都强化了这样一种观念，即某种独立于人类的原则、力量或动因在为人类存在立法，或者至少规约其中的某些方面。因此，把"天命"视为某种外在、客观存在的道德诫命就与天人的"合一"关系相抵触。因此，我们将论证："命"建构了存在的因果条件，这些条件既不是先定也不是不可动摇的。这也就是说，人是他自身在这个世界上存在的决定性力量，现有条件及其境遇都会因他的参与而改变。个体的成熟是对种种可能性做出回应的结果，而这些可能性本身是由个体行为与其环境相互作用决定的。

In the *Analects*, *t'ien ming* and *ming* are both used in this more general sense, and if there is an appreciable difference between them, it may lie principally in the fact that *ming* can be used in both a narrow and an extended sense. Where *t'ien ming* means the causal conditions constituting the whole of existence as perceived from a particular perspective, *ming* can mean the same, or can also mean the causal conditions constituting a particular phenomenon, without necessary reference to the whole.

Secondly, to translate *ming* as Fate or Destiny, and to explain *t'ien ming* as a moral imperative strongly hints at transcendence. The verb "to destine" in the Anglo-European tradition means "to make fast or firm," "to fix beforehand," "to predetermine." "Fate" similarly means "that which has been spoken"—the doom of the gods. Making proper nouns of these terms reinforces the sense that some principle, power, or agency independent of the human being legislates at least certain aspects of his existence. To thus cast *t'ien ming* as an external, objectively existing moral imperative is to challenge the integrity of the *t'ien-jen* relationship. We would argue that *ming* constitutes the causal conditions that sponsor the emergence of a particular human being, or any other phenomenon, and that these conditions are neither predetermined nor inexorable. That is, inasmuch as a human being is himself a determining force in the world, existing conditions and specifically his

将孔子诠释为命定论者最有力的例证就是《论语·雍也》中这段话:

> 伯牛有疾,子问之,自牖执其手,曰:"亡之,命矣夫!斯人也而有斯疾也!斯人也而有斯疾也!"

该章表明人几乎完全不能掌握自己的命运。但这并不就是说,人完全只能听之任之。实际上,《论语》中的子贡就同其经济和社会地位进行抗争:

> 回也其庶乎,屡空。赐不受命,而货殖焉,亿则屡中。(《论语·先进》)

君子也是可掌握自己生死权利的人:

> 今之成人者何必然?见利思义,见危授命。(《论语·宪问》)

显然,如果"命"先定而不可动摇,那么子贡既不能拒绝也无法

own circumstances are alterable through his own participation. An individual's maturation is the result of responding to possibilities which are themselves determined in the interchange between his actions and the emergence of yet other phenomena.

The strongest case in favor of a deterministic interpretation of Confucius can be made from passages such as (6.10):

> Po-niu was ill. Confucius went to look in on him, and, grasping his hand through the window, he lamented, "It is due to the force of circumstances (*ming*) that we are losing this man. That such a man could have such an illness! That such a man could have such an illness!"

This passage makes it clear that at the very least, man does not have complete control over his circumstances. However, this is not the same as saying that he exercises no control at all over them. In fact, the *Analects* describes Tzu-kung in revolt against his economic and social conditions (11.18):

> Yen Hui has almost made it, but he is consistently in poverty. Tzu-kung does not accept his circumstances (*ming*) and has gone into business. And in his ventures he is consistently on the mark.

The exemplary person is portrayed as one

改变它，君子的死生也不会受他自己支配。还有下面这章：

> 司马牛忧曰："人皆有兄弟，我独亡。"子夏曰："商闻之矣：'死生有命，富贵在天。'君子敬而无失，与人恭而有礼，四海之内皆兄弟也。君子何患乎无兄弟也？"（《论语·颜渊》）

该章常被引述论证"命"的"命中注定"（Destiny）的观点。刘殿爵将其视为最佳例证。但事实上这段话意思似乎恰恰相反。孔子的学生子夏引用了一句广为流传的名言，表明有些情况常被认为不是人力所能左右的。然后，他又以其中一个似乎肯定无法改变的情况（无兄弟）为例，说明情况可改变的条件。

首先，我们知道历史上的司马牛其实有一个兄弟——桓魋，这个人曾威胁过孔子的生命。司马牛在这里不认这个兄弟，不根据"确凿事实"来说"兄弟情谊"，变更了一个表面上无法变更的事实。子夏则给了一个更好的例子，说明反之

who chooses to determine the duration of his own lifespan (14.12):

> But to be a complete person in these times one need not go so far. He need only consider what is appropriate at the sight of personal profit, be willing to lay down his life (*ming*) at the sight of danger….

Clearly, if his *ming* were predetermined and inexorable, Tzu-kung could neither refuse it nor alter it, and the exemplary person's time of death would not be under his own sway. Further, there is the following passage (12.5):

> Ssu-ma Niu lamented, "Everyone has brothers except for me."
> Tzu-hsia said to him: "I have heard the saying: Life and death are a matter of *ming*; Wealth and honor lie with *t'ien*. The exemplary person (*chün tzu*) is deferential and faultless, respectful of others and refined, and everyone in the world is his brother. Why would the exemplary person worry about not having brothers?"

This passage is frequently cited to support the contention that *ming* means Destiny. Lau calls it his best illustration. But in fact this passage seems to have precisely the opposite meaning. Confucius' disciple, Tzu-hsia, repeats

亦是有效的——一个无兄弟的人可通过重新定义何谓有兄弟（即通过改变它的意义和指涉的基础，即其"名"）来改变这一使得他无兄无弟的状况（他的命）。他认为手足关系道德上（兄弟般）的标准胜过生物上（一奶同胞）的标准。这段话远非证明宿命论，而是说明"命"的变动性，说明描述个人的因果环境——"命"时，事实和价值的不可分离性。

"天命"和"命"之间的关系或许可这样表述：一个已获得像君子或圣人这样高级整体性的人建立了某种与"天"的内在关系，这种关系使他通过理解力和影响来运用"天命"。一个人自控力越弱，他将"命"视为无法抗拒的决定性条件的感觉就越强；一个人的自控能力越强，他自觉到自己在决定外在条件时所起的主导作用就越大。当世界尊重他的道德，他就为世界"言说"，即他为"天"说话。这样，从环境强加个人以意义还是个人主动为情境引入意义这两个不同角度，体现了个体语境意义的不同。

诚然，该诠释部分延续的是刘殿爵观点。此推论基于以下重要限

a popular maxim which suggests that there are circumstances that are commonly perceived as being beyond human influence. He then takes one of these circumstances (a man having no brothers) which would seem to be positively unalterable and explores a condition under which this situation can be changed.

First, we know that historically Ssu-ma Niu did in fact have a brother, Huan T'ui—the man who threatened Confucius' life. Here Ssu-ma Niu disowns him and alters the apparently unalterable by refusing to interpret "brotherliness" in terms of "facticity." Tzu-hsia then does him one better by demonstrating that the reverse can also be effected—a brotherless person can alter the conditions (that is, his *ming* 命) which cause him to be brotherless by redefining what it means to have brothers (that is, by changing its meaning and frame of reference, its "name," *ming** 名). He asserts that the criterion of brotherhood can be moral (fraternal) rather than biological (born of the same womb). This passage, far from justifying fatalism, demonstrates the fluidity of *ming* and the inseparability of fact and value in the description of one's causal context, one's *ming*.

The problem of the relation between *t'ien ming* and *ming* might be solved in such a manner as this: the individual who has attained a high degree of integration of the sort associated with the exemplary person (*chün tzu*) or the sage (*sheng jen*) has established a peculiarly immanent relationship with *t'ien* which permits

定：尽管或许最好把"命"理解为比"天命"更少为个体控制的环境条件，但控制力主要是由个体自我实现程度所决定的。同时，也是衡量是否值得个体为其付出最大努力的部分标准。为了为真正有意义的事业积蓄力量，终究有一些抗争我们是不会去做的。原则上君子或圣人富有意义的影响环境的能力是无限的。用西方哲学传统的一个至理名言来说就是："哲学无非是学习如何去死。"人只要能做出有意义的反应，甚至最"命中注定"的环境也会显著改变。

无论如何，孔子对"命"和"天命"的理解多少比传统认为的要开放得多。回想我们在讨论"成人"行为上对"义"（appropriateness/significating）的探讨，显然，"礼""义"的相互关系就像我们所诠释的"命"和"天命"的关系。因为，以"义"践行"礼"正是以一种有意义的方式对个体既定语境做出反应的典型例证。

（《通过孔子而思》，第 257—266 页）

当偶然的条件规定着一桩特定

him access to the *ming* of *t'ien* both in terms of understanding and of influence. The less intensely focused an individual is, the greater is his sense of *ming* as determining conditions over which he seems to exercise no control; the more intensely focused he is, the greater is his awareness of the role he can play in determining those conditions. Where the world defers to his excellence he "speaks" for the world; that is, he speaks for *t'ien*. The distinction, then, bears on the meaningfulness of one's context both in the sense of its given meaning and in the sense of one's capacity to introduce meaning into it.

Such an interpretation, admittedly speculative, in part sustains the position of Lau, with the following important qualification: although *ming* might best be understood as contextual conditions over which one has initially less control than those represented by *t'ien ming*, this lack of control is largely a function of the degree of self-realization possessed by a given individual. Also, it is partly a measure of the extent to which a given context is deemed worthy of one's best efforts. There are, after all, some battles one simply will not choose to fight in order to save energy for the truly important tasks. In principle there are no limits to the ability of the authoritative person, *chün tzu* or sage, to meaningfully influence his conditions. A truism of the Western philosophic tradition has it that "philosophy is nothing more than learning how to die." One's ability to respond meaningfully to even the most "fated"

的事件时，对于该事件，"命"既意味各种创造性的可能，又意味着一系列的限制。"命"是一种可能的前景，这种前景在起主导作用的各种环境的限度内得以兑现，而在那起主导作用的环境之中，处境本身先于任何派生和孤立的能力观念（notion of agency）。

（《切中伦常：〈中庸〉的新诠与新译》，第53页）

"命"习惯上翻译为"to command, to order"（动词）或者"command, mandate"（名词）。就词源学而言，《说文》将这个字分为"令"和"口"两个部分，并将这个字的意思解释为"使"。在早期的文献中，关于"令"和"命"可以互换使用，有大量的例证。这一点表明，"命"所表达的根本的意思，就是"命令"（to command）、"使发生"（to cause to happen）。

"命"这个字的"口"的部分也是很有意义的，它将"命"与有效的沟通联系起来。在儒家的字汇中，许多核心的概念都与"口"字有关。例如，"知""君子""和""恕""信""诚"等。或

of circumstances renders them significantly alterable.

When all qualifying remarks have been made, however, it remains true that Confucius' understanding of *ming* and *t'ien ming* is much less conservative than has traditionally been believed. Recalling the discussion of *yi* (appropriateness/significating) within the context of the activity of person making, it is clear that the interrelations of ritual action (*li*) and *yi* require something like our interpretation of *ming* and *t'ien ming*. For to perform ritual action (*li*) with *yi* is a paradigmatic instance of responding to one's given context in a meaningful manner.

(*Thinking through Confucius,* pp. 208-216)

As the causal conditions defining a particular event, *ming* is both its creative possibilities and its limitations. *Ming* is a possible future negotiated within the limitations of the sponsoring circumstances, where the situation itself is prior to any derived and isolatable notion of agency.

(*Focusing the Familiar: A Translation and Philosophical Interpretation of the Zhongyong,* p. 29)

Ming is conventionally translated as "to command, to order" and hence, a "command" or "mandate." Etymologically, the *Shuowen* lexicon analyzes the graph into its two components, *ling* 令 "to command," and *kou*

许，最明显的是，"命"与"名"同音，有时也可以与"名"互换使用。因此，就"口"这一部分而言，"命"的基本含义就是"通过有效的沟通来实现"。

有时，"命"是指那些特定的条件。那些条件规定着世间诸如一个人的寿命、社会经济地位、身体健康状况，等等，不仅是一个人一生中的"命运"，也指一个人的生命本身。至少早在周朝，就其政治上的使用来说，"天命"这个概念的出现，是作为统治者执政的条件的。

重要的是，在早期的文献中，"天"的这种"命"既不是武断的，也不是单向的。它更多地被描述为与统治权威的特定品格密切相关，依后者的具体情况而定，是对后者的一种回应。这样就使得我们在一种交互性的意义上来理解"天命"："天"对"君主"授予其不断的支持，而"君主"施行"天"对他的信任。在这个意义上，"天"和"君主"都是发"令"者。

当然，《中庸》最为重要的贡献之一，就是对于"诚"的阐发。《中庸》讲得很清楚，真正的"创造性"（诚）使自然而然的更新的出现成

口 "mouth," defining it as *shi* 使 "to cause to happen." There are numerous examples in the early literature of *ling* and *ming* being used interchangeably, suggesting that the fundamental idea represented by *ming* is "to command," "to cause to happen."

The "mouth(*kou*)" component of the character is significant, linking *ming* to effective communication, an association shared with many of the other core concepts in the Confucian vocabulary: *zhi* 知 "to know, to realize," *junzi* 君子 "exemplary person," *he* 和 "harmony," *shu* 恕 "deference," *xin* 信 "making good on one's word," *cheng* 誠 "sincerity/creativity," and so on. Perhaps most significantly, *ming* 命 is homophonous with *ming* 名 "to name", and is on occasion used interchangeably with this character. Hence, the basic idea is "to realize through effective communication."

At some point, *ming* came to designate those specific conditions that define existence in the world such as one's lifespan, one's social and economic status, one's physical health—not only one's "lot" in life, but one's life itself. Applied politically at least as early as the Zhou dynasty, the concept *tianming* 天命 "the command of tian," emerged as a condition for the ruler's continuance in office.

Importantly, in the early corpus, this "command" of *tian* is not arbitrary or unilateral, but is rather described as contingent upon and responsive to the particular character of the

为必然。这样一来,"创造"就不能够被化约为某种决定机制的预先存在的原因的推演。这显然符合对于"命"的一种更为决定论的诠释。

(《切中伦常:〈中庸〉的新诠与新译》,第90—91页)

诚

在以往英语世界的文献中,"诚"这个术语最为通常的翻译是"integrity"或"sincerity"。而在我们的翻译中,我们引入了"creativity",将其作为《中庸》中"诚"的最为重要的含义。

"creativity"作为"诚"的英文翻译之所以恰如其分,在于作为《中庸》世界观之基础的过程性的假

ruling authority. This allows us to understand *tianming* in a transactional sense: *Tian* and the ruler both "command" in the sense that *tian* confers its continuing support on the ruler and the ruler commands *tian*'s trust.

Certainly one of the most important contributions of the *Zhongyong* is its elaboration upon the term *cheng* 誠, making it clear that real creativity entails the spontaneous emergence of novelty, and cannot, therefore, be reducible to a calculus of prior causes of some determining agent. This significantly qualifies the more deterministic interpretations of *ming*.

(*Focusing the Familiar: A Translation and Philosophical Interpretation of the Zhongyong*, pp. 71-72)

Creativity (*Cheng*)

This term is most commonly translated in the early literature as either "integrity" or "sincerity." In our translation, we have introduced the term "creativity" as the most important meaning of *cheng* within the *Zhongyong*.

The appropriateness of "creativity" as a translation for *cheng* lies in the process assumptions underlying the world view of the *Zhongyong*. In a world of changing events, "integrity" suggests an active process of bringing circumstances together in a

定（process assumptions）。在一个由变化着的各种事件所组成的世界之中，"integrity"提示着以一种有意义的方式将各种情况聚合在一起的积极过程，目标是获得一种蕴涵着丰富意义的一贯性。就其本身而言，"integrity"提示着一种创造性的过程。"sincerity"包含着情感的主体形式，随着这种情感形式，创造过程得以进行。那就是说，"sincerity"提示着一种心境或情调，这种心境或情调推动着成功的整合。

这一连串三个相互可以取代的翻译在语源学上获得的支持来自于这样的事实："诚"这个字的"创造"感反映在其同源字"成"之中。"成"意味着"完成""成就""实现""圆满"。"成"和"言"一道构成了"诚（誠）"这个字。因此，作为"真诚"的"sincerity"、作为"完整性"的"integrity"以及作为导向这种完整性的成就过程的"creativity"，在不同的语脉之中，都可以作为"诚"的行之有效的翻译。

主要作为"creativity"而非"sincerity"或"integrity"，"诚"注重于作为《中庸》重要主题的宇宙创造性的核心地位。显而易见的人类

meaningful way to achieve the coherence that meaningfulness implies. As such, "integrity" suggests a creative process. "Sincerity" connotes the subjective form of feeling with which that creative process proceeds. That is, it suggests the mood or emotional tone that promotes successful integration.

This cluster of three alternative translations receives support etymologically from the fact that the "creative" sense of the graph *cheng* 诚 is reflected in the cognate *cheng* 成 —"to consummate, complete, finish, bring to fruition"—that together with the "speech" classifier *yan* 言 makes up the character. Thus "sincerity" as "the absence of duplicity," "integrity" as "wholeness," and "creativity" as the process leading to the achievement of such wholeness, can within different contexts all be viable translations.

The parsing of *cheng* principally as "creativity" rather than "sincerity" or "integrity" brings attention to the centrality of cosmic creativity as the main theme of the *Zhongyong*. The vital role of distinctly human creativity within its large cosmic context is described in *Zhongyong* 20:

Creativity is the way of *tian*（天之道）; creating is the proper way of becoming human（人之道）.

Building on a semantic extrapolation seemingly borrowed directly from the *Mencius*

创造性在其广大的宇宙脉络之中所扮演的至关重要的角色，在《中庸》第二十章中有如下的描述：

  诚者天之道也，诚之者人之道也。

正如我们第一章提到的，基于这样一种语义推断的做法似乎是直接借自《孟子·离娄上》第十二章的说法。如此一来，宇宙性共同创造性（cosmic co-creativity）的过程在《中庸》第二十五章中或许就得到了更为清晰和有力的阐发和描述。"诚"的意义从一种人类完整性的态度拓展到用来描述世界形成的过程。在这个过程中，作为共同创造者（co-creator），圣人发挥着关键的作用。由于所有的创造性都发生在关系性的脉络之中，"co-"这个限制前缀就可以抛开不计，"诚"在这里也就可以简单地翻译为"creativity"。

  诚者自成也，而道自道也。诚者，物之终始，不诚无物。是故君子诚之为贵。诚者非自成己而已也，所以成物也。成己，仁也；成物，知

形上学

4.12, this process of cosmic co-creativity is then elaborated upon and described perhaps most clearly and powerfully in *Zhongyong* 25. The meaning of *cheng* is extended from an attitude of human integrity to describe the process of world-making in which the sage (*shengren*) plays a key role as co-creator. Since all creativity occurs within a relational context, the qualifier "co-" is dropped, and *cheng* can be translated here simply as "creativity."

> Creativity (*cheng* 诚) is self-consummating (*zicheng* 自成), and its way is self-directing (*zidao* 自道). Creativity is a process taken from its beginning to its end, and without this creativity, there are no events. It is thus that, for exemplary persons, it is creativity that is prized. But creativity is not simply the self-consummating of one's own person; it is what consummates events. Consummating oneself is authoritative conduct; consummating other events is wisdom. This is the excellence of one's natural tendencies and is the way of integrating what is more internal and what is more external. Thus, whenever one applies this excellence, it is fitting.

The speech element of *cheng* mentioned above suggests that creativity involves a dynamic partnership between the living

59

也。性之德也，合外内之道也。故时措之宜也。

上面提到的"诚"的言说因素向我们提示：创造性涉及活生生的人类世界及其所在的各种自然、社会和文化脉络之间的一种动态的伙伴关系，那是通过在家庭和社群中的有效沟通所成就的一种圆满。

（《切中伦常：〈中庸〉的新诠与新译》，第80—82页）

细读《中庸》我们会发现，"诚"在这一儒家经典文本中的运用可在功能的意义上联想到"道"在道家文本中的运用。这也就是说，"诚"不仅是人之内在本源，而且也是万物之根本：

> 诚者自成也，而道自道也。诚者，物之终始，不诚无物。是故君子诚之为贵。诚者非自成己而已也，所以成物也。成己，仁也；成物，知也。

正如我们可以想到的那样，道家的"道"和儒家的"诚"的主要区别源自这样的事实，即前者是从

human world and its natural, social, and cultural contexts, achieving consummation through effective communication in family and community.

(*Focusing the Familiar: A Translation and Philosophical Interpretation of the Zhongyong*, pp. 61-63)

A careful reading of the *Chung-yung* reveals that *ch'eng* 诚 is used in this basically Confucian-oriented text in a manner that would associate it functionally with *tao* in the Taoist texts. That is to say, *ch'eng* is the immanental source not only of man, but of all things:

> *Ch'eng* means self-completing; and *tao* means self-*tao*-ing. *Ch'eng* is the full consequence of all things; to be not-*ch'eng* is to be nothing. It is for this reason that the exemplary person (*chün tzu*) prizes *ch'eng*. *Ch'eng* is not simply "self-completing," but is that whereby one completes things. To complete oneself is to become a "person" (*jen*); to complete things is "to realize" (*chih*).

As one would expect, the major distinction between the Taoist *tao* and this Confucian notion of *ch'eng* derives from the fact that the former interprets man through the structures of his natural environment, while the latter begins from human beings and tends to understand the cosmos through human categories. The focus

形上学

人的自然环境的框架中来解释人,而后者则从人开始且通过人来理解宇宙。道家注重通过存在的演变来理解人类,而儒家则寻求从人类的视角来理解所有存在。道家不愿仅依靠儒家的"圣人"(sage)涵盖对人的理解,因此,创造了他们自己的范畴"真人"(authentic person)。同样,儒家后来的诠释者将《中庸》的"诚"(integrity)拈出,亦是不愿用浓厚道家意味的"道"。这样,"诚"就成为实现真正人格的专门人类活动从人自身到存在过程所有成分的拓展。

(《通过孔子而思》,第63页)

"诚"通常译为"sincerity",或许更好的词是"integrity",它是又一个例词,用以表达经由交往而形成的"真正的关系"的作用。"诚(誠)"从词源上来说,是由"言"和"成"(to consummate 意为"使完成"、"使完善",to realize 意为"实现")所组成的,在文献中,道和诚有密切的关系:

诚者自成也,而道自道也。诚者,物之终始,不诚无物。是故君子诚之为贵。诚者

of the Taoist is to understand humanity from the perspective of the unfolding pattern of existence, while the Confucian direction is to pursue an understanding of all existence from the human perspective. The Taoists, being reluctant to rely exclusively upon the Confucian-laden term, *sheng jen* 聖人, "sage," as their comprehensive level of personhood, thus generate their own category, *chen jen* 真人, "authentic person." Similarly, the later interpreters of Confucius represented in the *Chung-yung* employ the term *ch'eng* 誠, "integrity," rather than the Taoist-burdened *tao* 道. *Ch'eng*, then, is the extending of the specifically human activity of actualizing genuine personhood from man himself to all constituents in the process of existence.

(*Thinking Through Confucius,* pp. 57-58)

"*Cheng* 誠," conventionally translated as "sincerity" or perhaps better, "integrity," is another example of a term that expresses the effecting of "true relations" through communication, being etymologically constituted by "to speak (*yan* 言)" and "to consummate, to realize (*cheng* 成)." There is a close association in the literature between *dao* 道 and *cheng* 誠:

Integrity (*cheng*) means self-consummating; *dao* means self-articulating (literally, self-*dao*-ing). For something to have integrity is the full substance of that thing from its

61

非自成己而已也，所以成物也。成己，仁也；成物，知也。性之德也，合外内之道也。故时措之宜也。（《中庸》第二十五章）

诚不仅限于对自己诚实。既然所有的自我都是由关系构成的，那么，诚就意味着在与人的交往中要可信、真诚。这是富有成效地将他自己整合到他的社会的、自然的和文化的环境中去。在宇宙论层面，诚之道发育万物，骏极于天。诚不是指事物是什么，而是指事物怎样才能够在它们的协同与联合中很好地、富有成果地存在和发挥作用。这种"丰富"、"大量"的意义，在"诚"的同根词"盛"中也很明显，"盛"的意思是"繁荣"、"茂盛"。

（《汉哲学思维的文化探源》，第167—168页）

《中庸》和《孟子》的联系更加复杂。在《中庸》中，被广泛发展了的最根本和最重要的观念之一，就是"诚"这一概念的拓展和详细阐述。习惯上，"诚"意味着"诚实"（integrity）或者"真诚"

beginning to its end; for it to be lacking in integrity is for it to be nothing. For this reason, the exemplary person (*junzi*) prizes integrity. Integrity is not simply the means to consummate oneself, but also the way to consummate other things. To consummate oneself is to distinguish oneself as a person (*ren* 仁); to consummate other things is to realize them (*zhi* 知).The persistent focus (*de* 德) of one's natural proclivities (*xing* 性) is the way to coordinate self in context. Thus, integrity is being appropriate anytime and anywhere.

Integrity is more than being true to oneself. Since all selves are constituted by relationships, integrity means being trustworthy and true in one's associations. It is effectively integrating oneself in one's social, natural, and cultural contexts. At a cosmological level, integrity is the ground from which self and other arise together to maximum benefit. It is not *what* things are, but *how well* and *how productively* they are able to fare in their synergistic alliances. This sense of "abundance" or "plenty" is evident in *cheng*'s cognate, *sheng* 盛, which means "to prosper," "to flourish."

(*Thinking from the Han,* pp. 161-162)

The connection between the *Zhongyong* and the *Mencius* is a bit more complex. One of the most original and remarkable ideas that （sincerity）这样一种情感。但是，在《中庸》中，"诚"已经逐步地开始拥有了宇宙论的意义。"诚"表达的是人们对于"宇宙创造性"（cosmic creativity）这一不断进程的参与。

（《切中伦常：〈中庸〉的新诠与新译》，第3页）

在《中庸》里，"诚"常常被翻译为"sincerity"，有时也翻译成"integrity"。而将其翻译为"creativity"，我们的理论说明如下：根据过程性的理解而非实体性的概念，我们对中国世界特质的理解会更好。如果说这一主张是合理的话，那么，我们就必须考虑到，在这样一个世界中，"物"是被理解为过程（process）和事件（events）的。通过诉诸一个过程的世界来加以理解，无论是没有口是心非的"sincerity"，还是健全完整的"integrity"，都必须涉及"成为一个个体"或"成为一个整全"的过程。就审美的角度来理解，成为整全的动态，恰恰是一个创造的过程所意味的东西。因此，"诚"被理解为创造性。

"诚"是一种由构成性关系（constitutive relationships）的独特性

is developed extensively in the *Zhongyong* is the extension and elaboration of the familiar notion of *cheng* 诚 that conventionally meant "integrity" or "sincerity" to express human participation in the ongoing process of "cosmic creativity."

(*Focusing the Familiar : A Translation and Philosophical Interpretation of the Zhongyong,* p. 134)

In the *Zhongyong, cheng* 誠 has most often been translated as "sincerity" or at times, as "integrity." Our rationale for also translating the term as "creativity" is as follows: If it may be reasonably claimed that the Chinese world is better characterized in terms of process understandings than in substantive concepts, then one must reckon that in such a world, "thing(*wu* 物)" are to be understood as processes (happenings) and events (happenings that have achieved some relative consummation). Construed by appeal to a world of process, both "sincerity," as the absence of duplicity, and "integrity," the state of being sound or whole, must involve the *process* of "becoming one" or "becoming whole." The dynamic of becoming whole, construed aesthetically, is precisely what is meant by a creative process. It is thus that *cheng* is to be understood as *creativity*.

Cheng 誠 is process defined by the uniqueness and persistence of the constitutive relationships that define a particular "event (*wu* （uniqueness）和持久性（persistence）所决定的过程，那种构成性关系决定了一个特定的"事物"。在根据上下文的脉络来翻译"物"时，不论是"过程"还是"事件"都可以使用。"过程"强调创造性生成的动态方面；"事件"则侧重于一个特定过程的结束或圆满完成。

（《切中伦常：〈中庸〉的新诠与新译》，第 56 页）

物）." Both the terms "process" and "event" may be used in translating *wu* depending upon context—the former when the dynamic aspect of creative becoming is stressed, the latter when one focuses upon the closure or consummation of a particular process.

(*Focusing the Familiar: A Translation and Philosophical Interpretation of the Zhongyong,* pp. 31-32)

气

Qi

"气"这个字有各种不同的翻译，如"hylozoistic vapors"、"psycho physical stuff"、"vital energizing field"等。"气"最初出现于商代的甲骨和周代青铜器的铭文上时，其写法是平行的三横，很像现代中文中的"三"字，只不过这三横通常较短且有起伏。《说文》将"气"解释为象形字，代表生起的雾气，也将其定义为"云气"。它描绘了云气升降的多种层次。

虽然阴阳五行宇宙论的系统化直到汉代才形成，世界及其现象源于并回归于被称为"气"的生命能量这样一种观念，却在公元前 4 世

This character *qi*, translated variously as "hylozoistic vapors," "psychophysical stuff," and "vital energizing field," first appears on the Shang oracle bones and on the Zhou bronze inscriptions as three horizontal lines, similar to the modern character for "three (*san* 三)," except the three lines are usually shorter and somewhat more fluid. The *Shuowen* lexicon explains this graph as a pictographic character representing rising mists, and defines it as "cloud vapors (*yunqi* 雲氣)." It depicts multiple layers of ascending and descending vapors.

Although the systematized and elaborate *yinyang wuxing* cosmology does not appear until Han dynasty sources, the idea that the world and its phenomena emerge out of and

纪晚期和公元前 3 世纪早期已经广泛流行。无论在《中庸》《道德经》还是《孟子》以及其他一些早期的文献中，都可以证明这一点。

"气"必须与"basic matter"和"animating vapors"区分开来。其原因在于："气"不会落于任何形式的精神—物质的两分（spiritual-material dichotomy）。"气"既是生命能量，又是被赋予生命能量的东西。不存在缺乏生气的东西，只有生命能量的场域及其焦点式的体现。转化的能力居于世界自身的内部，其表现正如《庄子》所谓的"物化"。

正是这种有关宇宙变化过程的焦点——场域式的理解，隐含在《庄子》之中，被假定为一种常识。

（《切中伦常：〈中庸〉的新诠与新译》，第 91 页）

fold back into a vital energizing field called *qi* was already widely held in the late fourth century and early third century BCE, attested to in the *Zhuangzi*, the *Daodejing*, and the *Mencius*, as well as other early texts.

Qi has to be distinguished from either "basic matter" or "animating vapors" in that it will not be resolved into any kind of spiritual-material dichotomy. *Qi* is both the animating energy and what is animated. There are no things to be animated; there is only the vital energizing field and its focal manifestations. The energy of transformation resides within the world itself, and is expressed in what *Zhuangzi* calls the perpetual "transforming of processes and events (*wuhua* 物化)."

It is this understanding of a focus-field process of cosmic change that is implicitly assumed in the *Zhongyong* as commonsense.

(*Focusing the Familiar: A Translation and Philosophical Interpretation of the Zhongyong*, pp. 72-73)

阴阳

Yin & Yang

阴与阳是一对相互关联的元素，它们在区分"此"与"彼"的过程中非常有实际效用。阴与阳不是通常所谓的亮和暗、男和女、动与静的二元原则，亮和暗相互排斥，

Yin and *yang* are elements of a correlative pairing which are pragmatically useful in sorting out "this" and "that." *Yin* and *yang* are not, as often claimed, dualistic principles of light and dark, male and female, action and passivity, where light and dark exclude each

逻辑上又相互需要，并且相互补充构成一个整体。而阴和阳首先是一对表示质的对比的词语，它们被用于特殊情境中，并且使得我们能够作出特定的区分。

由于一个命题必须只有唯一的含义，术语必须是严格地可限定的。而一个两极感悟方式（polar sensibility）则用最概括的术语排除了这种限定。这样，古代中国人将阴和阳理解为对举的概念，这并不必然导致二元的说明或解释。阴是一个正在形成的阳（a becoming-yang），阳是一个正在形成的阴（a becoming-yin）。

阴和阳总是描述独一无二的特殊个体之间的关系。最初，这两个术语指称山的有阳光的一面和没有阳光的一面，逐渐就用来表示，在两个事物相互关系的某一特殊方面一方胜过另一方。在这个配对中所捕捉到的对立的本性表达了动态的关系之间的相关性、相互依赖性、差异性以及创造的效验，而这种动态的关系被看成内在于世界之中并且维持世界的稳定。世界上的一切差异都被认为可以通过这个配对得到解释。总之，阴和阳是专门的解

other, logically entail each other, and in their complementarity constitute a totality. Rather *yin* and *yang* are, first and foremost, a vocabulary of qualitative contrasts which are applicable to specific situations, and which enable us to make specific distinctions.

For a proposition to have a univocal sense, terms must be strictly delimitable. A polar sensibility precludes such delimitation in any but the grossest terms. Thus, the classical Chinese understanding of *yin* and *yang* as contrastive concepts cannot coherently lead to dualistic translations or interpretations. *Yin* is a becoming-*yang*; *yang* is a becoming-*yin*.

Yin and *yang* always describe the relationships of unique particulars. Originally these terms designated the shady side and the sunny side of a hill, and gradually came to suggest the way in which one thing "overshadows" another in some particular aspect of their relationship. The nature of the opposition captured in this pairing expresses the mutuality, interdependence, diversity, and creative efficacy of the dynamic relationships that are deemed immanent in and valorize the world. The full range of difference in the world is deemed explicable through this pairing. In sum: *Yin* and *yang* are ad hoc-explanatory categories that report on interactions among immediate concrete things of the world.

For example, in a giving relationship, *this* older woman may by virtue of her wisdom be regarded as *yang* in contrast to *that* younger

释性范畴，它描述世界上相近的具体的事物之间的相互作用。

例如，在一个既定的关系中，此年长的女人可以因为她的智慧而被看作阳，相反，彼年轻的女人则是阴。但是，如果我们注意她们的生殖力，那么这种关系很可能完全相反。由于没有一样东西在所有的方面都是阳，所以总是有某种互补性的基础。

阴和阳描绘特殊关系之特性，总是会产生一个来自某特定视角的认识，这就使得人们能够揭示相关性之模式并且解释特殊的环境。当各种事物聚到一起并且构成了独特的组合的时候，阴和阳就提供了一套语汇来梳理它们之间的相互关系。只有通过一个概括的过程，女性和男性的性别特征才被分别解释为以阴与阳为主，并且出现了像阴门和阳道这样的词来将阴与阳的差别以"本质"特征表现出来。

在此，重要的是特殊的差别处于首要地位，并且缺少任何认定的相同性或严格的同一性。事物从来不是因为拥有同一的本质而被看成是相同的，相反，事物是基于类似角色或功能而被认为拥有相似性。

woman who is *yin*. But if we were to focus on their fecundity, the correlation would likely be the opposite. And since no one thing is *yang* in all respects, there is always some basis for complementarity.

Yin and *yang*, as characterizations of particular relationships, invariably entail a perception from some particular perspective that enables one to unravel patterns of relatedness and to interpret specific circumstances. They provide a vocabulary for sorting out the relationships among things as they come together and constitute them-selves in unique compositions. It is only through a process of generalization that feminine and male gender traits are construed as predominantly *yin* and *yang* respectively, and vocabulary such as vaginal orifce (*yin me*n 陰門) and virility (*yang dao* 陽道) emerges to "essentialize" the *yin* and *yang* contrast.

Important here is the primacy of particular difference and the absence of any assumed sameness or strict identity. Things are not purported to be the same because they own identical essences, but are deemed to have resemblances based upon analogous roles or functions. Hence, describing any particular phenomenon involves an unravelling of the relationships and conditions of the phenomenon's context, and its multiple correlations. And each phenomenon, in suggesting other similar phenomena, has the vagueness of a poetic image.

因此，描述任何特殊的现象都包括展开该现象之具体背景的条件及其关系，以及现象和背景之间的相互关系。每一个现象，让人联想到其他相似的现象，这就具有了一种诗意形象之模糊性。

因此，"阴—阳思维"是"关联性思维"的另一个名称，二者都包含了"语境化方法"。在《淮南子》后记——很可能是刘安本人写的——中，将该文本和传统著作所做的直接比较是和《易经》的比较。这个联系反映了这样一个印象，这两个文本在探索和理解世界的时候都借助于运用关联性范畴：

> 今易之乾坤，足以穷道通意也，八卦可以识吉凶、知祸福矣，然而伏羲为之六十四变，周室增以六爻，所以原测淑清之道，而捃逐万物之祖也。

（《期望中国：对中西文化的哲学思考》，第 313—315 页）

"Yin-yang thinking" is, then, another name for "correlative thinking," both involve "the art of contextualization." In the post face of the *Huainanzi*, very possibly written by Liu An himself, the immediate comparison drawn between this text and the traditional corpus is with the *Book of Changes*. This association reflects the perception that both texts have recourse to the application of correlative categories in exploring and understanding the world:

> Now, the "*qian*" and "*kun*" contrast in the *Book of Changes* is enough to exhaust *dao* and give a full account of its meaning, and the eight trigrams can be used to recognize what is auspicious and inauspicious, and to anticipate good fortune and calamity. But the reason the Fu Xi introduced the sixty-four changes and the House of Zhou (King Wen) increased the trigram to six lines was to fathom utterly the marvelous *dao* and to seek out the forbearers of the myriad things.

(*Anticipating China: Thinking through the Narratives of Chinese and Western Culture,* pp. 260-262)

神

常译为"spirits"或"gods"。其一系列意义展现了中国宇宙论的宗教性方面,这就是假定人类精神性与超自然或神性的统一。《说文解字》曰:"天神,引出万物者也",徐灏笺曰:"天地生万物,万物之主为神。"因此,神是与天地日月星辰山水林谷等自然现象相关的令人敬畏的精神。

然而,神又是中国古代思想各传统有争议的一个概念。它所带有的模糊性被认为正是其光辉与语义力量的一个要素。神的另一个意义即"神秘性"(mysteriousness),《易经》所谓"阴阳不测之谓神","神也者,妙万物而为言者也"。

重要的是,神不只指涉超自然的精神,它亦关涉人,意谓"生命"(life)与"精神"(spirit)。气成神生。此层面的神与道德行为和君子智慧相关。《淮南子》曰:"知人所不知谓之神";"神者,智之渊也。"《孟子》曰:"圣而不可知之之谓神。"

Spirits/Gods

Shen, often translated as "spirits" or "gods" has a range of meaning that is revealing of the religious aspect of Chinese cosmology that assumes a continuity between human spirituality and the numinous or divine. In the *Shuowen* lexicon, *tianshen* is "what calls forth the myriad things," and one of its commentaries suggests that "the heavens and the earth give birth to the myriad things, and what is master of these things is called *shen*." So *shen* is the numinous associated with natural phenomena such as the sky, sun, moon, stars, rivers, mountains, forests, valleys, and so on.

But *shen* was a contested concept in and among the various lineages of early Chinese thought, and it has been argued that the ambiguity that attends it is a significant element in its aura and semantic force. Another level of meaning of *shen* is "mysteriousness." The *Book of Changes* states that "what is unfathomable through the *yin* and *yang* distinction is called *shen*," and again, "as for *shen*, it is an expression for mysterious phenomena."

Importantly, *shen* does not simply reference the numinous; it can also refer to human beings, meaning "life" and "spirit." When *qi* takes form, *shen*—life and spirit—is born. At this level, it is associated with the moral conduct and wisdom of exemplary human beings. The *Huainanzi* it says that "to know what others do not know

(《生民之本：〈孝经〉的哲学诠释及英译》，第 103 页)

is shen," and "*shen* is a reservoir of wisdom." The Mencius says that "to be sagacious beyond comprehension is called *shen*."

(*The Chinese Classic of Family Reverence,* pp. 83-84)

几

"几"包含的意思从"最初的细微迹象或萌动""极其微小的""临近的"，直到"可能性""先兆""时机"；它由于将"机"的意思引申到"关键时刻""转折点""枢纽""危险"，因而又表示"动力""原动力""扳机""巧妙的设计"，然后还有"机会"与能够抓住机会的人，以及那些机敏、机智、机灵的人。这种意义上的秩序的不确定的方面，是一个"非常微小的""最初的萌动"，它作为自我再组织和再解释的"原动力"，是一个"关键性的转折点"。"危机"从字面上看，意为"危险—机会"，它是一个关键性的结合点，它在为转化提供"动力"时，既可能是一个"危险"，又可能是一个"机会"，这决定于一个人是否能够抓住机会，最大限度地利用好它。

Ji

Ji begins with the notion of "first inklings or stirrings", "minute," "imminent," "nearly," and then to "probability," "anticipation," "occasion," and with *ji* 機 extends to "critical point," "turning point," "pivot," "danger," hence to, "impetus," "motive force," "trigger," "clever device," and then to "opportunity" and one who can seize the opportunity, one who is "adroit," "flexible," "ingenious." The indeterminate aspect in this sense of order is "small," a "first stirring," which, as a "motive force" for self-reorganization and reconstrual, is a "critical turning point." As a critical juncture—*weiji* 危機, literally, "danger-opportunity"—it can be either a "danger" or an "opportunity" in providing "impetus" for trans-formation, depending on whether or not one is able to seize the opportunity and make the most of it.

This term, *ji* (幾), occurs in those canonical documents that have defined the classical Chinese worldview. For example, the "Great Treatise" of the *Yijing* (*Book of Changes*) contains the following passage,

"几"这个词出现于规定古典时期中国人的世界观的那些经典中。例如,《易传》包含有下面这段话,它将"几"与"深"和"神"相联系,具有代表性:

> 夫易,圣人之所以极深而研几也。唯深也,故能通天下之志。唯几也,故能成天下之务。唯神也,故不疾而速,不行而至。(《周易·系辞传上》)

在同一篇传中另外有一段这样说:

> 知几,其神乎。君子上交不谄,下交不渎,其知几乎。几者,动之微,吉之先见者也。君子见几而作,不俟终日。(《周易·系辞传下》)

古典时期中国人确立事件的秩序的思想,规定了不确定性,正是这种普遍的不确定性使得超越的语言不适用,并且引导我们返回中华世界本身之中,以寻求一种更方便的、更合适的语汇,它考虑到要强调生命和创造性,而唐君毅与牟宗

which typically associates *ji* 幾 with "deep, profound (*shen* 深)" and "spiritual, mysterious, inscrutable (*shen* 神):"

> The *Changes* is how the sage probes utterly what is profound and gets to the very bottom of things (*ji*). It is precisely because of the profundity of the *Changes* that the sage can penetrate thoroughly the purposes of the world; it is precisely because of its pivotal significance (*ji*) that he can be successful in the business of the world; it is precisely because of its mystery that he can be quick without haste and can arrive without going.

Another passage in the same text reports:

> To understand the first inklings (*ji*)—this is spiritual understanding. The exemplary person in his relationship with his superiors is not given to flattery; in his relationship to his sub-ordinates is not given to putting on airs. He understands the first inklings. The first inklings are the suggestion of movement, what is first shown of good fortune. The exemplary person on seeing the first inklings gets underway, and does not wait the duration of a single day.

三这样的现代新儒学哲学家赞颂了这种生命和创造性。

《庄子》中有一则故事直接讲到这一方面。两个大夫奉楚王之命去见庄子，当时庄子正垂钓于濮水之上。他们代表楚王邀请庄子随他们回楚，去治理楚国。庄子给这两个大夫提到神龟的事。他说楚有神龟，死了三千年了，现在它被包在布巾之中，藏于楚国庙堂之上。庄子问：此龟是愿意死而留骨以受尊崇，还是宁愿保持生命、摇尾于泥水之中？当然，大夫回答说，它愿保持生命、摇尾于泥水之中。庄子说，回去吧！别来烦我，我将摇尾于泥水之中。

因此，在论述古典时期中国人的世界观时，我们要么是诉诸超越的观念而舍弃这个世界，要么是仍然留在这个世界中而自由自在地摇尾于泥水之中。

（《汉哲学思维的文化探源》，第 237—238 页）

It is the general indeterminancy presupposed in the classical Chinese conception of the ordering of events that makes the language of transcendence inappropriate, and that returns us to the Chinese world itself in search of a more liberating and friendly vocabulary, one that allows for the emphasis on life and creativity celebrated by New Confucian philosophers such as Tang Junyi and Mou Zongsan.

There is an anecdote in the *Zhuangzi* which speaks directly to this point. Two high ministers are sent by the king of Chu to Zhuangzi who is fishing in the Pu River. On behalf of the king, they invite Zhuangzi to come back with them and govern the kingdom of Chu. Zhuangzi reminds the ministers of a sacred tortoise that has been dead for three thousand years, now wrapped in finery and stored in the ancestral temple of Chu. I ask you, says Zhuangzi, would the tortoise rather be so honored, or would it rather be alive to drag its tail in the mud? Of course, it would rather be alive and in the mud, reply the ministers. Get lost! said Zhuangzi, and leave me to drag my tail in the mud!

In interpreting the classical Chinese worldview, our choice then, is either to abandon that world by appeal to a notion of transcendence, or to remain in the world to drag our tails happily in the mud.

(*Thinking from the Han*, pp. 230-232)

变通 / 易

《大传》叙述的是传统本身的由来起源,讲的是人与自己所处环境,如何于以往、现在,常态性地与天地相合。远祖伏羲、神农近取诸身,远取诸物,始作八卦,类万物之情,通神明之德,知"变通"之道,并将此种"变通"之领悟视作人所处世界一以贯之的特点。两位圣贤"是以明于天之道,而察于民之故",画卦,以效之,象之,则之;举而措之天下之民。需要注意,两位古代圣贤并不是脱离价值观而探求客观自然界的科学家,恰好相反,他们致力于人们自己理解与叙述的事业:

《易》穷则变,变则通,通则久。

伏羲、神农所实践的是一种"域境化"做法,即有效地实现将人类经验与自然运行过程视作同一域境,且使其相合,努力将宇宙

The Perpetual Interface Between Flux and Persistence (*Biantong/Yi*)

This Great Tradition in telling the story of its own origins explains how a human responsiveness to context has in the past, and continues now, to enchant the cosmos. The remote ancestors Fu Xi 伏羲 and ShenNong 神農 established a rhythm in the human experience, enabling them to chime in with the cadence of the flux and persistence (*bian tong*) that they perceived as persistent characteristics of the world around them. Encouraged by the effcacy achieved in applying their insights into the workings of the cosmos to the human experience, they then represented their interpretation of life in the world in a hexagramic language of images, models, and patterns for the benefit of generations yet to come.Importantly, these antique sages were not natural scientists engaged in some disinterested interrogation of objective nature, but rather were fully occupied by a project of personal understanding and articulation:

According to the *Yijing*, when things run their course, there is flux (*bian*), where there is flux, there is continuity (*tong*), and where there is such continuity, it is enduring.

的可用性创造潜能,利用到最好程度——伏羲、神农在对《易经》一套深邃卦象的建构之中,培育出一种"文化"与"自然"之间厚重的不分性。这是一种被体悟到的人的经验与自然促使文化间相互接的和谐性,这种和谐状态显明地表达于对这一关系特点的描述性用语中,如"天人合一"(宗教性、自然、文化的域境与人经验的不分性)、"天人相应"或"天人感应"(精神领域与人经验的相互照应——不分)。值得注意,这种用语所表示的,是人类经验方面延续不分的共生相互性,而不是世界中两个原本分立不连的方面后有的结合性。人类的修养不是把世界与人类经验作为两件分立的事物而使它们结合在一起,而是让同属经验的两个本身不可分的部分,由于生态连续性(也即"我与我的世界")而更深度、紧密地相合。

其实,自然与人文(比如石头的自然条纹与岩画)之间那种可想而知的不分性,能够得到印证的事实是,同一词语既可用来表达人类的也可用来表述自然生态界的鼎新性。例如:"道"、"气"、"文"

By their efforts at *ars contextualis*—the art of effectively contextualizing and coordinating the experience of the human being within the processes of nature in an effort to optimize the creative possibilities of the cosmos—Fu Xi and Shen Nong cultivated a thick continuity between nurture and nature expressed in the evocative images that constitute the *Yijing*. This perceived resonance between the human experience and the natural and cultural forum in which it occurs is made explicit in expressions that have come to characterize the relationship, such as the continuity between the religious, natural, and cultural context, and the human experience (*tianren heyi* 天人合一), and the mutual responsiveness of the numinous context and the human experience (*tianren xiangying* 天人相應 or *tianren ganying* 天人感應). It is important to note that such expressions report on the continuing symbiotic mutuality of these dimensions of experience rather than on the reconciliation of two originally separate aspects of the world after the fact. Personal cultivation is *not* the bringing together and the "uniting" of the world and human experience, but is rather the deepening and intensifying of the productive continuities that conjoin two inseparable aspects of experience, that is, oneself and one's world.

Indeed, this assumed continuities between nature and nurture—between

（纹）、"理"、"阴阳"、"变通"，是既表达人文也表述自然世界的词语。

（《儒家角色伦理学：一套特色伦理学词汇》，第64—65页）

诸如思想/肉体、理论/实践互为排斥的二元主义，从未对中国互系的阴阳宇宙观造成负面影响。在中国宇宙观中，"身心"与"知行"从来就是人生经验中相辅相成、相连不分、相互兼有的偶对双方。其实，人经验的延续性与整体性是以"体用""变通"这样的观念表述的；这样的宇宙认识，对绝对性二元主义的范畴具有屏蔽性。

（《儒家角色伦理学：一套特色伦理学词汇》，第42页）

就《易经》的文本而言，它本身就是一堂刻意展示的世界观示范课。也就是说，当我们看待特别"事物"性质时，在一个过程性世界观中对它进行思考，这些特别视点与它们视域的关系呈现一种对世界系统的全息性认识。

（《儒家角色伦理学：一套特色伦理学词汇》，第61页）

petroglyphs and the striations in stone, for example—is reflected in the fact that the same vocabulary is used to express the creative advance in both the human and the natural ecologies. For example, "the way of things" (*dao* 道), vital energies (*qi* 氣), inscribed culture (*wen* 文), patternings (*li* 理), *yinyang* 陰陽, and the perpetual interface between flux and persistence (*biantong* 變通) itself are all terms that reference both the human and the natural worlds.

(*Confucian Role Ethics: A Vocabulary,* pp. 53-54)

Such an exclusive mind/body and theory/praxis dualism has never been a distraction in a Chinese correlative *yinyang* cosmology in which mind/body (*shenxin* 身心) and theory/praxis (*zhixing* 知行) have been taken to be collaborative, coterminous, and mutually entailing aspects of experience. Indeed, the continuity and wholeness of experience is defined in terms of "forming and functioning" (*tiyong* 體用), and "flux and persistence" (*biantong* 變通)—cosmological assumptions.

(*Confucian Role Ethics: A Vocabulary,* pp. 33-34)

The *Yijing,* or *Book of Changes,* as a text is itself an object lesson in the worldview that it attempts to present. That is, when we reflect on the nature of particular

《易经》的宗旨是协调处于永远变化的世界同人本身的经验活动之间的关系；它的目的是交代人实践经验的基本规范性和方略性，回应关切人生的紧迫问题：面对自然变化的过程，人的什么形式的参与活动，才能产生对现有世界最佳状态的利用？这是一种自然现象与人的行为现象相系不分、彼此互相塑造的状态。

（《儒家角色伦理学：一套特色伦理学词汇》，第62—63页）

events within this process worldview, the relationship between these particular foci and their fields lends itself to a holographic understanding of world systems.

(*Confucian Role Ethics: A Vocabulary*, p. 50)

The coordination of the relationship between the changing world and the human experience is the main axis of the *Yijing*. The purpose of this text is fundamentally normative and prescriptive. It purports to address life's most pressing question: What kind of participation in these natural processes can optimize the possibilities of a world in which natural and human events are two inseparable, mutually shaping aspects?

(*Confucian Role Ethics: A Vocabulary*, p. 52)

混沌

Hundun

理性的话语断定：末尾还没有出现，始初则已被混沌的晦暝之气所遮蔽。如若我们绕过了谐和秩序而潜近时间的起点，我们找到的只是非理性，因为作为我们把握第一原理的手段，理性仅止于把我们带到对混沌作出阐释后的那一刻。理性和推论是与对初始起源的构想相联系的。宇宙论是为理性的秩序

Reasonable words, certainly: the end hasn't come, and the beginning is lost in the obscurity of chaos. Were we to stalk the time of beginnings before there was order or harmony, we could find only irrationality, since reason as the means by which we grasp first principles would take us only as far as that moment after the illumining of chaos. Reason and reasoning are tied to the notion of primordial beginnings. Cosmologies are the groundworks

打下的底子。宇宙演化论预设了一种基本上是非理性、无理性的"时间",它提醒我们,在一个有序和谐的宇宙概念之外,还存在着虚无、疏离和混乱。为了对其寻根究底,在所有显示着我们盎格鲁—欧罗巴文化特性的理论、原则、规律和评价中,我们的混沌起源都被化成了一个大豁口、一片虚无、一团混乱。

《牛津英语辞典》告诉我们,"起源"(beginning)指"造成存在的活动或过程","事物通过这一活动或过程中得以萌生"。这一萌生的根源即为混沌($\chi\alpha o\varsigma$)——"基质"、"太初"、"深渊"。另外,"本原"(principle)(arche ἀρχή)这个词直接与 archon (ἄρχων 古雅典的执政官),即发布命令的权势者有关。本原是思想与活动的起点。不过"起源"这个自身富含诗意的词,经由原先与古英语 gínan 这个词的联系,也带有"大豁口",或混沌的"空空洞洞"的意思。本原和起源若究其根本,乃任意多变,纷披淆乱而莫可名状。

因此,始基、本原、起源都和太初、宇宙的第一状态——也即混沌有关。我们把混沌和作为有序、和谐世界的"宇宙"相对照。从混

of rational order. Cosmogonies, by presupposing a "time" characterized by a basic irrationality, or nonrationality, remind us that beyond the conception of an ordered and harmonious universe lies emptiness, alienation, confusion. Pursued to their ground, therefore, all theories, principles, laws, and valuations characteristic of our Anglo-European culture dissolve into the yawning gap, the emptiness, the confusion, of our chaotic beginnings.

The *Oxford English Dictionary* tells us that "beginning" refers to "the action or process of entering upon existence," "that out of which anything has its rise." The source of this arising is chaos ($\chi\alpha o\varsigma$)—"the elemental," "the first state of the universe," "the great deep or abyss." Further, "principle" (*arche* ἀρχή) is directly related to *archon* (ἄρχων), one authorized to *give orders*. Principles are beginning points of thought and action. But "beginning" itself is a richly poetic term carrying, through primary associations with the Old English *gínan*, the meaning of "the yawning gap," or "gaping void" of chaos. Principles and beginnings dissolve, at their roots, into arbitrariness and confusion.

Thus, *arche*, *principium*, beginning, all refer to the *origin*, "the first state of the universe"—namely, chaos. We contrast chaos with "cosmos" as the ordered or harmonious world. The idea of bringing

沌中衍生宇宙的观念植根于我们关于起源的构思。但认为"宇宙"有外部边缘，这还是一种相对较晚的看法。这种关于一个单一秩序的世界的推断并没有经过经验或逻辑的生成标准的检测。"宇宙"（cosmos）一词源自动词 kosmeo，在希腊语中它表示"建立秩序"。该词首先指做家务、军事组织或化妆打扮。因此 kosmos（宇宙）描绘了一种有条理、安排妥当或妆扮好的状态。

（《期望中国：对中西文化的哲学思考》，第3—4页）

自然

字面的意义就是"自我如此着"（self-so-ing）或"自我生成着"（self-deriving）。体味这个相当字面的意思，我们或许可以使用一下汉字双关语的模式，用"sow"（播种）和"sew"（缝纫）来替代"so"（如此），这就会引发各种各样有关耕作和培育的社会化的联想，对它的"裁剪"只是为了对个体及其周围环境种种倾向性的两相适应。

"自然"中"自"（self-）的成分

cosmos out of chaos is at the very root of our conception of beginnings. But "cosmos" as applied to the external surround is a relatively late notion. The presumption of a single-ordered world was by no means authorized by empirical or logical generative criteria. "Cosmos" comes from the verb *kosmeo* (κοσμεω), which means "to set in order." This word carries primary associations of housekeeping, military organization, or cosmetic adornment. Thus *kosmos* describes a state of being ordered, arranged, or adorned.

(*Anticipating China: Thinking through the Narratives of Chinese and Western Culture*, pp. 3-4)

Spontaneously so

"Spontaneously so" means literally "self-so-ing" or "self-deriving." We might play with this rather literal meaning in a Chinese "paronomastic" fashion by substituting "sow" and "sew" for "so," thereby evoking the protean images of "husbanding and cultivating" a world, and the "tailoring" of it to suit both one's own proclivities and those of one's context.

The "self-(*zi* 自)" element in *ziran* needs clarification. It is a non-reified and reflexive notion of "self-in-context," where "self-" refers to those roles and

需要作一下说明。它是一个非具体化和反身性的概念——是"语境中的自我",关涉那些将个体限定于某一社会中的角色和社会关系。它们构成个体行为业已养成的品质。在过程性的道家世界观中,创造性是逐步形成的,而且总是超越"自我"且与"自我"相关。因此,自发性的获得就同时表征为自我创造和共同创造。

在《道德经》第十七章中,"自然"被用来描述贤明君主非强制性统治下,老百姓自发形成的社会和政治秩序。在第二十三章中,自然秩序被看作是人类行为的范本,教条主义的行为受到批判:

> 天地尚不能久,而况于人乎?

尤为深远的是,在宇宙论意义上,"自然"被用来指称某种无上却又常常有语境化倾向的自发性,它比秩序的任何特定表达都更为根本。这就是第二十五章表达的意思:

> 人法地,地法天,天法道,道法自然。

transactional relationships that locate one in a world, and that constitute one's cultivated disposition to act. In the processual Daoist worldview, creativity is recursive, and is always exercised over and with respect to "self." Spontaneity thus conceived entails both *self*-creativity and *co*-creativity.

Ziran is used in chapter 17 to characterize the spontaneous social and political order of the people as it emerges under the non-coercive government of effective rulers. It is used in chapter 23 to recommend against being doctrinaire by invoking the natural order as a model for human conduct:

> And if the heavens and the earth cannot sustain things for long,
> How much less the human being.

More profoundly, however, it is used cosmologically as a kind of categorical yet always contextualized dispositional spontaneity that is more fundamental than any specific expression of order. This then is its import in chapter 25:

> Human beings emulate the earth,
> The earth emulates the heavens,
> The heavens emulate way-making,
> And way-making emulates what is spontaneously so.

In this cosmological usage, *ziran*

在该宇宙论意义上,"自然"就以与其同族词"自化"(self-transforming)相类似的含义(该词出现在第三十七和五十七章,描绘所有自然过程,包括人类世界在不被干扰情况下的自然发展)发挥作用。

"自然"的重要性在于事实上它是最初本原概念的一个替代。"自然"是新奇的自发产生,它就体现在那作为持续的现在"不断摆动的门"的种种事物的倾向性中。"本原"(beginnings)是"fetal"(始),而非"primordial"(初)。

第二十五、四十二、五十一、五十二章是最经常被从宇宙论意义上解读的章节,"道"在那里是被当作某种最初的"源头"和"发端"进行阐释的。对"道"的"资源性"理解自然可以说是适当的,但是这种理解如果被并到我们"一多"形而上学传统中对某种最初、决定性的第一原理或者诉诸某些初创行为——"起源"——的意义上来理解,就会变成一种误导。道家传统的自发性附带某种参与到经验永久持续过程的偶然性。"道"和万物只是观照这同一经验过程、同一现实的两

functions in a way similar to the cognate expression, "self-transforming (*zihua* 自化)," found in chapters 37 and 57 that describes the spontaneous unfolding of all of the natural processes, including the human world, when left free of interference.

The importance of *ziran* lies in the fact that it is an alternative to the notion of initial beginnings. *Ziran* is the spontaneous emergence of novelty that is manifest in the propensity of things as the "swinging gateway" of the continuing present. And "beginnings" are fetal (*shi* 始) rather than primordial.

Chapters such as 25, 42, 51, and 52 are most often read cosmogonically, wherein *dao* is interpreted as some initial "source" or "origin." While the sense of "resourcing" *dao* is certainly appropriate, such an understanding can become misleading if it is conflated with the sense of "origins" that we find in a "One-many" metaphysical tradition that appeals to some notion of originative and determinative first principles, and some initial creative act. Spontaneity in the Daoist tradition entails a contingency that attends the ever-continuing process of experience. And *dao* and the myriad things are simply two different ways of looking at the same process of experience, the same reality. They are the clearest statement of

个不同途径。它们是"一多不分观"最明白的宣称。

与此相一致,我们还必须承认,由于道家宇宙论中新奇的持续产生在适当的时候会否弃任何现存的认知范畴或说明性词汇,我们只能依赖现有的词汇描述这一持续过程的最新状态。

因此,在一种最初本原的意义上解读这一古典宇宙(发生)论,最好还是将其当成某种"认识发生论"来理解,这样,艺术和解释的术语就产生了。它不仅是产生于持存的现在的世界本身,而且也是我们对它的理解——把它看作有天地之别、气之阴阳、神灵和超自然、四季变化等等现象的世界。所有这些状态都是并行不悖且相互依托,以递推式地相互协作来创造这个经验世界。

必须超越现行的语言模式,把"道"当成某种"风格称谓"(字)来理解它高深莫测的多种可能性,而不是用某个专有名称定位它当下的特性。"道"是一个唤起想象力的名称,它的才能就是激发那些超越我们现实世界视野的行动。

认真观照中国古典宇宙论,会发现这是一个在动物、人类和神圣

"the inseparability of one and many, of continuity and multiplicity, of *dao* and *de* (*yiduo bufenguan* 一多不分觀)."

In order to be consistent, we would have to allow that the continuing emergence of novelty in this Daoist cosmogony in the fullness of time would overwhelm any existing cognitive categories or explanatory vocabulary. We can only rely on our present vocabulary to reflect upon the most recent phases in this continuing process.

Thus, what might be read as a classical cosmogony in the sense of an initial beginning might be better understood as a kind of "epistemogony" in which the terms of art and explanation are being born. It is not only the world as such that emerges in the continuing present, but our way of understanding it as being discriminated into the heavens and the earth, the *yin* and *yang qi*, the spiritual and the numinous, the four seasons, and so on. All of these conditions are collateral and mutually entailing, collaborating with each other recursively to produce the world of experience.

It is the need to reach beyond our current language that requires the use of *dao* as a style name that suggests its bottomless possibilities rather than as a proper name that captures its present character. *Dao* is a name that evokes the power of the imagination and its capacity to inspire activity that goes beyond the horizons of

世界之间涌动着偶发性和流动性的世界。虽则这所有世界之间共振式的相互依赖是古代中国宇宙论一个更广为人知的特征，但只有这些世界间真正地交互渗透，才使得"物化"宇宙论远比简单的协作、共生更为根本。中国的许多神话文学集中在生物身上，在这些著作中，人类和动物的身份是多变的，一种物态常是从另一种物态吸收幻化而成的。一种牢固树立的含糊性阻止任何将动物世界和人类世界分开的企图。而且"物化"宇宙论直觉到：在转化之流的不断进行中，一种存在秩序总是让位于另一种存在秩序。

例如，古典道家著作《庄子》就明确质疑人类特殊主义。它描绘了这样一种可能性，即人类形态在更大转化过程中有可能只是一种任意存在而且并不特别受欢迎的扰乱物。对于一个人可能濒临的"死"的不幸，庄子的反应是：一种状态的事物会不断需要经历转变为其他事物，而且，认识到这一点会获得一种真正的安慰，事实上，是会怀有一种宗教般的敬畏感。比如《庄子》中那个著名的蝴蝶的故事，通过意识中的解放将自身从贪婪、蠕

our present world.

A careful look at classical Chinese cosmology reveals a world in which there is a contingency and fluidity among the animal, human, and divine worlds. While this resonating interdependence among worlds is a much advertised feature of the early Chinese cosmology, it is the actual interpenetrating of these realms that makes the *wuhua* cosmology far more radical than simply synergy or symbiosis. Much of the mythological literature of China is populated with creatures in which human and animal identities are unstable, with one form assimilating elements from the other. There is an entrenched ambiguity that attends any attempt to separate out the animal and human worlds, and there is anticipation in the *wuhua* cosmology that one order of existence gives way to another in the ongoing flux and flow of transformation.

The classical Daoist text *Zhuangzi,* for example, is explicit in challenging human exceptionalism, describing the possibility of assuming a human form as an arbitrary and not especially welcome perturbation within the larger process of transformation. Zhuangzi's response to the misgivings one might have about"death" is that there is real comfort and indeed even a religious awe in the recognition that assuming the form of one kind of thing gives way to becoming

动的毛虫转化为五彩斑斓、欢快飞舞的蝴蝶,其潜台词是否就是在说庄周从一种生命状态转化成了另一种生命状态,还是可以商榷的。

使道家宇宙论区别于更为人熟知的其他宇宙发生论的最早、最清楚的宣称是《太一生水》(*The Great One Gives Birth to the Waters*)。《太一生水》是作为《道德经》的一部分在郭店被重新发现的,其产生可追溯到公元前300年左右。

(《道不远人:比较哲学视域中的〈老子〉》,第78—82页)

another in a ceaseless adventure. It can be argued, for example, that the *Zhuangzi*'s famous butterfly story, informed as it is by the perceived liberation from rapacious, wormlike caterpillar to the happy dance of the strikingly colored butterfly, really has as its subtext Zhuang Zhou himself dying out of one kind of life only to be transformed into another.

The earliest and clearest statement of this early Daoist cosmology that distinguishes it from more familiar cosmogonies is *The Great One Gives Birth to the Waters*, a document recovered as part of the *Daodejing* in the Guodian find dating to about 300 BCE.

(*Daodejing: Making This Life Significant,* pp. 68-71)

伦理学

德

"德"最常见的英文译法是"virtue"或"power"。如果我们从作为某个特定团体成员的个人品性和经历之中来感知人生的最高境界的话,"德"字与佛教 dharma 一语的意义更为接近。它们二者均暗示了我们能够做的和我们能够成为的。所以,我们将"德"译作"excellence",意为在实现自我的过程中卓尔不凡。已故法官瑟古德·马歇尔要求在墓碑上镌刻这样的墓志铭:"他在所能与所有两方面均臻于完美。""所有"即其德,马歇尔自信拥有至德。

"德"字不仅涵衍了一系列反映情境重于动作的观念的义项,而且兼具赋予及获得两种行为。作为对对方宽怀大度的回应,"德"既是恩惠也是感激(《论语》第十四篇第三十四章)。

De

De is conventionally translated as "virtue," or "power," but the Chinese term more nearly approximates dharma in signifying what we can do and be, if we "realize (*zhi*)" the most from our personal qualities and careers as contextualized members of a specific community. We translate *de* as "excellence" in the sense of excelling at becoming one's own person. The late justice Thurgood Marshall asked for his tombstone to read: "He did the best he could with what he had." What he "had" was his *de*, and he surely developed it to the fullest.

De has a range of meaning which again reflects the priority of situation over agency, characterizing both giving and getting. *De* is both the "beneficence" and the "gratitude" expressed in response to such largesse (cf.14.34).

(*The Analects of Confucius: A Philosophical Translation*, p. 57)

（《〈论语〉的哲学诠释》，导言第58页）

在早期的哲学文献中，"德"具有一种强烈的宇宙论含义，意味着事物持久的特性。正是由于这个原因，"德"习惯的译法是"virtue"或"power"，将这一特点定义为其自身经验领域内的能力焦点。鉴于个体在存在的过程观念之中的这种内在相关性，"德"可以被描述为尚未完成的总体的任何特定的倾向。《道德经》的核心问题就是个体如何将其所在的场域最富有成效地加以聚焦。

最早的儒家文献意在将其关注限定于人类的经验。在人的经验之中，"德"的这一质的向度几乎意味着：如果我们从自身作为一个特定社群的成员的个人生涯中最大限度地有所"实现"（"知"），那么，不论是"美德"（excellence）还是"成效"（efficacy），就都是作为我们真正能够的"所是"和"所为"（what we can truly be and do）。"德"的培养是通过完全参与到礼仪化的社群之中来寻求的。在一个礼仪化的社群中，一个人所成就的德行在构成其人格的各种角色和关系中使得该人

In the early philosophical literature, *de* has a strong cosmological sense, connoting the insistent particularity of things. It is for this reason that *de* is conventionally translated as "virtue," or "power," defining the particular as a focus of potency within its own field of experience. Given the intrinsic relatedness of particulars in a process conception of existence, *de* can be described as any particular disposition of the unsummed totality. The central issue of the *Daodejing*—literally, "the classic of *de* and its *dao*"— is how the particular brings its field most productively and effectively into focus.

The earliest Confucian literature tended to limit its concerns to human experience, where this qualitative dimension of *de* more nearly suggests both "excellence" and "efficacy" as what we can truly be and do if we "realize (*zhi*)" the most from our personal careers as members of a specific community. The cultivation of *de* is pursued through full participation in the ritualized community, where achieved excellence in the roles and relationships that constitute one's person makes one an object of the deference of others.

When located within the political realm, *de* describes the most appropriate relationship between a ruler and the people.

成为其他人敬重的对象。

当在政治领域中来加以定位时,"德"描绘的是统治者和百姓之间最为恰当的关系。在这一脉络中,"德"具有广泛的意义范围,它反映境域相对于行为主体的优先性,既凸显"予"(giving),也凸显"取"(getting)。换言之,"德"既是从统治者推展到老百姓的"仁慈"(beneficence),同时也是老百姓回应统治者那种"慷慨"(largesse)的"感激之情"(gratitude)。

在承认一个有教养的君子所具有的意义创造(meaning-creating)和意义彰显(meaning-disclosing)的力量的同时,《中庸》强调君子之道超越于人类社群之外而充拓到了宇宙本身。作为"德"的典范,圣人在将人类经验与其环境之间的共生关系发挥到极致的时候,便具有了一种宇宙论的意义。正是在环境之中,人类与环境的关系被境遇化。

(《切中伦常:〈中庸〉的新诠与新译》,第83—84页)

君子之教化未开化之人的"德"(personal focus)远非强制性或强迫接受的,而是其整合和参与到

In this context, *de* has a range of meaning that reflects the priority of situation over agency, characterizing both giving and getting. That is, *de* is both the "beneficence" extended to the people from the ruler, and the "gratitude" expressed in response to such largesse.

The *Zhongyong*, recognizing the meaning-creating and meaning-disclosing power of the cultivated human being, emphasizes the way in which this personal articulation extends beyond the human community to the cosmos itself. The sage (*shengren*), as the paragon of achieved excellence (*de*), has cosmological significance in maximizing the symbiotic relationship between the human experience and the environment within which that relationship is contextualized.

(*Focusing the Familiar: A Translation and Philosophical Interpretation of the Zhongyong,* pp. 64-65)

The personal focus (*te*) which the exemplary person uses to engage the uncultivated person, far from being impositional or coercive, is his potential from integrating with and participating in the intersubjective person making of his people.

(*Thinking Through Confucius,* p. 169)

Across the corpus of pre-Ch'in literature,

百姓主体间性的"成人"行动中的潜能。

（《通过孔子而思》，第206页）

通观先秦文献，"德"似乎拥有一个根本的宇宙论意义，其他涵义正是由此派生的。在道家文献中，"德"表示个体作为存在过程中潜在力量焦点的产生。作为整体场域的这一动态过程被称作"道"，而该场域中个体化存在——其不同的焦点，则称之为"德"。……"德"和"天"在本体论意义上并没什么不同，只是在聚焦或着重点方面才是有区别的。"德"表示整体的特定倾向性。

（《通过孔子而思》，第269—270页）

"德"尽管最常用来表示体察整体的独特视角，但它同时也是灵活可塑的，可跨越任何特定的部分—整体区分，且因此也涵容整体存在。

（《通过孔子而思》，第271页）

"德"在我们的哲学分析中既是"义"的原动力，又是"义"所追求的目标。

（《通过孔子而思》，第275页）

te seems to have a fundamental cosmological significance from which its other connotations are derived. In the Taoist literature, it denotes the arising of the particular as a focus of potency in the process of existence. As a total field this dynamic process is called *tao*; the individuated existents in this field, its various foci, are called *te*. ...*Te* and *t'ien* do not differ ontologically. They are differentiatable only as a matter of focus or emphasise. *Te* denotes any particular disposition of the whole.

(*Thinking Through Confucius,* pp. 218-219)

While *te* is most often used to denote a selected perspective on the whole, it is elastic, and can be extended through integration to overcome any presumed disjunction between part and whole, and in this sense, embraces the entire complex of existence.

(*Thinking Through Confucius,* p. 220)

We recall from our philosophical analysis that the character *te* implies both impetus and the pursuit of appropriateness.

(*Thinking Through Confucius,* p. 224)

As this person extends his *te*, his sphere of presencing becomes more influential and his capacity for focusing an interpretation becomes more pronounced. As artist, as

个体之德的拓展使其存在更有影响力，他志在于某一表达的能力也变得更明确。不管是作为艺术家、政治领导人物还是教师，他都能够组织好他的自然环境，表达他的种种可能性和谐——表达、诠释和展现他的文化。

（《通过孔子而思》，第 275 页）

从全息的观点看，"部分"与"整体"的关系最好根据"点域"（focus and field）的观念来描述。个别是一个焦点，它既为语境（它的场域）所限定又限定后者。域是全息性的，也即，它的建构方式使得每一个可识别的"部分"都包含整体。从根本上说，一个既定部分与其整体会在场域被以某种特别强烈的方式聚焦时变得完全一致。根据这一模式，"德"指称确定某一可识别"部分"（如一个人）诠释"整体"（即其社会环境）的模式的独特关注强度。就像我们上面所论，"天"是"德"（作为其确定关注点）的万物之域。

（《通过孔子而思》，第 293 页）

在《说文解字》中，"德"被解

political leader, as teacher, he is able to organize his natural environment and disclose its possibilities for harmony—to manifest, interpret, and display its culture.

(*Thinking Through Confucius,* p. 224)

In the hologrammatic view, the relations of "part" to "whole" are best characterized in terms of the notions of "focus" and "field." A particular is a focus that is both defined by and defines a context—a field. The field is hologrammatic; that is, it is so constituted that each discriminate "part" contains the adumbrated whole. Ultimately, a given part and its whole become identical when the field is focused in an especially intense manner. In terms of this model, *te* names the peculiar intensity of focus identifying the manner in which a discriminated "part"—an individual human being, for example—construes a "whole"—that is, its social context. T'ien 天, as discussed above, is the field of existing things for which *te* can serve as determinate focus.

(*Thinking Through Confucius,* p. 238)

In the *Shuowen* lexicon, *de* is defined as "to ascend", "to climb", "to arise", or "to presence"(*sheng* 升).

Knitting the various strands of the philological data together, it would seem that *de* denotes the emergence of particularity as a determining focus of the field that contextualizes it. The

释为"升"。

　　语言学上各方面的材料结合在一起，似乎表明"德"是指出现这样一种个性（particularity）：它是区域的起决定作用的中心，而区域又使它处于特定的环境中。它的特殊性的范围是可变的，这决定于它如何由其自身和其周围其他相关个人这两方面来说明。这就是说，它的环境（context），不论是在哪一方面和哪种程度上，总是可以解释为包括或唯有"我们"或"他人"。这种"升"不是随意的和胡乱的。相反，整体中的个人寻求一个适当的方向，据以在他自己的动力与其环境的变化之间保持平衡。这种个人是一个合成者（compositor），他总是在构造他的世界。他的方向是如此适当，以至于他能丰富其环境组成分子的特殊性。这是尊敬、服从与公认的卓越之间的交互作用。在一个人的世界中可以看到连贯和恒常，它们是他自己和他的环境组成分子的交互作用造成的定向趋势。升起的特殊个体的影响，决定于他的自我展示（self-construal）的范围和性质。整体中任何一个成员在受到其他成员敬重的情况下，就能与他们共同

range of its particularity is variable, contingent upon the way in which it is interpreted both by itself and by other environing particulars. That is to say, its context in whatever direction and degree, can always be construed inclusively or exclusively as either "us" or "other." This "arising" is not random and chaotic. Rather, there is an appropriate direction which the particular pursues, negotiated between its own agency and the flux of its context. The particular is a compositor, always composing its world. Its direction is appropriate to the extent that it enriches the particularity of the constituent elements of its context. This interplay is that of deference to recognized excellence. The coherence and regularity observable in one's world emerges as a vector negotiated out of the interplay between oneself and the elements of one's context. The influence of the arising particular is dependent upon the range and quality of its self-construal. Any particular can become coextensive with other particulars insofar as they defer to it. This can involve the inclusion of an increasingly broader field of "arising" within the sphere of one's own particularity. This then is the "getting" or "appropriating" aspect of *de—de* 德 as *de* 得.

(*Thinking from the Han*, p. 39)

发展。这包括了这种可能性：在某人自己的特殊性的范围内包容了日益广阔的区域的"升"（中译者注：此处"区域"指人的各种社会关系，"升"即德）。这就是"德"的"获得"方面，即作为"得"的"德"。

（《汉哲学思维的文化探源》，第43—44页）

中国宇宙论始于个体成就的独一无二性，宇宙本身正是万物不能简单累加的整体。世界是"多宇宙"（pluriverse）而非单一宇宙（universe）。没有任何置于其他事物之前作为统一原理的单一秩序存在——所有"事物"都可被视为相连于其他事物，取决于何时何地何因看待之。中国古典哲学著作中，"德"保有一种强烈的宇宙感。一般意指事物，而又常常专指人类"持存的特殊性"（insistent particularity）。由此，"德"经常习惯性地译为"virtue"或"power"，描述作为自身经验领域之潜在核心的个体。我们在对"德"的解读上已避免使用这些概念，部分原因是我们不太想读者按照亚里士多德的方式解释该文本，将之解读为道德伦理学

Chinese cosmology begins from the achieved uniqueness of the particular, and the cosmos itself is the unsummed totality of these myriad things. The world is a "pluriverse" rather than a universe, with no single order being privileged above all others as a unifying principle: every "thing" can be seen as concatenated with many other "things", depending on where you are seeing them from, and why, and when. In the early philosophical literature, *de* has a strong cosmological sense, connoting the insistent particularity of things, and usually, of human beings. It is for this reason that *de* is conventionally translated as "virtue" or "power", defining the particular as a focus of potency within its own field of experience. We have eschewed using these terms in rendering *de*, in part because we do not want the reader to impose an overly Aristotelian interpretation on the text—simply reading it as a naïve form of virtue ethics— and also because "power" usually has "coercion" lurking connotatively nearby, and as the *Classic of Familial Reverence* makes absolutely clear, Confucius detests coercion as a means of ordering society. We use "excellence" for *de*, and "consummate excellence" at times. It is also good to keep in mind that when developed as excellence, one's person （virtue ethics）的一种天真形式，也因为"power"常带有类似"强制"（coercion）的含义，而《孝经》在这上面表达得绝对清晰——孔子憎恨把强制作为一种管理社会的手段。我们用"character"译"德"，有时候用"consummate character"，偶尔也用"excellence"。记住这点也很有帮助：当一个人成为有德（excellence）之人时，其性格（character）也就带有超凡魅力的性质。一个成为典范的人，其性格（character）是会为人所效仿的，因其是优秀的（excellence）。

（《生民之本：〈孝经〉的哲学诠释及英译》，第87—88页）

甲骨文中"德"的字形是"𢛳"，意象为人行于道，眼睛凝视前方。这一组合意义给人以"正道"与"直行"的感觉，两个比喻之间所喻示的是身体与道德的"直"与"真"。"德"的铭文字形为"德"，加了一个"心"字，表达径直而行意识中的思想与情感因素。如前所述，几处不久前发掘的考古文本中，出现的"德"写法为"悳"，上为直，下为心，喻义为"诚实、正直、

takes on charismatic qualities, becoming a model whose conduct will be emulated because of this excellence.

(*The Chinese classic of family reverence: a philosophical translation of the Xiaojing*, pp. 68-69)

On the oracle bones, *de* appears as 𢛳, depicting a person walking on a road with eyes focused on moving straight ahead. This association provides a correlation between the metaphor of the "proper way" (*dao* 道) and walking straight ahead that has both the physical and the moral connotations of "straight" or "true". On the bronzes, the heartmind (*xin* 心) signific is added as an additional element in the character 德, underscoring the intellectual and affective dimension of the idea of walking the straight and narrow. As noted above, in several of the recently recovered archaeological texts, the character *de* 德 is written using an alternative graph, 悳, with a heartmind radical *xin* 心 placed underneath the character *zhi* 直 that means "honestly, straight, true, upright, forthright." There is a cognate relationship between the two characters *de* 德 and *zhi* 直, and in the archaic language where the latter occasionally appears as a loan character for the former they have a

真切、正道、直率"。"德"与"直"有同源关系,而且在古体语言中,"直"为"德"的通假字,二者发音相似。

(《儒家角色伦理学:一套特色伦理学词汇》,第 226 页)

similar pronunciation.

(*Confucian Role Ethics: A Vocabulary,* pp. 206-207)

性

"性",或者更具体地说"人性",习惯上被翻译为"human nature"。正如"天"被译为"Heaven"一样,通过将其与这种译法所带有的通常的一些假定分离开来,我们可以了解到许多东西。在英文中,"human nature"的含义所附加的东西并不比"Heaven"要少。尤其是就"人性"而言,如果我们无法明确我们并不是在将有关"human nature"的一种本质主义的理解附加到"人性"之上,那么,很可能我们的许多读者就会心照不宣地对这种理解不予理会。

一种固定不变的"human nature"的观念没有为创造性的社会理解力(social intelligence)留下空间,而在对古典儒学的仔细解读中,我们却能够发现那种创造性的社会理解

Xing

Xing, or more specifically, *renxing* 人性, is conventionally translated as "human nature." Like the translation "Heaven" for *tian* (天), much can be learned about *xing* by disassociating it from the common assumptions that attend this formulaic translation. In English, "human nature" is no less a conceptually laden expression than "Heaven." Specifically with regard to *renxing* 人性, if we fail to make clear that we are *not* ascribing an essentialist understanding of "human nature" to the expression, it is likely that many, if not most, of our readers will tacitly default to this understanding.

The idea of an invariant human nature leaves no room for the kind of creative social intelligence that we are able to find in a close reading of early Confucianism. It is better to think of *xing* as a spontaneous process that is continually altered through changing patterns of growth and extension.

力。将"性"理解为一种自发的过程,通过成长和拓展的各种变化着的模式,这种自发的过程不断得以改变,这样的理解要更好。这种理解将人性在一种过程或事件的宇宙论(process or event cosmology)中加以定位,而较之任何本质主义的解读,那种过程或事件的宇宙论与古典儒学都更为相关。

鉴于这种对"性"的过程性的理解,在一种始终是决定了的方式中,"人性"、"天"和"命"之间的关系一定是无法理解的。作为"性"的根源,"天"不能被理解为一种排斥性的自我决定(precluding self-determination)。正如我们对"阴"和"阳"的理解一样,如果我们将"天"和"仁"理解为一种关联性的功能,这种功能表达了过程与事件的变化着的各种模式,这样的理解会更好。

在其各自的条目中,我们已经讨论了"天"和"命"的关联性。这种关联性是由古典儒学焦点—场域的定义性的特征所提示的,那种特征就是"天人合一"(the continuity of tian and the human experience)。如果在被天赋予的同时,"人"赋予

Such an understanding locates *renxing* within a process or event cosmology that is far more relevant to classical Confucianism than any essentialist reading.

Given this processional understanding of *xing*, the relationship between *renxing*, *tian*, and *ming* must not be construed in an altogether deterministic manner. As the source of *xing*, *tian* 天 is not to be construed as precluding self-determination. It is better to think of *tian* and *ren* as we think of *yin* and *yang*—namely, as correlative functions that articulate the changing patterns of processes and events.

We have discussed the correlativity of *tian* and *ming* in their respective entries in this glossary. The correlative status of *tian* and *renxing* is suggested by the oft-cited defining feature of classical Chinese religiousness as *tianren heyi* 天人合一 the "continuity of *tian* and the human experience." If the human being, while being endowed by *tian*, contributes to the content of *tian*, then in some degree at least (certainly in the persons of sages and exemplary models), the human being has a role in continually renegotiating what it means to be human.

(*Focusing the Familiar: A Translation and Philosophical Interpretation of the Zhongyong,* p. 83)

In a Confucian world, because persons are born into family relations that are

"天"以内容的话,那么,至少在某种程度上(当然在圣人和君子这样的典范中),在与"做人意味着什么"进行不断协调的过程中,人就扮演着一个重要的角色。

(《切中伦常:〈中庸〉的新诠与新译》,第101—102页)

儒家世界的人生于家庭关系中,亦被认为是由家庭关系建构的。他们的"性"(nature)(或许更恰当地说是自然倾向[nature tendencies])是由其家庭场所和最初状况所提供的与生俱来的本能与养成的认识、道德、审美、宗教感受性的结合。

(《生民之本:〈孝经〉的哲学诠释及英译》,第52页)

我们作为人一出生就被置于家、国等多形态、多联系的角色与关系之中,而且正是这些厚重的初始条件,才使我们有恻隐之心,有羞怯、恭敬之心,有规矩之感和赞同与反对之心——其实,这就是伦理感。伦理感根植于心,是对人一出生就已有的条件的一个一般性概括。恰恰是这一伦理感,成为之后贯穿具体个人人生的特殊叙事话语,

considered constitutive of their persons, their "natures" (*xing* 性), or perhaps better, "natural tendencies", are a combination of native instinct and the cultivated cognitive, moral, aesthetic, religious sensibilities provided by their family locus and initial conditions.

(*The Chinese classic of family reverence: a philosophical translation of the Xiaojing*, p. 41)

We as persons are born into a manifold of family and community roles and relations, and by virtue of these thick initial conditions, we have feelings of pity at suffering, feelings of modesty and deference, a sense of propriety and a sense of approval and disapproval—indeed, an ethical sensorium. The ethical sensorium is rooted in the heartmind (*xin* 心) as a generalization of the conditions which obtain when a person is born, and it is this sensorium that is then articulated across the particular narrative of a distinctively human life as a collaboration between person and world to become one's *xing* 性.

(*Confucian Role Ethics: A Vocabulary*, pp. 142-143)

Human nature is a provisional generalization made with respect to the totality of human lives as they have

是人与世界协同而成的"性"的叙述。

（《儒家角色伦理学：一套特色伦理学词汇》，第 158 页）

人性是一种暂定的概括。它按照人生总体而概括并在它的自然与社会关系之中度过。

（《儒家角色伦理学：一套特色伦理学词汇》，第 173 页）

仁

本书将"仁"译为"authoritative conduct""to act authoritatively" 或"authoritative person"。"仁"是孔子提出的最为重要的范畴，而"仁"字也在《论语》中出现了百次之多。在《说文解字》中，"仁"并不是一个难以理解的字：它由"人""二"两字合成。这种语源学分析更加印证了孔子的观点：一个人不可能自我为人。也就是说，从出生起，我们就不可避免地社会化。对此，芬加勒特（Herbert Fingarette）曾言简意赅地指出："孔子认为，如果世界上只有不到两个人的话，便没有人

been lived within their natural and social relations.

(*Confucian Role Ethics: A Vocabulary*, p. 155)

Authoritative Person & Consummate Person / Conduct (*Ren*)

Ren, translated herein as "authoritative conduct," "to act authoritatively," or "authoritative person," is the foremost project taken up by Confucius, and occurs over one hundred times in the text. It is a fairly simple graph, and according to the *Shuowen* lexicon, is made up of the elements *ren* 人 "person", and *er* 二, the number "two." This etymological analysis underscores the Confucian assumption that one cannot become a person by oneself—we are, from our inchoate beginnings, irreducibly social. Herbert Fingarette has stated the matter concisely: "For Confucius, unless there are at least two human beings, there can be no human beings."

存在。"

当然，根据甲骨文的字形，"仁"字或许应作另外一种解释。在甲骨文中，"二"实际上是"上"字的雏形，"上"即写作"二"。这种诠释凸现出在"成仁"过程中日渐显著的高下之分。因而，我们就需要为人文社会制订一个标准，即："仁者乐山；……仁者静；……仁者寿。"（《论语》第六篇第二十三章；又见第二篇第一章和第十七篇第三章）。

在英文著作中，"仁"通常被译作"benevolence"、"goodness"、或"humanity"；有时也会见到"humanheartedness"的形式；在极少数情况下，可能还会遇到艰涩而强调男性至上的"manhood-at-its-best"。

诚然，"benevolence"和"goodness"可能是翻译"仁"字的最佳选择。但是，经过深思熟虑之后，我们决定采用相比之下不够雅致的"authoritative person"。首先，"仁"是指一个完整的人而言，即：在礼仪角色和人际关系中体现出来的，后天所获得的感性的、美学的、道德的和宗教的意识。正是人的"自我领域"，即重要人际关系的总和，使

An alternative explanation of the character *ren* 仁 we might derive from oracle bone inscriptions is that what appears to be the number "two 二" is in fact an early form of "above, to ascend *shang* 上," which was also written as 二. Such a reading would highlight the growing distinction one accrues in becoming *ren*, thereby setting a bearing for one's community and the world to come: "those authoritative in their conduct enjoy mountains... are still... [and] are long-enduring" (6.23; see also 2.1 and 17.3).

Ren is most commonly translated as "benevolence," "goodness," and "humanity," occasionally as "humanheartedness," and less occasionally by the clumsy and sexist "manhood-at-its-best."

While "benevolence" and "humanity" might be more comfortable choices for translating *ren* into English, our decision to use the less elegant "authoritative person" is a considered one. First, *ren* is one's entire person: one's cultivated cognitive, aesthetic, moral, and religious sensibilities as they are expressed in one's ritualized roles and relationships. It is one's "field of selves," the sum of significant relationships, that constitute one as a resolutely social person. *Ren* is not only mental, but physical as well: one's posture and comportment, gestures

人成为完全意义上的社会人。"仁"不仅体现在精神方面，而且还具有物质指向：比如人的举止与态度，手势和肢体语言。因此，如果把"仁"译为"benevolence"的话，那就是在一个并不以"精神"概念作为定义人类经验的方法的文化传统中，强行对"仁"进行心理分析。结果，不但因为截断与其他德行的联系大大削弱了"仁"的丰富内涵，而且得不偿失地将为人复杂化。

英文"humanity"中暗含了"所有社会成员共同分享"这样一个基本条件。可是，"仁"绝非如此简单。"仁"是一个美学范畴，是一项已经完成的工作（《论语》第十二篇第一章）。人并非我们所是；而是我们所为和我们所成为。或许，"成人"一词能够更加精确地勾勒出成为人的过程的和突发的特点。但是，这并不是一种天赋之能；个人能够成就为人的东西，恰恰划定了人的原初条件和自然、社会、文化环境之间的界限。

当然，作为各种关系枢纽的人具有天性（《论语》第十七篇第二章）。不过，"仁"首先是滋养这些关系，使之成为人类社会重要的、

and bodily communication. Hence, translating *ren* as "benevolence" is to "psychologize" it in a tradition that does not rely upon the notion of *psyche* as a way of defining the human experience. It is to impoverish *ren* by isolating one out of many moral dispositions at the expense of so much more that comes together in the complexity of becoming human.

Again, "humanity" suggests a shared, essential condition of being human owned by all members of the species. Yet *ren* does not come so easy. It is an aesthetic project, an accomplishment, something done (12.1). The human *being* is not something we are; it is something that we do, and become. Perhaps "human *becoming*" might thus be a more appropriate term to capture the processional and emergent nature of what it means to become human. It is not an essential endowed potential, but what one is able to make of oneself given the interface between one's initial conditions and one's natural, social, and cultural environments.

Certainly the human being as a focus of constitutive relationships has an initial disposition (17.2). But *ren* is foremost the process of "growing (*sheng* 生)" these relationships into vital, robust, and healthy participation in the human community.

有力的、健康的参与者的过程。

在《论语》中，弟子们非常频繁地向孔子问"仁"。这反映出，孔子总是根据不同的意图重新诠释"仁"；而与孔子问答的弟子们显然并不满意于各自的理解。在孔子以前的文献中，"仁"是一个罕见而且无足轻重的概念。这一点正好反衬出孔子对"仁"之内涵的创造性发明。在上古文献中，我们根本找不到"仁"的踪迹；在随后的典籍中，"仁"仅仅出现了三次；而在《论语》的499章中，"仁"在58章里出现了105次。

"仁"标志着一个独特的人的性质改变，不过，它的意义也相当模糊——因为它必须在与个人具体条件的参照下才能被理解。这里没有既定的规则，也没有完美的理想。"仁"就像一件艺术品，它是一个开放的而非封闭的过程，并自始至终地抵抗一成不变的解释和重复。

与"仁"本身一样，用"authoritative person"来翻译"仁"也是一个多少有点新奇的表达。而且，这种译法可能会让人急于澄清其内涵。"authoritative"与"authority"是同源词；后者是指一个人因成"仁"而成为团体的代表，并且通过礼仪活

The fact that Confucius is asked so often what he means by the ex-pression *ren* would suggest that he is reinventing this term for his own purposes, and that those in conversation with him are not comfortable in their understanding of it. Confucius' creative investment of new meaning in *ren* is borne out by a survey of its infrequent, and relatively unimportant usage in the earlier corpus. *Ren* does not occur in the earliest portions of the ancient classics, and only three times in the later parts. This unexceptional usage compares with 105 occurrences in the Analects in 58 of the 499 sections.

Given that *ren* denotes the qualitative transformation of a *particular* person, it is further ambiguous because it must be understood relative to the specific concrete conditions of that person. There is no formula, no ideal. Like a work of art, it is a process of disclosure rather than closure, resisting fixed definition and replication.

Our term "authoritative person" as a translation of *ren* then, is a somewhat novel expression, as was *ren* itself, and will probably prompt a similar desire for clarification. "Authoritative" entails the "authority" that a person comes to represent in community by becoming *ren*, embodying in oneself the values and customs of one's

动，在其身上体现出其文化传统的价值和习俗。在《论语》中，山的隐喻（《论语》第六篇第二十三章）贴切传神地刻画出"仁"的特点：沉静、庄严、极具精神内涵、永恒不朽、被视为地域文化与团体的分界石。

为道之路并不是已然设定的。仁者必须是一个开拓创新者，他参与创造了自己地域和时代的文化（《论语》第十五篇第二十九章）。而"礼"则是一个内在化的过程——"创造自己的传统"——将决定个人定位的社会角色和人际关系人格化。"仁"的创造性，恰恰就是在各自团体内成为权威代表所不可或缺的因素。

在严密的组织和被迫接受的权威命令，以及权威命令所暗含的倒置的、顺从的意义之间进行分析和对比，是一项大有裨益的工作。仁者是一个公认的典范。其他人在绝无外在强制的情况下，心悦诚服于其成就，并且遵循其模式，修养自己的人格。而对于政治运作中的上下级命令关系造就的权威主义者，和循规蹈矩的仪式化团体赋予法律制度的非强制性结构这两者，孔子均持明显的保留态度。

（《〈论语〉的哲学诠释》，第

tradition through the observance of ritual propriety (*li*). The prominence and visibility of the authoritative person is captured in the metaphor of the mountain (6.23): still, stately, spiritual, enduring, a landmark of the local culture and community.

At the same time, the way of becoming human (*dao*) is not a given; the authoritative person must be a "road builder," a participant in "authoring" the culture for one's own place and time (15.29). Observing ritual propriety (*li*) is, by definition, a process of internalization—"making the tradition one's own"—requiring personalization of the roles and relationships that locate one within community. It is this creative aspect of *ren* that is implicit in the process of becoming authoritative for one's own community.

The contrast between top-down and impositional "authoritarian" order, and the bottom-up, deferential sense of "authoritative" order is also salutary. The authoritative person is a model that others, recognizing the achievement, gladly and without coercion, defer to and appropriate in the construction of their own personhood. Confucius is as explicit in expressing the same reservations about authoritative relations becoming authoritarian as he is about a deference-driven ritualized community surrendering

48—51 页）

虽然人们都会认同，"仁"为翻译儒学的核心词汇，但是再努力搜索，能找到的对应英文，也必然是令人失望的。所以，对儒家思想做英文翻译，是不被立即采取的第二选择措施，第一选择措施是鼓励学习中国哲学的人直接学习中文术语。尽管如此，我还是倾向于以"consummate person"或"conduct"（极致、圆满的人或行为）作为对"仁"的暂定翻译。这是个经过认真考虑的选择。"consummate"的前缀"con-"含有"群体"（collective）与"集中"（intensive）感，意思是指"一起、合着"（together, jointly），可以恰当地用来对应不可简化（还原）的关系性，这样就可以对应"仁"的特殊性意义。还有，那种"summa"的"圆满"（completion）形态，具有"开放性"而非"封闭性"喻义，指一种事项处理意义的成熟与硕果，它远不是什么形而上学意义所讲的"外在赋予潜质变为现实"。"summa"表达的是至善效果，是特殊的成就，而且不是复制某些过去的成果。因为这样，

this noncoercive structure for the rule of law (2.3).

(*The Analects of Confucius: A Philosophical Translation,* pp. 48-51)

Although remaining persuaded that the search for inevitably disappointing English translations of the central Confucian vocabulary must stand as a distant second priority to urging the student of Chinese philosophy to learn the original Chinese terminology, I am inclined to use "consummate person or conduct" as a tentative translation for *ren*. This is a deliberate choice. "Consummate" has the virtue of using the collective and intensive prefix "con-," denoting the sense of "together, jointly" that does justice to the irreducible relationality and thus particularity of *ren*. In addition, *summa* is that form of "completion" that suggests disclosure more than closure, a transactional maturation and fruition more than the actualization of some given potential. *Summa* is the highest efficacy in some particular achievement and not merely a replication of something previously accomplished, and as such, is high praise by the community for someone's particular attainment (*summa cum laude*).

"summa"表达人群社会对一个人取得的特殊成就所给的高度颂扬（例如拉丁语"summa cum lauda"，意为学生在毕业典礼上被授予最高荣誉，因为他取得最优秀的学业成绩）。

（《儒家角色伦理学：一套特色伦理学词汇》，第198页）

(*Confucian Role Ethics: A Vocabulary*, p. 179)

义

在著名学者刘殿爵的《论语》英译本中，"义"字的译法并不统一。有时作"right"，有时为"duty"，偶尔被理解为"morality"，极个别情况下还写作"moral"。如果我们像刘殿爵一样，或多或少地按照西方观念，将孔子定位为一位"道德哲学家"的话，"义"字可能是汉语中对应于"moral"或"morality"的最佳选择。但是，在现代英语中，尤其是在后康德伦理学中，"morality"与"freedom"、"liberty"、"choice"、"ought"、"individual"、"reason"、"autonomy"、"dilemma"、"objective"、"subjective"诸词的语义联系极为密切。但是，我们恰恰无法在古代汉语中找到与

Appropriate (*Yi*)

In his translation of the Analects, the distinguished scholar D. C. Lau translates *yi* sometimes as "right," other times as "duty," and on occasion as "moral" or "morality" more generally. If one is committed, as Lau is, to portraying Confucius as a "moral philosopher" in more or less the Western sense, then *yi* is probably the best candidate as a Chinese lexical equivalent for "morals" or "morality." But the term "morality" in contemporary English, and particularly in post-Kantian ethics, is linked intimately with a number of other terms: "freedom," "liberty," "choice," "ought," "individual," "reason," "autonomy," "dilemma," "objective," "subjective." None of these English terms has a close analogue in classical Chinese, and hence in the absence of these associations, we are skeptical of using "morality" for *yi*, which is linked intimately with a very different

上述英文词汇一一对应的表达。正是汉语中这种相关语汇缺失的现象，使我们有充分理由质疑将"义"译作"morality"的选择。况且，在儒家思想中，"义"与"礼"、"仁"、"信"（第一篇第十三章）等迥异于西方文化的概念密不可分。

在商代甲骨文中，"义"有几种异体形式。这为诠释"义"之精髓提供了另外一种可能。从语源学的角度分析，"义（義）"的字形是"羊"字叠放在第一人称代词"我"之上。而"我"字的起源至今仍然晦涩难明。作为题外话，我们不妨提醒大家注意，在一个个人高度社会化的文化传统中，其语言不会刻意凸现单数"我"与复数"我们"之间的区别。单数的"我"已经融入社会之中，并与后者相互影响，相互作用。

代词"我"的几种早期写法以及《说文解字》中的诠释均显示，其字形是一只持戈的人手。而"羊"则是定期举行的礼仪活动中使用的牺牲（第三篇第十七章）。那么，我们似乎可以根据字形，将"义"理解为：某人对礼仪中用作牺牲的羔羊的态度和看法。

这种态度和看法使得此人成为

cluster of terms: "observing ritual propriety (*li* 礼)," "authoritative conduct (*ren* 仁)," "making good on one's word (*xin* 信)" (1.13), and so on.

Several variants of the original Shang dynasty characters for *yi* suggest another interpretation. *Yi*, etymologically, is an adumbrated picture of a sheep (*yang* 羊) over a first-person pronoun (*wo* 我) "I" "we," "me," "us," the origins of which are unknown. As an aside, it is revealing that in a tradition in which person is irreducibly social, the distinction between the singular "I" and the plural "we" is not indicated in the language. The "I" and the social context are reflexive and mutually entailing.

This pronoun *wo* is itself, in many of its early representations and attested in the *Shuowen* lexicon, a picture of a human hand holding a dagger-axe (*ge* 戈). When it is remembered that sheep were periodically sacrificed at large communal gatherings (3.17), we may gloss *yi* as the attitude one has, the stance one takes, when literally preparing the lamb for the ritual slaughter.

This attitude, this stance, is making oneself a sacred representative of the community, and thereby purifying and making appropriately sacred the sacrificial animal. If this be so, then *yi* should not be rendered as "moral" or

团体的神圣代表,并因而能够使献祭动物洁净无瑕,合适可用。如果上述分析是正确的话,"义"就不应该被翻译为"moral"或"morality";而"appropriate"和"fitting"可能更加接近中文"义"的原意。也就是说,"义"是人对适中的感觉和把握。这种感觉使人在既定的特殊环境下,能够从容恰当地应对(第四篇第十章,第九篇第四章和第十八篇第八章)。"义"的内涵也是由以"礼"的形式层累而成的传统所赋予的。"礼"限定了"义",即,个人遵循自己的各种角色和礼仪制度行事就是"义"。正因为"义"是对适中度的感觉和把握,所以一个相互信任的团体中的种种关系才更加耐人寻味。是以孔子曰:"信近于义。"

所以,我们在本书中用"appropriate"翻译"义",并请读者们牢牢记住:在理解"appropriate"的时候,不仅要注意到其美学的、道德的涵衍,还要充分发掘其社会的和宗教的意蕴。

(《〈论语〉的哲学诠释》,第54—56页)

《说文》可以证明,在其许多

"morality." "Appropriate" or "fitting" are perhaps closer English equivalents for *yi*, and that is how the term is translated herein. *Yi*, then, is one's sense of appropriateness that enables one to act in a proper and fitting manner, given the specific situation (4.10, 9.4,18.8). By extension, it is also the meaning invested by a cumulative tradition in the forms of ritual propriety that define it—import that can be appropriated by a person in the performance of these roles and rituals. It is because *yi* is the sense of appropriateness that makes relationships truly meaningful in a community of mutual trust, that Confucius says "making good on one's word (*xin* 信) gets one close to appropriateness."

The reader should keep in mind that "appropriate," as we use it for translating *yi*, should be understood in terms of not only its aesthetic and moral connotations, but also with its social and religious implications in mind as well.

(*The Analects of Confucius: A Philosophical Translation,* pp. 53-55)

In many of its early representations, attested in the *Shuowen* lexicon, the pronoun *wo* is a picture of a human hand holding a dagger-axe (*ge* 戈). Remembering that sheep were periodically sacrificed at large communal gatherings, we may gloss *yi* as

早期的表象中,"我"的形象是一个"人"持"戈"而力。"羊"是在大的公共集会上被定期用来进行祭祀的。如果我们记得这一点,那么,我们就可以将"义"解释为一个人在准备杀羊以为礼仪活动之用时所采取的姿势。

这种恭敬的姿势不仅使一个人成为社群的神圣代表,同时也使得祭祀的动物变得净化和具有恰当的神圣性。如果的确如此,那么,"义"就不能为翻译为"righteous"或"moral"。对"义"而言,"appropriate"或"fitting"或许是更为贴近的英文对应物。这里,我们就是用"appropriate"或"fitting"来翻译"义"的。

于是,"义"是一个人关于恰当、得体的感觉,这种感觉使一个人能够在具体的境况下以一种恰当和得体的方式去行为。当其居于一个人的品行之中时,"义"是对一种意义的肯定。事实上,在《中庸》第二十章中,恰恰以同音字互训的方式对"义"的这种含义进行了界定:

义者,宜也,尊贤为大。

通过扩展,它还具有一种礼仪

the stance one takes when preparing the lamb for the ritual slaughter.

This deferential stance not only makes one a sacred representative of the community, but also purifies and makes appropriately sacred the sacrificial animal. If this be so, then *yi* should not be rendered as "righteous" or "moral." "Appropriate" or "fitting" are perhaps closer English equivalents for *yi*, and that is how the term is translated herein.

Yi, then, is one's sense of appropriateness that enables one to act in a proper and fitting manner, given the specific situation. It is a recognition of meaning as it resides in personal character and conduct. In fact, *Zhongyong* 20 defines *yi* paronomastically in precisely these terms:

> Appropriateness (*yi* 義) means doing what is fitting (*yi* 宜), wherein esteeming those of superior character is most important.

By extension, it is also the meaning invested by a cumulative tradition in the forms of ritual propriety that define it. This import can be appropriated by a person in the performance of these roles and rituals. It is because *yi* is the sense of appropriateness that makes relationships truly meaningful in a community of credibility and mutual trust that Confucius in *Analects* 1.13 says "making good on one's word (*xin* 信) gets one close

形式下的累积性的传统所赋予的意义。这种意义可以通过一个人的礼仪活动以及社会角色的履行来获得。正是因为"义"意味着恰当、得体,才使得一个相互信赖的社群中的各种关系富有意义。正如《论语》第一篇《学而》第十三章所谓:"信近于义。"

(《切中伦常:〈中庸〉的新诠与新译》,第102—103页)

《说文解字》也根据人的身份的实际获得来定义"义":"义,己之威仪也。"基于"义"的这几种定义和讨论可以看出,"义"似乎是一个自我身份诠释的概念。有一点需要时刻铭记,即孔子思想的根基是语境本体论。这样,该语境中起作用的人乃是"过程性"而非"实体性"的。因而,"义"就很容易被认为既是自我诠释的身份又是自我的行为过程。

(《通过孔子而思》,第111页)

我们已认定,"义"是某种独为人类拥有的品格,它源于自我,也决定独一无二的"尊贵"(或实现的)自我,并且以某种积极、规范方式引导人的行为。"义"在其最根

to appropriateness."

(*Focusing the Familiar: A Translation and Philosophical Interpretation of the Zhongyong*, p. 84)

The *Shuo-wen* dictionary also defines *yi* in terms of the positive achievement of personal identity: "*Yi* means one's dignity of demeanor." It would seem on the basis of these several definitions and discussions of *yi* that it is a notion of self-construing identity. It is important to bear in mind the contextualist ontology in which the teachings of Confucius are grounded, and that the conception of person operative in this context is "processive" rather than "substantial." Hence, there is no difficulty in asserting that *yi* is both a self-construing identity and what one does.

(*Thinking Through Confucius,* pp. 92-93)

We have determined that *yi* is something exclusively human that has its origins in and defines the unique "exalted" or "realizing" self, and that informs human action in some positive, normative way. At its most fundamental level, *yi* denotes the importation of aesthetic, moral, and rational significance into personal action in the world. It is from this that the sense of *yi* as "meaning" or "significance" arises. A person, like a word, achieves meaning in the interplay between bestowing its own accumulated significance and appropriating meaning from its context.

本的层面表明将审美、道德和理性意义引入社会中的个人行为中。正由此,"义"作为"意义"(meaning, significance)的意义得以产生。一个人就像一个词,在将本身累积的意义赋予语境和从语境中获取意义的互动中获得意义。

(《通过孔子而思》,第 113 页)

对"义"的这一分析的根本价值在于,"语境中的人"将意义赋予世界。如果说孔子这一"成人"概念基于语境论宇宙观(contextualist cosmology),那么自然就是:存在过程中人类行为的本质体现即为新境况:来往内容不断推陈出新;其间,人将他的"义"赋予恒动而常新的情境之流。这必将意味着,任何两个人赋予世界的"义"都不会全然一样,而且,"得义"与否必须由个体与新情境的相互作用和融为一体所必需的灵活性来表征。陈大齐将这种灵活性称为"不固"。这是孔子思想的一个核心主题。它有力地强调了"义"的创造和创新维度。

(《通过孔子而思》,第 113—114 页)

(*Thinking Through Confucius*, pp. 94-95)

Of fundamental importance in this analysis of *yi* is that the person-in-context imports significance to the world. Given the contextualist, cosmology in which this Confucian conception of the realizing person is grounded, it follows that matters of human conduct within the process of existence characteristically represent novel situation which require a person to bestow his *yi* in perpetually changing and ever-unique sets of circumstances. This would have to mean that no two personal investments of *yi* in the world are ever the same and, further, that attaining *yi* (*te-yi* 得义)must be characterized by a flexibility necessary for a person to interact with and integrate into ever new situations. Ch'en Ta-ch'i terms this flexibility *pu ku* 不固. It is a central theme in Confucius, emphatically underscoring the creative and novel dimensions of *yi*.

(*Thinking Through Confucius,* p. 95)

Throughout the early philosophical and philological literature, *yi* 義 is consistently defined in terms of its homophone, *yi** 宜, "right, proper, appropriate, suitable." The two characters diverge, however, in that whereas *yi* denotes appropriateness to one's own person, *yi** refers to appropriateness to one's context. *Yi* is the active and contributory integrating of self with circumstances,

通观中国古代哲学和语言学文献,"义"都是根据它的同音字"宜"(right, proper, appropriate, suitable)来定义的。然而,由于"义"尽管表示"宜我"(appropriateness to one's own person),它也还指涉"宜境"(appropriateness to one's context),所以这两个字仍有区别。"义"是"我"主动地、有贡献地与环境融为一体,其中,"我"创造独特行动,并就此以一种创造性的方式诠释自我。它是"我"对"机体"这一概念的表达和贡献。而另一方面,"义"还表示自我为"宜"语境或环境意义的让步或放弃。"义"在关注"我"(即,语境中的人 [person-in-context])的同时也关注境(即,语境中的人 [person-in-*context*]);它既根本上是自我维护和意义的赋予者,又是自我牺牲和意义的派生者。

(《通过孔子而思》,第114—115页)

我们已将"义"确定为表征个人向世界赋予的意义。这意味着"人"是条件性的,不断由其自身在不断更新的环境中重塑。"义"不仅突显了某些人类独有的行为,而

where the self originates unique activity and construes itself on its own terms in a novel and creative way. It is the articulation and contribution of the self to the organism. The character yi*, on the other hand, denotes the yielding or giving up of oneself and "appropriating" meaning from the context or circumstances. Where the focus of yi is one's personal self (that is, person-in-context), the focus of yi* is on the environment (that is, person-in-*context*); where yi is fundamentally self-assertive and meaning-bestowing. yi* is self-sacrificing and meaning-deriving.

(*Thinking Through Confucius,* p. 96)

We have established that yi represents personal investment of meaning in the world. What it means to be human is contingent, being ever redefined by man himself in the emergence of new circumstances, Not only does yi distinguish certain actions as uniquely human, but a particular human action invested with and conditioned by yi is called li 禮 "proper form, moral conventions, ritual actions."

(*Thinking Through Confucius,* p. 97)

The Tuan Yü-ts'ai commentary on the *Shuo-wen* also defines yi with reference to its expression in ritual action: "The basic meaning of yi is each person's achieving his appropriateness (yi*宜) in the performance of ritual actions (li). Where one does so, he is good (shan 善)." Ritual actions are intimately

且,为"义"所贯注且以之为条件的特定人类行为还被称为"礼"（proper form, moral conventions, ritual actions）。

（《通过孔子而思》,第115页）

段玉裁《说文解字注》也参照"礼"来定义"义"："义之本训谓礼容各得其宜,礼容得宜则善矣。""义"是表达出个体所揭示的意义的公开的人类行为,"礼"与"义"有着密切关联。孔子之后日益流行的"礼义"这一表达就是明证。例如,《荀子》就有三分之一的"义"字是以"礼义"并陈的形式出现的。

（《通过孔子而思》,第116页）

"义"拥有规范力量,却并不是自行建构一个标准。实现"义"不是贯彻执行什么严格的方针。该行为至少在某种程度上是自发和具有创新性的。这意味着,"义"既是决意和行为的原因又是其结果。"义"从一开始就拥有规范化力量,尽管它是不完善的。诠释既定语境中的"义"涉及形成新的意识以判断是否与该情境相宜,且如何最大限度地

related to *yi*, those overt human actions which give expression to the personal disclosure of meaning. This is evident in the increasing popularity of the expression *li-yi* 禮義 after the death of Confucius. In *Hsün Tzu*, for example, more than a third of the occurrences of *yi* are in the binomial expression of *li-yi*.

(*Thinking Through Confucius,* pp. 97-98)

Yi has normative force without itself actually constituting a norm. The actions that realize *yi* are not performed in accordance with strict guidelines. Such actions are, at least to some degree, spontaneous, novel, and creative. This means that *yi* is as much the consequence of a particular decision or action as its cause. The normative force of *yi* exists in spite of its inchoate character at the beginning of *yi* acts. The articulation of *yi* with respect to a given situation involves the emerging awareness of what is or is not appropriate in that situation and how one might act so as to realize this appropriateness in its highest degree. This articulation occurs *pari passu* with the act itself. Neither determined nor determining, *yi* is actualized in the interplay between decision and circumstance; in this manner it achieves its appropriateness.

(*Thinking Through Confucius,* p. 102)

Yao and Shun, and the Duke of Chou, are known through their deeds. They serve as models of *yi* by virtue of their deeds. Their

做到与之相宜。诠释与行动本身同步发生。"义"既非决定者,也非被决定者,它实现于决意与语境的相互作用,且据此得获其"宜"。

(《通过孔子而思》,第120—121页)

尧、舜以及周公都以其行名世。他们由于嘉行而成为"义"的典范,其在中国传统中的岿然形象缘于他们的行为被认为是"义"。事实上,中国历史上对"义"行的证明更多援引的是历史人物,而非引述特定行为。而且,我们常常会发现援引的过程也是一个添加的过程——历史人物及其行为的轶事被一代又一代进行着再创造。但这些历史人物和他们的行为却从来都是不可分割地紧密联系在一起。我们效仿那些由其力量以及使之力量恢宏的行为所塑造的人。圣王和孔子自己之所以被视为"义"的典范,大概是因为他们高度持之以恒地在个体行为中实现"义"。因而,他们既是他们行为的创造者,也为行为所塑造。

(《通过孔子而思》,第125页)

persistent presence in the Chinese tradition is due to belief in the rightness of their actions. In fact, allusions to historical figures are more often than not allusions to specific acts as concrete instances of right behavior. And we can frequently observe a movement from allusion to attribution such that the historical figure and his repertoire of acts are recreated for subsequent generations. Neither the individual nor his action may be held in isolation one from the other, however. We model our actions upon the person who is constituted by both his agency and the act in which it culminates. The sage-kings and Confucius himself serve as models of *yi* because of the presumedly high degree of consistency with which they realized *yi* in their individual acts. They are thus authored by their deeds as well as being authors of them.

(*Thinking Through Confucius,* p. 106)

The vocabulary of *shu* and *zhong*—putting oneself in the others place and then doing one's utmost—resonates immediately with *yi* 義, a third term in this Confucian moral vocabulary. *Yi* is "achieving an optimal appropriateness in one's relations"—that is, the satisfaction of moral uncertainty through an acquired sense of what is most fitting in the situation. *Shu* can be thought of as rehearsing the possibilities for what would be most appropriate in a relationship, where the emphasis is on careful deliberation in identifying what the best course of action might be. *Shu* entails "other-directed"

"忠恕"二字——"尽己"和"推己及人",是与"义"直接关联的。"义"是孔子道德观第三核心词汇。"义"是"成就人关系之最恰宜",即以知晓"什么是"与情景最恰宜相合之涵义,作为对道德不确定的满意回应。"恕"可以被想成对关系最恰宜情景可能性的演练,它强调细致用心地去发现如何做将是最恰宜的行为。"恕"包括"敬人"之心,意思是只有在对他人的需要和意愿给以充分考虑之后,一个人的行为才得以确定。所以"忠"意为实行这样一种道德探询过程,随之在行事中做到尽己所能。

"义"在另一方面反映人的最恰当判断。在与他人关系上,为能做出最恰宜行为,为对合乎情势的恰宜做到胸有成竹,判断自己要采取什么态度。强调要根据自己对什么怀有恰当的感觉,要怎样最恰当地与人互动。"恕"是去发现,"忠"是去做的方式,"义"是在需要伦理考虑的场合中发挥。

"义"是"达到最恰宜",它所定位的即时行动,既具同步性又具历史性。同步性的"义"行动,意在将域境扩展得尽可能宽大,顾及

deference in the sense that one's action is shaped only after a full consideration of the needs and interests of others. And *zhong* then is giving this process of moral inquiry and the initiation of one's subsequent action the utmost in one's efforts.

Yi, on the other hand, reflects one's best judgment on how one might dispose oneself in one's relation to others in order to accomplish the recommended action, and confidence that what one is doing is appropriate in the circumstances. The emphasis is on following one's own sense of what is right in being responsive to the concerns of others. It entails a "self including" sense of how best to interact with others. The searching *shu*, the modality of action, *zhong*, and the consequent *yi* are at play in situations that require ethical consideration.

Yi as an "optimizing appropriateness" locates present action both synchronically and diachronically. Synchronically *yi* action attempts to extend the context as broadly as possible, attending to the full range of possibilities involved, and taking under consideration the sometimes competing yet still legitimate interests of all concerned. Diachronically *yi* action in the present moment locates the immediate circumstances within the continuities it has with both past and future activity, making a comprehensive consideration of the continuing present the best way to make full use of those resources inherited out of past experience and the most productive way of

场域全局的一切可能潜在力，把一些有竞争却仍是各方合理性的利益，也都考虑进去。历史性的"义"行动，在当下这一时刻把身处的直接环境，置入它与过去以及将来行动构成的延续中去，把仍在延续的当前，全面考虑为充分发挥那些资源的最佳方法，这些资源依据过去经验，是判断将来发生情况的最有效方法。

"义"在甲骨文的字形是"𦍌"，在铭文中的字形是"義"。在字形语义结构上，"义（義）"，从"羊"、从"我"。"羊"是与牺牲、祭祀相联系的象征，通常含吉利之义。"善""美""祥"等字皆从"羊"。这种情况告诉我们，在中国传统中"人"皆是不可简约的社会性的，单数的"我"与多数的"我们"二者之间的差异，是没有严格区分的。或许更甚者，更为独立性、主格性的"我"与社会嵌入性、宾格性的"我"，或者更为独立性、主格性的"我们"与社会嵌入性、宾格性的"我们"（于英语为"us"），在语言上都是不区分的。

另外，清朝语言学者段玉裁建议，取"义（義）"中"羊"与

anticipating what is yet to come.

Yi occurs in the oracle bones as 𦍌 and on the bronzes as 義. Etymologically the graph is a stylized picture of a sheep (*yang* 羊) in combination with the first-person pronoun for "I, we, me, us," (*wo* 我). The sheep signifier, carrying an association with sacrifice, is usually understood to suggest propitiousness. It occurs in characters such as "efficacy" (*shan* 善), "beautiful" (*mei* 美), "auspicious" (*xiang* 祥), and so on. Revealing here is that in a tradition in which persons are irreducibly social, the distinction between the singular "I" and the plural "we" is not marked. Perhaps even more telling, the distinction between the more independent, nominative "I" and the socially embedded, accusative "me" or the nominative "we" and the socially embedded accusative "us" is not indicated in the language.

But scholars of the classical language such as the Qing-dynasty philologist Duan Yucai 段玉裁 warn against making too much of the contemporary meanings of the two elements that constitute this character. This pronoun *wo*, as attested in the oracle bones and bronzes, depicts a dagger-axe (*ge* 戈): 我. On the basis of this information, it has been argued that the *wo* character references a long-handled weapon with serrated, saw-like teeth. At some point, for phonological reasons, it came to be used as a lone character for its homophone, the first person pronoun wo. When it is remembered that sheep were periodically sacrificed at large

"我"的现代涵义,不可过度。因为人称代词的"我",甲骨文与铭文中的字形为从戈"𢦏"。由此,有人就提出"我"是指一种长柄锯齿状兵器。在某种音韵学意义上,它又被作为同音异形异义单独代词的"我"来使用。古代"羊"是定期大规模祭祀活动的牺牲品,所以"义"可理解为准备献祭时人的严肃、庄重态度及其恰如其分的社会身份。"我"与"义"在献祭活动上的联系,与"牺"的"祭祀、牺牲、牲畜"意思是相合的;"牺"的原始甲骨文和铭文字形写作"羲"。另外,"义"的《说文解字》解释是"威仪",这里显出合乎身份的仪态的涵义在同根词"仪"上得到印证——"有仪态之人",尤指一位显出"威仪、端庄、礼数、恩慈"之人。这种礼仪身份及其恭敬仪态,不仅表示这个人代表社会的神圣性,同时牺牲祭品也获得净化,具有神圣性。

前面已做阐释,"仁"在郭店竹简的字形构成从身从心,表意妊娠妇人,将"仁"同一种轻柔仪态相联系;同样,"义"作为一个显出"庄重、威严",志坚意决,执戈备祭的人的形象,这中间有着内在的联系。这一鲜

communal gatherings, we may gloss *yi* as the solemn, dignified attitude one assumes and the proper social stance one takes when preparing the lamb for the ritual slaughter. This association of *wo* 我 and *yi* 义 with sacrifice is consistent with its cognate *xi* 犧. "to sacrifice, sacrificial animal," in that in its original form on the oracle bones and bronzes was written as *xi* 犧. Again, *yi* is defined in the *Shuowen* lexicon as "dignity, majesty" (*weiyi* 威儀), where the connotation of assuming a proper demeanor can be attested by this cognate character 儀 —"an *yi* person"— meaning specifically "a person with dignity, decorum, courtesy, graciousness." The propriety of this stance and its deferential attitude not only makes one a sacred representative of the community, but also purifies and consecrates the sacrificial animal.

Above we found a correlation of *ren* 仁 with concern for a pregnant women in the Guodian version of the graph that is composed of *shen* 身 over *xin* 心, associating *ren* with a kind of pliant and gentle attitude. Similarly, there is a correlation between *yi* 義 as "the solemn and dignified demeanor of a person using a dagger-axe to prepare a sacrifice" with a kind of firmness and resolve. This contrast is remarked upon explicitly in the recently recovered document, *Five Modes of Proper Conduct*:

To treat resolutely is how to be optimally appropriate (*yi* 義);to treat

明对照,在发掘出不久的《五行篇》中,可见到清晰的表述:

> 故义取闻而仁取匿。刚,义之方也,柔,仁之方也。(《五行篇》二十)

"义"历来被译为英语的"righteousness"和"meaning";一般译为"Rightness"(正确性)和"morality"(道德性)的情况,是较少的。"righteousness"这个英语词语与一种圣经涵义无法分开,即服从上帝的意志,它引进了一个具有独立性、客观性、神性旨意的正确、道德的标准,是一个与"义"不太相干的方程式。"正义"和"公平"涵义要求的是人的决断与坚定,而"义"则是人自己与所在场域的协调,需要的是宽阔胸怀、灵活和包容性。对孔子而言,就是我们不能手执已然准备好的、曾经的硕果,进入总是变化呈新的情况中来。因为这个原因,在尊重环境特殊性上,孔子十分坚决:

> 君子之于天下也,无适也,无莫也,义之与比。(《论语·里仁》)

leniently is how to be consummate in one's conduct (*ren* 仁).Standing firm is how to be optimally appropriate (*yi*); being flexible is how to be consummate in one's conduct (*ren*).

Yi has conventionally been translated into English as "righteousness" and "meaning," and less commonly as "rightness" and "morality." The decidedly biblical associations that attend the word "righteousness" as obedience to the will of God introduces an independent, objective, and divinely-sanctioned standard of what is right or "moral" into the equation that has little relevance for *yi*. While a sense of justice and fairness requires that one be resolved and stand firm, *yi* is still the outcome of a negotiation between self and the specific context that requires broadmindedness, flexibility, and accommodation. For Confucius, we cannot enter an always—novel situation with the best outcome ready to hand. It is for this reason that he is stanch in respecting the particularity of the circumstances:

Exemplary persons (*junzi* 君子) in making their way in the world are neither bent on nor against anything; rather, they go with what is most appropriate (*yi* 義).

This search for an optimal appropriateness is consistent with how Confucius himself is

追求至善（最好的恰宜性）是与经常描述的孔子生活态度相一致的：

子绝四：毋意，毋必，毋固，毋我。（《论语·子罕》）

在决定采取什么行为时，这样的灵活、包容态度并不排斥行动时的坚定意决。正如孔子所说："见义不为，无勇也。"（《论语·为政》）其实这样的意决是《论语》的一个主旨精神：

德之不修，学之不讲，闻义不能徙，不善不能改，是吾忧也。（《论语·述而》）

孔子对灵活性与意决的结合，在君子行道践行"义"中，做出阐述：

义以为质，礼以行之，孙以出之，信以成之。君子哉！（《论语·卫灵公》）

如果要确定一个对"义"的尝试性译法，域境包含性的

frequently described:

There were four things the Master abstained from entirely: he did not speculate, he did not claim or demand certainty, he was not inflexible, and he was not self-absorbed.

Such an attitude of flexibility and accommodation in determining a course of action does not preclude firmness and resolve in acting upon it. As Confucius remarks, "Failing to act on what one deems appropriate (*yi*) is a want of courage." Indeed, such resolve is a major theme in the *Analects*:

To fail to cultivate excellence (*de*), to fail to practice what I have learned, to be unable to follow through on what has been deemed to be the most appropriate course of action (*yi*), and to be unable to reform conduct that is not efficacious—these are the things I worry about.

Confucius summarizes this combination of flexibility and resolve in describing the process that the exemplary person goes through in determining and acting upon *yi*:

Having a sense of appropriate conduct (*yi*) as one's basic disposition, putting such conduct into practice by "appropriateness"（恰宜性）和"fittingness"（适合性）可能是意义最相近的英语词汇。这个翻译因与"义"常有同音联系的"宜"得到强化。"宜"像"义"一样具有一种基本宗教性指向，意思是"祭祀土地"，并由此引申为以"恰、和、适"进行调节。用"appropriate"作为"义"的英语翻译，它不仅具有审美和伦理涵义，还有思想的神圣与宗教意义。"至善"（最佳恰宜）关系不仅涵义丰富，而且正如我们将在下章讨论的，这样的关系也是我们与宗教群体相通的那种价值感与归属感意义充沛的源泉。

所以，"义"是一种人所成就的恰宜感，它使人能够根据一定情势的特别性，采取恰当的行为方式。进一步引申，因为关系的"恰宜性"是产生本身意义的根本来源，所以不应感到奇怪，"义"也有"意义"进入，正如它被表述以及它属于人本身的关系和行为。伴随时间的长久，"义"变成了一个充满活力的传统，遵行各种礼节，举手投足体现着聚合意义。"义"是一种何谓至善（最好恰宜性）的意义，表达于人的角色与关系构成中，确定着何谓

aspiring to propriety in one's roles and relations (*li*), carrying it out with modesty, and attaining it by making good on one's word (*xin* 信): this then is the exemplary person (*junzi*).

In looking for a tentative translation for *yi*, the contextually inclusive "appropriateness" and "fittingness" are perhaps the closest English equivalents. Such a translation is reinforced by the frequent paronomastic association of *yi* 义 with its near homophone, *yi* 宜, that like *yi* 义 has a primary religious reference in meaning "to sacrifice to the deity of the soil," and derivatively, to adjust to what is "right, proper, fitting." "Appropriate" as a translation for *yi* should be understood not only with its aesthetic and ethical connotations, but also with this sacred and religious import in mind. Optimally appropriate relations are not only meaningful; as we will explore in the next chapter, such relations are also the source of the intense sense of worth and belonging we associate with religious communion.

Yi, then, is an achieved sense of appropriateness that enables one to act in a proper and fitting manner, given the specifics of a situation. By extension, since appropriateness in relations is the ultimate source of meaning itself, it should not be surprising that *yi* also has the import of "meaning" as it is expressed and comes to reside in one's personal relations and conduct.

恰到适处。而且"义"是文化的施行，人们可以享用它，这样他们就会在践行同样的角色与礼数活动中，嵌入文化。这种社会形式的享用带有投入性意义——它使得一次敬礼，一次握手和一个婚礼，都充满意义；在这样的礼数践行活动中所实现与投入的"恰宜性"意义，使得人们对"义"的遵行具有深刻的自己的特色。

"义"是对待关系的恰宜性，随着时间的推移，它促进关系社会的信任与诚信度以及彼此的信心与依靠性，这样就能滋长人们对社会的真实归属感。孔子的话清晰地阐明了这一联系：

　　信近于义，言可复也。
（《论语·学而》）

（《儒家角色伦理学：一套特色伦理学词汇》，第221—225页）

拉丁字"proprius"（它的字面意思是"使某物成为自己的"），同根字还如"proper"（本身）、"appropriate"（适当）、"propriety"（得体）和"property"（属性）。这个字根"prop"

Over time, *yi* becomes the aggregating significance invested by a living tradition in the observance of the various gestures of propriety; it is a sense of what is optimally appropriate as expressed in those roles and institutions that come to be defining of what is truly proper. And *yi* is the cultural authority that can be appropriated by persons as they become enculturated in the performance of these same roles and rituals. It is this invested significance that one appropriates from the social form that makes a salute, a handshake, and a marriage ceremony meaningful, and it is the sense of achieved and invested appropriateness in the performance of these ritualized activities that makes their observance profoundly personal.

Yi is the fittingness in relations that over time galvanizes the trust and credibility of the fiduciary community and the feelings of mutual confidence and reliability that give members a true sense of belonging within that community. Confucius is reported to have made just this connection in the following passage:

That making good on one's word (*xin* 信) gets one close to appropriateness (*yi* 義) is because then what one says will bear repeating.

(*Confucian Role Ethics: A Vocabulary,* pp. 201-205)

提供了一系列同根词用语，对于翻译确定个人身份的儒家哲学术语十分合适，因为这样翻译是把人作为一个积极参与者，他尽己于人的各种（物性与社会性）生活形态的个人化，使这些生活形态成为属于一个具体人他自己的。这一对人的角色总是自反性的个性化（我是这个母亲的儿子），对于找到哲学语汇的有效翻译，是有直接效果的。例如，如果我们接受，对儒家"人"须是坚持一种关系性而不是质相性的理解，那么"义"就不会是"righteousness"（一种推定个体人服从外在神性的原则）。而应该，"义"必须是在那些与自己的具体家庭和社会的关系之中包容性的"自己的恰当行为"。也就是说，"义"是最符合具体情况的行为，而不是简单地执行一些外在的原则或法规——什么绝对正确的行为。

（《儒家角色伦理学：一套特色伦理学词汇》，第126页）

We find the Latin proprius—literally, "making something one's own"—as the root in words such as "proper," "appropriate," "propriety," and "property." This root provides us with a series of cognate expressions that are felicitous in translating those key Confucian philosophical terms defining of personal identity because such translations locate one as an active participant committed to personalizing one's various life forms—physical and social—and thus making them one's own. This always-reflexive personalization of one's roles—I am this son to this mother—has immediate consequence in the search for effective renderings of this philosophical vocabulary. For example, if we acknowledge the persistence of a relational rather than essential understanding of the Confucian person, *yi* 义 cannot be "righteousness"—putatively an individual's compliance with some external divine directive. Rather, *yi* must be an inclusive "conducting oneself appropriately" in those relations within one's particular family and Community. That is, *yi* is doing what is most fitting within the specific circumstances, as opposed to simply following some external principle or rule in doing what is deemed correct.

(*Confucian Role Ethics: A Vocabulary,* p. 112)

利

"利"的含义衍申，既有其褒义，也有其贬义。就其褒义而言，它常常被作为"害"的反义词来使用，其意思是有益于某事物。就其贬义而论，"利"则常常被用于同"义"做对比，其意思是指据其独特的地位或处境去谋取私利，而不是努力发扬道德意识，去做有助于公益或正义之事。这种对比似乎首先见于儒家《论语·里仁》中的一句话："君子喻于义，小人喻于利。"不管怎样，它很快成为中国古代文学中常用的一个典型的对比。

（《中国古代的统治艺术：〈淮南子·主术〉研究》，第 253 页）

人类经验具有多层面的重要性，需要公允、透明和更具客观的常规性理念；儒家传统长期以来也意识到这种需要。从"义"（最理想恰当性）与"利"（个人获益）二者之间的区分开始，儒家思想在其历史上就一直纠结在伦理行为与公允性二者间的必然关系上。然而不是借助于什么超越性道德标准

Profit (*Li*)

In its extended meaning of benefit, the character *li* has both a positive meaning and a derived pejorative connotation. In its positive sense, *li* frequently occurs as the rhyming antithesis of *hai* (harm) and means to benefit something. In its pejorative sense, li is frequently contrasted with *yi* ("rightness") that is, dedication to the furtherance of private interests as opposed to an effort to exert one's moral sense and do what is right in each unique situation. This contrast seems to have originated in the Confucian tradition with such passages as *Analects* 4.16: "The superior person understands what is right while the inferior person understands what is personally profitable." In any case it spread rapidly to become a characteristic comparison in early Chinese literature.

(*Art of Rulership: A Study of Ancient Chinese Political Thought,* pp.154-155)

But Confucian philosophy does have the internal resources for such revision and growth that might give it a more global appeal. There are many important dimensions of the human experience that require impartiality, transparency, and more objective regulative ideals, and the Confucian tradition has long been aware of this need. Beginning with the distinction between "optimal appropriateness"

或者什么客观理性能力（必将被环境性的偶然情况所捆绑），儒家传统坚持以家庭为比喻从而发展出一个"不偏不倚"观念。这是说，哪怕在主观性与客观性视角之间做出判断，"不偏不倚"实际是通过扩展人的关注范围而做到的，即从由受制于个人自私之利的"主观"（主人的视角）到为了所有牵涉方面着想而追求最适当性（义）的"客观"（客人的视角）。儒家"推己及人"之"恕"，与"尽己所能"之"忠"这样的说法，是另一种践行"谦恭"意图的转化性说法，它还保持了人所关注的范围的开放，去判断什么才是道德。关键点是，对传统来说，它是有自身资源的，要在自身资源之上建立更健康的防护措施，让它具有牵制过分偏颇的可能性。

（《儒家角色伦理学：一套特色伦理学词汇》，第296页）

他（孔子）认为，具有关系敏感性并有反应之人，是"仁"的最重要来源和最明智的判断者，因为他们所致力的，是做适合情景、对任何人都最适当的事，即"义"，

(*yi* 义) and "personal advantage" (*li* 利) that we find as early as the *Analects* and the *Mencius*, Confucianism has struggled across its history with the seemingly necessary relationship between ethical conduct and a sense of impartiality. Rather than invoking some transcendental moral standard or some faculty of impersonal reason as a strategy for claiming such impartiality—a strategy that is inevitably hobbled by the contingencies of circumstances—the Confucian tradition in developing a notion of impartiality has remained true to the family metaphor. That is, even in the distinction made between subjective and objective perspectives, impartiality is served practically by extending one's range of concern from "the master's-eye view" (*zhuguan* 主观) that might be limited by some self-serving personal advantage (*li* 利) to "the guest's-eye view" (*keguan* 客 观)that seeks what is most appropriate for all concerned (*yi* 义). The Confucian formula of "putting oneself in the other's place" (*shu* 恕) and then "doing one's best" (*zhong* 忠) is another variation on this deferential attempt to keep one's range of concern open in determining what is moral. The point is that there are resources indigenous to the tradition on which to build more robust safeguards that can rein in the possible excesses of partiality.

(*Confucian Role Ethics: A Vocabulary,* pp. 267-268)

而不是狭隘地只做对自己有利的事。

（《儒家角色伦理学：一套特色伦理学词汇》，第201页）

礼

在英文中，"礼"被译作"ritual"、"rites"、"customs"、"etiquette"、"propriety"、"morals"、"rules of proper behavior"和"worship"。在汉语里，这个合体字所表达的意义就是将牺牲放在神坛上祭祀神灵。《说文解字》以同韵部的"履"字训之，意为"开拓道路；实行，做"——即，"如何殷荐神灵以求多福"。在特定的语境下，上面列举出的"礼"的每一种英译都能够表达出"礼"的某一种含义；但是，在文言文中，"礼"字在每一次使用的时候，同时承载着它所有的义项。

He is observing that relationally aware and responsive persons are the foremost resource for and the best judges of consummate conduct because they are committed to doing what is most appropriate for everyone in the situation (*yi* 义) rather than just doing what is more narrowly to their own personal advantage (*li* 利).

(*Confucian Role Ethics: A Vocabulary*, p. 182)

Observing Ritual Propriety

Li has been translated as "ritual," "rites," "customs," "etiquette," "propriety," "morals," "rules of proper behavior," and "worship." The compound character is an ideograph connoting the presentation of sacrifices to the spirits at an altar (*li* 豊). It is defined in the *Shuowen* paronomasticahy as *lü* 履, meaning "to tread a path; hence, conduct, behavior"—that is, "how to serve the spirits to bring about good fortune." Properly contextualized, each of these English terms can render *li* on occasion, but in classical Chinese the character carries all of these meanings on every occasion of its use.

We have chosen to translate *li* as

经过一番慎重的比较推敲，我们决定将"礼"译作"observing ritual propriety"。

"礼"就是被赋予了种种隐喻的角色、关系和制度。所有这些都密切了社会成员之间的沟通交流，并且培养了一种集体感。诚然，"礼"的范围相当广泛：它包罗了所有礼仪——从宴饮酬唱到问候、告别、加冠和婚丧嫁娶；从表示敬服的各种肢体语言到庄严的祖先祭祀。所有这些以及其他相关内容均是"礼"。"礼"是在家庭、团体和政治结构中划定每个成员位置和地位的人文建构；是代代相传的生命形式，它是意义的源泉，它帮助年轻人掌握永恒的价值，确定各自的位置。

完全融入一个礼仪社会的先决条件就是接受它的各种习俗、制度和价值观。不同文化传统在自身的形成过程中，造就了礼与法（或是刑）的巨大差异。拉丁文 *proprius* 的含义为"独立做某事"；与英文 property 的词义相似。这一意蕴使我们能够在翻译中传神地表达出一系列重要儒家哲学词汇所暗藏的"参与"之意：于是，"义"不再被译作 "righteousness"，而

"observing ritual propriety." Again, this rendering is a considered choice.

Li are those meaning-invested roles, relationships, and institutions which facilitate communication, and which foster a sense of community. The compass is broad: all formal conduct, from table manners to patterns of greeting and leave-taking, to graduations, weddings, funerals, from gestures of deference to ancestral sacrifices—all of these, and more, are *li*. They are a social grammar that provides each member with a defined place and status within the family, community, and polity. *Li* are life forms transmitted from generation to generation as repositories of meaning, enabling the youth to appropriate persisting values and to make them appropriate to their own situations.

Full participation in a ritually-constituted community requires the personalization of prevailing customs, institutions, and values. What makes ritual profoundly different from law or rule is this process of making the tradition one's own. The Latin *proprius*, "making something one's own" as in "property," gives us a series of cognate expressions that are useful in translating key philosophical terms to capture this sense of participation: *yi* 义 is not "righteousness" but "appropriateness";

是 "appropriateness"；对于 "正" 字，我们放弃了 "rectification" 和 "correct conduct" 两种表达，采取了 "proper conduct" 的译法；至于 "政" 字，它绝不是指 "government"，而应该是 "governing properly"。

在西方人看来，粗俗与邪恶是两种截然不同的行为。而孔子认为，二者的性质完全相同，只是表现程度有所差异而已。在儒家观念中，个人行为的错误绝对不仅仅是恶习使然，更是道德责任的彻底堕落。

例如，孔子在解说 "孝" 的时候，其着眼点并不是衣食奉养——因为人们也以同样的方式豢养犬马之类的宠物。孝之根本在 "色"。也就是说，子女应以欣悦之心、恭敬之容侍奉年迈的父母（第二篇第八章）。

对于西方人来说，理解孔子之 "礼" 的最大障碍可能就是，在西方文化传统中，"礼" 就像仁爱那样，是一个众人非常熟悉的，属于日常范畴的概念。而且，在英文中，"礼" 大多用作贬义，讽喻了虚伪的行为，绝无风俗习惯之意。在深入研读《论语》的过程中，我们发现了一种精心编排最佳面部表情和肢

zheng 正 is not "rectification" or "correct conduct," but "proper conduct"; zheng 政 is not "government" but "governing properly" in our translation.

For Westerners, there is ostensibly a distinction to be made between being boorish and being immoral. For Confucius, however, there are simply varying degrees of inappropriate, demeaning, and hurtful behavior along a continuum on which a failure in personal responsiveness is not just bad manners, but fully a lapse in moral responsibility.

In defining filial piety (*xiao* 孝), for example, Confucius is not concerned about providing parents with food and shelter—we do as much for our domestic animals. The substance of filial piety lies in the "face (*se* 色)" one brings to filial responsibility—the bounce in the step, the cheerful heart, the goodwill with which one conducts the otherwise rather ordinary business of caring for aging parents (2.8).

Perhaps the greatest obstacle to understanding what *li* means in the world of Confucius is thinking that "ritual" is a familiar dimension of our own world, and like "benevolence," we fully understand what it entails. "Ritual" in English is almost always pejorative, suggesting as it often does compliance with hollow and hence meaningless social conventions. A careful reading of the *Analects*, however, uncovers a way of life carefully choreographed down to appropriate facial expressions and physical gestures, a world in which a life is a performance requiring enormous attention to detail. Importantly, this *li*-constituted performance begins from the insight that personal refinement is only possible through the discipline provided by formalized roles and behaviors. Form without creative personalization is coercive and dehumanizing law; creative personal expression without form is randomness at best, and license at worst. It is only with the appropriate combination of form and personalization that community can be self-regulating and refined.

(*The Analects of Confucius: A Philosophical Translation,* pp. 51-52)

体语言的生活方式。在这个世界中，生活是一种必须对细节付诸极大关注的表演。最为重要的一点就是，由"礼"构成的表演，始于对个人修养过程的深刻理解，即，人们只有遵循一定角色和行为所限定的各种规则，才能够涵养性情，提高自身的修为。没有创造性的个人化过程的形式，就是强制性的、无人性的法律制度；而没有形式作为规范的创造性的个人发挥，从好的方面说，是散漫，从坏的方面说，则是自由化。只有在强制性制度和个人化的完美结合下，社会才能自我调整，自我净化。

（《〈论语〉的哲学诠释》，第51—53页）

乐

Enjoyment/Music

乐(le)："enjoyment"或"happiness"。也就是说，在个人生活环境中找到共享的欣喜和快乐。这是个人的持存在其家庭、社群、宇宙关系中获得完善时才会获得的那种幸福感，其本身同时包含某种道德和宗教意义。正如斯宾诺莎所谓：此种快乐

Le is "enjoyment" or "happiness," that is, finding shared joy and rejoicing in the circumstances of one's life. It is that quality of happiness that is felt when the continuities of one's existence are consummated within the relationships of family, community, and cosmos, and as such, has both a moral and a religious meaning. As Spinoza suggests, such

不是道德的奖掖，而是道德本身。道德作为刚强、力量、卓越，是深入广泛的相关性的一种已获品格，其被既定群体表达为对有效典范的敬意模式。在坚实的个人纽带深处有某种强度，其所创造的意义成为社群本身的真正品格，成为其社会精神。与此同时，人际交往的质量又通过吸引合并一个始终扩展的参与域而变得广阔。

乐的宗教维度存在于当社群成员能够为整体培养和贡献其独特的个体性，且据此发现生活某种深刻持久的幸福感时产生的那种精神性。宗教因此被理解为是深远的特殊主义的，是通过真正独特的个人的全面参与来限定的。宗教本身是交往的社群的绽放，其中被启迪的有志之人就是一个精神性的人。

乐是保护与安定个体经受人类生活不可避免的兴衰变迁时深远的归属感。我们甚至在最不幸的情况下，都可维持某种深厚、稳定的情感和真正宗教意义的满足。儒家传统有个普遍深入的假定：人类经验最重要的事情乃确定个人在社群中的地位及建构其个人的诸关系的质量。

enjoyment is not the reward of virtue but is virtue itself. Virtue as virility, potency, and excellence is an achieved quality of intensive and extensive relatedness that is expressed as patterns of deference paid to effective models within a given population. There is an intensity in the deepening of robust personal bonds, where the meaning that is created becomes the very character of the community itself, its ethos. At the same time, the quality of interpersonal transactions is made extensive by attracting and incorporating an ever-expanding field of participation.

The religious dimension of *le* lies in the kind of spirituality that emerges as members of the community are able to cultivate and contribute their unique individuality to the whole and, in so doing, to find in life a deep and abiding happiness. Religion thus understood is profoundly particularistic, defined as it is through the full participation of truly distinctive persons. As such, religion is the flowering of the communicating community, where an aspiring and inspired people is a spiritual people.

Le is that profound sense of belonging that secures one and anchors one through the inevitable vicissitudes of a human life: Even in the most unfortunate circumstances, one can sustain a feeling of depth, stability, and contentment of truly religious proportions. There is a pervasive assumption in the Confucian tradition that the most important

《论语》中乐所出现的语境始终都是关系性的。乐与友（《学而》、《季氏》）与仁（《里仁》）、与知（《雍也》）、与礼（《季氏》）都息息相关。乐本身就是那些确定社会中我们的重要持久关系所激发的道德宗教欢乐。乐跟贫富（《学而》《雍也》《述而》）、享受（《季氏》）没有关系。这不是因为财产或感官享受本身必然徒然无益，而是因为它们会导致自我中心和心灵的冲突习性，后者在社会意义上是有腐蚀性和分裂性的。事实上，孔子在《学而》中表达得很清楚，如果社群成员的昌荣是基于他们共同铸造的生活质量，那么物质上的富有就没有问题。

"乐"字有两个不同读音：乐（le，enjoyment）、乐（yue，music）。这也很能说明问题。尼采有句流行的至理名言"恶人歌无乐（yue）"（Evil men sing no songs），而《孟子·梁惠王下》可谓其古老的中国版本。也就是说，如果百姓能够在仁慈的统治下欢乐地生活，那么，他们会真正欣赏宫廷之乐，反之，如果他们把自己的穷劳疾苦归结为朝廷的暴政，他们就会痛恨这种音乐。乐（樂）还跟"药（藥）"

thing in the human experience is the quality of the relationships that locate one in community and constitute one as a human being.

In the *Analects*, for example, the contexts in which *le* appears are invariably relational. *Le* is associated with friendship (1.1, 16.5), consummate conduct (4.2), efficacious knowing and social intelligence (6.20, 23), and full participation in ritualized roles and relationships (16.5). As such, *le* is that moral and religious enjoyment inspired by the vital and enduring relationships that locate and define us within our world. At the same time, *le* is disassociated from wealth (1.15, 6.11, 7.16) and sensual enjoyment (16.5), not because prosperity or sensuality in themselves are necessarily unproductive, but because they can lead to egoism and to conflicted habits of the heart that are socially corrosive and disintegrating. In fact, Confucius is explicit in claiming that material well-being can be unproblematic within the context of a community where the flourishing of its members is made possible by the quality of the life that they forge together (1.15).

Much is made of the fact that the same character, pronounced differently, is used for "enjoyment" (*le* 樂) and "music" (*yue* 樂). In *Mencius* 1.1, we have an early Chinese version of Nietzsche's popular adage "Evil men sing no songs." That is, while the people will truly celebrate the music (*yue* 樂)of the court if they are enjoying (*le* 樂) life under （medicinal remedies）是同源词，表明享受音乐（enjoyment of music）和欢乐的音乐（music of enjoyment）都是疗疾滋养的。

（《生民之本：〈孝经〉的哲学诠释及英译》，第 94—95 页）

乐（樂，*Yue*）："乐"是 "music" 或更恰当说 "making music"。乐由于总是与礼（the observance of ritual propriety）相连，其重要性不容忽视。礼是最佳化人类社群诸可能性，提升生活质量，且将日常生活模式转化为深远社会宗教实践的努力。正是在此意义上，礼常作为复名词"礼乐"（observing ritual propriety and the making of music）的缩写。

确实，古代经典中礼乐是不可分割的，其假定二者在强化社群关系上具有同等作用。《礼记·乐记》曰：

乐者，天地之和也。礼者，天地之序也。和故百物皆化，序故群物皆别。乐由天作，礼以地制。

乐及其同源词 "乐"（*le*, enjoyment）

its benign rule, they will resent the music bitterly if they attribute their dire straits to the court's misrule. *Le* is also cognate with "medicinal remedies" (*yao* 藥), suggesting that both the enjoyment of music and the music of enjoyment are therapeutic and restorative

(*The Chinese Classic of Family Reverence: A Philosophical Translation of the Xiaojing*, pp.75-76)

Yue is "music," or better, "making music." As the constant correlate of "the observance of ritual propriety" (*li* 禮), the importance of this term cannot be overstated. *Li* is an attempt to optimize the possibilities of the human community, to elevate the quality of life, and to transform the patterns of everyday living into profoundly socioreligious practices. It is in this sense that *li* is frequently read as an abbreviation for the binomial *liyue* 禮樂, "observing ritual propriety" and the "making of music."

Indeed, ritual propriety (*li*) and music (*yue*) are inseparable elements in the classical corpus, with the assumption that they have a collateral function in strengthening relationships within the community. In the "Record of Music" chapter of the Record of Rituals (*Liji*) it is stated:

Music is the harmony of the world; ritual propriety is the world's array. It is because the manifold of things are

和"药"(medicine，therapy)说明应如何理解礼。由关系性和过程性定义的礼，是调和"沟通的社群"(communicating community)进入全面和谐的策略，而社群成员各得其宜，获得社会交往中富有成果的共鸣。如交响乐般的社群，以其最小的不和谐，就不仅是疗疾之药(therapeutic)，亦是社群所有成员的快乐之源。人对彼此不同交往过程的熟谙，会产生某种相互依赖的和谐——于众音合一的齐唱中每个人又都拥有自己的独特声音。乐因此为我们提供了一个象征诠释，我们由之可得出一个个人与社群修养的综合语汇，而其中的礼本身又成为相宜生活的节奏。

（《生民之本：〈孝经〉的哲学诠释及英译》，第110—111页）

harmonious that they all transform; it is because they are arrayed that they are each distinct. Music is initiated in the heavens, and ritual propriety is established by the earth.

Yue and cognate expressions such as "enjoyment" (*le* 樂)(the same graph) and "medicine, therapy"(*yao* 藥)reveal how *li* is to be understood. *Li*, defined relationally and processually, is a strategy for orchestrating the "communicating community" into the fullest consonance, with appropriately disposed members resonating productively in their social transactions. To the extent that the community is symphonic, with minimal dissonance, it is not only therapeutic (*yao*) but also productive of enjoyment (*le*) for all who reside within it. To the extent that persons pursue virtuosity in the various discourses that dispose them one to another, they generate a mutually interdependent harmony in which everyone has his or her unique voice in a chorus that is at once one and many. Music thus provides us with an explanatory image from which we can derive a comprehensive vocabulary for personal and communal cultivation, where *li* itself becomes the rhythm of a proper life.

(*The Chinese Classic of Family Reverence: A Philosophical Translation of the Xiaojing,* pp. 90-91)

耻

既然孔子赋予"礼"以实现社会政治秩序手段的作用,那么,他也在积极寻求在百姓中培养一种知耻感。孔子关心的是"耻"(shame)而非"罪"(guilt),此点意义重大,因为这两个概念类似于礼与法的区分。由于"罪"标志着承认违犯了某规定行为,因此,它是以法为导向的。而"耻"则是以礼为导向的,因为它表达个体对他者如何看待自我的意识。"罪"是指向个体的,因为它以个体与法的关系为条件;而"耻"则趋向于社会性,是以个体与他者的关系为条件。

"罪"并不经常出现于《论语》中,且总是表达对某已立成规的侵犯:

> 子谓公冶长:"可妻也。虽在缧绁之中,非其罪也。"以其子妻之。(《论语·公冶长》)

反之,如果我们考察《论语》中许多出现"耻"的章节,会发现

Shame (ch'ih)

Given the importance that Confucius places on ritual action (*li*) as a means to sociopolitical order he seeks energetically to cultivate a sense of shame (*ch'ih* 耻) in the people. It is significant that Confucius is concerned with shame (*ch'ih*) rather than guilt (*tsui* 罪) in that these two concepts parallel the ritual/law distinction. Guilt is law-oriented in that it signals a personal acknowledgment that one has committed a breach of established conduct. Shame, on the other hand, is ritual-oriented in that it describes a consciousness of how one is perceived by others. Guilt tends to be individual as a condition of one's relationship to law; shame tends to be communal as a condition of one's relationship to others.

The concept, guilt (*tsui*), occurs infrequently in the *Analects*, and always indicates a transgression against some established standard(5.1):

> Confucius said that Kung-yeh Ch'ang could be allowed to marry his daughter. Even though Kung-yeh Ch'ang had spent some time in jail, it was not because of any guilt (*tsui*) on his part. On that, Confucius gave his daughter to him as wife.

它的运用总关涉疏忽责任，且常会因之受到他者欺侮、疏远和羞辱："……恭近于礼，远耻辱也。"（《论语·学而》）

我们可通过参考麦克奈特（Brian McKnight）近来在《仁慈的品格》（*The Quality of Mercy*）一书中对"赦免"（amnesties）和"宽恕"（pardons）的研究说明"耻"在中国文化传统中的重要意义。这一研究有一个清晰的推论，即在中国，诉讼发现原告"可耻"与发现他"有罪"的职责是一样的。这也就是说，法庭和监狱系统或许因为经济原因，并不是准备长期关押罪犯以作为对其不道德行为的惩罚。赦免与宽恕，不管是哪条指令，实际上每两三年都会打开监狱大门，放那些关押的人回家。在这种情况下，法庭不得不严厉对待罪大恶极的罪行，同时依赖诉讼过程中的"耻"来约束轻的次要的冒犯者，且恢复他们尽社会责任的义务。"耻"在判决中也是重要考虑的事项。断肢或肢解的惩罚就是通过使冒犯者无法以全身面觐祖先而使之背负违背"孝"道的耻辱。

理解孔子社会政治哲学很重

If, by contrast, we examine the many passages in which shame (*ch'ih*) occurs in the *Analects*, it is always used with reference to a lapse of responsibility, often accompanied by insult, estrangement, and humiliation at the hands of others (1.13):"… Being respectful to others is close to ritual action in that it keeps one at a distance from shame (*ch'ih*) and humiliation."

The importance of shame in this tradition can be illustrated by reference to Brian McKnight's recent study of amnesties and pardons: *The Quality of Mercy*. This study presents a clear inference that litigation in China functioned as much to find a plaintiff "shameful" as to find him "guilty." That is, the courts and prison system, probably for economic reasons, were not prepared to incarcerate criminals for lengthy periods as punishment for wrongdoings. Amnesties and pardons of one order or another opened the prison gates literally every two or three years and sent the inmates home. Under these circumstances, the courts had to act harshly in cases of heinous crime, and to rely on the shame entailed in the process of litigation to discipline the more minor and marginal offenders and restore their commitment to social responsibility, "Shame" was also an important consideration in sentencing. Punishment by amputation or dismemberment would be used to bring shame on the criminal by rendering him an

要的一点是，他青睐且追求审美和谐却并不排斥认识有实效价值的秩序，这些已经确立和规定的秩序发挥巩固作用，以避免内在产生的秩序的溃败。审美和谐的优先与对理性秩序实效价值的认可，二者之间质的张力可用《论语》中一段核心却常被曲解的话充分说明：

> 道之以政，齐之以刑，民免而无耻；道之以德，齐之以礼，有耻且格。(《论语·为政》)

显然，该节强调基于规章、法令的强制秩序与通过榜样、参与和道德教化实现的政治和谐截然不同。

该节实在太经常被解读为两种排他的二者必择其一的管理策略。但必须谨记的是，对孔子来说，社会是一种创造性成就。就此，已确立的政策和法律本身对最大可能丰富地实现社会和政治秩序就是不充分的。孔子相信要获得真正长治久安的政治和谐，就必须赋予在最根本意义上"源自"个人本身的转化性"教育"以优先性，因此，他划

offender against the filial injunction to return one's body to one's ancestors intact.

Important to an understanding of Confucius' social and political philosophy is that his preference for and pursuit of an aesthetic harmony does not preclude an awareness of the functional value of some order which, having been established and defined, can be applied as a reinforcement where intrinsically generated order breaks down. This qualitative tension between the preferred status of aesthetic harmony and an acknowledged functional value of rational order is well illustrated by reference to a central yet frequently misconstrued passage in the *Analects* (2.3):

> Lead the people with administrative policies and organize them with penal law, and they will avoid punishments but will be without a sense of shame. Lead them with *te* and organize them with ritual actions, and they will have a sense of shame and moreover will order themselves harmoniously.

In this passage, imposed order based on regulation and edict is contrasted with political harmony effected through example, participation, and moral edification.

This passage is all too frequently interpreted as offering two exclusive alternatives for government. It should be remembered,

出了灌输和教育之间的清晰界限。这种个人直接参与的最佳状态实现于一个自立、自制的社会。在该社会中，致力于修身会产生"德"，引起全社会的效仿和对构造和维持该社会的"礼"富有意义的践行。

孔子赋予具体特殊性的多元和多样性以优先权。该特征通过由"德"（particular focus）才可产生的效仿行为来表达，而非强调使用强制政策和法令来实现社会政治和谐。这表现在孔子倾向于个人对"礼"的践行，而反对运用很大程度上外在的法律和惩戒。这一点也体现在孔子不对个人利益和公共利益、社会领域和政治领域以及伦理学和政治学之间进行区分上。注重培养百姓的"知耻感"就是它的一个例证。它更体现在这一事实上，即从百姓的角度来说，社会政治秩序是他们实现而非为他们制造出来的东西。社会和国家的管理是签名性的，它展现特定参与者的性格，他们的差异，以及他们参与的性质。最后，我们从权力行使的秩序与创造性行为自发产生的秩序之间的对比，也可看到孔子对审美秩序的倾向。

however, that for Confucius, society is a creative achievement. As such, established political policies and penal laws are not in themselves a sufficient condition for achieving the richest possibilities of social and political organization. Confucius establishes a clear line between indoctrination and education in his belief that to achieve truly effective and enduring political harmony, transformative "education" in its original sense of "drawing out from" the particular person himself, must be given priority. This immediate participation of the particular person can be maximized by generating a self-sustaining, self-regulating society out of that commitment to self-cultivation which results in personal focus (te) and allows for integrative modeling and the meaningful performance of ritual actions which can structure and sustain such a society.

The characteristic Confucian priority of the plurality and diversity of the concrete particulars is expressed by reliance upon the modeling made possible by a particular focus (te 德), rather than the use of enforced policy and edict to effect social and political harmony. It is evidenced in Confucius' preference for personally performed ritual actions as against the application of largely external laws and punishments. It is illustrated by the absence of telling distinctions between the private and public interest, social and political spheres, and ethics and politics. It is exemplified in the

(《通过孔子而思》，第211—214页）

相反地，因为道德本身不过是那些有利于恰当关系的行为做法而已，所以，任何对家庭和人群关系有涣散影响的行为在性质上都被视为不道德的。人们认为有些生活方式散漫不羁的人对整个社会都会有腐蚀影响。所以生活方式极为重要，漫不经心不考虑他人利益的人会变为他人担心的对象。彬彬有礼很重要，因为人们很关注亲切与风度仪态带有的那种适宜性与恰当性。在很大程度上，道德与在别人接触时的稳重与举止是分不开的，其本质的正确性与否还在其次：

曾子言曰："……君子所贵乎道者三：动容貌，斯远暴慢矣；正颜色，斯近信矣；出辞气，斯远鄙倍矣。笾豆之事，则有司存。"（《论语·泰伯》）

这样的道德表现出的正直品格表达着一种社会责任心的"耻感"，是儒家文化的高尚价值。正如我们看到的，"耻"是如此强烈的

concern with cultivating a sense of shame in the people. It is further evidenced in the fact that, from the perspective of the people, sociopolitical order is something that they accomplish rather than have created for them. The disposition of the society and state is signatory, displaying the character of the specific participants, their diversity, and the quality of their participation. Finally, the preference for aesthetic order is found in the contrast established between order by the exercise of power and the emergent order of creative actions.

(*Thinking Through Confucius,* pp. 174-176)

Conversely, since morality itself is nothing more than those modalities of acting that conduce to enhancing relations, any kind of conduct that has a disintegrative effect on the fabric of family or community is perceived to be fundamentally immoral. Lifestyle takes on crucial import when we consider the corrosive consequences to the community of those persons who live lives without style. Carelessness becomes of major concern when we have to worry about those persons who couldn't care less. And graciousness has gravity when we reflect on the relevance that charm and deportment have for an overall sense of fittingness and propriety. Morality is associated more with poise and deportment in our transactions with other people than it is with any formal correctness:

一种道德意识表述，在一个人的教养之中，它可变为一种普遍流行价值使整个社会都充满亲和感和自律性。上面已论述过，适度地运用羞耻感作为道德规劝的手段，能够有力地发展社会的包容性与自我调整性（"有耻且格"《论语·为政》），否则"无耻"就是"井下之毒"（poison in the well），让不循规蹈矩的人不受约束、胡作非为，无视他们本来应有的在家庭、社会的"角色与关系"。这种自私之人对于道德人生所依赖的社会休戚与共的破坏性是巨大的。

孔子的"耻感"是很强的。《论语》的《子罕》《乡党》《先进》这几篇，人们一般不是很留意；这几篇贯穿一系列较为人性化细节，勾画出作为历史人物的孔子。即使我们对孔子这些个人情况有所注意，一般也不被认为有多大哲学意义并觉得与孔子道德人生观没太大关系。事实上，我们忽略了这些细节，就忽略了其中蕴含着的孔子心怀志向的确凿性。可以说，恰是这几篇，记录的是孔子本人人生的某些具体时刻；这些时刻才是最具写实性的，才最生动地呈现一个士大夫的儒雅

Master Zeng said: "...There are three things that exemplary persons consider of utmost importance in their vision of the consummate life (*dao*): By maintaining a dignified demeanor, they keep violent and rancorous conduct at a distance; by maintaining a proper countenance, they keep trust and confidence near at hand; by taking care in their choice of language and their mode of expression, they keep vulgarity and impropriety at a distance. As for the details in the arrangement of ritual vessels, there are minor officers to take care of such things."

The integrative nature of the moral experience means that a socially responsive "sense of shame" (*chi* 耻) is of high value in Confucian culture. As we have seen, shame is such a powerful expression of moral awareness that, when properly nurtured, can become a pervasive value that enables the community to be both inclusive and self-regulating (*Analects* 2.3). Shamelessness on the other hand is poison in the well, unleashing aberrant individuals to roam freely and to act arbitrarily without reference to the roles and relations that would properly locate them within their families and community. Such selfish individuals diminish in a dramatic way the communal solidarity

风度。他每日入朝觐见的举止，一下子既是形象化，也是深刻个性化的：衣服的剪裁、步履的节奏、域境与仪态适中的敏锐感、身姿与面部表情（"踧踖如也"，"怡怡如也"）、说话的语气声调、恭敬的举手投足，甚至包括气息节律等等。

（《儒家角色伦理学：一套特色伦理学词汇》，第 190—191 页）

on which the consummate life depends.

Confucius himself had a much-developed sense of shame. In reading the *Analects*, there is a tendency to give short shrift to the middle books nine through eleven that are comprised primarily of a series of intimate snapshots depicting the historical person, Confucius. If such personal information is taken into consideration at all, there is the tendency to deem it insufficiently philosophical to be relevant to his vision of the consummate life. In fact, in overlooking these very details we are in danger of missing the substance of Confucius' aspirations. At a general level, it is precisely these passages, remembering as they do the concrete moments in the life lived by Confucius himself, that are most revealing of the extent to which the appropriate conduct of a scholar-official participating in the daily activities of the court was at once formalized and intensely personal: the cut of his robes, the cadence of his stride, his keen sense of context and proprieties, his posture and facial demeanor, his profound expression of reverent attention, his tone of voice, his gestures of deference, even the rhythm of his breathing.

(*Confucian Role Ethics: A Vocabulary,* pp. 171-173)

信

在"符合"论中,认知性知识涉及事物真实状态的再现,这样一来,"知"(knowing)依赖的是客观实在的事实(相对于表象、思想或者语言)存在,以及思想与该实在的真正"相符"。

孔子的"知"(realizing)决然不同于这一"knowing"概念。现实是内在关联和或然性的。它是实现的,而非认识的。由于现实并不独立于实现者,自然,真理就不是简单相符的结果。它更关涉的是类似于"得当"(appropriateness)或"诚信"(genuineness)这样的行为。

(《通过孔子而思》,第61—62页)

作为有效社会、政治真理的"信"与作为本体论真理的"诚"之间这种亲密关系还有进一步的证明——《说文》中这两个字是互为定义的。段玉裁在《说文解字注》中强调"信"乃"人"之"信"这一孔子思想中最为突出的含义:"人言则无不信者,故从人言。"事实

Living Up to One's Word (*hsin**)

In a correspondence theory, cognitive knowledge involves the representation of a state of affairs as it really is. Knowing, then, is dependent upon the existence in fact (as opposed to appearance, thought, or language) of an objective reality, and the true correspondence between thought and this reality.

For Confucius, realizing (*chih*) is significantly different from this concept of knowing. Reality is immanent, relative, and contingent. It is something achieved rather than recognized. Since reality is not independent of a realizer, it follows that truth cannot be a consequence of simple correspondence. Rather, truth must involve something like "appropriateness" or "genuineness."

(*Thinking Through Confucius,* p. 56)

This intimate relationship between "living up to one's word"(*hsin** 信), as an aspect of effecting sociopolitical truth, and *ch'eng* 诚 , as the process of ontological truth, is further suggested by the fact that in the *Shuo-wen* lexicon, these two characters are each defined by the other. The Tuan Yi-ts'ai commentary to the *Shuo-wen* underscores the "person making" connotations of *hsin**, which are so prominent in Confucius: "Since when a 'person' speaks there is nothing that he fails to live up to (*hsin**), this character is constituted of 'person' (*jen* 人)

上，段玉裁这一评注的基础是《论语·为政》一章，在该章中，孔子将"信"作为人格形成的一个必要条件："人而无信，不知其可也。"

"信"是孔子思想的一个重要概念，在《论语》中共出现约四十次。事实上，它据说属孔子"文"、"行"、"忠"、"信"四教之一。它与"谨"（being sparing in one's word）和"忠"这两个概念不可分割地联系在一起。因为"信"不仅仅是愿意或承诺恪守诺言，它或许更近于古代的"盟誓"——宣称拥有足够的能力智慧和资本去履行和实现诺言。

如果"信"只是致力于践行诺言，那么，行动成功与否都无关紧要。然而，孔子把没能力实现诺言看作失"信"的一个条件："狂而不直，侗而不愿，悾悾而不信，吾不知之矣。"（《论语·泰伯》）孔子主张，"信"是个体在世界上实现或"成"（complete）（"成"乃"诚"[integrity, being true for oneself]的同源词）就自我之"义"（significance and appropriateness）的一种方式。孟子宣称"有诸己之谓信"也强调了"信"的这一意

and 'to speak' (yen 言)." In fact, it is likely that Tuan's commentary is based on an *Analects* passage in which Confucius makes "living up to one's word" a necessary condition for achieving personhood: "I am not aware that one can become a person without living up to his word (hsin*)."

Living up to one's word (hsin) is a major concept for Confucius, occurring some forty times in the *Analects*. In fact, it is said to be one of the four categories under which Confucius taught: culture (wen* 文), conduct (hsing 行), doing one's best as oneself (chung 忠), and living up to one's word (hsin* 信). It is integrally related to the notions of "being sparing in one's words" (chin 谨) and "doing one's best as oneself" (chung 忠). Because living up to one's word is more than simply a willingness or even a promise to accord with what one says, it is perhaps close to the archaic notion of "plighting one's troth": the claim that one has the acquired ability, acumen and resources to enact and make real what one says.

If *hsin** were nothing more than a commitment to try to carry out what one says, the success or failure of one's actions would not be an issue, yet Confucius makes a lack of ability a condition of failing to be *hsin**: "I do not understand persons who are reckless and not straightforward, who are ignorant and not attentive, and who are lacking in ability and do not live up to

义。正是因为"信"并非仅是一种承诺，所以孔子很高兴其弟子漆雕开就官时能说："吾斯之未能信。"（《论语·公冶长》）漆雕开当然不是自谓自己不值得信赖，正如韦利对该节的解释所言："我还没有充分完善自我。""信"更确切地说，是能够履行诺言的必要条件，因而也就能够使之实现。《论语》中"信"与"忠"多处同时出现，这一事实也表明，"信"根本上是述行性的。"信"是笃行诺言。

孔子强调的"信"的另一个特点即，它似乎是"与朋友交"和取"信"于民，赢得支持和拥戴的一个必要条件。这也就是说，"信"是建立人际信任的一个至关重要的因素。人际信任对孔子来说是人之为人的先决条件。

尽管"信"对做人来说是必要条件，但却不能就此推之为充分条件。"信"在一般被视为肯定特性的情况下，其"义"（得当性）还要依赖其所要践行的"言"。孔子将"士"（gentleman-scholar）按德行分为三等，他甚至将"信"这种品格归在最低的第三等。该德行本身似乎并没有什么非凡的可取之处

their word (*hsin**)." Confucius asserts that "living up to one's word" (*hsin**) is the way to realize or "complete" (*ch'eng** 成, cognate with *ch'eng* 诚, "integrity," "being true for oneself") one's own significance and appropriateness in the world. Mencius reiterates this aspect of "living up to one's word" when he claims that "having it in oneself" is called *hsin**. It was because *hsin** is more than simply a commitment that Confucius was pleased when his disciple, Ch'i-tiao K'ai, declined to take an official post, saying: "I do not think that I am yet able to live up to this (*hsin**)." The disciple was certainly not admitting that he was less than trustworthy, as Arthur Waley's rendering of this same passage might suggest: "I have not yet perfected myself in the virtue of good faith." *Hsin** rather entails as a necessary condition being able to carry out what one says and thus being able to make it true and real. The fact that many of the occurrences of *hsin** in the Analects are coupled with "doing one's best as oneself"(*chung* 忠) would suggest that *hsin** is fundamentally performative. *Hsin** 信 is the doing of what one says with earnestness.

Another feature of Confucius' emphasis on living up to one's word (*hsin**) is that it seems to be a necessary condition for establishing the relationship of "friendship"(*yu* 友), and for winning the continuing support of the people. That is, living up to one's word is an

使之足以提升到更高层次。对于孔子来说，道德低下者——一个"小人"——也仍然有"信"：

> 言必信，行必果，硁硁然小人哉！——抑亦可以为次矣。（《论语·子路》）

孔子即便在描述自己时也倾向于夸赞自己的好学，而不是"信"，他将后者视为某种更为普遍的特性。

最后需简要说明一下孔子如何看待"信"与"义"之间的重要关系。"义"这个概念是孔子思想中的一个范畴概念，它将审美、道德和理性意义的最终根源都植根于人本身。个体正是拥有赋"义"的能力，才得以从其文化传统中获取意义并展现自身的创造意义。

"信"要求对个体之"义"的阐明、展示和实现。如果一个人信守诺言，他就使自身成为这个世界意义的一个源泉，该意义能够被他者实现和承传。因此，《论语》有言："信近于义，言可复也。"当然，如果言不及义，那么，就自然无"信"，不值得"言"复了。

essential factor in establishing interpersonal credibility which, for Confucius, is a precondition for realizing oneself as a person.

In spite of the fact that living up to one's word is necessary to qualify as a person, it does not follow that it is sufficient. Where living up to one's word is generally regarded as a pusitive trait, the appropriateness of this characterization really depends upon the "word" that one is living up to. In distinguishing three levels of the gentleman-scholar, Confucius attributes living up to one's word even to the third and lowest. This virtue in and of itself does not, it would seem, prompt an unqualified recommendation for promotion to higher levels. For Confucius, then, it is possible for someone to be morally retarded— to be a "small person" (*hsiao jen* 小人)—and yet still live up to his word:

One who is certain to live up to his word and finish what he starts, even though this is no more than a small person being stubborn, can still qualify as a third level of the gentleman scholar.

Confucius, even in characterizing himself, tends to celebrate his love of learning (*hao hsieh* 好学) over his concern to live up to his word, regarding the latter as a more common trait.

Finally, there is an important relationship in Confucius between living up to one's word

"信"是个体之义阐明和获得的一个必要（尽管不是充分）条件。"信"只有立基于"义"，才能够为世界赋予意义。

（《通过孔子而思》，第66—68页）

(*hsin** 信) and "signification" (*yi* 義) which requires brief elaboration. This concept, *yi*, discussed more fully below in the context of the notion of self-articulation, is a categorical notion in Confucius which locates the ultimate source of aesthetic, moral, and rational significance in the human being himself. It is with this capacity to significate that a person appropriates meaning from his cultural tradition and discloses his own creativity.

*Hsin** requires the articulation, disclosure, and realization of personal significance. If a person is true to his word, he has made himself a source of meaning in the world, meaning that can be realized and transmitted by others. Thus, the Analects records: "Living up to one's word (*hsin** 信) comes close to significating (*yi* 義) in that these words (as articulations of significance) can then be repeated." Of course, where one's words are not grounded in, and informed by, significance (*yi*) and, as a consequence, are not lived up to, they hardly bear repeating.

The concept, *hsin**, is a necessary although not sufficient condition for the articulation and achievement of personal significance. To the extent that *hsin** is grounded in personal signification, the human being is capable of contributing meaning to his world.

(*Thinking Through Confucius,* pp. 60-62)

教

在说明儒家"教"的观念时，英文字"education"的语源学是有所帮助的。"education"有两个主要词根——"educere"和"educare"。第一个词根的意思是"引起"；第二个词根的意思是"培养"。作为被理性地加以规划的指南，"educare"是和"教"的意义相共鸣的，它是"教"的逻辑的模式以及被理性地加以安排的模式。另一方面，"educere"则提示了"教"的创造性方面，这一方面与审美性的理解是相互配合的。首先被理解为"educere"的"教"向我们提示了这样一种意义：通过一种自我修养（self-cultivation 修身）的方式——事实上那是一种自我创造（self-creation），一个人扩展延伸了其内在的倾向（"性"）。

当仁，不让于师。（《论语·卫灵公》）

如此理解的"教"是一种交往的过程，这一过程使连续性和创造性成为必要，而连续性和创造性既是这方面有能力的教师的成长，又

Education

The etymology of the English word "education" is helpful in articulating the Confucian notion of *jiao*. "Education" has two principal roots—*educere* and *educare*. The first means "to evoke, lead forth, draw out"; the second "to cultivate, rear, bring up." *Educare* resonates with the sense of education as rationally ordered guidance; it is the logical and rationally ordered mode of education. On the other hand, *educere* suggests the creative side of education that is complicit with aesthetic understanding. Education construed primarily as *educere* suggest that one "extends" one's inner tendencies through a mode of *self*-cultivation that is, in fact, self-*creation*.

In striving to be authoritative in your conduct, do not yield even to your teacher.

Education so construed is a transactional process that entails both continuity and creativity as the growth of both *this* able teacher and *that* able student.

(*Focusing the Familiar: A Translation and Philosophical Interpretation of the Zhongyong*, p. 50-51)

Granted, the purpose of education is to promote growth and extension. But to do this

是那方面有能力的学生的成长。

（《切中伦常：〈中庸〉的新诠与新译》，第 77 页）

"教"的目标无疑是推动成长和延伸。不过，这样做涉及如何阐明那些个人的、社会的以及建制性的脉络，那些脉络构成一个人的礼仪生活，而礼仪生活能够兴发和唤起一种特别的未经思虑营谋的经验。例如，作为被践行的礼仪形式，其当下直接的意义只是一种所拥有的审美的经验。可是，没有这种礼仪形式，所有这种直接当下性将会既是偶然的，又是短暂的。

"教"的"educere"和"educare"两方面之间必要的平衡，在《中庸》第二十一章中得到了把握：

> 自诚明，谓之性。自明诚，谓之教。诚则明矣，明则诚矣。

……创造性（新生事物当下的自发产生）是一种导向理解的自然的（不是强制的，不是被产生的）过程。在这种脉络中，当"某种东西被学到"时，"理解"首先意味着

involves the elaboration of those personal, social, and institutional contexts constituting one's ritual life that can evoke a particular unmediated experience. For example, the immediate meaning of a ritual forms as enacted is an aesthetic experience that is simply *had*. But without the ritual forms, all such immediacies would be both accidental and ephemeral.

The necessary balance between the educere and educare function of education is captured in *Zhongyong* 21:

> Understanding born of creativity (*cheng* 诚) is a gift of our natural tendencies (*xing* 性); creativity born of understanding is a gift of education(*jiao* 教). Where there is creativity there is understanding; where understanding, creativity.

…*Creativity* (the spontaneous emergence of novelty immediately, aesthetically entertained) is a natural (unforced, uncaused) process leading to *understanding*. In this context, "understanding" means primarily *logical*, rational understanding (*educare*) as "*what* is learned." The cyclical process continues, however, as creativity emerges again from *understanding*. "Understanding" in this new context is the aesthetic entertainment of experienced content acquired through education. Education now becomes *educere*—a process that allows for

逻辑的、理性的领会（educare）。但是，当创造性再次从理解中产生时，周期性的过程就处在持续当中。在这种新的脉络之中，"理解"是被经验的内容的审美享受，那种被经验的内容是经由"教"而获得的。这样一来，"教"就成为"educere"——一种顾及新生事物自发产生的过程。

（《切中伦常：〈中庸〉的新诠与新译》，第78页）

　　子曰："夫孝，德之本也，教之所由生也。"（《孝经·开宗明义》）

……孔子把"孝"和"教"互相联系起来，利用这两个字的同源词关系，"教"只是给"孝"加了个偏旁（攴）。它是出现在甲骨文中的"𤕫"（"教"），似乎给人一个熟悉却已不流行的"教"的意象；它的形象的最生动之处是"手""棍"和"学生"的适时结合。《说文》将"教"定义为相互性和辈分的"教，上所施，下所效也"。重要的是，"教"字本身已是强调，对于教育的实在内容与目的而言，以体悟"孝"为本；这也正如"孝""教"同时享

the spontaneous production of novelty.

(*Focusing the Familiar: A Translation and Philosophical Interpretation of the Zhongyong*, pp. 51-52)

"It is familial reverence (*xiao*)," said the Master, "that is the root of excellence (*de*), and whence education (*jiao*) itself is born."

…Confucius in correlating family reverence and education is taking advantage of the cognate relationship between the character for "education"(*jiao* 教) and that for "familial reverence" (*xiao* 孝), where the graph for "education" (*jiao* 教) simply adds on the "branch or stick" (*zhi* 攴) radical to *xiao*. This character *jiao* 𤕫 as it appears on the oracle bones seems to depict a familiar if no longer popular image of education as being best promoted through a timely correlation between hand, stick, and pupil. The classical *Shuowen* lexicon defines "education"(*jiao*) transactionally and generationally as "that which those above disseminate and those below emulate." Importantly the character for education(*jiao*) itself underscores the perceived centrality of familial reverence to the actual content and purposes of education, just as the term "emulating" (*xiao* 效) emphasizes the modeling role that the older generation has in instructing its progeny.

有和"效"字的同源词关系,强调长辈对其子孙施教的榜样作用。

(《儒家角色伦理学:一套特色伦理学词汇》,第 203—204 页)

"education"的词根"educare"与"educere"(唤起[to educe])是同源词。前一个的意思是"培养"(cultivate)、栽培(rear)、教育(bring up),后一个意思是"唤起"(to evoke)、引导(lead forth)、拉出(draw out)。"educare"跟教育作为理性规范的方针的意义相呼应,是与认知相联系的教育的逻辑和更系统化的模式。反之,"educere"则表明教育创造性的方面,跟审美理解贯通,暗含师生可同样新奇而富有想象力地阐明自我修身模式。教(education)因此可解读为富有才华的师生共同成长过程中既有连续性又有创造性的某种沟通过程。

儒家著作把教首先等同于道的弘进,这就同时投注了教之根本和创造性的两个方面。认为教(education)的作用首先不是传(transmission)和训(training),而是唤起(evocation)似乎有点误导,因为"educare"也在一代又一代弘扬

(*Confucian Role Ethics: A Vocabulary*, pp. 183-184)

The etymology of the English word "education" is helpful in articulating the Confucian notion of *jiao*. "Education," with its root *educare*, is cognate with *educere*, "to educe." The first means "to cultivate, rear, bring up," while the second means "to evoke, lead forth, draw out." *Educare* resonates with the sense of education as rationally ordered guidance; it is the logical and more systematic mode of education that we associate with cognitive understanding. By contrast, *educere* suggests the creative side of education that is complicit with aesthetic understanding and implicates both teacher and student equally through novel and imaginative elaborations of each one's mode of personal cultivation. Education so construed is a transactional process that entails both continuity and creativity in the growth of both *this* able teacher and *that* able student.

By identifying education primarily with improving upon and extending the proper way forward, the Confucian texts are invested in both the foundational and the creative aspects of education. To say that the function of education is not primarily that of transmission and training but of evocation would be misleading, because *educare* also has a role to play in passing on the details of the rich cultural heritage form one generation

丰富文化遗产上发挥着作用。

《孝经》一个核心观念就是所有教不过是亲情的扩展。君爱其父母，将此种情感扩之庶民便是要真正关心民之疾苦；子敬父，将此同样之敬扩之其君，便是忠。因此，转化和确保人类经验的教，就被自然化为孝向整个世界的扩充。

由于亲情对人类经验来说是根本的，教的过程就会通过家庭内部和国家中的模范和效仿的过程而得到最有效的实现。其既需"educare"——长幼之间努力传承知识，又需要"educere"——以一种自发和自然的方式"唤起"父母亲的慈爱和对父母的尊敬，巩固家庭内部彼此之间的关系，继而扩至整个国家。的确，《孝经》强调教育中效仿的作用，宣称"德教加于百姓，刑于四海"。（《孝经·天子》）

（《生民之本：〈孝经〉的哲学诠释及英译》，第 91—92 页）

to the next.

The *Classic of Family Reverence* has at its center the notion that all education is simply an extension of family felling. The Emperor loves his parents and extends that same affection to his people as sincere concern for their well-being; the son respects his father and extends that same respect to his sovereign as loyalty. Thus, education that transforms and secures the human experience is naturalized as the extension of family reverence(*xiao*) to the entire world.

Since family feeling is fundamental to the human experience the process of education is most effectively accomplished through a process of modeling and emulation both within the polity. It requires both *educare*— a labored transmission of knowledge from elders to the young—and *educere*—the spontaneous and natural way in which parental affection and parental reverence "educe" and reinforce each other within the family and, by extension, within the state. Indeed, the *Classic of Family Reverence* underscores the role of emulation in education, claiming that "such moral edification (*dejiao*) will transform the common people and will serve as exemplary in all corners of the world" (2).

(*The Chinese Classic of Family Reverence: A Philosophical Translation of the Xiaojing,* pp. 72-73)

孝

　　"孝"的英文直译是"filial piety"或"filial responsibility"。在儒家伦理中，正确的家庭观念不仅占据了家庭的核心位置，而且也是生活之路的源泉（第一篇第二章）。在将家庭作为一种秩序模式推而广之的过程中，儒家既不认为社会等级制度是必要的"恶"，也不认为简单的平均主义毫无价值。我们认为，注意到这一点是极其重要的。而将"孝"简单地理解为顺从，实则是对"孝"的极大误读。有时候，家庭里的至孝与朝堂上的忠臣一样，均表现为不畏强势的谏诤，而不是无条件的服从。但是，这种质疑权威的职责绝不是一种以下抗上的授权（第二篇第五章，第四篇第十八章）；它受到了种种严格的限制。

（《论语的哲学诠释》，第60页）

　　"孝"直接的意思就是"filial piety"或"filial responsibility"。鉴于家庭在儒学中的核心地位，恰当的亲情是一种"道"所由而"生"的"本"。正如《论语》第一篇《学而》

Family Reverence (*Xiao*)

Xiao is, straightforwardly, "filial piety" or "filial responsibility." Given the central place of the family for the Confucian way, appropriate family feelings are that resource from which a pathway through life emerges (1.2). It is important to note that in promoting the family as the pervasive model of order, the Confucian worldview does not accept that hierarchical social institutions are necessarily pernicious, or that simple egalitarianism should be an uncritical value. Having said this, an obstacle to understanding *xiao* can arise from a simplistic equation between filial responsibility and obedience. At times being truly filial within the family, like being a loyal minister within the court, requires remonstrance rather than automatic compliance, yet such a responsibility to question authority has its limits, and is not a warrant to pit one's own opinions against one's elders. (2.5, 4.18).

(*The Analects of Confucius: A Philosophical Translation,* pp. 58-59)

Xiao means rather straightforwardly "filial piety" or "filial responsibility." Given the central place of the family in Confucianism, appropriate family feelings are that resource from which a pathway through life emerges (*Analects*

第二章所谓:"其为人也孝弟而好犯上者,鲜矣。不好犯上而好作乱者,未之有也。君子务本,本立而道生。孝弟也者,其为仁之本与!"在推动作为一种普遍的秩序典范的家庭的过程中,儒学的世界观并不接受这样一种看法:等级的社会制度必然是有害的,或者说,朴素的平均主义就应当是一种无须批判的价值,意识到这一点很重要。因为当这样说时,很容易妨碍我们对于"孝"的理解,而这种妨碍来自将"孝"简单地等同于服从。在家庭中真正的"孝",就像在朝廷中真正的"忠"一样,所需要的与其说是自动的顺服,不如说是劝谏。不过,这种质疑权威的责任是有其限制的,它不能成为将自己的意见强加于长者的一种担保。

在《中庸》第十九章中,对于"孝"的界定很清楚,所谓:

> 夫孝者,善继人之志,善述人之事者也。

在《中庸》第十五至第十九章中,一连串的历史人物和文化英雄对于这一段文字中关于教育的转

1.2). It is important to note that in promoting the family as the pervasive model of order, the Confucian world view does not accept that hierarchical social institutions are necessarily pernicious, or that simple egalitarianism should be an uncritical value. Having said this, an obstacle to understanding *xiao* can arise from a simplistic equation between filial responsibility and obedience. At times being truly filial within the family, like being a loyal minister within the court, requires remonstrance rather than automatic compliance. Yet such a responsibility to question authority has its limits and is not a warrant to pit one's own opinions against one's elders.

Zhongyong 19 defines *xiao* explicitly:

> Filial piety means being good at continuing the purposes of one's predecessors and maintaining their ways.

The mustering of historical figures and cultural heroes in *Zhongyong* 15-19 to support this text's emphasis upon the transformative power of education exploits the cognate relationship between "education(*jiao* 教)" and "filial responsibility(*xiao* 孝)." Indeed, just as family is the pervasive metaphor in the Confucian world view, filial piety is the

化性力量的强调,都利用"教"与"孝"之间的同源关系。的确,正如家庭在儒学中是一种普遍性的隐喻,"孝"是儒学的核心。

(《切中伦常:〈中庸〉的新诠与新译》,第 99—100 页)

heart of Confucian learning.

(*Focusing the Familiar: A Translation and Philosophical Interpretation of the Zhongyong*, pp. 81-82)

谏

理解儒家社会批判性参与的一个主要观念,是要区分强调辩证论争和"谏"观念的重大不同;前者假定有两个独立排他的竞争视角,后者作为劝导的包容模式,假定是要致力于共同的目标。该区分也体现在对"protest"(反抗)两个相当不同的使用上。前一个用法,是反对某种事情(我反对战争)(I protest against the war),而后一个则是严肃的确定(我申明我的清白)(I protest my innocence)。反抗的前一个意义是辩证和剑拔弩张的——我试图取代对方,从而也取代跟我"相反的"观点。其指导方针的立场乃是排他的,一个是对的,另一个就是错的。反抗的后一个意思假定有一个共同的关心,寻求用我真诚的品质为我

Remonstrance (*Jian*)

A key notion to understanding critical engagement in the Confucian world is the important difference between an emphasis on dialectical dispute that assumes two exclusive, competing perspectives, and the idea of remonstrance as an inclusive mode of persuasion that assumes a shared commitment to a common goal. This distinction is echoed in the two rather different uses of the term "protest": The first usage is to take exception to something ("I protest against the war"), while the second is to affirm with solemnity ("I protest my innocence"). The first sense of protest is dialectical and agonistic—I seek to displace the opposite and thus "opposing" point of view with my own. The guiding assumption is that the positions are exclusive—one is right, the other wrong. The second sense of protest assumes a shared concern and seeks to persuade the other through the quality of my sincerity for our common end.

们的共同目标劝导他人。

论辩参与和劝诫参与这两种模式都试图改进和提升某种情况。前者更纯粹理性和决断，立基于某种允许争论双方保持自我尊严与其平等意识的外在关系感。后者更具修辞性、劝勉性，假定有诸内在关系限定着相互包容的家庭成员或其他团体成员，他们尽管有等级差别的关系，但都是为了维持家庭或社团共同的完整性，而非某一个体成员的完整性。

《孝经》沿袭《论语》，在解决差异上也主张将谏而非争作为最首要适宜的方法。家庭和政府中等级较低的成员不仅有谏的权利，而且还负有谏的责任，因为就像《谏诤章》所强调的，此种劝勉关涉到每个人的利益。

谏的几种情况不容忽视。首先，公认的目标是要改变行为。为达到这一目的，就必须最机智最尊敬地表达关心——如果希望它们产生影响。过分坦率很容易被视为侮辱和冒犯，被视为一种盛气凌人而非尊重敬重。其次，劝诫中抱持的真诚是说服力的关键。真正共同怀有的关心与非难二者之间有极大差

Both dialectical and remonstrative modes of engagement are attempts to improve and advance a situation. The former is more purely rational and assertive, based upon a sense of external relations that allows each disputant to maintain her/his own integrity and sense of equality. The latter is more rhetorical and exhortative, assuming intrinsic relations that locate the differences among mutually accommodating family members, or members of other groups, who, although hierarchically related, are all concerned to sustain the shared integrity of the family or group rather than just the integrity of its individual members.

The *Classic of Family Reverence* follows the *Analects* in advocating remonstrance rather than dialectical engagement as the primary and most appropriate method of resolving differences. The hierarchically subordinate persons in family and in government not only have a right to remonstrate but an obligation to do so, because such exhortation is in the best interests of everyone concerned, as Chapter 15 insists.

There are several conditions of remonstrance that must not be overlooked. First, the putative goal is behavioral change, and to this end, concerns must be expressed with the utmost tact and respect if they are to be effective. Excessive candor can easily be heard as insulting and offensive, replacing erstwhile deference with condescension. Second, the sincerity with which the admonishment is proffered is the key to its persuasiveness; there is a world of difference

异。再次，谏不是一种选择，而是责任。谏得少就是没能完成某一严肃神圣的职责。顺与谏一前一后构成"忠"（或者更宽泛理解"尽忠"[doing one's best]）的实质。最后，谏有其限度，而且只能到此为止。到了某种程度谏者就必须和缓下来：进谏者绝不能就认定他们的判断比他们的父母或长者好。但再说一遍，儒家作为特殊主义者，是从来不会事先指定或抽象出哪一点上我们必须缓下来。

（《生民之本：〈孝经〉的哲学诠释及英译》，第90—91页）

孔子在这里提倡人群、社会，最后是政体这一理念，它所滋养的黏合力，来自组织结构；而家庭成员之间享有的忠诚、信赖关系，就是这种组织结构。他将自然平常心看到的事情诉诸官府，不是我们处理家里人犯小过失应做的事情；这种做法，只是在别无他法之时的最后一种选择——最起码，我们几乎完全确定，已为解决问题千方百计地做了努力。只要是牵涉家人甚至是牵涉邻居与朋友的问题，我们在对情况进行处置上，须优先考虑

between real shared concern and rebuke. Third, remonstrance is not an option, but an obligation; and to do less is to fail in a solemn and sacred duty. It is in tandem that obedience and remonstrance constitute the substance of loyalty (*zhong* 忠), or, more broadly understood, of "doing one's best." Fourth, remonstrance has its limits and can only be taken so far. There is a point at which the remonstrator must relent: The remonstrating party must not simply assume that her/his judgment is better than that of the parent or elder. But again, being particularistic, Confucians would never attempt to specify the point at which one must relent in advance, or abstractly.

(*The Chinese Classic of Family Reverence,* pp.71-72)

The position that Confucius is advocating here is that a true and trusting relationship among members of a family is the fabric from which the norms of community, society, and ultimately polity draw their tensile strength. He perceives quite plausibly that calling in the police is not what we would do in response to such a lapse on the part of a family member, but is something we would only do if at all as a last resort; initially at least we would almost surely try other means to remedy the problem. As far as our family is concerned, and very probably our neighbors and friends as well, there are priorities in our response to situations that require ingenuity and imagination.

并要求我们有主观能动创造力和想象力。

我们以儒家"角色伦理"的内在要求,即在具体特殊的情况下,如何做到最好程度地把握恰当性,使形势得到好转——"义"。对这件事情的意义进行阐明,同时也让情况变得有些复杂。为此,"谏",即为人子你有义务,当家长有错误行为之时,必须表示反对并加以纠正,成为儒家经典讲"孝"中很突出、关键的内容。考虑到这一点,我们就必须要能想到,对孔子在这件事情上的看法的期待,作为"子为父隐"当事者,必然要想一切办法,对因为自己父亲行为而遭受损失的任何社会成员做出弥补,而且还要更进一步,规劝父亲改过自新。

儒家"角色伦理"不是抽象理论,不是指对那些我们经常碰到的特殊情形的错误状况,根据"原则"做出道德判断;"角色伦理"也不是把主导地位交给为达到一定道德目的,而刻意去开拓的理性手段。在总结伦理"理论化"背后那些一般假设的特征过程中,"理论化"是把作为相关因素理由的家庭角色排斥在外的。

What sheds light on this case while at the same time making the situation somewhat more complex, is the internal demand in Confucian role ethics to make the situation right by achieving optimal appropriateness in the particular situation (*yi*). To this end, "remonstrance" (*jian* 谏)—that is, the obligation that a child has to protest against and to rectify the conduct of an erring parent—has a prominent and crucial role in the Confucian literature on family reverence (*xiao* 孝). With this in mind, we would have to assume that the expectation of Confucius in his evaluation of this case would be that the concerned son in "covering for his father" would necessarily do his best to set the ledger right with any members of the community who had suffered loss on account of the conduct of his parent, and further, would do what is needed to return his father to the straight and narrow.

Confucian role ethics is not an abstract theory that provides principled moral judgments for those particular problematic situations we might encounter along the way, nor does it give primacy to developing a deliberate, rational means to achieve some moral end. In characterizing those general assumptions behind much ethical theorizing that preclude the consideration of family roles as relevant factors.

(*Confucian Role Ethics: A Vocabulary*, pp.163-164)

But deference is only the more obvious part

（《儒家角色伦理学：一套特色伦理学词汇》，第181页）

然而，"遵从"只是"孝"比较明显的一方面，它还有不时被忽略的另一方面：时常在家庭中做到"孝"，如同朝廷上的忠君之臣，需要进"谏"，并非只是恭顺而已。进"谏"不是随意的或可做可不做的，而是要严格问责要求的。例如《孝经》中学生问"孝"是否可认为是顺从，孔子很不认同：

> 曾子曰："……敢问子从父之令，可谓孝乎？"子曰："是何言与？是何言与？……故当不义，则子不可以不争于父，臣不可以不争于君。故当不义则争之。从父之令，又焉得为孝乎？"（《孝经·谏诤》）

《荀子》一书也是这样的观点，《子道》篇一大半内容都在阐述复杂的关系，都是对把"孝"或"忠"理解为盲目顺从的批驳，并以大量现成事例说明，对长辈或上级权威要求不加分析地顺从，恰是不孝、不忠。

of the equation, having as it does a sometimes overlooked complement. At times being truly filial within the family, like being a loyal minister within the court, requires remonstrance (*jian* 谏) rather than compliance. And this remonstrance, far from being discretionary or optional, is considered a stern obligation. In the *Classic of Family Reverence*, for example, Confucius responds impatiently to his student's suggestion that family reverence can be reduced to simple obedience:

> Zeng asks:"I would presume to ask whether children can be deemed filial simply by obeying every command of their father?"
>
> "What on earth are you saying? What on earth are you saying?" said the Master, "…If confronted by reprehensible behavior on his father's part, a son has no choice but to remonstrate with his father, and if confronted by reprehensible behavior on his ruler's part, a minister has no choice but to remonstrate with his ruler. Hence, remonstrance is the only response to immorality. How could simply obeying the commands of one's father be deemed filial?"

In the *Xunzi* too, much of an entire chapter is devoted to the complexity of these

进"谏"是一件包容性和思考性的事情，思考集中点在于"我们"，是对"我们"的询问："'我们'怎样才能做得更好？"面对这种情况，进"谏"必须与那种抗议性的表达行动区别开来，抗议性批评是排斥性和对立性的，是一种反对：只是针对"你"的。当然，为了有效地使人接受行"谏"，改变原来的做法，进"谏"说服别人，必须对对方的感受与态度保持敏感，并善于应对，有丰富想象力。不过，这种对上级权威的进"谏"是有底线的，它决不容许顽固地以自己的判断与长辈抗争。虽说作为后辈对父母有进"谏"之责，却并不意味着长辈就一定有听后辈进谏的道理。孔子这样说：

事父母几谏。见志不从，又敬不违，劳而不怨。(《论语·里仁》)

(《儒家角色伦理学：一套特色伦理学词汇》，第206—207页)

relations, challenging any simple reading of family reverence or loyalty to one's lord as blind obedience. It provides many ready examples of where it is in fact unfilial and *dis*loyal to comply *un*critically with the demands of one's senior or superior.

Remonstrance is an inclusive and reflexive concern; it is focused on the "we" in enjoining us to ask "How can *we* do better?" As such, it must be distinguished from the kind of protest that is exclusive and dialectical—an objection directed at "you" alone. Of course, to be effective in altering patterns of behavior, such remonstrance must be pursued with enormous sensitivity and tact, and with considerable imagination as well. Yet such an obligation to question authority also has its limits, and is never a warrant to pit one's own judgment stubbornly against that of one's elders. Just because a child has the responsibility to remonstrate with the parent, it does not follow that the child invariably has on offer advice that should be heeded. As Confucius remarks:

In serving your father and mother, remonstrate with them gently. On seeing that they do not heed your suggestions, remain respectful and do not act contrary. Although concerned, voice no resentment.

(*Confucian Role Ethics: A Vocabulary*, pp.186-187)

伦

"伦"——"协调的家庭关系",也干脆即字面意思上中国(一个特殊性民族纽带)意思的"纶"。

(《儒家角色伦理学：一套特色伦理学词汇》,第117页)

如果我们谈及人伦(角色)是什么,或者有关人伦的更为根本进行时态的一种表述——去"活"人的角色与关系——正如我们在古汉语中对这一过程的理解,其实"伦"字是一组直接同源汉字之一,这些汉字是各种对辐射秩序不同的表述。我们可以从"輪"(轮子、轮流)字开始。我们身份角色的"纽带"性,在表"挑选"含义的"掄"字和表"拧绳、织线"含义的"綸"字上被加强了。这一簇汉字连在一起,共同喻示对关系作用形态以及理想秩序的发展、巩固。但是,对于"活"我们身份角色动态的、叙述的话语方面,恐怕最能通过同源表意的是"論""淪"和"侖"。其实,"侖"字可追溯至甲骨文,字形为"开口"(亼)

Lun

Coordinated family relations (*lun* 伦) then are quite literally the fabric (*lun* 纶) of the Chinese as a particular "people."
(*Confucian Role Ethics: A Vocabulary*, p. 104.)

In fact, if we ask after the meaning of personal "roles"(*lun* 伦) or perhaps a more primarily gerundive expression of them—"the living of one's roles and relations"—as this process is understood in the classical Chinese language, this character *lun* is one of a cluster of immediately cognate terms that offer various ways of characterizing radial order. We might begin from the notion of "a wheel, or taking turns"(*lun* 輪). And the notion of "bonding" in our roles is reinforces by cognates such as "selecting out"(*lun* 掄) and "twisting a cord, the woof"(*lun* 綸). This family of terms shares in the association of developing and strengthening a functional pattern of relations and of achieving a desired order. But the dynamic, articulate, and discursive aspects of living our roles are perhaps best captured in cognates such as "conversing, conversation"(*lun* 論), "rippling, ripples"(*lun* 淪), and the root character, "turning over in one's mind, thoughts, ordering, achieving coherence"(*lun* 侖). Indeed, this root character *lun* 侖 dates back

与编为"册"的一串竹简"⿻",意指一书写而成文献,表达着条理有序的思维。

(《儒家角色伦理学:一套特色伦理学词汇》,第110页)

to the oracle bones, and is constructed from an "opened mouth" and "an orderly bundle of bamboo written strips," ⿻ suggesting a coherent exposition that elicits from and brings coherence to a particular written document.

(*Confucian Role Ethics: A Vocabulary*, p. 97)

直

叶公语孔子曰:"吾党有直躬者,其父攘羊而子证之。"孔子曰:"吾党之直者异于是:父为子隐,子为父隐,直在其中矣。"(《论语·子路》)

这段话道出了儒家角色伦理学家庭和道德想象的实质。……

当我们发现我们十来岁的孩子在当地的商店偷东西,我们很可能不会打911来逮捕他。我们需要更多的思想摆正事情恢复和谐。这很可能需要我们陪着做错事的孩子去商店把东西还回去并且道歉——从感受明显的羞耻感开始依次分担所有后果。知耻是儒家道德哲学的一个极重大因素。其与诉诸(义务论

True Person

The Governor of She in conversation with Confucius said, "In our village there is someone called 'True Person.' When his father took a sheep on the sly, he reported him to the authorities." Confucius replied, "Those who are true in my village conduct themselves differently. A father covers for his son, and a son covers for his father. And being true lies in this." (13.18)

This passage goes to the heart of both the family and moral imagination in Confucian role ethics….

When we discover that our teenage child has shoplifted at the local store, we are probably not inclined to dial 911 and have him or her arrested. We need more imagination to set the situation right and

或功利主义)原理完全不同，前者常对犯错有预防功能（preempt）。在孔子看来，叶公所描述的"直"人是有缺陷的，因其缺乏依情理处事的道德想象力。羊的主人当然应获得补偿，父亲通过劝谏也必然应认识到偷羊是不可接受的行为。然而，亲情是儒家角色伦理学的道德基础，是发展我们道德感受性之所在，我们不能为解决问题而丢弃该基础。

（《生民之本：〈孝经〉的哲学诠释及英译》，第73—74页）

对儿子来讲，要做到得当处理（直）与父亲的关系，一定要有想象力，思维有前瞻性与预见性，以此为基础决定自己行为。甲骨文"𣆶"与青铜器铭文"𥄂""直"，"目"上加竖线，表示行路时目光须有深刻性与前瞻性。其实，如根据《说文》则是："直，正见也。"此外，"直"的道德意义是明确的，因为它与"德"字构型直接相关。"德"在马王堆出土竹简上的字形是"悳"，上有"直"，下是"心"。其次，"直"的道德涵义还明显表现为它常作为另一同源字"值"借用字。孔子在这里讲的道理是，从有利家庭和人

restore harmony. This would likely require that we accompany the offending child to the store to return the merchandise and apologize—and share in whatever consequences are in order, beginning with the feeling of an acute sense of shame. Shame is a hugely important factor in Confucian moral philosophy because, unlike appeal to principle (deontic or utilitarian), it usually preempts the offence. Confucius' point is that the True Person as described by the Governor of She was deficient in not having had the moral imagination to deal with the situation appropriately. Certainly the owner of sheep has to be compensated, and certainly the father through remonstrance has to understand that stealing the sheep was not acceptable conduct. But family feeling is the ground of morality in Confucian role ethics—it is where we develop our moral sensibilities. And we cannot abandon this ground when resolving the situation.

(*The Chinese classic of family reverence: a philosophical translation of the Xiaojing*, pp. 57-58)

For the son, to "true" his relationship with his father requires the imagination necessary to be prospective and prescient in the thinking that informs his conduct. The character "true" *zhi* 直 occurs on the oracle bones as 𣆶 and

群和睦方面而言，儿子对自己父亲的诉讼行为，并以此视为最正确做法的行为，是令人不齿的，最终也是有悖于国运昌隆的。"直"是表达道德正当性的比喻，它允许家庭找到举措方位。"直"是件很难做的事情，它要求丰富的想象力及其有力发挥，为扭转形势，坚持自己路向，找到最适当的做法。

（《儒家角色伦理学：一套特色伦理学词汇》，第184页）

on the bronzes as ![img], where the centrality of the "eye" element suggests the need for both insight and foresight in finding one's way. Indeed, the *Shuowen* lexicon defines *zhi* as "seeing properly"(*zhengjian* 正見). In addition, the character *zhi* carries with it a decidedly moral aspect in its immediate association with "moral excellence" (*de* 德), a character that on the Mawangdui bamboo strips is in fact written as 悳, constituted in this alternative graph of "true"(*zhi* 直) with "heartmind"(*xin* 心) beneath it. Again the moral connotation of *zhi* is apparent from it frequent use as a loan character for the cognate character "value"(*zhi* 值).The assumption on the part of Confucius here would be that endorsing a litigious course of action on the part of a son as the most appropriate way to behave would not only be anathema to the interests of familial and communal harmony, but ultimately it would be detrimental to the prospects of a prosperous state. With *zhi* invoking the metaphor of being true to the moral "path or way"(*dao* 道) that allows the family to find its bearing, being "true" is the taxing job of accruing and exercising sufficient imagination to discern the best way to adjust the situation and to hold one's course.

(*Confucian Role Ethics: A Vocabulary*, pp.165-166.)

家

在《政治学》中，亚里士多德将 oikos（家庭）的目标与 polis（城邦）的目标加以区分，前者的目标是家庭事务，后者的目标是公众论坛。对亚里士多德而言，oikos 是一个有关自然的必然性和不平等的领域。这种私生活所受到的谴责是其"贫乏性"。与此相反，polis 则使不平等的家庭关系在平等的公众领域中得以克服。私人领域和公众领域没有被视为本来就是相关的。换言之，polis 不应当被看作 oikos 的自然的辐射性延伸，就像一个自由人不过是奴隶的自然进化那样。它们的旨归彼此不同。这一观点迥然有别于中国古代思想，在后者看来，家庭是社会、政治甚至宗教等各种关系的普泛性隐喻。

因此，在古典儒家那里，我们必须承认，确定家庭日常事务中所遵守的适当礼节应当首先取决于家庭，进而扩展到社群和国家。《中庸》第二十章强调了家庭与其延伸之间的根本关系，家庭的延伸，即社群和国家，就是社会和政治秩序的基础：

Family

In the *Politics*, Aristotle distinguishes between the aims of the *oikos*, the household, and those of the *polis*, the public forum. For Aristotle, the *oikos* is a realm of natural necessity and inequality. To be condemned to this private life is thus privation. By contrast, the *polis* is the overcoming of unequal familial relations in the public realm of equals. The private and the public spheres are not seen as intrinsically connected. That is, the *polis* is not seen as a natural radial extension of the *oikos* any more than the freeman is seen as a natural development of the slave. They have different ends. This view contrasts starkly with classical China in which family (*jia* 家) serves as a pervasive metaphor for social, political, and even religious relations.

In classical Confucianism, then, we must allow that the locus for observing ritual properly in the familiar affairs of the day lies first with the family, and by extension, the community and the state. *Zhongyong* 20 highlights the radial relationship between family and its extension as the ground of social and political order:

> In general there are nine guidelines in administering the world, the state, and the family, yet the way

> 凡为天下国家有九经，所以行之者一也。

《论语》第一篇《学而》第二章中也非常明确地指出，人之所以为人的行为模式，是从强烈的亲情关系中获得的：

> 君子务本，本立而道生。孝弟也者，其为仁之本与。

其潜在的前提是，相比于其他人类社会的建制，人更有可能完全地、无条件地将自身投入到家庭中。因此，作为一种社会建制，通过允诺构成家庭的人们投入到他们的人生经历中并能从中获取最大收益，家庭为人的发展提供了典范。提升家庭关系的中心地位，即想要确保所有的人，无一例外地投身于他们的每次行为之中。

当自然的家庭和群体关系不被理解与其他更为根本的各种关系相脱离、相对立时，作为人类发展的基本中心，家庭发挥作用的力量就得到了更大的加强。正是在从家庭向外的扩展过程中，人逐渐成为深

of implementing them is one and the same.

The *Analects* 1.2 states explicitly that the way of conducting one-self as a human being emerges out of the achievement of robust filial relations:

> Exemplary persons (*junzi* 君子) concentrate their efforts on the root, for the root having taken hold, the proper way (*dao* 道) will grow therefrom. As for filial and fraternal responsibility, it is, I suspect, the root of authoritative conduct (*ren* 仁).

The underlying assumption is that persons are more likely to give themselves utterly and unconditionally to their families than to any other human institution. Thus, the family as an institution provides the model for the process of making one's way by allowing the persons who constitute it both to invest in and to get the most out of the human experience. Promoting the centrality of family relations is an attempt to assure that entire persons, without remainder, are invested in each of their actions.

The power of the family to function as the radial locus for human growth is much enhanced when natural family and communal relations are not perceived as being a distraction from, in competition with, or dependent upon

刻的群体、文化和宗教敬畏的对象。

除了通过日常生活经验而获得一种强烈的宗教性之外,"君子"对"天"也作出了自己的贡献,"天"界定了作为一种传统的中国文化。正是这些文化英雄使得"天"作为祖先的遗产,一代又一代地流传下去,坚定而意义深远。

在古典儒家看来,在其最根本的意义上,"神"(spirituality)是指一个人对现存各种事物的全部场域(total field)的复杂意义和价值达到了一种聚焦化的领悟(focused appreciation),这种领悟是透过对于一个人自己创造性角色的极致的反身觉悟(reflexive awakening)而获得的,并且,一个人的创造性角色是各种相互依赖的创造性中心的其中之一。

通常而言,正是各种表示敬意的模式,建构了家庭以及家庭成员之间正当的相互作用,这一作用产生、规定并授权特定的"礼"来探求人类经验的不断进化和完善。正如《中庸》第二十章所揭示的那样:

> 亲亲之杀,尊贤之等,礼所生也。

any more fundamental relations. It is from the family expanding outward that persons emerge as objects of profound communal, cultural, and religious deference.

Beyond the achievement of an intense religious quality felt in the everyday experience of their lives, these exemplary persons emerge as contributors to the ancestral legacy (*tian* 天) that defines Chinese culture as a tradition. It is such cultural heroes that make *tian* as the ancestral legacy passed down from generation to generation determinate and meaningful.

For classical Confucianism, spirituality in its most fundamental sense refers to a person's attainment of a focused appreciation of the complex meaning and value of the total field of existing things through a reflexive awakening to the tremendum of one's own creative role as one among other interdependent centers of creativity.

Speaking generally, it is the patterns of deference that makeup the family itself and the appropriate transactions among its members that give rise to, define, and authorize the specific ritualized roles and relationships (*li* 禮) through which the process of refinement is pursued. As *Zhongyong* 20 explains:

> The degree of devotion due different kin and the degree of esteem accorded those who are different in

（《切中伦常：〈中庸〉的新诠与新译》，第62—64页）

对孔子思想超越时空的宏大诉求，是从几乎对每一个人的生活都适用的深刻理解开始的，无论何时何地，都多多少少是在他/她自己具体家庭环境中反映的。对孔子以及对他出现之后的世世代代中国人来说，人的基本单位指的是：这个家庭的"这个"具体人；而不是"单独、互不联系"的"个人"或者什么"平等地抽象"且"类属性"的家庭概念。其实，在读孔子之时，我们读不到其中有什么"核心本质"之人，是基于"核心本质"，我们在"本质上"是"人"；是它，当我们把家庭和社群关系层层全部剥掉之后，仍保持着不变。也就是说，在我们复杂与动态性的行为习惯背后，没有什么"我"（"己"），没有"灵魂"，不存在什么互不相系的"个体人"。我们每一个人，都是不可简化的（社会的），都是作为我们要去"活"它们的，是各种角色的总和——它们不是演剧那种角色，而是我们与他人关系与相互性中的。这样，人生目的是为自己、为他人

character is what gives rise to ritual propriety (*li* 禮).

(*Focusing the Familiar: A Translation and Philosophical Interpretation of the Zhongyong,* pp.38-40)

The timelessness and broad appeal of the teachings of Confucius begins from the insight that the life of almost every human being, regardless of where or when, is played out within the context of his or her own particular family, for better or for worse. For Confucius and for generations of Chinese that have followed after him, the basic unit of humanity is *this* particular person in *this* particular family rather than either the solitary, discrete individual or the equally abstract and generic notion of family. In fact, in reading Confucius, there is no reference to some core human *being* as the site of who we *really* are and that remains once the particular layers of family and community relations are peeled away. That is, there is no "self," no "soul," no discrete individual behind our complex and dynamic habits of conduct. Each of us is irreducibly social as the sum of the roles we *live*—not *play*—in our relationships and transactions with others. The goal of living, then, is to achieve harmony and enjoyment for oneself and for others through behaving in an optimally appropriate way in those

求得和谐和睦的愉悦，途径则是在实行那些角色与关系上达到一种恰到好处的适当行为方式；是那些角色与关系构成着我们的独特性。这里用音乐作比喻，是最妥当不过了。和谐性要求每一组成成分保持自己之纯正，并同时加入、与其他成分融为一体，构成一个与所有组成成分之总和明显不同且更具意义的有机个体。我们每个人的统一性，是来自我们追求一种交响乐队的队员角色与关系的那种包容的和谐。

儒家思想之根基为人们日常之生活；家庭生活无处不有的那种自然敬畏，为其活生生之源泉。对儒学而言，家庭关系之意义与价值，不仅是社会秩序性之根本基础，家庭关系还具有宇宙及宗教性的喻义。对我们每一个人之于延展开去的关系网都具有道德的责任，关系所到之处，远不止我们各种角色自我所在之处，要达到这样的理解，出发点则是维护好家庭的纽带。

家庭对个人成长影响之深，始于婴儿从出生起就全部地对家庭关系的依赖。如果说婴儿期让我们学到了什么，它教给我们的最要紧的第一课就是人之经验的无可逃避的

roles and relationships that make us uniquely who we are. The analogy with music here is irresistible. Harmony requires that each component maintain its own integrity and be itself while simultaneously joining in and integrating with the other participants to form an organic unity distinct from, and more than, the sum of its parts. The unity of each of us emerges as we pursue this inclusive harmony within the orchestra of our roles and relations.

Confucianism is grounded in the everyday lives of the people, and has as its source of animation the natural deference that pervades family living. For Confucianism, the meaning and value of family relations is not just the primary ground of social order, family relations have cosmological and religious implications as well. Family bonds properly observed are the point of departure for understanding that we each have moral responsibility for an expanding web of relations that reach far beyond our own localized selves.

The profound influence of family on personal development begins from the utter dependency of the infant upon the family relations into which it is born. If infancy teaches us anything, and it teaches us much, its first lesson should be the inescapably interdependent nature of the human experience. Indeed, when Confucius's rather unremarkable student, Zai Wo, resists the

相互依存性。其实，当孔子不太有出息的学生宰我，不愿为父母遵行守丧三年传统之时，孔子加以申斥，指出父母在婴儿身上也是要悉心三年养育他们，为他们成长为人而尽责。

家庭被视为社会和宇宙所有秩序的核心，正如我们在《大学》中读到，从个人于家庭内部的修养开始，所有意义的涟漪，都围绕一个中心一圈一圈向外散射而去，而后则又返回来抚养这个本源。如果我们谈及人伦（角色）是什么，或者有关人伦的更为根本进行时态的一种表述——去"活"人的角色与关系——正如我们在古汉语中对这一过程的理解，其实"伦"字是一组直接同源汉字之一，这些汉字是各种对辐射秩序不同的表述。我们可以从"輪"（轮子、轮流）字开始。我们身份角色的"纽带"性，在表"挑选"含义的"掄"字和表"拧绳、织线"含义的"綸"字上被加强了。这一簇汉字连在一起，共同喻示对关系作用形态以及理想秩序的发展、巩固。但是，对于"活"我们的身份角色动态的、叙述的话语方面，恐怕最能通过同源表意

burden and inconvenience of the traditional three-year mourning period for his parents, Confucius chides him by observing that parents quite literally give to infants three years of themselves, nourishing them and ensuring the continuing viability of their offspring as persons.

The family is conceived as the center of all order, social and cosmic, and as we have seen in the *Great Learning*, all meaning ripples out in concentric circles from personal cultivation within family, and then returns again to nourish this primary source. In fact, if we ask after the meaning of personal roles (*lun* 倫) or perhaps a more primarily gerundive expression of them—"the living of one's roles and relations"—as this process is understood in the classical Chinese language, this character *lun* is one of a cluster of immediately cognate terms that offer various ways of characterizing radial order. We might begin from the notion of "a wheel, or taking turns" (*lun* 輪). And the notion of "bonding" in our roles is reinforced by cognates such as "selecting out" (*lun* 掄) and "twisting a cord, the woof" (*lun* 綸). This family of terms shares in the association of developing and strengthening a functional pattern of relations and of achieving a desired order. But the dynamic, articulate, and discursive aspects of living our roles are perhaps best captured in cognates such as "conversing, conversation" (*lun* 論), "rippling, ripples"(*lun* 淪), and the

的是"諭""淪"和"侖"。其实,"侖"字可追溯至甲骨文,字形为"开口"(亼)与编为"册"的一串竹简"龠",意指一书写而成文献,表达着条理有序的思维。

当我们将这一组同源汉字的各种各样联系放到一起看的时候,容易洞悉的是,人们认为的恰宜"关系"的滋养而成为来源,从根本上是话语的:在家庭及延伸到社会的环境中,在人所有身份的圈子之内,人自己所具有关系的聚合及人对自己给予的表述。简而言之,蒸蒸日上、"家庭为本"的社会,形成于人与人的不间断、家庭模式的有效交流。换句话说,所有人要去"活"的角色,其最广之意义,是"言说"家庭角色,是人类经验之内在延续与一致的根本渊源。家庭角色,是对关系做出最大限度发挥的大思维,也因此成为一种对秩序(社会、政治和宇宙秩序)实现更宽宏阐释的灵感。对儒学而言,是通过不断沟通交流的家庭和社会这种话语性的生活,人才能做到对日常生活加以赞美,对一般生活加以礼仪化,让习以为常之事显出活力,向社风习俗注入生命灵感。这是在根本上去

root character, "turning over in one's mind, thoughts, ordering, achieving coherence"(*lun* 侖). Indeed, this root character *lun* 侖 dates back to the oracle bones, and is constructed from an "opened mouth" and "an orderly bundle of bamboo written strips," 龠 suggesting a coherent exposition that elicits from and brings coherence to a particular written document.

When we bring these various associations of this family of characters together, the insight gleaned is that the perceived source of growing proper "relations" is fundamentally discursive: an aggregating "relating to" and "giving an account of oneself" within the compass of one's roles that define family, and by extension, community. Simply put, a thriving, family-based community derives from continuing familial patterns of effective communicating. Said another way, "speaking" family roles in the broadest sense of living them is the ultimate source of coherence and order within the human experience. Family roles as a strategy for getting the most out of relations are thus an inspiration for order more broadly construed—social, political, and cosmic order. We might say that Confucianism is nothing more than a sustained attempt "to family" the lived human experience. For Confucianism, it is through discursive living in a communicating family and community that we are able to enchant the ordinary, to ritualize the routine, to invigorate the familiar, to inspire

做每日普通精神的沟通。

（《儒家角色伦理学：一套特色伦理学词汇》，第 109—111 页）

the customary habits of life, and ultimately, to commune spiritually in the common and the everyday.

(*Confucian Role Ethics: A Vocabulary*, pp. 96-98)

爱

这里一个有趣的问题是：在孔子"成仁"的方案中，古典"家"的观念是其中一个必要还是或然的要素？假定我们所谓人类生命赖以历练的种种依赖语境的结构和制度具有可塑性的观点成立，自然，任何特定的形式结构甚至家庭都不是必不可少的。当然，可以通过传统家庭组织关系详述的各种性质各异的"爱"具有毫无疑问的丰富性：孝（filiality）、慈（paternal affection）、悌（fraternity）、友（camaraderie），不一而足。首先，家庭组织关系本身是从种种本身也总是独特、具体的关系中抽象出来的。但即便是一种抽象，如果需要调整结构以适应环境和种种可能状态，那家庭或许最好被认为是某种可在各种不同情况下被另一不同且更为相宜、更富有意义的社会组织替换的或然机构。

Loving（*Ai*）

An interesting question here is whether the classical notion of family is a necessary or a contingent factor in Confucius' project of becoming authoritatively human. Given what we have said about the malleability of the context-dependent structures and institutions through which human life is experienced and refined, it would follow that no specific formal structure, even family, is necessary. Of course, the various kinds and qualities of love that can be elaborated through the traditional institution of the family have an unquestionable richness: filiality (*hsiao* 孝), paternal affection (*tz'u* 慈), fraternity (*t'i* 悌), camaraderie (*yu* 友), and so forth. To begin with, the institution of family is itself an abstraction from particular concrete relationships that are themselves always unique. But even as an abstraction, given the need to adjust structure to circumstances and the wealth of possible worlds, the family is perhaps best regarded as a contingent institution that could, under different

我们只需想一下孔子时代以族系为主导扩充的家庭系统与当代中国体现这种或然意识的核心家庭模式的巨大反差就一目了然了。

孔子以及他后来的许多追随者都根据"爱人"来定义"仁"。古典中国传统中"爱"这一概念与"成人"过程"受"（taking in）的方面一致，传达了某种"宜"的意识。"爱"是将某人纳入个体关心的范围，且据此使之成为自我整体的一部分。当这一领受处在互给的情况的时候，"爱"就是自我可参照其所爱来描述的盟约。

（《通过孔子而思》，第 142 页）

四端

为便于对"人性"作一种过程性理解，我们以"始端"为例："修成身份及关系之礼。"就一个婴儿而言，出生于它所在的家庭生命形态环境中，必然是有素质和习性倾向的。随着时间推移，它成长为这个社会体的一位既响应又有责任的成

conditions, be replaced by a different, more appropriate, more meaningful communal organization. One need only reflect on the gross distance between the clan-oriented extended family of Confucius' own world and the nuclear family of contemporary China to entertain this sense of contingency.

Confucius, and subsequently many of his followers, defined authoritative humanity in terms of loving others (*ai jen*). This concept of love in the classical Chinese tradition, consistent with the "taking in" aspect of person making, conveys a sense of appropriation. *Ai* is to take someone into one's sphere of concern, and in so doing, make him an integral aspect of one's own person. Where this taking in is reciprocated, *ai* is a bond that allows one's own person to be defined by reference to those he loves.

(*Thinking Through Confucius,* pp. 120-121)

Four Inklings (*siduan*)

To make the case for a processual understanding of "human nature" (*renxing*), we might take one of these "beginnings" as an example: "achieved propriety in our roles and relationships" (*li*). On the side of the infant, born within the context of its familial life forms, there is certainly a predisposition and a propensity to develop over time into a responsive and thus

员。但是当我们把关于人性讨论排斥性地置于抽象个体婴儿而非包容的具体家庭关系网内时，我们思维的扭曲性局限就产生了。无论我们如何看待一个人的出生，他对群体生活组织和结构最初始的回应，使得家庭成为未成形人与社会和文化的连接点——作为信仰、技能、志趣、是非观、职业等方面和富有意义集中点——这是对人从中生长带有支配性创造力的源泉，成仁之人最终也对它报以特殊意义。

婴儿从小就有交流倾向，它出生在文化意义的世界，世界向它提供交流资源，这是婴儿有效参与它所在家庭与人群的必要资源。如果需要证明"人性"的重要性，去给一个独特的人意味着什么做出定义，在于具体社会情况，个人是社会的一部分，而不是排他性、未成形的单子个体人。我们必须要参照的，是截然不同的人类文化内部思维与生活惊人多元化的方式。另一方面，人的初始条件并非不变质相的人，惊人相似的野孩现象可以证明这一点。他们生活在没有家庭生活环境的动物性世界，与人类生活脱离了联系。因此，他们不可避免地成为野孩。

responsible member of this social unit. But a distorting limitation in our thinking arises when we locate the discussion of *renxing* exclusively within the abstracted individual infant rather than within the inclusive and concrete web of family relations. Regardless of how we describe a human nativity and its initial responsiveness to the institutions and structures of communal living, it is the family as the articulated social and cultural locus of otherwise inchoate persons—an invested and meaningful concentration of beliefs, skills, interests, values, occupations, and so on—that is the predominant creative source out of which persons grow, and to which grown persons ultimately contribute their particular meanings.

Infants have a predisposition to communicate, but it is the world of cultural meanings into which they are born that provide them with the communicative resources necessary to participate effectively in their specific families and communities. If there is proof needed that the weight of "human nature" as defining of what it means to become distinctively human lies in the concrete social situation of which the individual is a part, rather than exclusively in inchoate individuals themselves, we have simply to reference the staggering diversity of ways of thinking and living within the vastly disparate human cultures. On the other hand, proof that the initial conditions are not the substance of what it means to become human

其实，我在下面想要阐明孟子提出的关系构成的"成人"观点，此观点是对"人"的认识，是一个需在根本不同于任何将人类做后溯性（追溯到神造人——译者）和质相概想认识的观点。进一步来说，最近出土的儒家典籍《五行篇》不少方面都呼应着《孟子》，有力证明了对孟子"人性"观点的解释，"什么是成仁"，它讲的是一种前瞻的、过程的、相互联合的和彻底的域境。

正如我在别处阐述的，要理解《孟子》的人性，第一步是把它清晰地与另一个起重要作用的观念区别开来。孟子有一套词汇用来阐述修身养性的人生观，那个重要观念就是"心"（heartmind）。诠释孟子思想的学者有一种显著倾向，就是忽略"性"与"心"的重要差别。这种混淆是因为"性"作为创造性过程，是根植于"心"的，而作为自然性的初始人性条件，人一般是确有一些特定根本倾向。但恰是看这些特定根本倾向，我们才会认识到，正是变化、成长、向善的创造性过程构成"人性"。

《孟子》明确地阐明，人皆有

might be the phenomenon of remarkably similar feral children who seem to be the ineluctable consequence of disconnected and dislocated "human being" living out their animality without the resource of family life.

Indeed, I will argue in what follows that the *Mencius* is positing the notion of a relationally constituted "human becoming," a notion of person that requires an understanding fundamentally different from any retrospective, essentialistic conception of the human being. I am further persuaded that the recently recovered Confucian document, *Five Modes of Proper Conduct* (*Wuxingpian* 五行篇), resonates in many ways with the *Mencius* and corroborates this interpretation of the Mencian *renxing* as a prospective, processual, transactional, and radically contextual understanding of what it means to become human.

As I have argued elsewhere, a first step in understanding *renxing* 人性 in the *Mencius* is to distinguish it clearly from a second notion that also has an important role in the cluster of terms through which Mencius explicates the project of personal cultivation, that is, the "heartmind" (*xin* 心). There has been a decided tendency on the part of scholars in interpreting Mencius to elide *xing* and *xin* without respecting their important differences. This confusion emerges because the *xing* as a creative process is rooted in the heartmind (*xin*), and human beings in general do have certain determinative propensities as a function of their initial natural conditions. But it

心，心皆存向善行为之始端，被比喻地表述为"四端"：

> 恻隐之心，仁之端也；羞恶之心，义之端也；辞让之心，礼之端也；是非之心，智之端也。人之有是四端也，犹其有四体也。有是四端而自谓不能者，自贼者也；谓其君不能者，贼其君者也。凡有四端于我者，知皆扩而充之矣，若火之始然，泉之始达。苟能充之，足以保四海；苟不充之，不足以事父母。（《孟子·公孙丑上》）

这一段阐述的是"心"的初始条件。不过，我们得想到"性"的字形是"心"和"生"（初生、生长、生活），要把"生"的意思考虑到"心"中去。为进一步辅助理解，《孟子》又明确指出：

> 君子所性，虽大行不加焉，虽穷居不损焉，分定故也。君子所性，仁义礼智根于心。其生色也睟然，见于面，盎于背，施于四体，四体不言而喻。（《孟子·尽心上》）

is precisely over and against these determinate propensities that we are able to observe the creative process of change, growth, and refinement that constitutes *xing*.

We are told explicitly in the *Mencius* that persons all have heartminds (*xin*), and that these heartminds share a given incipient propensity for moral conduct that is metaphorically described as "the four inklings" (*siduan* 四端):

> The heartmind in feeling pity at suffering has the first inkling of consummate conduct; the heartmind in feeling shame at crudeness has the first inkling of appropriate conduct; the heartmind in feeling a sense of modesty and deference has the first inkling of propriety in conduct; the heartmind in feeling a sense of approval and disapproval has the first inkling of wise conduct. Persons having these four inklings (*siduan*) is like their having four limbs... Now acknowledging these four inklings in me, the process of realizing the development and fruition of them all is like a fire beginning to burn or a spring of water beginning to break through. Persons who are able to bring them fully to fruition can sustain all within the four seas; persons unable to do so cannot even serve their own parents.

如果我们把这段与上段比喻的说法（"人之有是四端也，犹其有四体也"）联系起来看，即可领略到，"四端"与"四体"都是成长的起始所由。其实，只有通过勤勉的修养过程，"性"才可充分得到发挥：

> 孟子曰："尽其心者，知其性也。知其性，则知天矣。存其心，养其性，所以事天也。"（《孟子·尽心上》）

一个"心"和"性"不加区分而产生问题的例子，是张岱年提出"既然圣人也是人，因此圣人之性也是人人所备之性"的观点。对《孟子》小心细读，张先生肯定地断言，圣人之心也是与人人相似之心。其实，《孟子》所说之心，是拿它作为器官来对待的，与有视觉和听觉的器官同样。而张先生认为的似乎是，"性"与"心"一样，是人人皆有的天赋潜能，而圣人无非是成功做到实现潜能的人。不过唐君毅指出，"性"的潜能不在于"性"本身之中，而是一物同所处各种环境之间创造性的协同过程。人是个"人"并不把他造为一个"圣人"，而"成

This passage describes the initial conditions of the heartmind, but we have to remember that the graph for *xing* 性 is comprised of both "heartmind" (*xin*) and "to be born, to grow, to live" (*sheng* 生). Taking this verbal "growth" (*sheng* 生) complement to heartmind as an important further consideration, in the *Mencius* we are again told explicitly that:

> ... Consummatory conduct (*ren*), a sense of appropriateness (*yi*), an achieved propriety in roles and relations (*li*), and a capacity to live wisely (*zhi*) that exemplary persons engender and grow (*xing*) as their habits of conduct is rooted in their heartminds, and grows in their countenance. The luster of this conduct is manifest in their faces, is discernible in their posture, and extends throughout their bodies. They do not need to explain what they are doing to be understood by others.

If we couple this passage with the analogical claim in the passage cited above that "persons having these four inklings (*siduan*) is like their having four limbs," we can appreciate that the four inklings and the body are both incipient sites of growth. Indeed, it is only through this assiduous process of cultivation that the *xing* can be fully developed:

为"圣人能最充分造就一个人。说"人人皆备圣人之性"与说"如圣人般行为的是圣人",二者之间区别很大。成为圣人的潜力与相互联系的活动是一起呈现的,没有分别的,人与人的相互联系性是人生命生活的本质构成。孟子把这一点讲得很清楚:

> 曹交问曰:"人皆可以为尧舜,有诸?"孟子曰:"……尧舜之道,孝弟而已矣。子服尧之服,诵尧之言,行尧之行,是尧而已矣。"(《孟子·告子下》)

学者们一般都要引用的《孟子》中的一段,把孟子的"性善"理解为"人性在本质上是善的"(Human nature is essentially good),是这样说的:

> 孟子曰:"乃若其情,则可以为善矣,乃所谓善也。若夫为不善,非才之罪也。恻隐之心,人皆有之;羞恶之心,人皆有之;恭敬之心,人皆有之;是非之心,人皆有之。恻隐之心,仁也;羞恶之心,义也;

Those who exhaust their heartminds (*xin*) realize their *xing*, and to realize their *xing* is to realize *tian*. Preserving their *xin* and nurturing their *xing* is the way to serve *tian*.

As one example of this problem of conflating *xin* and *xing*, Zhang Dainian suggests that "since the sage is also a man, the *xing* that the sage has is the *xing* that all people have." On a careful reading of the Mencius, Zhang could certainly assert that the sage has a *xin* that is similar to that of all people. In fact, the *Mencius* describes the *xin* as an organ (*guan* 官) on a plane with the organs of sight and hearing. But Zhang's assumption would seem to be that *xing* like *xin* is a given potential shared by all, and the sage is simply the one who successfully actualizes it. However, as Tang Junyi has argued, the possibility of *xing* does not lie within *xing* itself; *xing* is a creative collaboration between something and its various environments. Being a person does not make one a sage; becoming a sage makes one most fully a person. There is an important difference between saying that everyone has the nature of a sage and saying that everyone who conducts themselves as a sage is a sage. The potential for becoming a sage emerges *pari passu* in the transactional events that constitute the substance of a human life. Mencius makes this point explicitly:

Cao Jiao inquired: "Is it the case that

恭敬之心，礼也；是非之心，智也。仁义礼智，非由外铄我也，我固有之也，弗思耳矣。故曰：'求则得之，舍则失之。'或相倍蓰而无算者，不能尽其才者也。"（《孟子·告子上》）

我想指出，基本上对这段做了误读的，都是因为把"内"和"外"之间的不同理解为互相排斥和本质性的，而不是作为互系的、经验的和环境的作用。类似的误读可能是颜回把"仁"说成"自爱"，"自爱"被理解成排他的而不是关系性的。这里的重点是，这些行为倾向，是将关系构成的人，置于经验之中，这样他们的主观性意向和客观行为必须都得到承认。道德行为是人与世界之间的协同，而不只是从外在或内在派生的行为模式。

（《儒家角色伦理学：一套特色伦理学词汇》，第152—156页）

……孟子的心之"四端"不是生来固有、质相本质的，不是其"自我"性才使我们是"人"（human beings：人的本体存在）。"四端"当然是天生与原始的，是作为起始的

we can all become Yaos and Shuns?"

Mencius replied: "...The way of Yao and Shun is nothing but family reverence and fraternal deference. If you wear Yao's clothes, speak his words, and do what he does, then you *are* a Yao."

The passage that is generally cited from the *Mencius* as defining of his understanding that human nature is essentially good (*xingshan* 性善) is the following:

As respects one's actual circumstances that one can act efficaciously is what is meant by *shan*. As respects one acting ineptly, this is not the fault of one's native ability. All people have a heartmind that feels pity at suffering, that feels shame at crudeness, that feels a sense of modesty and deference, and that feels a sense of approval and disapproval. The feeling of pity at suffering leads to consummate conduct; the feeling of shame at crudeness leads to appropriate conduct; the feeling of a sense of modesty and deference leads to propriety in conduct; the feeling of sense of approval and disapproval leads to wisdom in conduct. These four inklings in conduct do not illuminate me from without. They are tendencies that I have but have simply failed to

关系条件，是它将我们植入家庭纽带的。但它只是成长过程大体依赖之"端"，关键在于联系在一起生活，需要给予营养使我们吃饱，成为家庭与社会的积极参与者。"四端"所讲的，是具体伦理的、美感的、认知的和宗教的"端"，人从这里成长而来。所以，儒家的人生观是将未成形却是有机、相互依存的人纳入家庭纽带并将他们转变为一个在生机勃勃、精力充沛社会中的积极参加者。

（《儒家角色伦理学：一套特色伦理学词汇》，第 167—168 页）

acknowledge. It is for this reason that it is said: "If you seek it you will get it; if you don't you will lose it." That some people are twice, five times, and indeed infinitely better than others is because there are those who fail to make the most of their native ability.

I would argue that the basic misreading of this passage arises from interpreting the distinction between inside and outside as exclusive and essential rather than as correlative, experiential, and a function of circumstances. It is the same misreading that is possible when Yan Hui's definition of ren as "self-loving" (*ziai* 自爱) is understood to be exclusive of others rather than relational. The point is that these inclinations in conduct locate relationally constituted persons within experience in which their subjective dispositions as well as their objective behavior must both be acknowledged. Moral conduct is a collaboration between persons and their worlds rather than being a pattern of behavior derived solely from the outside, or solely from the inside.

(*Confucian Role Ethics: A Vocabulary,* pp. 137-140)

"Inklings" (*siduan*) of the heartmind are not inborn and essential qualities that in and of themselves make us human "beings." These "inklings" are certainly native and incipient as the initial relational conditions that bind us into our families. But they are only the largely dependent beginnings of a process of growth in associated living that need to be nourished to make us full, active participants in family and community. The *siduan* describe the particular ethical, aesthetic, cognitive, and religious beginnings whence human beings emerge. The Confucian project, then, is to incorporate inchoate yet organically interdependent persons within the family nexus and to transform them into eager participants in a flourishing and thus spiritual community.

(*Confucian Role Ethics: A Vocabulary*, pp. 150-151)

Doing One's Best (*Chung*)

Lau provides us with a significant corrective for the popular understanding of *chung* as simply "loyalty" by reconstructing its more primitive meaning— "doing one's best":

> Translators tend to use "loyal" as the sole equivalent for *chung* even when translating early texts. This mistake is due to a failure to appreciate that the meaning of the word changed in the course of time... Chung is the doing of one's best and it is through *chung* that one puts into effect what one had found

忠

"忠"的流行翻译为"loyalty"。刘殿爵认为此译过于狭隘，对此提出了重大意义的纠正，重建了该概念更源初的意义——"doing one's best"（尽己）：

> 译者们甚至在翻译古代著作时也倾向于把"loyal"作为"忠"唯一的对称词。他们所犯的错误在于不能够充分理解该词随时间变化而产生的意义变

更……"忠"有"尽己"之意，只有"忠"才能行之有效地实现"恕"。

刘殿爵对"忠"的解释可在《说文》中找到根据，《说文》将"忠"定义为"敬"（reverence）。以后，注者们又对《说文》的概念做了进一步阐明："尽己曰忠，忠乃有诚。"这就是说，"忠"有为当下责任竭尽其力的意思。把刘殿爵的解释再推进一步，这一概念中的"己"乃指个体独一无二的特殊性。因此，"忠"的意思即"以己尽己"（doing one's best as one's authentic self）。

（《通过孔子而思》，第351—352页）

忠字由"中"（into, interior）和"心"（heart-and-mind）两个成分构成，意思是对手头的任务"尽我所能"或"竭尽全力"（giving oneself fully）——实际相当于对你所做的事情尽心尽意。当忠被用于君臣关系上时，"尽力"就被窄化为"loyalty"。

《论语》中，忠恕被一起用作行义之途。只有设定了此种相互性与共同关心，我们才会判断出何为

out by the method of *shu*.

Lau's interpretation of *chung* is reinforced by the *Shuo-wen* lexicon which defines *chung* as *ching* 敬, "reverence." Commentary on the *Shuo-wen* further clarifies this concept: "It is because exhausting oneself (*chin chi* 盡己) means *chung* 忠 that *chung* has the import of 'having integrity' (*yu ch'eng* 有誠)." That is, *chung* 忠 means "doing one's best" or "giving of oneself fully" to the task at hand. Taking Lau's clarification one step further, the "oneself" in this definition of *chung* is one's unique particularity. Thus *chung* means "doing one's best as one's authentic self."

(*Thinking Through Confucius*, p. 285)

The character *zhong* that is constituted by components "into, interior" (*zhong* 中) and "heart-and-mind" (*xin* 心) means "doing one's best" or "giving oneself fully" to the task at hand— quite literally putting one's heart into what one does. When *zhong* is used in the context of the relationship between ruler and subject, "doing one's best" becomes more narrowly focused as "loyalty."

In the Analects, *zhong* appears together with *shu* 恕 as a strategy for appropriate behavior: "putting oneself in the other's place." It is only by assuming this kind of mutuality and shared concern that one can exercise one's judgment on how to do one's best, entailing as *zhong* does both enthusiastic obedience and sincere

尽力,像"忠"那样既有热切的顺,又有真挚的谏。正如《孝经》所言,上下彼此相亲,需要事上者能"将顺其美,匡救其恶"。(《事君章》)

(《生民之本:〈孝经〉的哲学诠释及英译》,第 111—112 页)

《说文解字》把"忠"解释为"敬",这对刘殿爵解释的"忠",是一个印证。后来人们把《论语》里的"忠"解释为"尽己"。

"忠"的青铜器铭文字形为"忠","从中从心"。前面对"中"字意义已有分析,意思是以旗鼓聚众。"心"可以说既是思想也有情感。这两字组成一字,意为"尽己所能"或"尽己"于事——准确地说,就是全心全意做事。显而易见,当把"忠"用于君主与臣民政治关系的语境中时,"尽己所能"就变成更为狭义的"效忠",即使如此,"效忠"也是具有思想而非盲目效忠的。

"忠"作为"尽己所能",是对自己所用心思与行为的诚心诚意。不难看出,具有抗辩性格的孔子,对自己被说成"好学",并没有不好意思。孔子总是以身为榜样教给学生"怎样"做人成仁,而不是空讲

remonstrance (*jian*). As the *Classic of Family Reverence* observes, superiors and subordinates can appreciate each other only if subordinates "are fully compliant (*shun*) in carrying out what is commendable in the instructions of those above and take steps to remedy what cannot be condoned."

(*The Chinese Classic of Family Reverence: A Philosophical Translation of the Xiaojing*, pp.91-92)

Lau's interpretation of *zhong* is reinforced by the *Shuowen* lexicon that defines *zhong* as being "respectfully attentive" (*jing* 敬). Later commentary on the *Analects* defines *zhong* explicitly as "giving of oneself utterly" (*jinji* 盡己).

The character *zhong* 忠 appears on the bronzes as 忠, constituted by the components "centering, into, interior, focus" (*zhong* 中) and "heartmind" (*xin* 心), The character *zhong* 中 was analyzed earlier in this chapter as suggesting ways of assembling the people visually and aurally with banners and drums respectively. The second element is the "heartmind" (*xin*), or perhaps better, "thinking and feeling." In combination, the graph means "doing one's best" or "giving oneself fully" to the task at hand—quite literally putting one's whole heart and mind into what one is doing. It is easy to see that when *zhong* comes to be used in the context of the political relationship between ruler and

"仁"的道理,因为人的具体行为是复杂条件,总是需要在特殊的具体情境和情势之中具备品格性。因此道德行为不能成为一种一般处方。

(《儒家角色伦理学:一套特色伦理学词汇》,第 220—221 页)

subject, "doing one's best" becomes more narrowly focused as "loyalty," but even here, an intelligent as opposed to a blind loyalty.

Zhong, "doing one's utmost," is thus a conscientiousness in one's deliberations and actions. We have seen that an otherwise demurring Confucius is not shy about being described as "caring deeply for learning"(*haoxue* 好學). Confucius in his exhortations is given to recommending the more modal *how* to live morally because the *what* of one's specific actions is a complex variable that will always need to be qualified by the uniqueness and exigencies of the circumstances. Moral actions are thus resistant to general prescription.

(*Confucian Role Ethics: A Vocabulary,* pp. 200-201)

恕

孔子把"恕"视为自己的方法论——他"一以贯之"之"道"。孔子实际恰是这样来描述"恕"的:"子贡问曰:'有一言而可以终身行之者乎?'子曰:'其恕乎!己所不欲,勿施于人。'"(《论语·卫灵公》)"己所不欲,勿施于人"这一原则在《论语》中反复出现,《中庸》和《大学》也都有新表达。尤

Shu

There can be no doubt that Confucius saw it as his methodology, his "unifying thread." In fact, he defines it for us in precisely these terms(15.24): "Tzu-kung asked, 'Is there one expression that one can act on to the end of his days?' The Master replied, 'There is *shu*: do not impose on others what you yourself do not desire.' " This formula, "do not impose on others what you yourself do not desire," is repeated on several other occasions in the Analects, and reformulated in both the *Chung-*

其是《中庸》将"恕"专门描述为"人""己"建构的关系域中彼此的譬比，而且，似乎更恰合孔子的意思：

> 子曰："道不远人。人之为道而远人，不可以为道。《诗》云：'伐柯伐柯，其则不远。'执柯以伐柯，睨而视之，犹以为远。故君子以人治人，改而止。忠恕违道不远，施诸己而不愿，亦勿施于人。"

该段道出了孔子思想几个很核心的观点。首先，人之"道"，即人的秩序或模式始终就在身边——就出自特定、具体的个人。引《诗》的那段话以及《中庸》的评论都形象地描述了这一点。尽管"道"并不远，然而在范型与产物、已建模式和当下所塑模式之间却始终存在着必不可少的差异。独特的新柯不仅依靠已有之柯伐之，而且现有的柯本身实际主动参与到创造新柯形式的活动中。人类世界同样如此——"以人治人"。

或许，该段最能说明道理的一句是"改而止"。也就是说，就

yung and T*a-hsueh*. The *Chung-yung* passage is particularly important in that it describes the method of *shu* specifically as evoking analogy between oneself and other people, or perhaps stated in more appropriately Confucian terms, within the field of the relationship constituted by self and other:

> The Master said, "The *tao* is not far from man. where someone takes as *tao* something distant from man, it cannot be the *tao*. The *Book of Songs* states: 'In hewing an axe-handle, in hewing an axe-handle, the pattern is not far off.' We grasp an axe-handle to hew an axe-handle, but, when we look from one to the other with a critical eye, they still seem far apart. Thus, the exemplary person brings proper order to man with man, and having effected the change, stops. *Chung* and *shu* are not far from the *tao*: what you do not want done to yourself, do not do to others."

This passage makes several points that are central in the philosophy of Confucius. To begin with, the *tao* of man, that is, the order or mode of man, always emerges out of what is close at hand—out of the particular, concrete person. The *Book of Songs* passage cited and the *Chung-yung* commentary on it describe this emergence analogically. Although the pattern is close, there always remains a critical difference between the

像打造出的新柯,尽管与旧柯相似却仍可看出差异,因此,人的塑造也一样,其目的是向着"和"而非"同"。已有模式与新塑造物比拟的这一动态过程用到人类秩序的创造,在概念上就表现为"忠""恕"二字。

《中庸》这段揭示"人""己"之间适当关系的话尚有更深的意义。"恕"在古典著作中常用"仁"来定义。《说文》就是一个例子。在第二章对"仁"的讨论中,我们已指出"仁"从词源上由"人"和"二"两部分组成,合在一起强调的是"成人"不可化约的关系性。"仁"与"恕"的这一关联有助于我们理解该关系的譬比性质。"仁"不是两个相同的人之间的关系,而是由相似性与差异性、美德与敬意共同建构起的人与人之间的和谐。"恕"之"道"(methodology)需要突出或承认美德,作为引起或表达敬意的方法。"恕"作为一种"道",则要求在任何既定情形下,一个人或是展示其自身美德(因而可期望从他人那儿获得敬意),或是尊敬别人的美德。而且,"恕"总是个人性的,因为它体现"忠":"以己尽己"(doing

template and the product, between the established pattern and the one that is presently being fashioned. The new and unique axe-handle is not only hewn against the pattern of the existing one, the existing axe-handle itself actually participates actively in bringing the new axe-handle into proper form. Similarly in the human world, man is used to bring order to man.

Perhaps the most telling phrase in this passage is "and having effected the change, he stops." That is, just as the fashioning of the new axe-handle results in something similar yet discernibly different, so the fashioning of one man in relation to another is directed at harmony, not sameness. The dynamics of this analogizing between the existing pattern and the newly fashioned article, when applied to the proper ordering of man, is captured conceptually in *chung* and *shu*.

This *Chung-yung* passage has further significance in disclosing the appropriate relationship in the interaction between one man and another. The concept *shu* is defined frequently in the classical texts in terms of *jen** 仁 , "authoritative person." The *Shuo-wen* is a case in point. In our extended discussion of *jen** above in Chapter II, we indicated that *jen** 仁 etymologically reduces to "person" and "two," a combination of ideas indicating that achieved person as *jen** is irreducibly relational. This association between *jen** and *shu* helps us understand the analogical nature of this relationship. *Jen** is not a relationship between one's best as one's authentic self）。

"恕"以个人为出发点以及它的人际关系的种种含义，在孔子对"仁"的定义中一目了然：

> 夫仁者，己欲立而立人，己欲达而达人。能近取譬，可谓仁之方也已。(《论语·雍也》)

芬格莱特在讨论该节时，反对把"恕"做全然康德式的解读。他认为康德面临着这样的困难：虽然他想达到普遍性公则，但是存在无法推行公则的"相关类似情境"问题，所以公则本身阻碍人们运用它。也即只要运用"绝对命令"（categorical imperative），就需要道德立法者来制定出涵盖一切可能情况的道德规范。芬格莱特提出了和我们类似的对"恕"的另一诠释，即在孔子那里，"恕"有"譬"的作用：

> 这里关键的一个词是"譬"。"譬"相当频繁地出现在《论语》中。尽管在英汉词典中"譬"被译为"to compare"，但

two identical persons; it is a harmony existing between persons that is constituted by both similarity and difference, and by both excellence and deference. The methodology of *shu* requires the projection or recognition of excellence as a means of eliciting or of expressing deference. *Shu* as a methodology requires that in any given situation one either display excellence in oneself (and thus anticipate deference from others) or defer to excellence in another. Again, *shu* is always personal in that it entails *chung*: "doing one's best as one's authentic self."

The personal starting point and the interpersonal implications of this process of *shu* are made apparent when Confucius turns to define *jen** in the *Analects*(6.30):

> **The authoritative person (*jen** 仁) establishes others in seeking to establish himself, and promotes others in seeking to get there himself. To be able to take the analogy from what is closest to oneself can be called the methodology of becoming an authoritative person.**

Herbert Fingarette, in his reflections on this passage from the *Analects*, rejects a strictly Kantian interpretation of *shu*, because of the difficulty faced in arriving at universal maxims that are not themselves thwarted by the problem of "relevantly similar circumstances." That is, the application of the categorical imperative would require the moral equivalent of a legislator

我认为值得注意的是它在《论语》中运用的几个重要特征：首先，在《论语》中，"譬"总是相似性而非差异性的"比较"。因而，译成"analogy"跟它更相称。其次，"比较"根据的是人、事态和行为的形象化描述而非抽象特征表达的。因此，《论语》中的"譬"是典型的比喻……取"譬"是孔子授教的特点……它与抽象分析、理论建构和概括方法形成鲜明对照。这样，"恕"就是一种特殊的"譬"——从当前（"己"）把握与他者（"人"）的类似，且基此推己及人——这就是"恕"。

芬格莱特用"譬"来定义"恕"当然有其词源学的支持。"恕"由它的同源词"如"和"心"（heart-and-mind）构成。"如"的意思即为"像"（like, as if, to resemble）。但如果再进一步论述则仍然有两个重要问题没有解决。首先，如果说"恕"像《论语》的传统注者们所解释的那样是"推己及物"和"以己量人"，那么似乎（正像芬格莱特所论）"己"之判断力就是"恕"的起

to formulate an inexhaustible code that would cover all possible situations. As an alter-native explanation of *shu*, he, like us, suggests that it functions as analogy in Confucius:

> One key word here is *p'i* 譬, a word used with some frequency in the *Analects*. Although it is rendered in bi-lingual dictionaries by the English "to compare," the important features of its use in the *Analects* to which I would direct attention are these: First, *p'i* in the *Analects* is always a "comparison" of likenesses, not differences. Hence "analogy" is an appropriate term. Second, the comparison is expressed in terms of imagery, of persons, situations or activities, not in terms of abstract traits. Hence, *p'i* is in the *Analects* typically met aphorical.... The use of *p'i* is characteristic of Confucius' way of teaching.... It contrasts sharply with the method of abstract analysis, theory building, universalizing. *Shu*, in turn, is a specific kind of *p'i*. To be able from what is close—i.e., oneself—to grasp analogy with the other person, and in that light to treat him as you would be treated—that is *shu*.

Fingarette's definition of *shu* in terms of analogy is certainly borne out by the etymology of the character 恕, composed of its cognate *ju* 如, which means "like, as if, to resemble,"

点。如果确乎如此,那么,"恕"似乎就是单向度的,个人的自我成就(己之德)成了他人如何行事的标尺。这样一来,"敬"何以产生?什么情况下"恕"能够被理解为"敬"呢?第二个问题是:为什么"恕"的"己所不欲,勿施于人"的定义用的是否定表达而非肯定表达?

回答第一个问题,我们可以研究一下《孟子》中唯一出现的一处"恕":

> 孟子曰:"万物皆备于我矣。反身而诚,乐莫大焉。强恕而行,求仁莫近焉。"(《孟子·尽心上》)

该节表明了这样几个观点。首先,"我"是根据"我"与万物的关系来界定的。正是这个原因,"万物皆备于我"。行"恕"之道,"我"必须首先"反身"——由人及己,而后明己。说"反身而诚,乐莫大焉"就是说个体必须清醒地意识到"我",并且以此赤诚之"我"行事。"义"(appropriate)始于"诚",而且以"诚"为基础建立与其语境的和谐关系。这是"乐"的源泉,因

and *hsin* 心, "heart-and-mind." Proceeding one step further, there are two important questions that are still unresolved. First, if *shu* is "extending oneself to other things" (*t'ui chi chi wu* 推己及物) and "weighing others with oneself" (*yi chi liang jen* 以己量人) as explained in the traditional commentaries on the *Analects*, it would seem (as Fingarette indeed suggests) that one's own judgment is the starting point of *shu*. If this is the case, it would seem that *shu* is one-directional. This personal judgment on how to act with respect to another is then going to be qualified by one's own achievement as a person, one's own excellence. Under these circumstances, it is difficult to understand how deference enters into it. In what way is *shu* to be understood as "deference"? The second question is: why is the definition of *shu* as, "do not extend to others what you yourself do not desire," persistently framed in negative rather than positive terms?

We can respond to the first question by examining the only occurrence of *shu* to be found in the *Mencius*:

> Mencius said, "Everything is complete here in me. There is no greater source of enjoyment than, upon introspection, to find that one is true to oneself. And there is no method of pursuing authoritative humanity more immediate than carrying *shu* into practice with earnestness."

为"乐"就是"顺"各人之"志"。

个体只有在由人及己,继而明己的情况下,才有可能"反身"及人,确定什么行为是适当的。同样的观点也表现在"克己复礼为仁"(《论语·颜渊》)的表达中。"克己"是据"人"而向内明"己"的行为,"复礼"则是向外延"己"的行为。这样,"恕"就是双向性的,因此可被界定为互惠性的,可根据美德和敬意来描述。"恕"不只是将自己视为典范而以己之心度他人;它毋宁是首先因人明己,然后,或是展现己之德,或是敬"人"之德。这样,"恕"就既是一种敬意行为,又是对敬意的需要。我们下文要说明的"譬"的方法就是以"敬"的这种意义为基础的。

为什么"恕"总是被以一种否定的形式表达?"恕"作为一种"譬",既有连续性也关涉创新性。像"礼"这样现成的模式关心连续性,一个人只有按"礼"行事,才能肯定地明确他应做之事。但现成的"礼"并不能涵盖所有有意义的行为,而且由于任何礼仪行为都必然是个人性的,因此,它确实会某种程度上融入创新。那么,是什么

This passage suggests several points. First, one's own self is defined in terms of one's relations with all other things. It is for this reason that "everything is complete here in me." In exercising the methodology of *shu*, one must first move from other to self in order to clarify self. To say that "there is no greater source of enjoyment than, upon introspection, to find that one is true to oneself" is to say that one must have a clear awareness of one's own self and act in such a way as to be true to that self. Being "appropriate" (*yi* 義) begins with being true to oneself, and, on that basis, negotiating harmony with one's context. This is a source of enjoyment because enjoyment involves attuning the dispositions represented by the constituent particulars.

It is only once one has moved from other to self in order to clarify oneself that one can move in the opposite direction and extend oneself to the other in order to determine appropriate conduct. This same point is made in stating: "to discipline oneself and to practice ritual action is to become authoritative as a person(12.1)". To discipline oneself is the movement inward to clarify self in terms of other, and "to practice ritual action" is the extension of self outward in the direction of other. Thus, it is because *shu* is bi-directional that it can be defined as reciprocity and described in terms of excellence and deference. *Shu* is not simply taking oneself as the model and projecting it onto others; rather, it is first clarifying oneself in terms of

制约了这种创新？鉴于我们并不能充分意识到他者会做什么，因此，"恕"要容纳创新，就只能加以否定地表达。创新不能够被指定，它能受的唯一束缚就是个体本身的局限：我们会发现与己所不相容者。

例如，声乐老师对歌手要负什么责任？他要使歌手的发声符合规范，与此同时还要为其留出创造性表达的空间。那么，他对歌手的创新有什么限制呢？他只有通过总结自己的经验并用它们来分析歌手的个人风格，才会发现向什么方向发展是徒然无益的。他必须在那些技术指导不适用的情况下，用"否定的"语言提出建议，从而为歌手的创新留有余地。

当我们坚持根据给予和获得敬意来理解"恕"时，实际上我们的意思还要更深。因为如果孔子确实认为"恕"是统一他思想的一贯之道，而且，如果我们可以根据"敬"的关系来理解"恕"，那么"敬"就必然可在诠释的意义上从各种不同途径成为理解孔子哲学的手段。我们讨论作为敬意的"恕"一个最重要的意义就是：一定要根据"恕"来理解思想活动本身——这正是我

others, and then either displaying excellence oneself or deferring to the excellence of others in personal relations. *Shu*, then, is both the act of deferring and the demand for deference. It is the sense of deference we are employing that grounds the approach in a specific sort of analogical procedure which we shall seek to articulate in the following pages.

Why is *shu* always expressed negatively? *Shu* as an analogy involves both continuity and novelty. The existing structures, such as ritual action, take care of the continuity. To the extent that one can positively specify what ought to be done, one must "do ritual action." But not all meaningful actions are covered by existing ritual and, because any performance of ritual action is necessarily personal, it does in some measure introduce novelty. What are the constraints upon this novelty? Since one cannot be fully aware of the possibilities represented by another, *shu*, in covering this novelty, can only be expressed negatively. This novelty cannot be specified. The only bounds that can be drawn on it emerge out of the limitations of one's own possibilities: what one would find discordant for himself.

What, for example, is the responsibility of a voice coach to a singer? He must discipline the voice through existing forms while at the same time giving the voice room for creative expression. What limits can the voice coach place upon the creative side? Only what the coach, plumbing his own experience and

们将要开始论证的一点。然而，要使这一观点说得通，我们首先必须深入探究一种语言，该语言既是作为敬意、譬喻行为的思想活动的前提，又以之为先决条件。

（《通过孔子而思》，第352—357页）

"恕"是儒家伦理核心的重要词语。"恕"所表达的，既是道德困惑，也是对找到最恰宜回答所做的开创性探索。儒家经典对"恕"进行过多次阐明，《说文解字》也将"恕"解释为"仁"之最理想效果。"恕"与"仁"是一种体用关系。正如"仁"是类比，即人的既相似又相异的角色与关系的恰宜协调，"恕"也是相对于他人行为，自己做出的相应行为。

赋予"恕"如此核心性的意义，是根据人做出有效相应性行为以及确定人的道德判断时，想象力所发挥的无可比拟的重要性。想象之发生，不是什么附加性、附属性或补救性的，而是一种感同身受力，产生于人的必要的教育和修养所需的所有资源。如同任何审美性的判断，想象是花费气力，成就特殊细

focusing it with respect to the idiosyncrasies of the singer, finds creatively unproductive. He must leave the opportunity for novelty open by advising in "negative" terms in those situations in which technical advice is not pertinent.

In asserting that *shu* is to be understood in terms of giving and receiving deference, we are making a rather far-reaching claim. For if it is true that Confucius believed *shu* to be the single thread that served as the unifying theme of his thinking, and if *shu* may appropriately be understood in terms of deferential relations, then the notion of deference must be employed interpretively in a variety of ways as a means of understanding Confucius' philosophy. One of the most significant implications of our discussion of *shu* as deference is, as we shall now begin to argue, that the activity of thinking itself must be understood in terms of *shu*. To make sense of this claim we must consider, in somewhat greater detail, the sort of language that both presupposes and is presupposed by thinking as a deferential, analogical activity.

(*Thinking Through Confucius,* pp. 285-290)

There can be no question about the central importance of *shu* in the Confucian ethical vocabulary. *Shu* expresses both moral perplexity and the creative search for the most appropriate response. *Shu* is defined frequently in the classical texts and in the *Shuowen* lexicon by reference to *ren*, "consummate conduct," as the desired outcome of *shu*. The association

节与整体效果之间的相应,这是在一个整体环境中达到的,而且这样做,扩展了道德考虑的场景及其深刻性。

"恕"有"胸怀宽阔"与"宽容"的含义,在哲学上被译为"altruism"(利他主义——陈荣捷)、"reciprocity"(互惠主义——杜维明和雷蒙·道森)、"consideration"(虑及——阿瑟·韦利)、"mutuality in human relations"(人人关系的相互性——芬格莱特)、"understanding"(体谅——森舸澜)、"using oneself as a measure in gauging the wishes of others"(以自己为忖度虑及他人意愿——刘殿爵)等种种说法。"恕"是一种虑及他人的宽阔胸怀,它伴随着类比性意想,明确地蕴含在字形构成的语义当中:"如"意思是"像、如同、好似、相似"等;"心"含情感性与理智性。"如"的甲骨文字形为"𡥀",意为"质问人"。"恕"是"虑及他人":在自己做事的时候想到他人,对他人表示尊重。这一类比尊重理念也体现在同源字"汝"(你)的含义里。

相较于用更抽象和计算分析或者理论方法对道德行为进行定义,"恕"的含义是明显不同的。如果懂

between *shu* and *ren* is one of function. Just as *ren* is analogical—a coordination of both similarity and difference in one's roles and relations—so too is *shu* a matter of correlating one's own conduct with the behavior of others.

The centrality given to *shu* respects the unparalleled importance that imagination plays in the productive correlating of one's conduct and in the refining of one's moral judgment. Imagination is not invoked as supplemental or subsidiary or remedial, but as an empathetic capacity drawing on all one's resources that require education and nurturance. Like any aesthetic judgment, imagination is an attempt to correlate specific details with the totality of the effect achieved within the circumstances as a whole, and in so doing, to broaden the context for and depth of moral consideration.

Shu has the meaning of "generous" and "indulgent," and has been translated within the philosophical literature variously as "altruism" (Wing-tsit Chan), as "reciprocity" (Tu Wei-ming and Raymond Dawson), as "consideration" (Waley), as "mutuality in human relations" (Fingarette), as "understanding" (Slingerland), and as "using oneself as a measure in gauging the wishes of others" (Lau). That *shu* 恕 is an "other-regarding" generosity that entails analogical projection is clearly borne out by the etymology of the character, constituted by the cognate character, *ru* 如, meaning "as to, like, as if, to resemble" and *xin* 心 "heartmind." *Ru*

得"推己及人",这种具体、场景性的道德倾向,是最有效用的形态表现。其中蕴含的意义,是对直至有了道德答案为止所做的"尊重"行为重要性的认同,同时还包括将他人的利益考虑在内。

"恕"在根本上是一种审美倾向,源于由"孝""悌"主导的家庭纽带,在这种纽带中,"人格"在努力践行自己角色和关系过程中实现——祖孙之间,孙子既把祖母作为尊重对象,也将她作为自己人格成长的资源。在全部时间中,"恕"被扩展为塑造和深化家庭范畴之外关系的相应素质。如此之"推己及人",成为一种机敏性、思虑全面性人生的无所不在、无可不有的性情。

"恕"的思想由捉摸不定的情势而生,即对一种特殊情况感到困惑,不知如何对待。那么解决这种状态就在于:人通过丰富想象而找到转机,使自己从窘境中走出来,最后终于知道如何去做才是最恰宜的行为取向。通过一个类比性思维过程,人有了自己去应对的态度,将面对的情况与记忆中以及可想象的情况互相联系起来。我们可以将这样一个过程进行总结,"恕"就是

如 occurs in the oracle bones as 㕯, interpreted as one person being questioned by another. That is, *shu* is consideration: a thoughtful and heartfelt deference to others in what we do. This notion of analogical deference is also suggested in the cognate *ru* 汝 —"you."

Shu contrasts sharply with more abstract and calculative analytic or theoretical strategies for determining moral conduct. Understood as "putting oneself in the other's place," it is the most fundamental gesture of a concrete, contextualizing moral disposition. It entails a recognition of the importance of "deference" both in the sense of deferring action until we overcome uncertainty in our moral inquiry, and in the sense of taking under consideration the interests of others in that process.

Shu is a fundamentally aesthetic disposition initially shaped within the *xiao* 孝 and *ti* 悌 governed family bonds where one's "person" emerges in the process of striving to optimize concrete roles and relations—this grandson responding to this grandmother, taking her both as an object of his deference and as a resource for his own personal growth. In the fullness of time, *shu* is then extended as a quality of responsiveness in shaping and deepening relations outside of the home. "Putting oneself in the other's place" (*shu*) is thus an omnipresent and indispensable disposition for living life responsively and thoughtfully.

Shu is prompted by uncertainty—a perplexity in how to respond in a particular

为一种域境化困惑寻找解决方法的意念，从而确定自己该如何行为。"恕"最好的状态，是呼唤清晰的记忆，想到各种类比的情形，能把最为妥帖的相互联系性建立起一种穿透性智慧，同时也能提供一系列创造性想象为可能出现的局面及后果做出预想。这样的类比思维过程正是《论语》中经常被引用的话："能近取譬，可谓仁之方也已。"（《论语·雍也》）

"恕"有一种认知与谋虑功用。但是我们要适当地"理性化"（rationalize）地认识这个认知、谋虑过程。"恕"需要的是一种全面性对待。与"恕"在一起的，也许还有为达到更有效探讨而更核心性的过程，即通过感受而知——它要求做到的是以感同身受的心理对情势环境的审视。正如同一种批判性疑问可变成一个思智习惯问题，一种对待他人的感同身受回应也可变成一种习惯成自然的情感备至行为模式。实际上，"恕"习惯成自然这种模式的形成，就发生在潜在性成长之中，从一种谋虑性做法变成人与人关系行为上的一种即时性、无自我意识的道德智力。

situation. It then requires a conjuring forth of how the alternative possibilities one can imaginatively construct might play themselves out. Finally it eventuates in crafting what one determines to be the most appropriate disposition for conduct. One shapes a response through a process of analogical thinking, taking the present situation and associating it with other remembered or imagined correlates. We might summarize this process by saying that *shu* is a contextualized doubt in search of a guiding idea to stabilize one's actions. *Shu* at its best requires a keen memory that recalls analogous situations, a penetrating intelligence that is able to make the most felicitous correlations, and a creative imagination that can provide a serial rehearsal of possible scenarios in anticipation of their consequences. This analogical process captured in a much-cited passage in the *Analects*:

> Correlating one's conduct with what is near at hand can be said to be the way of becoming consummate in one's conduct.

There is a role for cognition and deliberation in *shu* certainly, but we do not want to overly rationalize this process. *Shu* requires a holistic responsiveness. With *shu* there is perhaps an even more central role for an affective inquiry—a knowing through feeling—that requires a weighing of the circumstances with empathy and concern. Just as a critical skepticism can

在儒学经典中对角色伦理智慧与想象力做出核心强调的,当然是《中庸》对"恕"观念所做的阐述:

子曰:"道不远人。人之为道而远人,不可以为道。诗云:'伐柯伐柯,其则不远。'执柯以伐柯,睨而视之,犹以为远。故君子以人治人,改而止。忠恕违道不远,施诸己而不愿,亦勿施于人。"(《中庸》第十三章)

"仁道"不是远在天边、虚无缥缈之物,而是就在日常事务的"恕"与"忠"的践行之中实现。这段话及"伐柯"过程的意象,对践行"忠""恕"有重大指导效果。首先,人们指导自己行为的恰当方式,总是从身边存在的资源出发,直接从特殊、具体环境之处可得的资源中,类比地形成。再者,在这一过程中,没有什么单一原因性。虽然"伐柯"样式是近身的,但是这种样式与"伐柯"成品、原有样式与正在"伐"的具体的"柯"(斧柄)之间那种必须解决的差别,只能以细致观察、做出决断去消除。

become a matter of intelligent habit, so too can an empathetic responsiveness to others become a sedimented, spontaneous pattern of compassionate conduct. In fact, the evolution of a *shu* habitude lies in its potential to grow from a more deliberative exercise to become a kind of extemporaneous, unselfconscious moral artistry in one's interpersonal activities.

Certainly one of the most revealing passages in the canonical literature that stresses the central place of artistry and imagination in Confucian role ethics is the *Zhongyong* elaboration on this notion of *shu*:

The Master said, "The vision of the consummate life (*dao*) is not at all remote. If someone considers this consummate life to be something that is distant and inaccessible, they have taken a wrong turn. In the *Book of Odes* it says:

In hewing an axe handle, in hewing an axe handle—The model is not far away.

But in grasping one axe handle to hew another, if one only looks obliquely at the axe handle in one's hand, the two handles still seem far apart. Exemplary persons (*junzi*) in taking one person to work upon another relent only after having improved upon them. Putting oneself in the place of others (*shu*) and doing one's best on their behalf (*zhong*)

现有"伐柯"样式既有示范也有工具意义,新开出且有特质的"柯"(斧柄)并不完全是在现有样式上的雕琢。进一步说,现有"伐柯"样式本身,其实是为开出新成品所用的一种手段,只为造出一新工具而其自己作为其他物之样式。在这个"伐柯"例子中,具有效力的原因只有一种,即解决手段与目的之间的常有差别;"仁"的行为对"仁"行为的理想效果产生影响,成就它的是自己的"仁"。

在现有样式与新造型成品之间类比所具有的鲜活性,将它运用到不可繁而化简的做人方式中去,得到的观念表达就是"恕"。首先在人与人的相互交往中,绝不能斜视他人或心怀不信任。在互相影响中,这种影响产生于彼此的尊重方式以及在尊重方式里所包含的一定模式,这样在我们塑造对方、对方也塑造我们的情况下,要求我们具有最集中的精神以及对一切资源最充分的发挥——我们的记忆力、智力与想象力。在人世间,一个人的行为会对别人产生人格成长的效果,这一人格塑造过程的成品是"仁",成"仁"的他人又反过来塑造另外的

is not staying far from the proper way. 'Do not treat others as you yourself would not wish to be treated.'"

The vision of the consummate life (*dao*), far from referencing something distant and obscure, emerges out of the exercise of *shu* and *zhong* in the ordinary business of the day. This passage and its image of the process of shaping an axe handle is hugely instructive. First, the proper way of conducting oneself always emerges analogically from those resources close at hand—from what is immediately available in the particular, concrete circumstances. Still, there is nothing casual about this process. Although the pattern of the axe handle is close, the critical distance between the model and the product, between the established pattern and the particular axe handle that is presently being fashioned, can only be closed through painstaking scrutiny and resolve. The existing axe handle is both exemplar and instrument. The new and always unique axe handle is not only hewn on the model of the existing one, but further, the existing axe handle itself is the means that is used to shape the emerging product, only to produce an instrument that will itself serve as a model for others. In this example of crafting an axe handle, the formal and efficient causes are one and the same, collapsing the familiar distinction between means and ends. Consummate conduct effects the desired end of consummate conduct by itself

人。在整个过程中，手段与目的是呈现为一体的。我们行仁，为的也是行仁。

对于"尊重"，还有可进一步说明之点，这点可从《中庸》得出。在《中庸》与《论语》中，"恕"作为"设身处地"，表达了另一种特点，即"恕"是从消极意义而言的——"己所不欲，勿施于人"。这一"金律"的"消极意义"说法是谦虚性的；它不去做假设推定——人必须遵行某些客观和普世性的标准，这个标准是命令性的："你要人家怎样对待你，你就怎样对待人家。"正如"伐柯"用的是"样式"，而不是"模板"，与别人联系的人格塑造是一种引导性的融洽和谐，而不是强加的同质。不是简单性"复制"，而是需要很大程度的艺术造诣。的确，"推己及人"所需要的，是对"己"与"人"的差异性的敏感。反之，在不存在什么假设推定普世标准的情况下，出发点如果是认为一个人已经晓得对另一个人说什么才是最合适的，那么这是一种不尊重地看待他人的态度。我们要有开放与灵活的心态，要在如何最好地培养出一种关系上尽心，而这

being consummate.

The dynamics of analogizing between the existing pattern and the newly fashioned article when applied to the irreducibly social way of becoming human is captured conceptually by *shu*. First, in our interactions, we must not look askance at each other (*ni* 睨). We must get beyond viewing each other obliquely and with distrust. In the mutual shaping that occurs through both patterns of deference and the modeling that such patterns entail, we require the utmost focus and concentration and the fullest application of all of our resources: our memory and our intelligence as well as our imagination. In the human world, the conduct of one person serves as a model that shapes the conduct of others, where that process of being shaped eventuates in consummate persons who will in their turn shape others. In all of this, the means and the ends are the same. We act consummately in order to act consummately.

There is a further point with regard to deference that can be inferred from this *Zhongyong* text. In this passage and in the *Analects* too, *shu*, "putting oneself in the other's place," is given an alternative characterization: *Shu* is defined negatively as "do not impose on others what you yourself do not want." This "negative" version of the Golden Rule is modest; it does not presuppose that one has access to some objective and universal standard that would serve as warrant for "doing unto others as you would have them do unto you."

只能通过悉心地考虑对方的需要和所在具体环境可能性中实现。尽管如此，在我们努力发挥一切可能性发展与他人的关系时，"己所不欲，勿施于人"，这至少是开始的一个很好的切入点。不过，除此之外，人面对的是一个充满偶然变化的世界，是需要谋略与想象开发力的。

不过《中庸》这段文字还有更多意思。根据上面的引述，接下来讲的还是同一要点，即被视为"中庸"的观念——由人践行的具体的"仁"。《中庸》中有段文字描述直接的家庭角色与人伦修养出"恕"与"忠"的人格：

> 君子之道四，丘未能一焉：所求乎子，以事父，未能也；所求乎臣，以事君，未能也；所求乎弟，以事兄，未能也；所求乎朋友，先施之，未能也。庸德之行，庸言之谨，有所不足，不敢不勉，有余不敢尽。言顾行，行顾言，君子胡不慥慥尔。（《中庸》第十三章）

这里所讲的，就是人要在最直

Just as the hewing of the axe handle uses a model rather than a template, so the shaping of one person in relation to another is directed at an accommodating harmony rather than an imposed uniformity. Rather than mere replication an important degree of artistry is needed. Indeed, what is required in "putting oneself in the other's place" is the awareness that these are different places. Stated conversely, in the absence of some assumed universal standard, to begin from the presumption that one already knows what is most appropriate for someone else is disrespectful and condescending. Instead, one needs to be open and provisional, and to assume that deliberation on how to best grow a relationship can only be pursued through a careful consideration of the needs of this specific person and the possibilities of these specific circumstances. Even so, in our search for a way to optimize the possibilities in this relationship, to refrain from doing to someone else what we do not want done to us would at the very least be a good place to start. Beyond this rather obvious beginning, however, there is a world of contingencies that require thoughtful and imaginative exploration.

But this same *Zhongyong* passage has more to say. As in the section cited above, here again in what follows, the locus of the discussion is identified as the "everyday" (*yong* 庸): the concrete consummate life as it is lived. And here again this text associates the cultivation of a capacity to *shu* and to *zhong* with immediate

接的家庭与社群伦理关系中，采取恰宜的"敬"的人格修养取向。《论语》中有很多孔子恭敬对待他人的例子，不同情况下涉及不同的人。在几个不同场合，心怀困惑的弟子请教孔子"仁"为何意，虽然孔子每次的回答都是"恕"，但都考虑到不同学生各自的情况，给出适合于该学生的回答。

这种做事情必须要对实际情形有恰如其分的反应的做法，又一次明显地体现在冉有和子路同时询问"怎样为仁"这个问题时，孔子给他们的是相反的教导这件事上。之后有人问为什么会对同一问题给出明显矛盾的回答，孔子明确指出二人的不同情况："求也退，故进之；由也兼人，故退之。"（《论语·先进》）

事实上，因为"恕"必须要理解成为欣欣向荣的社会培养出人与人之间的相敬风气，孔子对此看得很重。在社会中每个人都置身自己角色和关系的活泼动态环境之中，这些角色与关系的践行只有在人与人之间的相互恭敬条件下才能实现积极地驱动。当学生在课堂上对老师传给的智慧怀有恭敬之心时，激活的是学生自己的学习潜能。当老

family roles and relations:

> Of the four requirements of the exemplary person's consummate vision, I am not yet able to satisfy even one of them, I am not yet able to serve my father as I would expect my son to serve me; I am not yet able to serve my lord as I would expect my minister to serve me; I am not yet able to serve my elder brother as I would expect my younger brother to serve me; I am not yet able to be first in treating my friends as I myself would wish them to treat me.
>
> Where there are deficiencies in my everyday moral conduct and in my everyday speech, I must make every effort to address them; where there arc excesses, I must make every effort to constrain myself. Speech that is accountable to conduct; conduct that is accountable to what is said—How could the exemplary person do other than earnestly aspire to such behavior?

At issue here is one's cultivated propensity for appropriate deference in ones most immediate family and community relations. There are many examples in the *Analects* of Confucius himself exhibiting proper deference to others. One consideration in each novel situation is the specific people involved. As I have noted above, on several different occasions

师对学生在课堂做出的互动加以重视时，课堂气氛就会进一步激发且热烈，因而呈现教学相长，学生与老师均能备受裨益。

（《儒家角色伦理学：一套特色伦理学词汇》，第 215—220 页）

puzzled students ask Confucius what he means by the expression *ren*, and each time he acts on his *shu* disposition by being responsive to the specific profile of the individual student in giving an answer he deems appropriate to that student.

This need to tailor one's responses to the concrete situation is again captured nicely in the conflicting advice Confucius gives to Ranyou and Zilu when they ask him about acting on what they have learned. On being queried by a third party about what are clearly contradictory answers to the same question, Confucius simply references their different needs: "Ranyou is reticent, and so I urged him on. But Zilu has the energy of two, and so I sought to rein him in."

In fact, it is because *shu* must be understood as the evolving patterns of deference necessary for a flourishing community that Confucius invests such singular importance in it. In a world constituted of unique individuals located within a dynamic matrix of roles and relationships, the performance of these roles and relationships can only be effectively driven by the giving and the receiving of deference. When students in the classroom defer to the wisdom of their teacher, it activates the possibilities of their learning. When the teacher defers to important interventions on the part of the students, the class is further motivated, and everyone including the teacher is the beneficiary.

(*Confucian Role Ethics: A Vocabulary,* pp. 195-200)

善

　　"善"字通常译为"good",它由两个部分构成。在上面的"羊"这个偏旁部首与"牺牲"(sacrifice)有关。在其他一些类似构成的字如"义(義)"和"美"中,"羊"则意味着"吉利"(auspiciousness)。在下面的部分是"口"。根据《说文》这个字的古体最初是两个"言"部首。正如其他许多包括"口"和"言"这两个部首的古代中国哲学术语一样,看起来作为"吉利"的"善"是有效沟通的结果。

　　尽管"善"常常译为"good",但是,这种理解却有不利之处,即将关系性的东西本质化了。"善"在根本上是情境性的。它首先是"felicity"(恰当)或"efficacy"(效力)。它是"good to"、"good for"、"good with"、"good in"或"good at"。在翻译中,我们将其翻译为"felicity"或"efficacy",是要努力保持"善"的这种关系性的意义。正如"义"一样,"善"的这种理解说明了古典儒学的审美属性。在古典儒学中,善的获得是在繁荣社群的

Felicity/Efficacy

The character *shan*, conventionally translated "good," is composed of two elements. The "sheep (*yang* 羊)" radical is associated with "sacrifice," and, as in other similarly constructed characters such as "appropriate (*yi* 義)", and "beautiful(*mei* 美)," suggests "auspiciousness." The second element on the bottom is the "mouth (*kou* 口)," that, according to the *Shuowen* lexicon, in an archaic version of the character, was originally two "speech (*yan* 言)" radicals. Like many of the classical Chinese philosophical terms that contain the "mouth" and "speech" elements, it would seem that auspiciousness is the product of effective communication.

Although *shan* is most frequently translated as "good," such a rendering has the disadvantage of essentializing what is fundamentally relational. *Shan* is radically contextual. It is first and foremost "felicity" or "efficacy." It is to be "good to" or "good for" or "good with" or "good in" or "good at." In the translation, we have struggled to retain this relational sense of *Shan*, translating it as "felicity" or "efficacy." This understanding of *Shan*, like "appropriateness (*yi* 義)," highlights the fundamentally aesthetic nature of classical Confucianism, wherein the common good is achieved in the productive relationships

富有成果的各种关系之中。人或者社群的品格或精神气质是一种持续性的审美成就。

（《切中伦常：〈中庸〉的新诠与新译》，第 93—94 页）

of a thriving community. The character or ethos of person or community is an ongoing aesthetic achievement.

(*Focusing the Familiar: A Translation and Philosophical Interpretation of the Zhongyong,* pp. 75-76)

友

在儒家关系网之内，朋友之情具有转化的力量。这种转化力量只有在将其作为一种"家"本身的延伸与扩展理解时才能够恰当解释。作为儒家"家为中心"伦理的一个层面，"友"是一种确定、有时是补偿性的意义与价值来源。直接家庭关系一般都是出生就有的、血缘性的，而朋友关系的结成是偶然的，必然是多样的和刻意选择的。我们应该可以将"友谊"看为门道，老朋友们走这个门道进入这个家，加入这个家，为这个家的各种关系层次，增添明显深刻的含义。

对于儒学而言，朋友的重要性在于它的作用好似开放的通道，使得从港湾性安全平静的家能通往外部，与更具不确定性且时而需花大气力的社会、政治和文化世界衔接。

Friendship

Within the web of Confucian relations, intimate friendships take on a transformative force that can only be adequately explained by understanding them as an extension and amplification of the family itself. As a dimension of a Confucian family-centered ethic, friendship serves as a definite, sometimes compensatory source of meaning and value. While immediate family relations are usually a matter of birth and blood, developed friendships are contingent, and entail diversity and deliberate choice. We might describe the role of friendship as a doorway through which erstwhile outsiders enter to join and add a remarkable depth to the ranks of family relations.

The vital importance of friendship for Confucianism lies in its function as an open conduit that leads from the security and stability of one's own family out into the more uncertain and sometimes taxing social, political, and cultural realm. When Zilu asks after the makings of a scholar-official, Confucius says

当子路问"何如斯可谓之士矣",孔子只是答:

> 切切、偲偲、怡怡如也。可谓士矣。朋友切切、偲偲,兄弟怡怡。(《论语·子路》)

在这里孔子想到的是朋友可能在某种意义上比亲情关系更要难做。从亲属那里得到关爱与呵护,人可想当然地接受,而在社会事务上,成功的人生对关系则要求有更高的觉察与原则性。但是,从一生的长期友谊关系上所获得的受益切实是巨大的,它为人引来使个人成长得以实现的非同小可、更深的资源。在这样的儒家思想中,"交友"是十分平白意义的参与到彼此的"交"上去,直到让友谊本身成为最具体实在的东西,而使关系获得发展的这些"个人"则会越来越成为一种抽象的存在。

在选择朋友上,孔子强调:"君子……无友不如己者。"这种态度表明孔子对人生的认识。他认为个人品格的成长或消退,都是"人活的是关系"对人的影响。我们不禁又要问:"富有意义"的友谊,这意 plainly:

> Persons who are critical and demanding, yet amicable can be called scholar officials. Persons need to be critical and demanding with their friends, and amicable and acquiescent with their older and younger brothers.

Confucius thus anticipates that friendships can in some ways be more challenging than intimate family relations. One can fairly take for granted the love and protection of one's immediate family, while successful life in the public sphere requires a higher degree of discrimination and a more critical sense of engagement. But then again the dividends to be reaped from enduring friendships over a lifetime are truly substantial, introducing into the project of personal growth resources that provide a deeper degree of difference. In this Confucian tradition, to "make" friends is quite literally to participate in the "making" of each other to the extent that it is the friendship itself that becomes what is most concrete, while the "individuals" who participate in the growth of the relationship become increasingly an abstraction from it.

In choosing one's friends, Confucius is emphatic:"Exemplary persons ... do not have as a friend anyone who is not as good as they are." This declaration is a clear acknowledgment of his understanding that personal growth and diminution are a function of associated living. It prompts us to ask again: For Confucius, where does the meaning in a "meaningful" friendship

义从何而来？在柏拉图—基督教世界观中，"意义"具有超越性来源，"友谊"是工具化的，是献身一个共同的目的。柏拉图论述友谊的《斐德罗篇》的结论是：朋友是有共同性的人。而当"人们的共同性"是一种朝向超越之善的爱时，他们是真朋友。同样，对基督教而言，"菲利亚"（*philia*）作为朋友间或者亲人间之爱，是附属于"阿伽培"（*agape*）——对超越上帝之爱的；对上帝之爱通过的渠道是他所创造之物彼此之间的爱。

亚里士多德与柏拉图一样，将人的共同点视为友谊的基础。在这两种情况中，自给自足都有很高价值。在亚里士多德看来，有一种低级层次的偶然性友谊，是以功利与快乐感为目的的；但是"真"朋友是比照之下的"另一个自己"或者"第二个自己"，因为它们都反映一个人自己能力特质与心灵智力活动，这是一切人共有的认同之点。亚里士多德确实使用了"镜子"的比喻，用来阐明为什么真朋友的相同能力特质是个自知之源。他赞同"冥思式朋友"比实际型的更高；具有这种能力性质的友谊并不多，具有同

come from? In a Platonic-come-Christian world wherein meaning has a transcendent reference, friendship is instrumentalized as a commitment to a common end. The conclusion of the reflection on friendship in the *Phaedrus* is that friends hold all things in common. And when what they hold in common is an *eros* directed toward the transcendent Good, they are true friends. Similarly, for the Christian, *philia* as the love among friends and family members is subordinated to *agape*, the love of a transcendent God channeled through His creatures as their love for one another.

Aristotle, like Plato, takes commonality as the basis for friendship. In both cases, there is a high value invested in self-sufficiency. For Aristotle, there is a lower level of incidental friendship that seeks utility and pleasure. But true friends by contrast are "another self" or "a second self" because they mirror one's own virtuous character and the intellectual activity of *nous* that is identical in all people. Indeed, Aristotle appeals to the mirror metaphor to illustrate how the real friend in being similarly virtuous is a source of self-knowledge. He allows that "contemplative friendships" are higher than the practical kind, and that such virtue friendships are rare; they are only available to an elite circle of equally virtuous people. There is a superiority of the theoretical life over the practical, and of the speculative vision over daily moral activities. Thus, for Aristotle, the eternal truth that can be grasped by *nous* must be given priority over friendship, even when it means turning one's back on one's

样能力特质的人只是一个小圈子的精英们。理论之于实际生活，思辨性视野之于日常道德活动，具有一种高尚性。所以对亚里士多德来说，可被心灵捕捉的永恒真实，必须给予超然于友谊的优先地位，甚至是当它意味着人必须对自己的老师也要反戈一击时，就像他对柏拉图那样：

> 我们或许必得考虑普适之善，彻底弄清它的含义，尽管这一探求是爬坡之径，因为事实是：这种"形式"（"forms"，本体之真实——译者注）是我们"自己朋友"提出……虽然二者皆可贵，虔诚之心要求我们将真实置于朋友之上。

有点像他们的古希腊同行，孔子及其弟子也认为朋友在某种意义上有共同点的看法：

> 曾子曰：君子以文会友，以友辅仁。（《论语·颜渊》）

沈美华发现孔子与亚里士多德在"朋友"观念上，有许多点都是相近的，对二者的重要类似点做了

own teacher—in his case, Plato:

> We had perhaps better consider the universal good and discuss thoroughly what is meant by it, although such an inquiry is made an uphill one by the fact that the Forms have been introduced by friends of our own... While both are dear, piety requires us to honor truth above our friends.

For Confucius, like his Greek cousins, friendships are in some ways a matter of common cause:

> Master Zeng said, "Exemplary persons attract friends through their refinement, and through these friends promote consummate conduct (ren)."

May Sim has identified many resonances between the Confucian and Aristotelian models of friendship, taking careful account of their important similarities. But beyond these commonalities, it must be allowed that there is significant distance between the accounts of friendship we find in Aristotle and Confucius. We must take into account the metaphysical and biological uniformities in Aristotle's foundational individualism, the self-sufficiency of final and unchanging first principles and causes that are the object of contemplation, and the centrality of rationality as the ground in making moral decisions. For Confucius, contra Plato and Aristotle, the ultimate source of

认真阐述。但是除了这些共性之外，也必须要考虑到亚里士多德和孔子关于友谊的观点还是有很大距离的。亚里士多德是根本性的个人主义，其中蕴含着：人具有形而上学与生物学同一性，遵循终极与不变原始法则以始因的独立性为思考对象，并进行以理性中心性为基础的道德抉择。而孔子与柏拉图和亚里士多德不一样，认为朋友之意义的根本不是来源于外在，而是友谊本身发展过程的呈现。朋友的人品尊贵是各有千秋的，也是由于彼此不同，才具有协同共进的机会。"君子和而不同，小人同而不和"可谓是儒家友谊观的一个经典论断。当卫公孙朝问于子贡曰"仲尼焉学"，子贡的回答很有包罗性：

> 文武之道，未坠于地，在人。贤者识其大者，不贤者识其小者，莫不有文武之道焉。夫子焉不学？而亦何常师之有？（《论语·子张》）

我们得到的启示是，每个人都不同，孔子向每个人学习，有的学得多，有的学得少，对绝大多数与

meaning is not external, but emerges through the nurturing process of the friendship itself. And it is the ways in which friends are qualitatively superior to and different from each other that provides the opportunity for a collaborative advancement. Confucian friendship is a classic illustration of the mantra: "Exemplary persons seek harmony not conformity; petty persons are the opposite." When Zigong was asked who Confucius had as his teacher, his reply is inclusive:

> The moral vision (*dao*) of Kings Wen and Wu has not collapsed utterly—it lives on in the people. Those of superior character have grasped the greater part of it, while those of lesser quality have grasped a bit. Everyone has something of Wen and Wu's way in them. Who then did the Master not learn from? Again, how could there have been a single constant teacher for him?

The message here is that since each person is different, Confucius had something—sometimes more, sometimes less—to learn from everyone. This generous appreciation of both the positive and negative possibilities that most relations with other people provide us for moral development is made abundantly clear:

> The Master said, "In strolling together with just two other persons, I am bound to find a teacher in their company. Identifying their strengths, I follow them,

他人关系，既有正面也有负面考虑，这样的宽宏大度有利于一个人的道德提高。孔子在很多地方都传达着这种思想：

> 子曰："三人行，必有我师焉。择其善者而从之，其不善者而改之。"（《论语·述而》）

个人成长是亲朋关系达到很积极的状态导致的结果。在向外寻求和发展丰富含义的友谊方面，我们有空间、有自由度，这与我们的亲属血缘关系性质不一样。孔子有强烈的意识，认为发展、扩大人们的友谊，可以大力弥补亲属关系的局限性，这对个人成长切实是个机会。但是如果择友不当，朋友也可能是有损自己成长的源头。他提出：

> 益者三友，损者三友。友直，友谅，友多闻，益矣。友便辟，友善柔，友便佞，损矣。（《论语·季氏》）

孔子这里的意思是，"友"在家庭亲属关系的外围开辟了一个疏松环境，这样为更有意识、有意志地

and identifying their weaknesses, I reform myself accordingly."

Personal growth is a function of the quality of the specific productive relations achieved among family and friends. In seeking out and developing meaningful friendships, we have latitude and a degree of freedom that is not characteristic of our relations with blood relatives. Confucius is keenly aware that broadening and expansive friendships, compensating to an important degree for family constraints, can serve as a real opportunity for personal growth. Poorly chosen, however, these erstwhile friendships can also be a source of personal diminution. He observes:

> Having three kinds of friends will be a source of personal improvement; having three other kinds of friends will be a source of personal injury. One stands to be improved by friends who are true, who make good on their word, and who are broadly informed; one stands to be injured by friends who are ingratiating, who feign compliance, and who are glib talkers.

Confucius' point here is that friendship provides a porous border on the institution of family that allows for a more deliberate and purposeful shaping of one's own personal relations, and hence, one's own person. These voluntarily chosen relations are still to be construed as familial, and yet they have a

造就有个人特殊性的关系，也为具体个人人格提供了可能。"友"是自愿选择的关系，但仍被理解为是家庭性的，而且它有潜力，可为个人提供经常超出正式亲属纽带的成长意义与复杂性。

"友"的共同性与重合性，包含在"朋"这个表示"友谊"的汉字中。在甲骨文中，这个字的原形是一个两串贝壳的货币单位：▨。后来它所表达的具体含义是同一师傅的"同门"或"师兄弟"。"同学"和"学长/姐"的称呼直到现在还继续流行，不过它们的儒家含义强调的是互相依赖关系和"不同"，而不是同一性和自足。"友谊"作为一种发挥想象力的成长机会，是建构在关系之中的，这正是使用频率大一些的"友"呼唤的意思。"友"字在甲骨文中是两只手▨，有时两只手还牵在一起▨，喻示一种共同友谊纽带。"友"起初与"右"同源，即"右手"，其引申含义为受尊崇。它的进一步同源字是"佑"（"护佑"）和"祐"（"福祐"）。将这些连带关系结合着看，我们就能领会到，一个真正的朋友是一个被尊崇和恭敬的对象，宛如助人成

potential to provide a degree of growth and complexity that can often go beyond our more formal family bonds.

Commonality and overlap is covered in the vocabulary of friendship by the term *peng* 朋. In the oracle bone script this character originally identified a denomination of two strings of cowry shell currency as ▨ and later came to mean "peer" or "comrade" in the specific sense of being students of the same master. Although the power of the role of "classmate"(*tongxue* 同學)and "student older brother/sister" (*xuexiong/jie* 學兄/姐)continues down to the present day, the emphasis in Confucian friendship is on interdependence and difference rather than on sameness and self-sufficiency. Friendship as an opportunity for creative growth is built into the associations that the more frequently used term for "friend"—*you* 友 —evokes. The oracle bone version of this character has "two hands" ▨ that are sometimes joined together ▨, suggesting a common bond of friendship. *You* is first cognate with *you* 右, "the right hand," and by extension, with what is to be honored and revered. It is further cognate with *you* 佑 "to assist," and *you* 祐 "a blessing." Combining these several associations, we might observe that a true friend is an object of deference to be honored and esteemed as a blessing that assists in one's personal growth.

A second philological correlation for "friend" (*you* 友) is its cognate and homophonous relationship with *you* 有, "to have, to be around (=wealth)," a term that also appears as a loan character for it. *You* 有 is depicted suggestively

长的福佑。

"友"还有第二个语言学相通字"有",它与"有"(富有)是同源也同音关系。"有"也作为"友"的通假字出现。"有"在青铜器铭文中,是以尊贵的右手抓着一块肉,表示一种农业社会罕见、贵重及有时神性的物品形象:🤚。这里的启示:真正的朋友讲的就是亲近,与你咫尺不离,是蕴藏个人生活日益深厚意义的资源。

孔子对"友"有严格的具体定义,这体现在两个跟他关系很近的学生——子夏和子张对于"与人交"的理解有分歧的对话中。孔子过世数年后,两个学生各成为自己一派的掌门,对孔子说的话及他当时的意思是什么,各有解释:

> 子夏之门人问交于子张。子张曰:"子夏云何?"对曰:"子夏曰:'可者与之,其不可者拒之。'"(《论语·子张》)

从这段对话看,似乎子夏对"交"的理解保留了孔子本人交友的严格选择性。但是这样的狭义理解遇到了争执。子张不同意,指出:

on the bronzes specifically as the honored right hand grasping a piece of meat, a scarce, valuable, and sometimes sacred commodity in an agrarian community: 🤚. Again, the implication is that a true friend is a matter of proximity—someone who is there for you—and a resource whence to garner increased meaning in one's life.

That Confucius insists upon this restricted and specific use of "friend" (*you*) is suggested in a disagreement on the meaning of "establishing relations with others" (*jiao* 交) that involves two of his closest proteges, Zixia and Zizhang. In the years following the death of the Master, these two disciples matured into patriarchs in their own right and had their own interpretations of what Confucius had said and what he had meant by it:

> The disciples of Zixia asked Zizhang about establishing relations with others. Zizhang queried, "What has Zixia told you?" They replied, "Associate with those who are worthy of your efforts; spurn those who are not."

It would seem from Zixia's definition of "establishing relations with others" that he is retaining the strictness and the discrimination with which Confucius himself approaches friendship. But such a narrow reading does not go unchallenged. Zizhang counters:

> This is different from what I have learned. Exemplary persons exalt

异乎吾所闻：君子尊贤而容众，嘉善而矜不能。我之大贤与，于人何所不容？我之不贤与，人将拒我，如之何其拒人也？(《论语·子张》)

我们现在对孔子之"交"态度的两种很不同的理解，如何去明辨——如果想想两个弟子各自的性格气质将很有帮助。《论语》及其他典籍，常有提及二人性情和言谈举止之处。

子张因无条件的利他主义，时常受到孔子的批评，说他注意外表而不注重实质，使用语言不确切。有一段讲道：

子张问善人之道。子曰："不践迹，亦不入于室。"(《论语·先进》)

在这里，孔子特别批评子张的是他对有德君子——那些可称为真朋友的人不够恭敬，这样导致自己将不会有与人建立君子朋友关系的机会，这种关系是通向建立真正人格的大门。

子夏则是另外一种人，文采飞

those of superior character and are accommodating of everyone, praise those who are truly efficacious, and are sympathetic with those who are less so. If in comparison with others, I am truly superior in character, who am I not able to accommodate? If I am not superior in the comparison, and people are thus going to spurn me, what basis do I have to spurn others?

In evaluating these two very different interpretations of Confucius' attitude to establishing relationships, it is helpful to recall the profile of these two students that emerges from frequent reference in the *Analects* and elsewhere.

Zizhang with his free-wheeling altruism is repeatedly rebuked by Confucius for paying more attention to appearances than to substance, and for using language without due care. In one telling passage:

Zizhang asked about the way of the truly efficacious person (*shanren* 善人). The Master replied, "Not following in the footsteps of others, one does not gain entrance to the inner sanctum."

Confucius, is here criticizing Zizhang specifically for not deferring sufficiently to moral exemplar— those who would be true friends—thereby precluding the possibility of his ever having access to those relations that open the door to real personal worth.

扬，是孔子学生当中被老师夸赞有学问次数最多的。在儒家传统中，他是一个对儒家经典传承有重要贡献的人。子夏是《论语》后五章的中心人物，他十分强调学的重要性。为弥补他可能给人的学究印象，子夏提出，在"仁"方面做得好，才是学问的真正意义。其实连孔子都承认他本人从与子夏谈话中学到了不少东西。头脑中有了子张、子夏两个人的基本印象，我们就会想到，不少人可能赞成子张的逻辑，倾向于认为对"友"意义的恰当表述似乎就是他那种平等主义与广泛包容的观点。但是子夏强调友谊的重大意义是有益个人成长，才更准确传达了孔子本人关于交友的思想。

不过如果说孔子真是从子夏那里学到不少东西，那么他承认的是从颜回（他最爱的学生）那里学到了更多。在《论语》中，孔子从头至尾都反复特殊地提到颜回，给他很高评价，而且唯一给这个杰出学生以"仁"和"真好学"的评价。其实，在好学方面他甚至把颜回置于比他自己和所有其他人还高的地位：

Zixia, on the other hand, is a man of letters, and being credited more than any other of Confucius' proteges for his scholarship, he is remembered by tradition as having played a major role in the transmission of the Confucian classics. Zixia has a central place in the last five chapters of the *Analects* where he underscores the importance of learning. Trying to compensate for his image as a pendent, Zixia insists that virtuosity in one's personal relationships is what learning is all about. Indeed, Confucius allows that he himself has gained a great deal from his conversations with Zixia. With these two profiles in mind, then, we can speculate that while many of us might admire the logic of Zizhang and prefer his seemingly more egalitarian and inclusive sentiments on the proper expression of what it means to be a friend, it is probably Zixia who, in underscoring the vital function of friendship for the possibility of personal growth, is transmitting the more genuine understanding of what Confucius himself expected from friendship.

But if Confucius has learned a great deal from Zixia, he has on his own admission learned much more from his favorite disciple, Yan Hui. Throughout the *Analects*, Confucius repeatedly singles out Yan Hui for high praise, according this one exceptional student alone the description of being consummate in his conduct (*ren*) and of being truly fond of learning (*haoxue*). Indeed, he places Yan Hui far above himself and everyone else in his capacity for learning:

子谓子贡曰："女与回也孰愈？"对曰："赐也何敢望回？回也闻一以知十，赐也闻一以知二。"子曰："弗如也！吾与女弗如也。"（《论语·公冶长》）

当然，这里的"学"有直接的道德与宗教感，是指通过勤勉修养的个人成长，以及在处理齐家理政关系方面表现的卓越才能，孔子本人之于其学生，一点也不显得神秘和超然，而在教导学生的局限性方面，十分坦诚，他说：

二三子以我为隐乎？吾无隐乎尔。吾无行而不与二三子者，是丘也。（《论语·述而》）

同时孔子也提出，人值得尊重的是他对社会的贡献，而不是他的年纪大。他鼓励对尚未显露头角的后生要给予适当的尊重：

子曰："后生可畏，焉知来者之不如今也？四十、五十而无闻焉，斯亦不足畏也已。"（《论语·子罕》）

The Master remarked to Zigong, "Comparing yourself with Yan Hui, who is the better person?" Zigong replied, "How dare I have such expectations. With Yan Hui, learning one thing he will know ten; with me, learning one thing I will know two." The Master said, "You are not his match. Neither you nor I are a match for Yan Hui."

Of course, "learning" here has an immediate moral and religious reference to personal growth achieved through assiduous cultivation and a demonstrated relational virtuosity in family and community. Confucius himself, far from being mysterious and aloof with his students, is candid about the limits of the mentorship that he can offer them:

The Master said, "My young friends, you think that I have something hidden away, but I do not. There is nothing I do that I do not share with you—this is the person I am."

At the same time, Confucius insists that it is one's contribution to the community rather than one's seniority that is deserving of deference. And he encourages an appropriate respect for the as-yet undisclosed potential and possibilities that might well attend the next generation:

The Master said, "The young should be held in high esteem. After all, how do

鉴于孔子对于其时代人的批评态度，以及对学生超群表现的恰当到位赞许，我们可以领略到，他对导师性友谊的严格定义是基于一种更实质性人的不同，而不是什么等级的高低。毕竟是，好老师从好学生身上学的多。我们必能总结出：就孔子身边情况而言，他承认学生也是丰富意义友谊的源泉。他对颜回极其赞赏的态度，或许就是这种情况：

> 颜渊死，子哭之恸。从者曰："子恸矣！"曰："有恸乎？非夫人之为恸而谁为？"（《论语·先进》）

（《儒家角色伦理学：一套特色伦理学词汇》，第128—135页）

we know that those yet to come will not surpass our contemporaries? It is only when one reaches forty or fifty years of age and yet has done nothing of note that we should withhold our esteem."

Given Confucius' critical attitude toward his contemporaries and his judicious admiration for the ways in which his students excel, we can surmise that his strict understanding of a mentoring friendship is more a matter of substantial difference than it is of hierarchical superiority. After all, since good teachers learn much from good students, we would have to conclude that on his own premises, Confucius would allow that students too can be a source of meaningful friendship. This would certainly seem to have been the case in his fervent admiration for Yan Hui:

> When Yan Hui died, the Master grieved for him with sheer abandon. His followers cautioned, "Sir, you grieve with such abandon." The Master replied, "I grieve with abandon? If I don't grieve with abandon for him, then for whom?"

(*Confucian Role Ethics: A Vocabulary*, pp.114-121)

认识论

智／知

无论是否有下面的"曰"这个部首,"智"(或"知")通常都译为"knowledge"、"wisdom"或"to know"。不过,我们常常将"智"翻译为"to realize"。在英文中,"to realize"具有和"to know"、"knowledge"同样强度的认识论意义上的内涵。你可以说你"相信"你所喜欢的任何东西,但是,在最为真实的意义上,你只能说"know"或"realize"某种东西。此外,"realize"强调"智"的实行性的意义(performative meaning),即需要去创造一种境况并"使之成为真实"(make it real)。进而言之,将"智"翻译为"realize",我们认为我们恰当地注意到了通常被描述为"知行合一"这一儒家的格言。古代汉语中"知"的这种实践的蕴涵排除了我们所熟悉的那种在英文中可以发现的知识(knowledge)和

To Realize (*Zhi*)

Zhi (知), with or without the "to speak" radical 曰 beneath it, is usually translated as "knowledge," "wisdom," and "to know." We often translate it as "to realize." "To realize" has the same strong epistemic connotations as the original associations of "to know" or "knowledge" in English. You may say you believe whatever you like, but you can only know or realize something in the truest sense, if that something is or becomes the case. In addition, "realize" underscores the performative meaning of *zhi*—the need to author a situation and "make it real." Furthermore, by translating *zhi* as to *realize*, we believe we are paying proper attention to the Confucian precept generally described as "the continuity of knowledge and action (*zhixing heyi* 知行合一)"—that is, "to know is to authenticate in action." This practical entailment of the classical Chinese *zhi* precludes the familiar distinction between knowledge and wisdom that we find in English.

当"智"名义上作为"wisdom"或"the wise"出现时,《中庸》继续着那种在《论语》中被大量运用的语义学的思想关联(semantic association)。在儒家的文献中,"智"反复与"仁"相并列,这一点排除了任何事实与价值的区分(fact/value distinction)。认识一个世界并在其中保持明智,也就是以与"那种"相对的"这种"方式来托付这个世界。因此,认知具有非常真实的规范性的含义(normative implication)。在界定这种创造性的过程时,《中庸》第二十五章的观察是这样的:

诚者非自成己而已也,所以成物也。成己,仁也;成物,知也。

这一段话让我们想起《论语》第六篇《雍也》第二十三章,其中,"知"和"仁"也被作为世界形成过程中(world-making)的共生的成就(symbiotic achievements)。《论语》中的这段话是这样的:

子曰:"知者乐水,仁者

When *zhi* appears nominally as "wisdom" or "the wise," the *Zhongyong* continues a semantic association that is richly exploited in the *Analects*. *Zhi* occurs repeatedly in the Confucian literature in juxtaposition with "authoritative person/conduct (*ren* 仁)," precluding any fact/value distinction. To know a world and thus be wise in it is to recommend it in *this* as opposed to *that* way. Thus, knowing has very real normative implications. In defining this creative process, *Zhongyong* 25 observes:

> But creativity is not simply the self-consummating of one's own person; it is what consummates events. Consummating oneself is authoritative conduct (*ren* 仁); consummating other events is wisdom (*zhi* 知).

This passage is reminiscent of *Analects* 6.23 in which "wisdom" and "authoritative conduct" are also presented as symbiotic achievements in world-making:

> The Master said, "The wise (*zhi* 知) enjoy water; those authoritative in their conduct (*ren* 仁) enjoy mountains. The wise are active; the authoritative are still. The wise find enjoyment; the authoritative are

乐山；知者动，仁者静；知者乐，仁者寿。"

"智"始终蕴涵着恰如其分和恰到好处（appropriateness to context）。因此，一个人实现自我的过程，同时也就是在实现其境况。

（《切中伦常：〈中庸〉的新诠与新译》第103—104页）

如果把"仁"理解为对待关系的艺术，就可立刻与"智"（活得聪明）形成一种互为性的联系，而且这样也就没有什么奇怪，这两个词语，就如同雨水冲刷山脉，山脉造成雨水，在儒家语词上，从来是不可分的。

　　子曰："知者乐水，仁者乐山；知者动，仁者静；知者乐，仁者寿。"（《论语·雍也》）。

孔夫子还认为，"仁者安仁，知者利仁。"（《论语·里仁》）

"知"字，或者字形下边多了表达"说"的"曰"或"太阳、日子"的"日"的"智"字，在英文里一般被译为"knowing""knowledge"或

long-enduring."

Wisdom always entails appropriateness to context (see *Analects* 6.22). Thus, in realizing oneself, one at the same time brings realization to one's situation.
(*Focusing the Familiar: A Translation and Philosophical Interpretation of the Zhongyong,* pp. 84-85)

Ren understood as relational virtuosity has an immediate correlation with living wisely (*zhi* 知), and so it ought to come as no surprise that these two terms, like the rain water that shapes the mountains and the mountains that occasion the rain, are never far apart in the Confucian vocabulary:

The Master said, "The wise (*zhi* 知) enjoy water; those consummate in their conduct(*ren* 仁) enjoy mountains. The wise are active; the consummate are still. The wise find enjoyment; the consummate are long-enduring."

For Confucius, "Consummate persons (*ren*) find satisfaction in acting consummately; wise (*zhi*) persons flourish in it."
The character *zhi* 知 , with or without the "speaking" (*yue* 曰)or "sun, day"

209

"wisdom"。"知"还指"知己"，是将"知意味着什么"的问题人格化，将它作为"可信赖的人际关系形态"，这种关系形态作为家国之人可智慧地生活在一起的条件。从"智"的甲骨文字形"𤔲"去探讨"智"的语义，一种解释是，一个大人以口头或文字形式向下一代传授智慧。"智"还有一个甲骨文字形是"𤔲"，而一些晚期青铜铭文"智"或"知"的字形是"𤔲"："矢"和"口"；"口"以及表示交流意思的其他字如"言""示""耳"和"心"等，是经典中国哲学重要术语出现次数很多，却不是最多的字。与"曰"的语义一起存在于"智"字中，这种结合关系反映着作为社会的、交流的"知"的重要性。其实，欧洲著名语言学家高本汉，或许受到一些甲骨文不同字形的启发，推测"智"字中的"矢"原本是指代"人"的。如果这一说法正确，那么"智"就包含了社会学知识的范畴，而不是什么与世隔绝的知识。鉴于儒家的"人"具有不可简约的社会性，所以所知范畴不是个体人之所知，而是社会之所知，这样"知"作为实用智慧，是作为一种社会幸福的直接

(*ri* 日) signifier beneath it as *zhi* 智, is usually translated as "knowing, knowledge, wisdom." *Zhi* 知 also means "an intimate or friend," thus putting a human face on what it means to know as "a pattern of relations one can trust in" that allows the community to live wisely together. In analyzing the etymology of the character *zhi* 智 as it appears on the oracle bones 𤔲, one version has been interpreted as a big person handing wisdom down to the younger generation both orally and on written documents. On other oracle bones 𤔲 and some of the later bronzes 𤔲, 智 / 知 is composed of an arrow (*shi* 矢) and a mouth (*kou* 口). This "mouth" element and other related ways of indicating communicating such as "speaking" (*yan* 言), "showing" (*shi* 示), "listening" (*er* 耳), and "thinking and feeling" (*xin* 心) appear in many, if not most, of the key philosophical terminologies in classical Chinese philosophy. Together with the "speaking" (*yue* 曰) semantic indicator in "wisdom" (*zhi* 智), this association with speaking reflects the importance of the social, communicative aspect of knowing. In fact, the distinguished philologist, Bernhard Karlgren, perhaps persuaded by some of the oracle bone variants, speculates that the "arrow" element in the character *zhi* was originally "persons" (*ren* 人), which if true reinforces the sense that *zhi* entails

资源被感知的。

"智"的社会层面性引出第二种看法:"智"是具有改良含义的,它所求的是改善世界。孔子说:

> 知之者不如好之者,好之者不如乐之者。(《论语·雍也》)

这里的"知",当然有认知层面的意思。但是对这个认知的理解,必须是一种延伸出去的意义,且已经修养为沟通的性质,人之乐由此而出。导引之下、目的性强的知识,比起简单性认知,是受到推崇的;而事实上有益于家国社群享有欢乐的知识是更好的。斯宾诺莎《伦理学》的最后一个命题说"福佑不是'德'的回报而是'德'本身",如果我们对这句话做点随意改动,我们可能会说:幸福不是智慧生活的回报,而是智慧本身。也许更确切一点,我们应该说,幸福不是智慧生活的目的,而是智慧人生的情感特点。

古汉语没有把"知"与"智"分开。由于没有"理论/实践""我/他"的那种严格二分性,所以必须经过社会性行动检验为真,才有

a sociology of knowledge rather than any solitary knower. Given the irreducibly social character of the Confucian person, the locus of knowing is not the individual knower, but a knowing community wherein knowledge as an applied wisdom is perceived as an immediate resource for communal happiness.

This social aspect of *zhi* leads to a second observation: *Zhi* is meliorative—it seeks to make the world better. Confucius observes:

> **Cherishing it is better than just knowing it, and finding enjoyment in it is better than just cherishing it.**

As suggested here, *zhi* certainly has a cognitive dimension. But the expectation is that this cognitive capacity must be extended and cultivated into a quality of communing that is productive of human happiness. The kind of knowledge that is directed and purposeful has privilege over simple cognition, and that kind of knowledge that actually conduces to communal enjoyment is better yet. If we were to take liberties with the last proposition of Spinoza's *Ethics* that reads: "Blessedness is not the reward of virtue, but is virtue itself," we might say that happiness is not the reward of living wisely, but is wisdom itself. Said perhaps more clearly, rather than taking happiness to be

资格被称为"知识"。它必须是具实际效果的。由于"知"有这样重要的实用内涵，我们可以将这种"智慧"理解得更充分，将它作为"智性社会实践"（intelligent social practice）。而且因为"知/智"总是包含"实践"，所以它总是特地性的（localized）知识、情景性的智慧。什么时候也不会有"无定位的观点"，没有"上帝眼之观"，可提供严格的"客观"角度。如果事情是这样的话，认知世界就是反身性和价值性的：是从这个视点向外推荐这个世界。

可以说，"认知"被理解成智性社会实践，不仅具有信息量，也具有行动力量。"知"是作为，作为改变世界。按这个意思，"知"还可以译为 realizing（实现），以此突出"将预想结果变为现实"这种含义，即创造一个特别的世界。"知"是规范性地创造世界。在此还要重申，"知"包含"行动"的力量：它必然导引一种感受认识论。"知"对于那些相互感同身受的人们的感受、信仰和心境产生直接、重大的影响。这样的"知"切实地改变他们的感情和思想。

我们知道，中国人的认知语汇

the goal of living wisely, we might say that happiness is the affective character of wise living.

The classical Chinese language does not distinguish between "knowledge" and "wisdom." In the absence of a severe theory/praxis and self/other dichotomy, the assumption is that "knowledge" must be authenticated in communal action for it to qualify as knowledge. It must be practically efficacious. Since *zhi* has this important pragmatic entailment, we might understand this kind of "wisdom" more fully as "intelligent social practice." And since *zhi* involves practice, it is always a localized knowledge, a situated wisdom. There is no putative "view from nowhere," no "God's eye view" that would provide a strictly "objective" perspective. This being the case, knowing a world is reflexive and evaluative: It is to recommend this world from this point of view.

We can say that "knowing" thus understood as intelligent social practice is not only informative, but also has performative force. "Knowing" does something; it changes the world. In this sense, *zhi* might also be translated as "realizing" in order to highlight this sense of "making the desired outcome real"—that is, bringing a particular world into being. Knowing is a normative world-making. Again, *zhi* has a perlocutionary force: It entails an epistemology of feeling.

传达一种对"事务安排"(mapping out)与"开辟路径"(making one's way)的意念。这样的"知"语言,相当于我们一起行路时观察标识,以便走上正确的方向。这种意念一直传承延续到现代汉语之中,"我知道"这种说法在语言上可清晰地表述为"我知道路径"或"我走这条道",呈现为一种语感性的东西,传达给别人的既是举止姿态,也是一种到达彼地的最佳途径。"知"对显而易见的具体条件具有意识性和想象力,能看到可能性,并且通过思考的仁性,在自己的家国环境中,赢得聚合支持与迎接未来的热情所必需的向心力。"知"之于古代儒家世界,的确是一种"乐知"(joyful wisdom)源泉。这种思想是社会智性,在广泛普遍性上,在重要方面屏蔽掉需要"伦理意志"(ethical deliberation)的具体硬实的情况,也屏蔽掉与之伴随的对"常规性理念"(regulative ideals)的诉求。

值得注意的是,"我知道"是一种及物语法,但"道"并不是这种语法的"谓语",而是包含实实在在的"主语"意义。这种情况就像"生活""历史"或"经验",不

"Knowing" has a direct and significant effect on the feelings, beliefs, and the mood of those who come to know each other empathetically. Such knowledge quite literally changes their hearts as well as their minds.

As we have seen, the Chinese epistemic vocabulary suggests "mapping out" and "making one's way" (*dao*) as its dominant image. The language of knowing is to read the signposts as we walk together in the proper direction. This sense of mapping carries over into modern Chinese in which the expression for "I know" is quite literally "I know the way" or "I am walking the way" (*wo zhidao* 我知道), suggesting both a specific bearing and how best to get there. To know is to be cognizant of prevailing conditions, to have the imagination to see their possibilities, and through relational virtuosity (*ren* 仁) within one's own community, to have achieved the deference necessary to rally support behind and enthusiasm for a chosen future. "To know" in this classical Confucian world is indeed a source of a joyful wisdom. And the assumption is that such social intelligence, broadly diffused, will in important measure preclude the hard cases that require ethical deliberation and its attendant appeal to regulative ideals.

Importantly, in the transitive "I know the way" (*wo zhidao*), "the way" (*dao*) is not the "object" of knowledge as such,

能以二元论意义去对待。"道"表示指导在世间生活的一种质量道路（qualitative way），它既包含主观性，也包含客观性，是不可分的。"主语"的属性及其做出的行为形式同样是不可分的。"道"不承认亚里士多德的"范畴"，而是同时与主语、谓语条件保持联系性，同时也与"知"的质量以及所知世界的条件保持相关性。"知"既给予其主体"仁"的质量，也给予我们其所知之物，既给予我们采取行为的具体情势，也给予我们采取行为的本身形式。

（《儒家角色伦理学：一套特色伦理学词汇》，第 210—213 页）

"知"通常翻译为"to know, to realize, to be wise, wisdom"（这几个英文词分别意为认识、了解、明智的、智慧），我们要从几方面将它与主要是作为理论活动的"认知"（knowing）区别开来。第一，根据伯恩哈德·卡尔格伦（Bernhard Karlgren），"知"的词源大概是"人"和"口"的结合，这表明知是社会学上的事，而不是心理学上的事。知是在富有成效的交流中产生的共同成就。

知的特点是，它总是与人的特

but has a real subjective dimension. It is a term like "life" or "history" or "experience" that does not resolve into dualisms. *Dao* is a qualitative way of conducting one's life in the world that entails both subject and object, and the attributes of the subject as well as the modality of the actions being carried out. *Dao* defies Aristotle's categories, having as much to do with the conditions of the subject as with the object, and having as much to do with the quality of understanding as it does with the conditions of the world as understood. Knowing tells us as much about the *ren* quality of the person who "knows" as it does about something known, as much about a particular disposition to act as it does about the modality of acting itself.

(*Confucian Role Ethics: A Vocabulary*. pp. 190-193)

Zhi 知, is conventionally translated "to know, to realize, to be wise, wisdom," and is to be distinguished in several ways from knowing as a primarily theoretical activity. First, the etymology of *zhi* 知, according to Bernhard Karlgren, is probably the combination of "person" (*ren* 人) and "mouth" (*kou* 口) = 佝, suggesting that *zhi* is a sociological rather than psychological event. *Zhi* is a communal achievement that emerges out of effective

殊的、不断展开的情境相联系，它不能归结为精神状态。它不是一个抽象的过程，而是非常具体的活动，目的是最大限度地增加现有的可能性和有用条件。认知是从任何一个情境中获取最多。它是展示世界潜在的东西，或者说是"体悟"世界。就此而言，"体悟者"并不独立于被体悟的环境之外，相反，他是构造世界的创造性活动中的构成因素。

由于这种浓厚的实行涵义（performative connotation），知经常被理解为"预知"（foreknowledge）。它不是要获得天启的预兆，而是一种预知特殊的未来的能力，又是一种能够实际地安定人类社会的品格力量。

仁与知在早期儒家文本中经常一起出现，这表明知以某种程度的仁为前提。仁所涵衍的健全的关系是社群和谐的必要条件，这种和谐产生了知。

与知相联系的另外一个词是"乐"（enjoyment）。知识与幸福是相互促进的。思想与感情是不相分离的，它们作为特定环境中的心的合乎人性的具体表达，总是一起出现。因此，知像"理"和"心"，也完全

communication.

Zhi is always characteristic of a particular, unfolding human situation that cannot be reduced to mental states. It is not an abstractive process, but a profoundly concrete activity that seeks to maximize existing possibilities and contributing conditions. Knowing is getting the most out of any situation. It is to "*actualize*" or "*realize*" the world. As such, the "realizer" is not independent of the realized circumstances, but rather is a constituent element in the creative enterprise of making a world.

Zhi is often understood as "foreknowledge" because of this strong performative connotation. It is not access to some revelatory source, but rather the ability to anticipate a particular future, and the strength of character to consolidate the human community in such a manner as to make it happen. That the presence of some achieved authoritative person (*ren* 仁) is a precondition for *zhi* is suggested by the fact that *ren* and *zhi* are so often found together in the formative Confucian texts. The robust relationships that are entailed by *ren* are necessary conditions for the communal harmony that produces *zhi*.

Another association with *zhi* is "enjoyment." Knowledge and happiness are mutually entailing. Thinking and feeling are not separate, but occur together as the concrete human expression of the resolutely

处于情境中，它将人的世界与其自然的、社会的和文化的环境整合在一起。

（《汉哲学思维的文化探源》，第34页）

contextualized "heart-mind." *Zhi*, like *li* and *xin*, is thus radically situated, integrating the human world and its natural, social, and cultural environments.

(*Thinking from the Han,* pp. 30-31)

物

"物"常常译为"things"。我们也遵从这种翻译，但是却有一个重要的附加条件。在《中庸》的宇宙论中，过程优于实体，连续性优于离散性。因此，"物"应该更恰当地被理解为不是静态的事物，而是动态的过程以及在"事件"（events）意义上这些过程的暂时的停顿。所以，我们必须将"物"理解为既是过程又是事件。

正是不断流动的过程进入特定事件这样一种停顿，使得世界得以确定和可以理解。"万物"的表达是指，当所有特定的过程和/或事件交互性地构成这个世界时，这些过程和/或事件的无法汇总的总体。庄子"物化"（transforming of processes and events）的表述提示着，当一个"事物"转化为另一个时，

Things

Wu is most frequently translated as "things." We follow that translation, with the following important proviso: In the *Zhongyong* cosmology, process is privileged over substance and continuity over discreteness. Thus, *wu* is more appropriately understood not as static things, but as processes and the conventional and transitory punctuation of these processes in the terms of "events." Thus we must understand "things (*wu* 物)" as both processes (happenings) and events (happenings that have achieved some relative completion).

It is the punctuation of the ongoing fluid process into particular events that makes the world determinate and intelligible. The expression *wanwu* 萬物 or "ten thousand processes and events" refers to the unsummed totality of all particular processes and/or events as they transactionally constitute this world. Zhuangzi's expression *wuhua* 物化 —"the

各种过程的所有形式之间的相互性和彼此渗透。

（《切中伦常：〈中庸〉的新诠与新译》，第 99 页）

transforming of processes and events"—suggests the mutuality and interpenetration of all forms of process as one "thing" transforms to become another.

(*Focusing the Familiar: A Translation and Philosophical Interpretation of the Zhongyong*, pp. 81)

名

中国的类书是有等级的，尽管这种等级不是立足于种属的划分或是抽象形式的原则。人被有意识地安排在中心。但是，这里的"人"并非先验的人性，而是指特定朝代的中国人，他被嵌牢在一套特殊的历史环境中。

类书显示的是我们所谓的"伦理的"或"美学的"而非"逻辑的"组织原则。单个的条目以最"尊贵的"人开始，止于最"底层的"；动物始于"狮子"和"大象"，止于"老鼠"和"狐狸"；树始于"松树"和"柏树"，止于"蓟"和"刺藤"。

世界不是根据客观的本质来描述，而是按照通常规定将其分为自然成分和文化成分，当这些成分处于接近中心的位置时，就对中国

Ming

The Chinese *leishu* is hierarchical, though the hierarchy is not based upon distinctions such as genera/species or principles of abstract form. The human being is placed *self-consciously* at the center. However, "human being" here dose not refer to a transcendental "humanity," but to the specific imperial Chinese person embedded within a particular set of historical circumstances.

The *leishu* illustrates what we should call an "ethical" or "aesthetic," rather than a "logical," principle of organization. Individual entries begin with the most "noble" and conclude with the most "base": animals begin with "lion" and "elephant" and finish with "rat" and "fox"; trees begin with "pine tree" and "cypress" and end with "thistles" and "brambles."

The world is not described in terms of objective essences but is divided, prescriptively, into natural and cultural elements which have

当朝之经历发挥日益强大的影响。遍及该传统的那种趋向性唯名论（tropic nommalism）意味着，统治者在给他的世界以名时就是命令其各得其位。

an increasing influence upon the experience of the Chinese court as they stand in proximity to the center. An implication of the tropic nominalism which pervades this tradition is that the ruler, in "naming" (*ming* 名) his world, is "commanding" (*ming* 命) it to be a certain way.

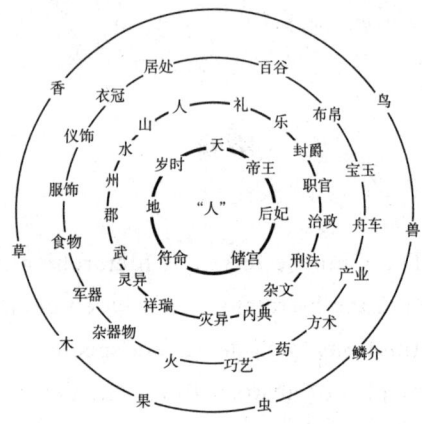

《艺文类聚》中的类书圆圈
（取自梁从诫 1986）

处于圆圈上半部分的范畴，由于它们提供给朝廷的利益，因此就更为高贵；而处于下半部分的范畴，则由于它们可能带来的有害影响而更为低等。中国的文化经验在位居中心的统治者那里得到体现，而且类书不仅以这种特殊的方式组织了其世界，而且赞许了它。当朝廷强大的时候，向心的和谐就被维持着，所有一切各得其位；当中心不可避免地衰落的时候，那些处于边缘的因素就开始发挥越来越大的影响。例如，那些看来无

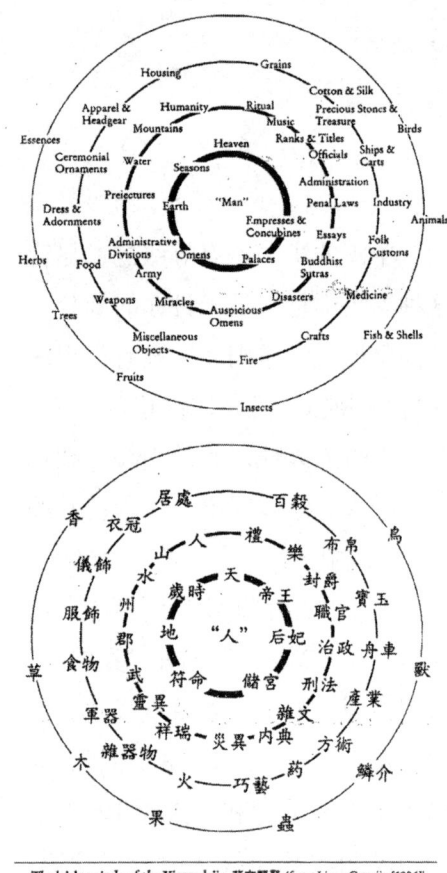

The leishu circle of the Yiwen leiju 藝文類聚 *(from Liang Congjie [1986])*

Categories on the upper portion of the circle, by virtue of the benefits they provide the court, are more noble, while those on the lower half of the circle, by virtue of their possible noxious influences, are more base.

218

关紧要的自然异象都反映了朝廷的无序，如果不作出及时的反应，就可能对统治中心产生戏剧性的甚至是改朝换代的影响。

（《期望中国：对中西文化的哲学思考》，第 306—308 页）

The Chinese cultural experience is embodied in the ruler at the center, and the *leishu* not only organizes his world in this particular way—it recommends it. When the court is strong, the centripetal harmony is maintained and everything is kept in its proper place; as the center inevitably weakens, elements which were on the periphery come to exert increasing influence. Seemingly insignificant abnormalities in the natural world, for example, reflect disorder at the court, and if not responded to in a timely way, can exert a dramatic even transformative influence on the reigning center.

(*Anticipating China: Thinking through the Narratives of Chinese and Western Culture*, pp. 254-256)

象

最常见的译法是"image"（意象、形象），我们就在这个意义上运用此术语。"象"是知觉的、想象的或回忆的经验的一种感观的（即视觉、听觉、触觉、嗅觉）呈现。知觉、记忆或想象的形式可以与其呈现的模式相区别，例如，对于一朵玫瑰的嗅觉或视觉经验可以用诗句来描绘，由诗的欣赏者所体验到的文字意境，而不（必定）是诗人的

Image (*Xiang*)

Xiang is most frequently translated as "image." In the sense in which we shall be using the term, an image is a sensory (that is, visual, auditory, tactile, olfactory) presentation of a perceptual, imaginative, or recollected experience. The form of the perception, memory, or imagination may be distinct from the mode of its presentation. For example, the olfactory or visual experience of a rose may be imaged in the words of the poet. The word-picture as experienced by the

个人体验，才构成有社会效验的意象。因此，讨论"象"最富成效的方法是根据其可共同体验的特征，只有这样的象才有直接的效用。

与《易经》六爻相联系的卦象是"象"的一个绝好的例子，因为它们都是特殊性的。卦象"火"可以说是使人想起对于"火"现象的特殊经验，这种经验由于人们依靠社会记忆和共同经验（传统、机构、礼、音乐、文学等）而贮存于求助于《易经》的人的心中。

在认识论的讨论中，我们希望能够以下面的方式区分形象和象征：一个形象是随着任意的、特定的，或仅仅是约定俗成的联想而呈现的一个客体或事件。通过一种特殊的叙述（一部小说、一出戏剧、一个历史解释、一首史诗）过程中形成相互一致的一组意义，一个形象可以成为一种象征。纳博科夫（Nabokov）的《暗淡之火》（Pale Fire）用这样一种方法表现了以书名命名的形象：它的叙述在各种语境里出现的过程中逐渐采用了解释性的"现金价值"（cash-value）。在更理性化的西方，单义规定的术语的明晰高于隐喻和想象的模糊，这使

celebrant of the poem, and not (necessarily) the private experience of the poet, constitutes the image as socially efficacious. The most productive manner of discussing images, therefore, is in terms of their communally experienceable character. Only such images have direct efficacy.

The images associated with the hexagrams of the *Yijing* (*Zhouyi* or *Book of Changes*) are good examples of *xiang* since they are particularistic. That is, the image "fire" may be said to bring to mind particular experiences of the phenomenon of "fire" that are housed in the individual consulting the *Yijing* by virtue of his or her recourse to social memory and communal experiences (traditions, institutions, ritual practices, music, literature, and so on).

In epistemological discussions we may wish to distinguish between the image and the symbol in something like the following manner: An image is an object or event presented with arbitrary, ad hoc, or merely conventional associations. An image may become a symbol by accruing in the course of a particular narrative (a novel, a play, an historical account, an epic poem) a consistent set of significances. Nabokov's *Pale Fire* presents the image named in its title in such a manner that it gradually takes on interpretive "cash-value" in the course of its occurrence in a variety of contexts in the narrative. Privileging the clarity of univocally defined terms over the vagueness of metaphor and

诗人和小说家摆脱文学批评中的理性化解释、维护他们想象的丰富性，已经非常困难。

在古代中国模式中，形象是表象而不是一个在具体的和历史的层面上成形的世界的再现，所构建的形象比一种逻辑阐释更具有解释力。事实上，威拉德·彼德森论证说，一般将《易经》的"象"这个术语译作"image"或"model"，但从"给出或显出形状"意义上看，应当译作"figure"。

……既定的形象之内在的意义是创造和重塑形象本身的反省行为。与幼稚的预期相反，人们在艺术作品中最终看到的是产生作品的创造行为。创造的过程，而不是物品，才是意义的宝库。被想象的一个东西是一个过程。

（《期望中国：对中西文化的哲学思考》，第262—265页）

心

"心"的字形最初像是大动脉。但是在英文中，却出现了"mind"和"heart"两种并行的译法。我们

imagery in the more rationalistic West has made it difficult for poets and novelists to protect the richness of their imagery from the rationalizing interpretations of literary critics.

In the classical Chinese model, image is the presentation rather than re-presentation of a configured world at the concrete and historical levels. The constructed image assumes considerably more explanatory force than would a logical account. Willard Peterson in fact argues that the term *xiang*, generally translated "image" or "model" in the *Yijing*, ought to be rendered "figure," in the sense of "to give or to bring into shape."

…The meaning resident in an established image is the reflexive act of creating, and recreating, the image itself. Contrary to naive expectations, what one finally sees in a work of art is the creative act that produced it. The creative process, not the object, is the repository of meaning. What is imaged is the process.

(*Anticipating China: Thinking through the Narratives of Chinese and Western Culture*, pp. 216-218)

Heart-and-mind (*Xin*)

Xin was originally a picture of the aorta, but the character has been rendered as "mind" as often as "heart." There is much justification for this, for there are many

可以找出许多理由来解释这一现象：如果心不能够思考的话，许多中国古典文献就没有什么意义和价值了。但是，将头脑与心情剥离——即，将认知与情感相分立，却是再次进入西方形而上学的领域——尤其是在无历史、无文化的唯理性观念的背景下进行身心两分。为了避免出现上述情况，我们将"心"译为"heart-and-mind"。这种译法或许不够雅致，但却能够不断提醒读者：对于孔子来说，不存在完全无实体支撑的思想，也没有全然缺少感知内容的痛觉。

在古代中国人的世界观里，过程和变化是高于形式和静止的。说到人体，我们也不难发现，生理学理解远远重于解剖学认识，脏器的功能优先于其位置。这个例子恰好可以证明，"心"是指"思想与感情"。如果进一步引申理解的话，我们可以说，各种经验也都是产生并汇集于心中的。

（《〈论语〉的哲学诠释》，第 57 页）

"心"这个字是心脏主动脉的象形字，它与"heart"及其所表示的情感的含义直接相关。我们翻译为

passages in the classical texts which do not make much sense in English unless the *xin* thinks. But to divorce the mind from the heart—the cognitive from the affective is to reenter the Western metaphysical realm again, most especially via the mind-body dichotomy, and embrace the notion of an ahistorical, acultural seat of pure rationality. To avoid this reference, we render *xin* as "heart-and-mind," which is inelegant perhaps, but serves to remind the reader that there are no altogether disembodied thoughts for Confucius, nor any raw feelings altogether lacking (what in English would be called) "cognitive content."

In the classical Chinese worldview, in which process and change have priority over form and stasis, it is frequently observed that, with respect to the human body, physiology has priority over anatomy, and function takes precedence over site. This being the case, it might well be argued that *xin* means "thoughts and feeling," and then derivatively and metaphorically, the organ with which these experiences are to be associated.

(*The Analects of Confucius: A Philosophical Translation*, p. 56)

The character *xin* is a stylized pictograph of the aorta, associating it quite immediately with the "heart" and "emotions"或"feelings"的"情"这个字,是这个"心"和音旁"青"这个字的复合。这一事实证明了以上的理解。事实上,有许多包含"情"的意义的中国字中都有"心"这个部首。

"心"常常译为"mind"。有许多指涉"思维"不同程态(modalities)的中国字中也都包含"心"的部首。的确,除非"心"既包含"思考"(thinks)的理智的向度,又包含"感受"(feels)的情感的向度,在英文中,许多中国古代文献中的文字是没有意义的。

当然,关键在于,在古代中国的世界观中,认知上的"心"(mind)不能与情感意义上的"心"(heart)相脱离。为了避免这种两分,我们宁可不那么优雅地将"心"翻译为"heart-and-mind",意在提醒读者没有脱离情感的理性思考,也没有任何缺乏认知内容的原始情感。

在古代中国的世界观中,过程与变化优先于实体和持久。因此,经常可以看到的是,就人体而言,生理学(physiology)优先于解剖学(anatomy)。在这种情况下,或许可以很好地论证,"心"意味着"思与

the emotional connotations that attend it. The fact that the character 情 that we translate as "emotions" or "feelings" is a combination of this *xin* 心 and a phonetic element, *qing* 青, justifies this understanding. In fact, many if not most of the characters that entail "feeling" have *xin* as a component element.

Xin has as often been rendered as "mind." Many if not most of the characters that refer to different modalities of "thinking" are also constructed with *xin* as a component. Indeed, there are many passages in these classical texts that would not make sense in English unless *xin thinks*, as well as *feels*.

The point, of course, is that in this classical Chinese world view, the mind cannot be divorced from the heart. The cognitive is inseparable from the affective. To avoid such a dichotomy, we have translated *xin* rather inelegantly as "heart-and-mind" with the intention of reminding the reader that there are no rational thoughts devoid of feeling, nor any raw feelings altogether lacking in cognitive content.

In the classical Chinese world view, process and change have priority over substance and permanence. Thus, it is frequently observed that, with respect to the human body, physiology has priority over anatomy. This being the case, it might well be argued that *xin* means "thinking and feeling," and then derivatively and

感"（thinking and feeling），并且，在引申的意义上和隐喻的意义上，通过"心"，"思"与"感"这两种经验得以联系起来。

（《切中伦常：〈中庸〉的新诠与新译》，第 100—101 页）

"志"这个词通常用以翻译西方的概念"will"（意为"意志"）。从词源上看，"志"是由"心"和"之"或"止"合成的，表示"意欲"或"决心得到"。在经典性的辞书《说文解字》中，"志"注为"意"。它表示一个人心中所想。与"意志"的概念相比，它更接近于"意愿"的概念。

（《汉哲学思维的文化探源》，第 42—43 页）

精神

现在，一提"气"字，就会联想到健康、医学、强身健体这种领域的"生命能量场"。将"体"理解为"气"是很有帮助的。但就古代互系性宇宙观而言，"体"字，如同对"气"的任何预想，使用必须

metaphorically, the organ with which these experiences are to be associated.

(*Focusing the Familiar: A Translation and Philosophical Interpretation of the Zhongyong,* p. 82)

Zhi 志 is the term conventionally translated with the Western concept of "will." Etymologically, *zhi* combines *xin* 心 "heart-and-mind" with "to go to" (*zhi* 之) or "to abide in" (*zhi* 止), and means "to have in (heart) mind" or "to set one's heart on." In the classical *Shuowen* lexicon, *zhi* is glossed as "meaning" or "idea" (*yi* 意). It means what one has in (heart) mind. It is much closer to the notion of "disposition" than the concept of "will."

(*Thinking from the Han,* p. 38)

Spirit (*Jingshen*)

Today we are most familiar with *qi* as a vital energy field in the areas of health, medicine, and exercises leading to bodily well-being. Understanding "body" as *qi* can be helpful. But in this classical correlative cosmology, the term "body," like any predication of *qi*, must of course be used

认 识 论

得当,任何事物都是一个相续不分的气场,都会立即显示自己既是一个"生命体"又是一个"环境",为"肉体"亦为"精神",为"体"亦为"用",为"世"亦为"界",为"通"亦为"变"。正因为"身"是被如此理解的,所以传统中医为我们提供了一个理解"气宇宙观"的窗口,我们可从一种与众不同角度理解万物,万物构成着这个世界。

……

虽然"精神"一词被译成英文"mind"或"spirit",可无论怎么说它也是属于"身体"的。……作为根本的"精"是提供能量转化过程的基础,能量是由食物精化而来;"精"因为"获得性精"而实现浓缩与强化。中医理论将精与气("air""breath""vital energy")视为同一生命能。集而谓之精,散而谓之气。如果说"精"作为"生命能"的养育性一面,气则是作为它的活性结构一面。……如果说"精""气"作为生命之本,神则是生命之貌。……换句话说,神是生命活动本身的现象。

advisedly; everything is a continuous field of *qi* manifesting itself at once as "lived body" and as "environs," as "physical" and as "spiritual", as "forming" (*ti* 體) and as "functioning" (*yong* 用), as "temporal" (*shi* 世) and as "spatial" (*jie* 界), as "persistent" (*tong* 通) and as "flux" (*bian* 變). It is because of just such assumptions about the "body" that traditional Chinese medicine can provide us with a useful explanatory window on *qi* cosmology and a significantly different way of understanding the myriad "things" that constitute this world.

…

Although *jing shen* 精神 is translated in English as "mind" or "spirit", it is very much part of *shenti*. … Primary *jing* provides the basis for the process of transforming the energy distilled from food and is enriched and strengthened by "acquired *jing*." Chinese medical theories view *jing* and *qi* 氣 (air, breath, vital energy) as the same life-giving energy. When it is concentrated, it is *jing*; when it is dispersed it turns into *qi*. If *jing* is the nurturing aspect of this energy, *qi* is the active configurational aspect of the same energy. ... If *jing* and *qi* are the basis of life, then *shen* 神 is the manifestation of that life.... In other words, *shen* is the phenomenon of life activity itself.

225

生命能的流动需要协调性与方向性。"心"作为指导方向的力量,它是一种具体情形内在的能动潜力所进行的调节与导向。

(《儒家角色伦理学:一套特色伦理学词汇》,第68—71页)

身/体

在中国宇宙观中,"身心"与"知行"从来就是人生经验中相辅相成、相连不分、相互兼有的偶对双方。其实,人经验的延续性与整体性是以"体用""变通"这样的观念表述的。

(《儒家角色伦理学:一套特色伦理学词汇》,第42页)

将"体"理解为"气"是很有帮助的。但就古代互系性宇宙观而言,"体"字,如同对"气"的任何预想,使用必须得当,任何事物都是一个相续不分的气场,都会立即显示自己既是一个"生命体"又是一个"环境",为"肉体"亦为"精神",为"体"亦为"用",为"世"亦为"界",为"通"亦为"变"。

The flow of life energy requires coordination and direction. The heartmind (*xin* 心) provides the directive force negotiated in and guided by the efficacious possibilities inherent in the particular circumstances.

(*Confucian Role Ethics: A Vocabulary,* pp. 57-59)

Body

Such as exclusive mind/body and theory/praxis dualism has never been a distraction in a Chinese correlative *yinyang* cosmology in which mind/body (*shenxi* 身心) and theory/praxis (*zhixin* 知行) have been taken to be collaborative, coterminous, and mutually entailing aspects of experience. Indeed, the continuity and wholeness of experience is defined in terms of "forming and functioning"(*tiyong* 體用), and "flux and persistence"(*biantong* 變通).

(*Confucian Role Ethics: A Vocabulary,* pp. 33-34)

Understanding "body" as *qi* can be helpful. But in this classical correlative cosmology, the term "body", like any predication of *qi*, must of course be used advisedly; everything is a continuous field of *qi* manifesting itself at once as "lived body" and as "environs," as "physical" and as "spiritual," as "forming"(*ti* 體) and as

（《儒家角色伦理学：一套特色伦理学词汇》，第 68 页）

这种互系宇宙观对形式结构的功能理解是根本"域境性"的，即将"事物"（如"生命肉身"或"作为经验之身"）置于它总是处在变化状态的"环境"中去，这样形成一种内在与外在的"场景"；身体被从内外两方面看待，作为或多或少的主观，亦作为或多或少的客观。"形成状态"（体）与"功能状态"（用）之间，有不可简化错综复杂的关系，它在"身"这个象形字中被抓住；"身"字常被一般化、简单化地译为"body"，而它却需要更细微得多的理解。"身"不仅指一个具体和主观生命的人身，更是甲骨文"𠂤"和金石文"𩩙"中所表示的，它的古字体清晰显示了一个怀孕身体的象形，强调着嵌含的内外含义，即它的特殊生命力，它的生殖功能性，它的社会性，它的旺盛的、生育的延续性。

（《儒家角色伦理学：一套特色伦理学词汇》，第 69 页）

"体"是知识文化素材的分流中

"functioning"(*yong* 用), as "temporal"(*shi* 世) and as "spatial"(*jie* 界), as "persistent"(*tong* 通) and as "flux"(*bian* 變).

(*Confucian Role Ethics: A Vocabulary,* p. 57)

This functional understanding of formal structures in correlative cosmology is radically contextual, locating "things" such as the "lived body" or "the body as experienced" within its ever-changing circumstances—thus forming a collaboration between an internal and an external landscape. Body is understood from the inside and from the outside, as more or less subjective and more or less objective. The irreducible complexity of the relationship between "forming" and "functioning" is captured in the graph *shen* 身, often translated generically and simplistically as "body", but which requires a much more nuanced understanding. *Shen* means not only particular and subjective "lived-body", but in its archaic oracle bones and bronze forms, 𠂤 and 𩩙 respectively, the graph is clearly the profile of a "pregnant lived-body," underscoring its nested sense of inside and outside, its vital particularity, its procreative functionality, its sociality, and its fecund, generational continuity.

(*Confucian Role Ethics: A Vocabulary,* pp. 57-58)

The body is the site of a conveyance of the cultural corpus of knowledge—

枢——语言的便利与娴熟，宗教礼仪与方式，厨艺美感，歌曲和舞蹈，道德观念与价值的形体感，认知技术的教授与学习等等——作为一种生生不已、辈辈相传过程，通过它，一个生生不息的文明得以绵延不绝。

（《儒家角色伦理学：一套特色伦理学词汇》，第124页）

儒家角色伦理学十分重视"体"在成就人格与"仁"行为中的能动统一角色——以体为本，接受滋养与培育，人的行为呈现光彩。"体"作为"體"的简写，不是偶然的，也就是说，字面就很清楚，"体"的蕴意即"人之本"。"体"总是作为人与世界、生命体与环境之间的协同，在同一时间既是肉体也是生机，是所见到的也是生活着的，是接纳的也是反应的。不仅是世界塑造人的身体，而且也是我们通过身体感官，对经验的世界进行构造，进行概念化与理论化。其实，正是因为"身体"是中介，通过它，我们祖先及其文化才得以活在我们身上，所以才有说"身体发肤，受之父母，不敢毁伤，孝之始也"。

（《儒家角色伦理学：一套特色伦理学词汇》，中文版序言第4—5页）

linguistic facility and proficiency, religious rituals and mythologies, the aesthetics of cooking, song, and dance, the modeling of mores and values, instruction and apprenticeship in cognitive technologies, and so on—as a continuing, intergenerational process through which a living civilization itself is perpetuated.

(*Confucian Role Ethics: A Vocabulary*, p.111)

Confucian role ethicists appreciate the dramatic role that body has as integral to achieving personal identity and consummate conduct—the body as the root through which human conduct, being nourished and grown, becomes refulgent. It is no coincidence that the simplified graph for body 體 is 体 —that is, quite literally, the graphic denotation of the root of a person. The body—always a collaboration between person and world, between organism and environment—is at once carnal and vital, seen and lived, receptive and responsive. Not only does the world shape the body, but through our bodily sensorium we structure, conceptualize, and theorize our world of experience. Indeed, it is because the body is the medium through which our ancestors and their culture live on in us that keeping one's body intact has been the first among the several precepts of family reverence (*xiao* 孝).①

---

① 中文版序言的部分内容在英文原书中没有对应，为后来补充。

政治哲学

政

"政"最好被理解为"对社会政治秩序(在其最宽泛的意义上是人际秩序)的影响(effecting sociopolitical order)",而非更为政治化的专门的"政府管理"(administering government)。有人曾从严格"做官从政"的意义上,问孔子为何不"为政",孔子的回答显然表明他是以我们上面所论的方式来理解"政"的:

> 或谓孔子曰:"子奚不为政?"子曰:"《书》云:'孝乎惟孝,友于兄弟,施于有政。'是亦为政,奚其为为政?"(《论语·为政》)

其次,《论语》中"政"确实有正反两义。前者指涉一种审美秩序,是君主和臣民共同参与的自然和谐

Effecting Sociopolitical Order (*Cheng*)

Cheng is better understood as "effecting sociopolitical order" (interpersonal order in its broadest sense), rather than the more politically specific "administering government." That Confucius understood it in this way is made clear in his response to an interlocutor who uses *cheng** restrictively in the sense of formal government (2.21):

> Someone asked Confucius, "Why are you not in government?" Confucius replied, "*The Book of Documents* says: 'Filiality! Simply extended filiality and fraternity into government.' This filiality then is also taking part in 'government.' Why must one take part in formal government?"

Secondly, there is indeed a positive and a negative sense of *cheng** 政 as it occurs in the *Analects*. The former refers to an aesthetic order that involves the participation

的表达，该和谐是由个人在礼仪行为中体现的意义和价值决定的。该秩序的理想状态是一个在上者修身激励在下者效仿所实现的模范过程。社会秩序的独特性尽管立基于对传统的承续，但却是由其独特参与者赋予的意义限定的，因此，它总是常新且独有的。

"政"的反面意义是因个人修身需要努力投入引起的。我们已看到，有意义的礼仪行为需要个人践行"义"的才能。即便百姓有君主模范行为的影响，也不可避免会有一撮人因缺乏智慧或修养而冥顽不化，只知追求个人私利而不顾及其行为后果。为了整体的和谐，这些人就必须受到由法律表达和行使的为规约行为的底线的制裁。此乃"政"的第二个派生意义：发表的（继而成为正式的）社会和政治标准，最低限度保证符合普遍的秩序感。此第二性、补助的秩序意义之所以是反面的，是因为它不要求那些它所针对的人的"义"。这些人被假定为不能够主动参与秩序，因此，必须强制使之服从。尽管孔子显然支持共享秩序调整的权利，但正如我们下面将要详细阐明的，他是一个完

of both rulers and people in an emergent harmony defined by the personal display of meaning and value in the performance of ritual action. Ideally, this order is effected by a modeling process in which personal cultivation above inspires emulation below. The specific disposition of a society's order, although grounded in the continuity provided by tradition, is qualified by the meanings invested by its specific participants, and hence, is always novel and unique.

The negative sense of *cheng** arises because personal cultivation requires commitment and effort. As we have seen, ritual actions, to be meaningful, require that particular people exercise their capacities to "significate" (*yi* 義). Even with the influence of the ruler's exemplary conduct on the people, there will inevitably be a recalcitrant fringe who, for want of wit or refinement, will pursue their own personal advantage without concern for the consequences of their actions. For the sake of general harmony, these persons must be held to a minimum standard of orderly conduct described and enforced as the rule of law. This then is the second, derived meaning of *cheng**: articulated (and hence formal) social and political measures taken to insure a minimum degree of compliance with the prevailing sense of order. This second, ancillary, order is negative in that it does not require "signification" (*yi*) from those whom it most immediately affects. The assumption is that these persons have failed

全的现实主义者，承认必须有强制顺从作为备用措施。

（《通过孔子而思》，第190—191页）

正名

"正名"，我们将之译为"the ordering of names"，但更流行的译法是"the rectification of names"。依照我们所谓圣人是沟通大师的主张来考察"正名说"是有启发意义的。如果说人以及人与人之间的关系需要不断协调且富有意义，那么自然这些人所借以组织、关联和行为的媒介或形式——诸如语言、礼仪和音乐这样的介质——也需要关注。

在孔子的内在宇宙中，思想和行为、理性和经验以及理论与实践之间有一种彼此关联的关系。另外，儒家哲学始于某种人之不可化约的人际关系的概念，其中，自我、社会和国家都是由交流和沟通

to participate voluntarily, and hence must be compelled. Although Confucius' sympathies clearly lie with participatory ordering, as we shall detail, he was realist enough to acknowledge the need for enforced compliance as a backup measure.

(*Thinking Through Confucius,* pp. 157-158)

The Ordering of Names (*Cheng Ming*)

Cheng ming* 正名, translated by us as "the ordering of names," but more popularly rendered as "the rectification of names." It will be instructive for us to examine the doctrine of *cheng ming** in light of our claim that the sage is a master of communication. If persons and personal relationships require a constant attuning to be meaningful, it would follow that the media or forms through which these persons are composed, related, and performed—mediums such as language, ritual actions, and music—also require attention.

In the immanental cosmos of Confucius, a correlative relationship obtains between idea and action, reason and experience, theory and praxis. Further, Confucian philosophy begins from an irreducibly interpersonal conception of the human being in which self, society, and state are correlates determined through communication. Under these conditions, naming

决定的彼此关联。在这种情况下，命名对孔子来说，就不仅是一种对某种已有的实在适当地贴上相应标签的过程。语言的述行力量表达了这样的结论——通过语言诠释世界就是推动它趋向某特定现实，使其以某种方式被"知"。而且，一个人能够影响世界的程度是他能够以唤起别人敬意反应的方式表达个体意义、价值和目的的一个功能。由于对语言寄予这种期望，因此，就不难理解为什么孔子的许多主要概念的词源都有指示人际沟通的成分。"知"（to realize）与"信"（to live up to one's word）都表明了对言的信奉。表达人的不同成就的"君子"和"善人"以及实现"命"（to cause certain possibilities to be realized）、"和"（aesthetic harmony），还有"名"本身，其词根都是"口"，都表示口头表达的意思。

在分析孔子"正名说"时，我们想先指出孔子对恰当使用语言的重要性的强调。在《论语·子路》这一经典章节中，孔子认为为政必先"正名"：

子路曰："卫君待子而为

for Confucius cannot simply be a process of attaching appropriately corresponding labels to an already existing reality. The performative force of language entails the consequence that to interpret the world through language is to impel it towards a certain realization, to make it known in a certain way. And the extent to which one is able to influence the world is a function of the extent to which one can articulate his meaning, value, and purpose in such manner as to evoke deferential responses from others. Given such an expectation of language, it is not really surprising to find components indicative of interpersonal communication in the etymologies of many of Confucius' major concepts. "To realize" (*chih* 知) and "to live up to one's word" (*hsin** 信) both indicate a commitment to speech. Exemplary person (*chun tzu* 君子) and "good person" (*shan jen* 善人) as levels of personal achievement, to "*ming*" 命, "to cause certain possibilities to be realized," the achievement of "aesthetic harmony" (*ho* 和) and "naming" (*ming** 名) itself all contain the mouth radical, perhaps indicating verbal articulation.

In this analysis of the doctrine of *cheng ming**, we want to begin by noting the importance Confucius invested in the appropriate use of language. In a classic passage, he describes the proper ordering of language as the immediate priority in the proper ordering of society (13.3):

Tzu-lu asked Confucius, "If the Lord of Wei was waiting for you to bring order

政，子将奚先？"子曰："必也正名乎！"子路曰："有是哉，子之迂也！奚其正？"

子路的惊讶表明他完全没有领会孔子的哲学观念，以致孔子变得很不耐烦，回答道：

> 野哉由也！君子于其所不知，盖阙如也。名不正则言不顺，言不顺则事不成，事不成则礼乐不兴，礼乐不兴则刑罚不中，刑罚不中则民无所措手足。故君子名之必可言也，言之必可行也。君子于其言，无所苟而已矣。

因此，对孔子来说，"正名"是"政"的出发点。但我们这样解释该概念必须小心不要分离了思想和行动。这就是说，我们必须对命名的述行力量给予充分说明。正名的流行译法"rectification of names"则未做到这一点。它试图依照某些外在于该传统的理论框架来处理"名"，使之实体化因而能够为满足固定理论架构的行为所"正"。这种诠释或许源于过于简单地理解了《论语》

to his state, to what would you give first priority?"

Confucius replied, "Without question it would be to order names properly."

"Would you be as impractical as that?" Tzu-lu responded, "What is there to order?"…

Tzu-lu's surprise showed such a total lack of sympathy with Confucius' philosophical insight that the Master became uncharacteristically impatient, replying:

> How can you be so coarse! An exemplary person (*chun tzu*) remains silent about things that he does not understand! When names are not properly ordered, what is said is not attuned; when what is said is not attuned, things will not be done successfully; when things are not done successfully, the use of ritual action and music will not prevail; when the use of ritual action and music does not prevail, the application of laws and punishments will not be on the mark; and when laws and punishments are not on the mark, the people will not know what to do with themselves. Thus, when the exemplary person (*chun tzu*) puts a name to something, it can certainly be spoken, and when spoken it can certainly be done. There is nothing careless in the attitude of the exemplary person (*chun tzu*) toward what he says.

中表达"正名"的章节：

觚不觚，觚哉！觚哉！
（《论语·雍也》）
齐景公问政于孔子，孔子对曰："君君，臣臣，父父，子子。"（《论语·颜渊》）

通常对"正名"的解释是："觚"或"君"都有一个（根据他们的特征和作用）已确立的定义，因此，理论定义和实际行为之间有任何错离都将是不正之源。萧公权是这一观点最为突出的代表：

孔子政治思想的出发点是"从周"。他的具体措施是正名（rectification of names）。用现代术语来解释，他所谓的"正名"就是根据周朝封建社会鼎盛时期的制度重新调整君臣、上下的权利和责任……"正名"要有个具体标准，孔子标准的基础就是周朝盛期的制度系统。

萧公权公正地批判了顾立雅，后者认为"正名"不是孔子的概

For Confucius, then, this doctrine of "ordering names" (*cheng ming**), is the starting point of sociopolitical order. In so construing this concept, however, we must be careful not to separate idea and action. That is, we must give full account to the performative force of naming. The prevailing interpretation of ordering names (*cheng ming**), as the "rectification of names" fails to do so. It tends to treat names in terms of some theoretical schema that has been inherited out of the tradition, and that can be hypostatized and hence rectified by behaviors that satisfy the standing theoretical construct. This kind of interpretation is perhaps based on a too simple reading of the presentation of *cheng ming** in the *Analects* (6.25 and 12.11):

Is a ritual goblet (*ku*) that is not a ritual goblet really a ritual goblet? Is it a ritual goblet!
Duke Ching of Ch'i asked Confucius about effecting sociopolitical order, and Confucius replied, "The ruler ought to be ruler, the subject subject, the father father and son son."

The standard interpretation of *cheng ming** has it that there is an established definition—characteristics and function—of what it means to be a ritual goblet (*ku*) or a ruler (*chun*), and that any breach between theoretical definition and actual performance is a source of disorder. Hsiao Kung-chuan is a prominent representative of this position:

政治哲学

念，有可能是后来法家的篡改。顾立雅的观点受韦利的影响，韦利坚持认为"正名"是一种时代错误，根本与"孔子学说并不相容"，但这却实际并不能证明顾立雅的结论。然而，顾立雅的认识还是有可取之处的，他认为与法家相连的"正名"概念（实际是萧公权的一个解释）并不符合孔子的思想。尽管如此，对顾立雅来说，更为明智的做法还是应在诠释层面质疑与孔子思想根本宗旨不相符的"正名"的诠释，而非质疑其作为儒家概念之根本的合法性。

萧公权的解释符合理性模式，其中定义先于实在：君主施政应遵循已确立的规范行事，服从一系列既定的规章、制度。这种诠释表面上因有文本支持，一直以来都很有影响，因此，孔子就成了极端保守分子。正如萧公权所论，"正名说"，"显然说明孔子的政治态度就是从周制，其政治观是保守的"。我们认为，"正名"的这一流行诠释部分是正确的，但它高度强调孔子思想中与传统的一致性，与此同时，却忽视了孔子真正看重的文化多样性、原创性和丰富性，则损害了对孔子

The starting point of Confucius' political thought was to "follow the Chou," and his concrete proposal for carrying it out was the rectification of names. Explained in modern terms, what he called the rectification of names meant readjusting the powers and duties of ruler and minister, superior and inferior, according to the institutions of the Chou feudal world's most flourishing period......The rectification of names demands reliance upon a concrete standard. The standard that Confucius took as his basis was the institutional system of the Chou's flourishing period.

Hsiao Kung-chuan is rightly critical of Creel, who rather denies that *cheng ming** is a Confucian concept and attributes it to later, probably Legalist, interpolation. Creel's arguments, inspired by Waley's insistence that *cheng ming** is anachronistic and has a basic "incompatibility with the doctrines of Confucius," do not in fact warrant his conclusions. But there is merit in Creel's insight that the sort of interpretation of this doctrine associable with Legalism (an interpretation of *cheng ming** in fact advocated by Hsiao Kung-chuan himself) does not square with Confucius' teachings. It would seem more reasonable on Creel's part, however, to question an interpretation of *cheng ming** that is inconsistent with the basic tenets of Confucius' thought at the level of interpretation, rather than questioning its basic legitimacy as a Confucian concept.

Hsiao Kung-chuan's interpretation fits the

思想的理解。要知道，据载，孔子自己就曾说：

> 愚而好自用，贱而好自专，生乎今之世，反古之道。如此者，灾及其身者也。(《中庸》第二十八章)

无疑，孔子确实崇敬古制旧典，但这种敬仰绝不是简单重建古老的周朝制度和文化。它要求选择和创造性的综合：

> 颜渊问为邦。子曰："行夏之时，乘殷之辂，服周之冕，乐则《韶》舞，放郑声……"(《论语·卫灵公》)

另外，孔子崇"古"亦是出于实际考虑，他认为应不断改进重组继承的智慧和制度以适应新的世界不断变化的环境。(例如可参见《为政》和《子路》相关章节。)总而言之，孔子相信人类文化是不断累积且不断进步的。然而世人更多注意的是他的崇"古"，却未能足够重视他对未来的期望。说明一个可能的世界并使之与他世界沟通，就是试图实现它。

rational paradigm in which definition precedes realization: a ruler must, in carrying out his office, act according to a preestablished norm and satisfy a set of given specifications. Such an interpretation, with its apparent textual support, has been influential in rendering Confucius as extremely conservative. As Hsiao Kung-chuan observes, the doctrine of *cheng ming** thus understood "clearly demonstrates that Confucius' political attitude was that of a compliant Chou subject, and that his political views were conservative." We want to argue that this popular interpretation of "ordering names" is partially correct, but that it has the deleterious effect of highlighting an emphasis on traditional continuity in Confucius' thought at the immediate expense of overlooking a real concern for cultural diversity, originality, and enrichment. After all, Confucius is reported to have said himself:

> To be stupid yet fond of relying on oneself, to be base yet fond of being one's own advocate, to be born into the present age yet attempt to return to the ways of the past—a person like this is disaster's prey.

Unquestionably Confucius evidences a profound respect for the institutions of the past, but this respect is by no means equatable with a simple reconstruction of early Chou institutions and culture. It requires selectivity and creative synthesis (15.11):

命名就是促使它"现实化"。

"名"这个词既有"给出意义"（to mean）又有"给出名称"（to name）的意思。"给出名称"（命名）就是奉献意义，而"给出意义"就是阐释名称。我们会发现《论语》中的尧作为传统中意义的创造者，虽然百姓无可"名"之，但他本人却负有运用他所贡献的意义塑造文化的责任：

> 大哉尧之为君也！巍巍乎！唯天为大，唯尧则之。荡荡乎！民无能名焉。巍巍乎！其有成功也，焕乎，其有文章！（《论语·泰伯》）

同样，泰伯高尚的行为在导致周朝建立的一系列事件中起决定性的作用，他所体现的无私的道德成为后世公认的标准。泰伯和尧一样，他的行为是新意义的源泉，百姓难以名之："泰伯，其可谓至德也已矣！三以天下让，民无得而称焉。"（《论语·泰伯》）

当然，最直接最明显体现个体意义的"名"就是一个人自己的名声。这也说明了孔子为什么非常关

Yen Yüan (Hui) asked how to order a state. Confucius replied, "Use the calendar of Hsia, ride about the state carriage of Yin, wear the ceremonial cap of Chou, and as for music, there are the Shao dances (of Shun). Ban the sounds of Cheng...."

Further, Confucius tempers his respect for antiquity with the practical consideration that inherited wisdom and institutions must be constantly revamped to accommodate the shifting circumstances of an always unique world. In short, Confucius believes that human culture is cumulative and generally progressive. While his emulation of the past is much noticed, not enough has been made of his expectations for the future. To articulate a possible world and communicate it to others is an attempt to realize it. To name it is a prompting to "actualize" it.

The term *ming** 名 means both "to mean" and "to name." "To name" is to contribute meaning, and "to mean" is to construe names. In the *Analects*, we find that Yao, as a creator of meaning in the tradition, could not be "named" by his people, yet he himself was responsible for the patterning of culture in such manner as to accommodate his contributed meaning (8.19):

How great indeed was Yao as a ruler! How majestic! Only *t'ien* is truly great, and only Yao took it as his model. How expansive was he—the people had no name to do him justice. How majestic was he in his accomplishments, and

心个人名声:"君子疾没世而名不称焉。"(《论语·卫灵公》)

命名的述行性以及它与意义的关系,可从"名"常用"命"(to cause certain possibilities to be realized)定义这一点清楚看到。

事实上,早期中国著作中,这两个词常是互换使用的。《说文》将"名"定义为"自命"(self-selected causal possibilities)。

要想充分说明孔子的"正名说",除了揭示他深察"言"之传扬历史成就的方式,还必须说明如何创造性地用"命名"来实现一个新的世界。实际上,孔子"名"的概念可解释为一种与"礼"类似的"行"(performance)(形式创造[making of form])。据《左传》所载,"名"和"礼"之间的这种关联实际是孔子自己建立起来的:

> 既,卫人赏之(仲叔于奚)以邑,辞,请曲县、繁缨以朝。许之。仲尼闻之曰:"惜也,不如多与之邑。唯器与名,不可以假人,君之所司也。名以出信,信以守器,器以藏礼,礼以行义,义以生

how brilliant was he in his cultural achievements.

Similarly, T'ai Po, whose exemplary conduct was a critical factor in the series of events leading up to the establishment of the Chou dynasty, exhibited a selfless morality that would emerge in later generations as a recognized standard. Like Yao's, his actions constituted a source of novel meaning that defied description by the people (8.1): "T'ai Po can certainly be called a person of highest *te*. Several times he ceded his rightful claim to the empire, leaving the masses searching for language to describe him."

Of course, the most immediate and apparent "name" in which one invests meaning is his own reputation. This notion that one's name has contributed meaning explains Confucius' concern for Personal reputation (15.20): "The exemplary person (*chun tzu*) hates the prospect of arriving at the end of his life without having made a name for himself."

The performative dimension of naming and its relationship to meaning is evidenced in the fact that "name" (*ming** 名) is frequently defined as "to cause certain possibilities to be realized" (*ming* 命). In the early Chinese corpus, in fact, these two terms are frequently used interchangeably. The *Shuo-wen* defines "name"(*ming** 名) as "self-selected causal possibilities" (*tzu ming* 自命).

A full explanation of Confucius' doctrine of "ordering names", in addition to reflecting his appreciation for the way in which language

利，利以平民，政之大节也。若以假人，与人政也。政亡，则国家从之，弗可止也已。"（《左传·成公二年》）

"名"和"礼"都可被视为保存和传承"义"的形式。富有意义的称名或执礼，就是引出过去和现在环境中的相似之处，以唤起其中灌注的"义"。"名"和"礼"都具有一个重要特征，即它们二者都具有语境特指性（context-specific），是由一系列独特语境限定的。这也就是说，它们的"义"不可能被只说明其本身意义的语源分析所穷尽。既然"义"并非仅仅源于"名"或"礼"本身，那么完整的说明就必然需要借助它们在独特、永恒变化的语境中的意义以及它们与这些意义的关系。

一个既定的"名"或"礼"尽管可在某种抽象层面描述，但却只有作为"义"之独特个体性的展现才真正富有意义。这可以从"礼"通常的另一个译法"propriety"得到证明，假定"propriety"根据其原意"所有权，特有"（to make one's own）来理解的话，那么，"适当"

conveys past realizations of the world, must provide some account of how naming can be used creatively to realize new worlds appropriate to emerging circumstances. We shall argue that Confucius' concept of "naming" (ming*) is to be explained as a "performance" (that is, a making of form) similar to ritual action (li). This association between "name" (ming*) and "ritual action" (li) is in fact established by Confucius himself in a passage recorded in the Tso-chuan:

> Thereafter, the people of Wei wanted to make a present of a city to Chung-shu Yü-hsi. Chung-shu Yü-hsi declined, instead asking for suspended musical instruments, and ornamental bridles like those used by the nobility to appear at court. The Lord of Wei granted this request.
>
> On hearing of this, Confucius observed, "It is a pity. It would have been better to have given him more cities. Ritual vessels and names (titles) alone cannot be loaned to others—they are what the ruler controls. Names are used to generate credibility, credibility is used to protect the ritual vessels, ritual vessels are used to embody ritual actions, ritual actions are used to enact significance (yi), significance is used to produce benefit, and benefit is used to bring peace to the people. These are the important measures for effecting sociopolitical order. To loan them to others is to give them control

（appropriate）的"礼"和"专有的"（proper）语言都要求一种个人化改造以适应个体自己专门的状况。正是这一原因，像"觚"和"君"这样抽象的"名"尽管承载历史衍生的意义，也必须在展现"义"时保持开放，以适应特殊环境。正如"礼"只有获得现时特定情境下的尊重、体现、重塑和拓展才可能存在，"名"和"正名"也是一项动态的规划，其中，现有结构和定义必须这样理解：即"名"以及它们所获得的和谐总需要不断协调，它们是流动性的，总是需要语境的不断重塑。

"命名"的述行力量巩固了"名"及其种种表达模式的流动性，反对"正名"概念的纯逻辑、指向性诠释。"礼"不仅由人履行，而且由于它们积极唤起某种形式的反应，因而在某种重要的意义上，它们"实现"人。同样，"名"不仅表征，它们也产生效果，因为它们推动人趋向某特定经验。给一个替代物一个"*gu*"的名字（且赋予适当的"义"），就能够有效地将这个替代物转换成名字为"觚"的礼器。"名"不仅用来指称秩序，它们也用

of the sociopolitical order. And when sociopolitical order is lost, that the state will follow is an inexorable fact."

Both name and ritual action can be viewed as formal structures used to capture and transmit meaning (*yi*). To use the name or perform the ritual action meaningfully entails drawing an analogy between past and present circumstances to evoke this vested significance. An important characteristic of both name and ritual action is that they are context-specific, qualified by a unique set of circumstances. That is, their significance cannot be exhausted by a genetic analysis that only accounts for what they mean for themselves. Since meaning is not simply derived from the name or the ritual action per se, a complete accounting must also have recourse to an explanation that reveals their relationship to and meaning for their ever-particular, ever-changing context.

A given name or ritual action, although describable at an abstract level, is truly meaningful only as a particular and personal disclosure of meaning. This can be made evident in the common alternative translation of "ritual action" (*li* 禮)as "propriety," provided "propriety" is understood in light of its primitive sense as "to make one's own." Thus, both "appropriate" ritual actions and the "proper" use of language require a personalization and a making over fitting to one's own specific conditions. For this reason, abstract names such as "ritual goblet" (*ku*) and "ruler" (*chun*), while laden with their historically derived meanings,

来实现所命名的秩序。《管子》描述了"名"的这个功能:"名者,圣人之所以纪万物也。"(《管子·心术上》)

我们诠释的"正名"这一概念反对形式结构的优先论。我们不同意所谓孔子仅是用"名"来组织规划人类经验,以使其符合某种界定生命之意义、价值和目的先定模式的观念。我们认为,孔子把特别环境中的特定个人视为"义"之根源,这说明他强调审美秩序的优先性。通过优先将人视为某一特定焦点,孔子让"名"之网络构成的诠释模型变得一致和连贯,与此同时,这些模型也成为新奇性和独特性得以显露的可塑构架。

(《通过孔子而思》,第330—338页)

对在中国古典文本中看到的语言修辞用法作最稳妥的归纳,可以说它们关涉到"类比推理"。〔中国人〕所使用的那种类比论证必须理解为"关联思维"(correlative thinking)的一种模式。我们的《期望中国》的相当大一部分是用来阐发这种思维模式的。我

must remain open to particularization in their display of significance, just as ritual actions exist only to the extent that they are considered, embodied, reformulated, and extended via the peculiar conditions of the present moment, so naming and the attuning of names is a dynamic enterprise in which the existing structure and definition is qualified by the understanding that names and their achieved harmonies are always fluid within the parameters of a context, and are in continual need of attunement.

The challenge that this fluidity of names, and their patternings represents to a purely logical, referential explanation of *cheng ming** is reinforced by the performative force of naming. Ritual actions are not only performed by people, but, because they actively evoke a certain kind of response, in an important sense they "perform" people. Similarly, not only do names describe, they act in that they impel a person towards a certain kind of experience. Giving a substitute vessel the name of a *ku* ritual goblet can, where appropriate significance is invested, effectively transform this substitute vessel into a *ku*. Not only are names used to name the order, they are also used for effecting order in what is to be named. The *Kuan Tzu* describes this function of names: "Names (*ming**)are the means whereby the sages organize the myriad phenomena."

Our interpretation of "ordering names" (*cheng ming**) argues against the priority of formal constructions by rejecting the suggestion that Confucius simply uses names reductionistically to organize the process of

们向读者提到这本著作是为了阐明以下的论点。

就像大部分中国哲学家所使用的那样，类比程序在上文所讨论的这个词的意义上说，是修辞的用法。它们诉诸传统的权威和榜样（圣人和文化上的杰出人物）。虽然这样诉诸权威性可能会将论证变成为气质类的论证，然而，礼的制度和习俗保证了情感也包容于其中。

将"正名"理解为寻求单义性，是解释上的一个错误，这样的错误经常发生。之所以说是错误的，是因为，那种正名的努力是一种功能性的和实用的程序，而不是逻辑的或严格语义的程序。这意味着正名关涉到确立已由礼清楚地规定的名分之间的连贯性，还关涉到个体（夫、父、臣、子）的特定的行为，这些个体作为社会成员的表面身份并非讨论的对象。

（《汉哲学思维文化探源》，第142—143页）

中国的过程宇宙论将伽达默尔对语言的这一深刻见解，向更深层推进，并提出：语言在广义上远比"媒介"的意义更深，语言的意义由

human experience into some preestablished pattern that is held to define the meaning, value and purpose of life. It argues for the priority of aesthetic order by insisting that Confucius regarded the particular person in a specific context as the source of signification. Confucius, in giving this priority to the person as a particular focus, regards the interpretive patternings constituted by the network of names to serve a sense of continuity and coherence and, at the same time, to be a malleable framework through which novelty and uniqueness are disclosed.

(*Thinking Through Confucius,* pp. 268-275)

The safest generalization concerning the rhetorical uses of language found in classical Chinese texts is that they involve "analogical reasoning." Analogical argumentation of the sort employed must be understood as a mode of "correlative thinking." A significant portion of our *Anticipating China* is given over to the explication of this mode of thinking. We refer the reader to that work for an elaboration of the following remarks.

As employed by the majority of Chinese philosophers, analogical procedures are rhetorical in the senses of the term discussed above. They appeal to the authority of tradition and to the exemplars (the sages and cultural heroes) of that tradition. And though this appeal to authoritativeness might seem to shape the arguments into those of the *ethos* variety, the institution of ritual behavior insures that *pathos* is involved as well.

"我们是谁"构成;"我们"是关系相连的、不可简约的"民"。交流具有话语的塑造人功能,《易经大传》对这一点讲得十分清楚。一个人的认同,当然是位置确定的"体"与"家";它的定义实际是通过积极的话语而形成或建立一种聚焦式的敬畏关系,它包括"体"和"举止",还包括文字和语言、音乐、礼仪化的身份和关系、会餐等。在整个儒学经典中,争论主题是如何正确、高效地使用语言,即"正名",认为关系是根本性的,是一个繁荣社会在其所有斑驳重叠的方方面面所达到的基本点。"正名"是如何才能达到人与人互相关系最恰宜的度,因而也是最富于意义的度。其实,恰当性的行为和蕴义性的"素质",都表达在"义"字中,"义"是儒家观点的一个核心术语,指的是人生的圆成。"正名",作为带来社会秩序效果的本源,在孔子思想之中得到阐述:

子路曰:"卫君待子而为政,子将奚先?"子曰:"必也正名乎!"子路曰:"有是哉,子之迂也!奚其正?"子曰:

It is an interpretative misstep to understand the "rectification of names" (*zhengming* 正名) as a search for univocity, as it so often is. For the attempt to properly order names is a functional and pragmatic, rather than a logical or strictly semantic, procedure. This means that ordering names involves establishing coherence between roles already spelled out by tradition (*li* 禮), and the specific actions of individuals (husbands, fathers, ministers, sons) whose ostensive identity as functionaries within the society is not in question.

(*Thinking from the Han,* pp. 137-138)

The Chinese processual cosmology would perhaps take this Gadamerian insight into language one step further and claim that, in its broadest sense, "language," more than a medium, is constitutive of who we are as irreducibly relational people. The *Great Commentary* of the *Book of Changes* turns explicitly to the way in which communication functions to form persons discursively. The identity of a person, while certainly localized by "body" and "home," is in fact defined as a concentrated focus of patterns of deference established and fostered through effective discourses that entail body and gesture, but that also include the written and spoken language, music, ritualized roles and relationships, food, and so on. Throughout classical Confucianism, the contention is that the proper and effective use of language (*zhengming* 正名) is the substance of relationships, and is basic to the flourishing community in all of

"野哉由也！君子于其所不知，盖阙如也。名不正，则言不顺；言不顺，则事不成；事不成，则礼乐不兴；礼乐不兴，则刑罚不中；刑罚不中，则民无所措手足。故君子名之必可言也，言之必可行也。君子于其言，无所苟而已矣。"（《论语·子路》）

"正名"一词，一直被译为英语的"the rectification of names"（"校正名称"），指的是我们所有行为应与我们"名号"与"阶层"所规定的意义相符；"正名"当然是含此一必要之义。对孔子而言，"正名"所指的是在严格使用官阶名号与政府清廉之间存在的一种必然联系。《春秋左传》中记载：有一个人因救了一个地位尊贵的人，得到奖赏。但他拒绝了赏赐的一座城池，却希望以公子等级配备穿戴。孔子听说此事后，怒斥此人，与上面摘引《论语》那段话甚是相似：

仲尼闻之曰："惜也，不如多与之邑。唯器与名，不

its overlapping dimensions. Using language properly is how we achieve what is most *appropriate* in our associations, and hence what is most *meaningful*. Indeed, both of these qualities of Conduct—appropriateness and meaningfulness—are captured in the term *yi* 義, a central terminology in this Confucian vision of the consummate life. This power of language as the primary source for effecting social order is not lost on Confucius:

"Were the Lord of Wey to turn the administration of his state over to you, what would be your first priority?" asked Zilu.

"Without question it would be to insure that names are used properly (*zhengming*)," replied the Master.

"Would you be as impractical as that?" responded Zilu. "What is it for names to be used properly anyway?"

"How can you be so dense!" replied Confucius. "Exemplary persons defer on matters they do not understand. When names are not used properly, language will not be used effectively; when language is not used effectively, matters will not be taken care of; when matters are not taken care of, the achievement of a ritual propriety in roles and relations and the playing of music will not flourish; when the achievement of ritual propriety and the playing of music do not flourish, the application of laws and punishments

可以假人，君之所司也。名以出信，信以守器，器以藏礼，礼以行义，义以生利，利以平民，政之大节也。若以假人，与人政也。政亡，则国家从之，弗可止也已。"（《左传·成公二年》）

贯穿《论语》的一个重要主题就是孔子所强调的礼，这一点也不能疏忽，正式礼仪活动必须与相应官阶恪守一致，否则，朝政倾塌之危将至。（如《论语·八佾》："子曰：'禘自既灌而往者，吾不欲观之矣。'"《论语·八佾》："'然则管仲知礼乎？'曰：'邦君树塞门，管氏亦树塞门；邦君为两君之好，有反坫，管氏亦有反坫。管氏而知礼，孰不知礼？'"《论语·先进》："南容三复白圭，孔子以其兄之子妻之。"《论语·先进》："季氏富于周公，而求也为之聚敛而附益之。子曰：'非吾徒也。小子鸣鼓而攻之，可也。'"）具体言之，孔子沮丧不已，是因为在自己的国家鲁国，季氏僭礼篡权，主持只有国君才有特权做的礼乐仪式。（如《论语·八佾》："孔子谓季氏：'八

will not be on the mark; when the application of laws and punishments is not on the mark, the people will not know what to do with themselves. Thus, when exemplary persons put a name to something, it can certainly be spoken, and when spoken it can certainly be acted upon. There is nothing careless in the attitude of exemplary persons toward what is said."

This notion of *zhengming* has conventionally been translated as "the rectification of names," suggesting that in our conduct we need to satisfy the stipulated definition of names and ranks. And this requisite is certainly part of the story. For Confucius, there is an immediate association between using political titles of office strictly, and the integrity of the state. In the *Zuozhuan* commentary on *the Spring and Autumn Annals* there is an account of a person who in being rewarded for saving a prominent man's life declines the offer of a city and asks instead to be allowed to use the dress and accoutrements of a prince. On hearing of this, Confucius denounces this charade bitterly in language reminiscent of the *Analects* passage cited above:

What a pity! It would have been better to give him many cities. It is insignias of office and titles alone that cannot be conceded to pretenders— they must be managed by the ruler. Proper titles give rise to confidence, and confidence

俏舞于庭，是可忍也，孰不可忍也？'""三家者以《雍》彻。子曰：'相维辟公，天子穆穆'，奚取于三家之堂？'""季氏旅于泰山。子谓冉有曰：'女弗能救与？'对曰：'不能。'子曰：'呜呼！曾谓泰山，不如林放乎？'"）

当然，活着的语言拥有自己的历史，其内容具有约定俗成的意义。从这一方面来说，它在意思上是回溯性的。但是"正名"并非到此为止，它有前瞻性。也即，它是一种正活着的语言，必须在使用时带有一种对总是变动不已的环境的敏感性，而且必须尊重谈话参与者的特殊性。这是《论语》中时而可见的，在六处不同地方，学生问孔子"何谓仁"，而每一次对话，孔子都是对不同学生有不同的回答。原因是，颜回是一个贫穷、少言寡语、谦恭谨慎的人，他不像子贡，很有钱、自信、坚定、个性强。我们可能要想到，语言有文法与形态性含义，也有语义性的力量，这种情况要求它具有一种整体合意性的恰当到位的语感。并不简单的是，人说话的内容传达着意义，语言传达意义还在于场合、时机和对象。

is what protects the insignias of office. It is insignias in which the meaning of ritual propriety is invested, and it is ritual propriety that carries appropriate conduct (*yi*) into practice; appropriate conduct is what gives rise to benefit, and it is benefit that brings equanimity to the people. Such things are what structure government, and if you concede them to pretenders, you concede the government along with them. If the government is lost, the country will follow, and there can be no stopping it.

A major theme that runs through the *Analects* is Confucius' insistence that unrelenting attention must be given to retaining a strict correspondence between formal ritual practices and the ranks of office, with the risk of political collapse being the consequence of doing otherwise. More specifically, in his home state of Lu, Confucius was repeatedly chagrined at the powerful Ji family's usurpation of practices and privileges appropriate to the royal house.

Certainly, living language is informed by a history of usage that allows for its content to be stipulated, and in this sense, is retrospective in its meaning. But the need to *zhengming* does not end here. It is also prospective. That is, it is a living language and has to be used in a way that is sensitive to the specifics of the always changing context and in a way that respects the uniqueness of the persons involved in the conversation. It is often remarked upon that on six different occasions in the *Analects*, Confucius is reported to have been asked by his proteges about

的确，作为一个君子，说话的效果，不仅对社会有直接影响，而且对整个天下也具有流传下去的深刻影响。君子作为有效言行之本源，可以理解为对社会环境构成内部发生一系列特定现象起到促成作用。

> 君子居其室，出其言善，则千里之外应之，况其迩者乎？居其室，出其言不善，则千里之外违之，况其迩者乎？言出乎身，加乎民；行发乎迩，见乎远。言行，君子之枢机。枢机之发，荣辱之主也。言行，君子之所以动天地也，可不慎乎？（《周易·系辞上》）

话语的质量在于其适当度（宜）；这种"适当性"的感觉，是当人产生出一种真挚的付出感与对富于意义关系的归属感。其实，它是话语洋溢的一种真挚性的实感，是交流的有效性基础。它区别于那种操纵行为，是十分有造诣的和谐结合；它区别于宣传，是伦理劝说；它不是侵犯个性，而是开放的亲密

the meaning of "consummate conduct" (*ren*), and on each of these occasions he gives each of these different students a different answer. This is because an impoverished, reticent, respectful, and conscientious Yan Hui would need a different understanding of what it means to become consummate in his conduct than a wealthy, self-possessed, assertive, and sometimes self-serving Zigong. We might reflect on the fact that language has syntactical and morphological implications as well as semantic force, and as such, requires a sensitivity to "positioning and place" (*wei* 位) as being integral to its meaning. It is not just what one says that conveys meaning, but where, when, and to whom one is speaking.

Indeed, the efficacy of what the exemplary person has to say not only influences the immediate community, but also has a profound and lasting effect on the world broadly. The exemplary person as the source of effective speech and action has to be understood as catalytic within a configuration of circumstances in precipitating a certain course of events:

> If what the exemplary persons say even while remaining at home is felicitous, those in distant quarters will respond to it; how much more so those near at hand. If what is said is not felicitous, those in distant quarters will oppose it; how much more so those near at hand. What is said comes from one's person but has an effect on the people; actions arise near at hand but are seen from

性；它不是煽情，而是激动人心的鼓舞。

（《儒家角色伦理学：一套特色伦理学词汇》，第112—115页）

a distance. Words and actions are the hinge and trigger of exemplary persons. And the operations of hinge and trigger control honor and disgrace. Since it is with words and actions that exemplary persons move the heavens and the earth, how could they be but circumspect with respect to them?

The quality of discourse is measured by its degree of appropriateness (*yi*), and this feeling of appropriateness is whence a sense of genuine commitment and of belonging within meaningful relations emerges. Indeed, it is the quality of genuineness within the discourse that is the ground of effective communication, and that distinguishes virtuosic orchestration from manipulation, ethical exhortation from propaganda, liberating intimacy from an invasion of privacy, and inspiration from sensationalism.

(*Confucian Role Ethics: A Vocabulary,* pp. 99-102)

民

有一大批同源词是由"民"字为词根导源出的。这些词几乎全都带有提升"愚昧，昏聩"原意的意味：如"泯"（troubled, confused, disorderly）、"瞀"（blinded, distracted, confused）、"昏"（dusk, darkness,

Min

The character, *min* 民, is the root from which a large field of cognate characters derive. These characters almost uniformly convey refinements on the primitive meaning of "blindness and confusion": *min* 泯 "troubled, confused, disorderly"; *hun* 瞀 "blinded, distracted, confused"; *hun*

benighted, blinded, mentally dark)、"惛"（darked in mind, stupid）等等。另一个同源词"珉"，意思是"玉石"，实际是随处可得的"假玉"，因为它缺乏真玉的光泽而为君子所不取。古典著作中有一些在双关意义上将"民"（masses）定义为"冥"（dark）或其同源词"瞑"（shut the eyes, troubled sight）的情况，都突出了该术语所反映的无知、黑暗、模糊不明的混沌状态这一核心意义。董仲舒《春秋繁露》就有现成的例子：

> 民之号取之瞑也。使性而已善，则何故以瞑为号？……性有似目，目卧幽而瞑……譬如瞑者待觉，教之然后善。当其未觉，可谓有质，而不可谓善……民之为言，固犹瞑也，随其名号以入其理，则得之矣。（《春秋繁露·深察名号》）

早期周代铭文上有"民"的一个最基本形式"中"，该字形一直被解读为"目盲"的象形字，因为中间没有瞳孔。与"人"的"核"的概念相对照，"民"则是无"睛"（核）之目。段玉裁强调，《说文》

昏 "dusk, darkness, benighted, blinded, mentally dark"; *hun* 惛 "darkened in mind, stupid"; and so on. Another cognate, *min* 珉, which denotes "jade," is in fact an abundantly available pseudo-jade which, because it lacks the luster of real jade, is disdained by the exemplary person. This core meaning of dark and undiscriminated chaos that is reflected in the term "masses"(*min* 民) is underscored by the several classical texts that define *min* paronomastically as "dark" (*ming* 冥), or its cognate, "shut the eyes, troubled sight" (*mien* 瞑). Tung Chung-shu is a ready example:

> The designation for "the masses" (*min* 民) is derived from "closed eyes" (*mien* 瞑). If by natural tendency the masses are already good, why should "closed eyes" (*mien*) be taken as their designation?....It can be likened to the eye. When the eye is sleeping, it is closed.... Just as the closed eye needs to be awakened, so the masses need to be instructed before they can be good. Before they have been awakened, we might say they have the potential, but we cannot say that they are good. ... The way we express "the masses". (*min* 民) is certainly similar to "closed eyes" (*mien* 瞑). We can get at

249

将"民"定义为"众萌",即在用"萌"专门表达某种精神的蒙昧和无知状态:"懵懵无知貌也。""萌"字另一个意义是"萌芽",其显然与董仲舒将"民"形容为"卧幽待觉"之论相应。

《论语》中"民"的地位显然是低下的,其常被用来与"上"(those above = superior)作对比。例如:"子曰:'上好礼,则民易使也。'"(《论语·宪问》)

作为"子民"的"民"倾向于被动。用以描述在上者对待"民"的适当态度的语言通常也是有意屈尊的:他们"服"于上者,而上者却以"临"与"惠"的姿态来管理和对待他们。是"在上者"而非"民"自己代表"民",前者决定"务民"之"义";而"民"作为"子民"一般来说都要受制于"刑罚"。"民"应"敬""上",且"从"其行。"民"的德性和潜能是以是否践行"中庸"之德来表达的:"中庸之为德也,其至矣乎!民鲜久矣。"(《论语·雍也》)杨伯峻解读该章时指出:"'民'在这里不是专门指平民(common people),因此我将它翻译为'everybody'(人人)。"然而,

this meaning when we pursue its conceptual structure by analyzing the term.

One of the primitive forms of the character *min* 民 given to us on the earliest Chou inscriptions is ㄇ: which has been interpreted as a pictograph of an eye blind because it lacks a pupil. In contrast to *jen* 人 as the kernel of the fruit, *min* 民 is the eye lacking in its most essential element, the pupil. Tuan Yü-tsai is insistent that the *Shuo-wen* dictionary in defining *min* as *chung meng* 眾萌 uses the character *meng* 萌 specifically to indicate an attitude of mental darkness and ignorance: hence, "the ignorant masses." The second meaning of *meng* 萌 as "sprout" resonates clearly with Tung Chung-shu's description of the *min* 民 as sleeping with the potential to be awakened.

The low status of *min* is clear in the *Analects* where it is frequently contrasted with "those above =superiors" (*shang* 上). For example(14.41): "The Master said: 'When superiors (*shang*) are fond of ritual action, the masses (*min*) will be easy to employ.'"

The *min* as *min* tend to be passive. The language that is used to characterize the appropriate attitude of their superiors to them is generally condescending: they are to submit (*fu* 服) to those above whose

恰恰正因为他们是"民",才应当致力于公共事务(common affairs)。既然"民"与"时"有关,那么"使民"(proper employment)似乎就是在适当时间耕种或服劳役。而"使人"则指服务于公共事务。

《论语》用了几个不同的表达来指称民,如其中有"众"(the multitude)、"百姓"(the hundred surnames)和"庶人"(the many)。这些指称各自含义有重大不同,但它们却与"民"本身有一个共同差异,即他们都是指集合在一起的单个人或者至少单个部族,而"民"似乎是意指身份模糊的平民大众。第二个重要区分在于其他这些称呼并不必然排除上层社会,但"民"却几乎确实如此。

当孔子用"民"来指称那些无可名状的普通大众时,他的态度可以说是蔑视的。他们是不能"视"的盲者:"困而不学,民斯为下矣。"(《论语·季氏》)如果我们将"德"理解为一个"特点"(particular focus),那么孔子所用"民德"的表达或许进一步表明"民"是可以被用一个总称一概而论的。上面我们谈到"礼"最突出的特性即在于它

posture in administering to them is to oversee (*lin* 临) them and treat them with magnanimity (*hui* 惠). It is the superiors on behalf of the masses, rather than the masses themselves, who work on what is appropriate (*yi* 义) for them; the masses as masses are generally governed by the rule of law and its attendant punishments. The masses should be reverent (*ching* 敬) in their attitude to those above, and model themselves upon them. The virtue and potency of the masses is to be expressed in the proper execution of their everyday occupations (6.29): "Taking hitting the mark in common affairs as their *te* 德 is of the utmost importance, yet it has been lacking in the masses for a long time." Yang Po-chün in his interpretation of this passage argues that "*min* here does not exclusively refer to the common people, and for this reason I have rendered it 'everybody'". But it is precisely because they are *min* that they ought to exert themselves in common affairs. And given the association between *min* and the proper seasons, it would appear that their proper employment (*shih min* 使民) is specifically tilling the land and performing corvée duties at the appropriate times. The employment of the *jen* (*shih jen* 使人), on the other hand, can often refer to public office.

The *Analects* uses several different expressions to designate the people: "the

要求投注个体之"义"。那么，在这一意义上，作为全体而非作为独特个人的"民"，其践行"礼"的能力也是折中的。

（《通过孔子而思》，第171—173页）

multitude" (*chung* 眾), "the hundred surnames" (*paihsing* 百姓) and "the many" (*shu jen* 庶人) among them. These terms have important differences in connotation; but they may share one common difference from *min* itself in that while they all suggest an assembly of discrete persons, or at least discrete clans, *min* would seem to connote the common people as an undiscriminated mass. A second important difference would be that these alternative designations would not necessarily exclude the upper echelons of society, while *min* almost certainly would.

When Confucius uses *min* as the amorphous mass of commoners, he can be deprecatory. These are the blind who will not see: "the masses who will not learn even when vexed with difficulties" (16.9). That Confucius uses the expression, the *te* of the masses (*minte* 民德), if we understand *te* to be a "particular focus," might further suggest that the *min* can be treated as a whole. We have seen above that the distinguishing characteristic of ritual action is that it requires a personal investment of significance (*yi* 義). To the extent, then, that the *min* act en masse rather than as unique persons, their capacity for performing ritual actions is compromised.

(*Thinking Through Confucius,* pp. 140-142)

无为

儒家的统治者能以身作则，故他的活动反映出某种信念，即确信其道德表现可以影响并教化他的臣民。这是通过道德的榜样来教化其臣民的政治原则。君主的"无为"即在于只是通过其个人的修养与民众产生相互影响，而不需要以专制的方法统辖其臣民。他同臣民的关系特点具有完全的非强迫性。而其臣民由于共同参与了道德秩序创建，因而他们个性的实现亦能够与统治者保持一致。应当注意的是，道家的"无为"观念与儒家的有一基本差异：道家是无意以人类的道德范畴去解释宇宙之运动的；儒家则坚持人类之道德完善与宇宙之和谐相一致的观点。对早期儒家来说，"义"表示了道德完善的某种可能性，每个人的此一道德之完善即意味着个人的天赋必须同其生存的自然和社会环境相一致。……由于在孔子的伦理学说中，道德纯系自然的和内在的，因此统治者不需要为了社会和政治的秩序去主动地扩充其臣民的品性。相反，这只是一种

Wu-wei

The Confucian ruler, regulating his conduct so that his activities reflect a commitment to the expression of his moral nature, is able to influence his subordinates and transform his people. This is the political principle of the guidance and transformation of the people through moral example. The ruler "does nothing" inasmuch as his personal cultivation, possible only through interaction with his people, does not require the projection of arbitrary demands on his subordinates. His relationship with these subordinates is characterized by a total absence of compulsion. That the particular realization of these subordinates happens to be congruent with that of the ruler is due to their common participation in a creative moral order. It should be noted that there is a fundamental difference between the Taoist notion of *Wu-wei* and its Confucian counterpart: Taoism is unwilling to interpret cosmic activity in terms of human moral categories; Confucianism insists on the coincidence of human moral achievement and cosmic harmony. For the early Confucians, *yi* is a possibility for moral achievement which ties the natural endowment of individuals to their natural and social environments. … Since in Confucian ethical theory morality is entirely natural and intrinsic, it is not necessary for the ruler actively to augment the character of his subordinates in order to

他如何去参与其臣民共同实现他们本性中已然之善端的事情。在这一对话当中,君主与其臣民共同追求其自然之善端的完美实现。臣民则把君主看作实现了人类善端的一个典范,当然是他们自己也可以企及的某种典范。

(《中国古代的统治艺术:〈淮南子·主术〉研究》,第 56 页)

天之道与圣人之道之间的这种类似在《老子》中通过直接比较得到了更进一步的强调:

> 天地不仁,以万物为刍狗;
> 圣人不仁,以百姓为刍狗。
> (五章)
> 天之道,利而不害。圣人之道,为而不争。(八十一章)

这些有关天之道与其现象世界和圣人与百姓间关系的种种特征之描述,大都会推导出"无为"的概念——就是说,这些都体现了"顺其自然"的途径或方法。正如天道并不强制万物一样,圣人也不会以强制的社会和政治规范限制其百姓的自然发展。《老子》的政治思想是

achieve social and political order. Rather, it is a matter of his participating with them in the realization of the incipient virtue which is already theirs by nature. Both the ruler and the subordinate pursue the consummation of their natural possibilities in this dialogue. The subordinate looks to the ruler as an actualizing model of human potential—a model of what he himself can achieve.

(*Art of Rulership: A Study of Ancient Chinese Political Thought,* pp. 29)

The analogy between the natural *tao* and the *tao* of the ruler as consummate human being is reinforced even further by direct parallels in the text:

> Heaven and earth are amoral;
> They consider the myriad things to be straw dogs.
> The sage is amoral;
> He considers the common people to be straw dogs.
> The natural *tao* benefits without injuring;
> The *tao* of the sage does without contending.

These characteristics which are attributed to both the natural *tao* in its relationship to the phenomenal world and the sage-ruler in his relationship to the people are, for the most part, corollary to the notion of *wu-wei*—that is, they are alternative ways of saying "pursue only natural activity." Just as the

政治哲学

一种颇具特色的道家无政府主义，"无为"则是其推行的主要方法：当权者不干涉个人的发展并为之创造一个最有益的环境。如儒家的政治理论一样，君主及其社会地位被看作是自然形成的。虽然他的职责是使社会的运行秩序化从而使之得以维持下去，但是他与百姓的关系与其说是专制的，不如说是权威的。他在国家中的地位极类似于家庭中父亲的角色。他作为一个君主，在完成自身自然角色的同时，也为其臣民的成就创造了一个十分有利的环境。

（《中国古代的统治艺术：〈淮南子·主术〉研究》，第72页）

主术中或许首要的就是"无为"及其内涵。在我们上面提到的国家概念中，君主与大臣的职责与权力是明确规定的，大臣只是作为一个整体的、实际行使日常职能的官僚体系中的组成部分。而君主则不然，他是整个国家机器的权力象征与化身。因此，对其地位的任何冒犯行为都会破坏这一个人体系的结构。如对君主重法表示不满，鼓吹另一种具有无政府主义的自动职

natural *tao* does not impose consiraints on the myriad phenomena, the sage too refrains from inhibiting the natural development of his people by subjecting them to imposed social and political regulation. *Wu-wei* is the main precept behind the *Lao Tzu*'s conception of government as a peculiarly *Tao*istic anarchism: the minimum amount of external interference projected onto the individual from those in power combined with an environment most conducive to the individual's quest for personal fulfillment. As in Confucian political theory, the ruler and his position in society are taken as natural conditions. While he functions to facilitate the orderly operation necessary to sustain social living, he is authoritative rather than authoritarian in his relationship to the people. His position in the state is best seen as an analog to the role of the father in the family. In realizing himself in his natural role as ruler he creates a situation fertile for the realization of his subordinates.

(*Art of Rulership: A Study of Ancient Chinese Political Thought,* pp. 41-42)

Of these techniques of rulership, perhaps the foremost is *wu-wei* and its corollary implications. In the conception of the state outlined above, the positions and occupations of ruler and minister are clearly defined. The ministers are integral, functioning, and active components in the bureaucratic system; the ruler is not. Rather, he is the human embodiment of the authority of the

能体系，那么，即使不破坏公众对法律至上信念的基础，也必然会严重地动摇它。此外，如果官僚制度遭到人们的反对，那么也同样会动摇官员们通过尽职尽责去获得财富和晋升的信心。

《韩非子》中的"无为"思想正同道家和儒家一样，亦试图沟通天道运行与政府职能之间的联系。赋予形上之道的许多特征，也被用来形容理想之君主：

> 故曰：道不同于万物，德不同于阴阳，衡不同于轻重，绳不同于出入，和不同于燥湿，君不同于群臣。凡此六者，道之出也。道无双，故曰一。是故明君贵独道之容。君臣不同道，下以名祷。君操其名，臣效其形。形名参同，上下和调也。（《韩非子·扬权》）

君主恒处于无为，便不会受聪明人的蒙骗，因为他无法揣摩主上想要做些什么。这些人与其去猜测君主的想法，倒不如老老实实以法律及其应尽的职责为标准行事。进而，君主也可以因成功而坦然接受

governmental machinery as a whole. As such, any activity on his part violently disrupts the structure of the individual systems. Any intervention on his part with respect to law, for example, introduces an arbitrary element into an otherwise automatically functioning system, seriously threatening if not undermining public conviction in the absoluteness of law. Any personal intervention with respect to the bureaucracy, moreover, disturbs the faith of officialdom in the certainty of wealth and promotion through fulfillment of responsibility and devotion to duty.

Just as in the Taoist and Confucian interpretations of *wu-wei*, in the *Han Fei Tzu* there is an attempt to correlate the operations of the cosmos and the proper functioning of the political state. Characteristics attributed to the metaphysical *tao* are projected onto the ideal ruler:

> Therefore it is said: The *tao* is not the same as the myriad things, virtue (*te*) is not the same as the *yin* and *yang*, a pair of scales is not the same as heaviness and lightness, the marking line is not the same as the variations it measures, the *ho* flute [a reed instrument unaffected by humidity] is not the same as wetness and dryness, and a ruler is not the same as his various ministers. All six of these come out of the *tao*, but because the *tao* is not a plurality, it is called the One. Therefore the perspicacious ruler values the disposition of the solitary *tao*. The

臣下的颂扬，却不必承受因失败而带来的指责。他还可以避免同他的那些事实上在各个方面都比他强的臣下发生正面冲突。这就是说，一位平庸的君主——并非所有方面都平庸——也能够维持他的统治。《韩非子》中有许多地方都讨论了"无为"的统治术，这些形形色色的统治术实际上构成了"无为"思想的真正内涵。譬如，"无见"即不表现人之好恶，不对任何议题发表意见，不显露个人志向和愿望。君主若能长处此道，即可在公众面前维持其睿智的形象。此外，由于他深居简出，行为诡秘，不与人直接交流或接触，便可以保留自己的意见，增加个人的神秘色彩。由于君主让公众难以捉摸，因此他就成了至高无上的理想代表。由于他的臣民不了解他的实际水平，所以授予了他远超其实际能力所能承担的权力。《韩非子》对这样的君主作了如下描写：

> 凡听之道，以其所出，反以为之入，故审名以定位，明分以辩类。听言之道，溶若甚醉。唇乎齿乎，吾不为始乎，齿乎唇乎，愈惛惛乎。彼自离

ruler and his ministers do not have the same *tao*. The subordinates define their proposals and the ruler takes a firm hold on these definitions. The ministers then deliver their performance, and where definition and performance are congruent there is harmony between ruler and subordinate.

By maintaining his attitude of *wu-wei*, the ruler cannot be deceived by clever people who are able to anticipate his reactions. Rather than trying to second-guess the ruler, these people look to the laws and to their responsibilities of office as their standards of conduct. Further, the ruler can avoid censure for any failures while basking in the praise of his subordinates for any successes. He can avoid personal competition with his subjects who, collectively, surpass him in virtually all respects. This means that even a ruler of very common parts—not an altogether uncommon phenomenon— can maintain political control. In the *Han Fei Tzu* passages which discuss the political technique of *wu-wei*, there are a variety of corollary techniques which are really implications of the *wu-wei* attitude. There is, for example, "showing nothing" (*wu-hsien*)— not demonstrating one's likes and dislikes, not proffering an opinion on any given subject, not revealing ambitions or personal desires. In maintaining this posture, the ruler shields the contours of his character and intellect from public sight. There is also personal solitude and secrecy, keeping one's own counsel and the encouragement of a personal mystique by

之，吾因以知之；是非辐凑，上不与构。虚静无为，道之情也；参伍比物，事之形也。参之以比物，伍之以合虚。根干不革，则动泄不失矣。动之溶之，无为而改之。喜之，则多事；恶之，则生怨。故去喜去恶，虚心以为道舍。上不与共之，民乃宠之；上不与义之，使独为之。上固闭内扃，从室视庭，参咫尺已具，皆之其处。(《韩非子·扬权》)

这段话十分清楚地说明了法家的"无为"政治理论及与之相关的统治术，其意在防止任何深入了解君主以操纵国家机器的个人能力的企图。

(《中国古代的统治艺术：〈淮南子·主术〉研究》，第85—87页)

a lack of direct contact. By remaining beyond the range of public scrutiny, the ruler becomes an ideal invested with a superlative degree of all things worthwhile. Because his subordinates have no knowledge of his actual limitations, they attribute powers to him far beyond his real capacities. The *Han Fei Tzu* describes this ruler in the following terms (32.10):

Now, the Way of listening is to match the performance against the proposal. Therefore examine proposals carefully in fixing offices and clarify duties in making distinctions. The Way of listening is to say to yourself: Assume the characteristics of drunkenness. Lips! Teeth! I am not the first to move! Teeth! Lips! Be ever more inscrutable! I will take advantage of other people exposing themselves to understand them. Different opinions converge on the ruler at the hub, but do no play any part. Vacuity, stillness, and nonaction— this is the shape of affairs. Examine subordinates by comparing what has come to light and scrutinize them by bringing these into the hub. Where the trunk and roots do not change, things will not go astray. In motion, in stillness, make all changes through nonaction. When you like subordinates, affairs will proliferate; when you dislike them, you will give rise to resentment. Therefore abandon likes and dislikes, and make your heart vacuous in order to become

政治哲学

the lodging place of the Way. The ruler does not join together with his subjects in administering affairs, and the people respect him. He does not discuss things with them, and makes them carry them out by themselves. He bolts his chamber door firmly and from his room watches the courtyard. The standards already being set in place, everyone takes up his proper role.

As this passage makes clear, in Legalist political theory *wu-wei* and the related techniques of rulership were intended to prevent any insight into the ruler's personality which might interfere with the operations of the governmental machinery.

(*Art of Rulership: A Study of Ancient Chinese Political Thought,* pp. 51-53)

法 / Laws (*Fa*)

西方传统中,"法"或者作为神圣命令,其超验根源为它们提供了最强有力的正当性;或者作为种种理性原则,借此说明体现社会最大稳定性的公正和繁荣的行为和交往规范,这二者都是立法者的产物。

(《通过孔子而思》,第 207 页)

人的个体性力量源于外在规

In the Western tradition, laws as divine commands, whose transcendent source provides their strongest justification, or laws as rational principles articulating norms of behavior and interaction characterized by fairness and productive of the greatest social stability, are products of lawgivers.

(*Thinking Through Confucius, p. 170*)

One of the consequences of the claim that the strength of one's individuality is a function

259

范这一主张的一个结论就是超验的"法"。一个突出由个人主义塑造的社会必须使法成为秩序外在决定的根源。因为公论在一个高度个人主义的社会中几乎不可能实现。在这种情况下,"法"就必须首先用于外在行为,且必须拥有制裁力量以惩罚的威胁来确保一致。

(《通过孔子而思》,第207页)

确保理性秩序依赖已有的关系模式,在其真正意义上几乎不依赖任何具体情境。我们这里可以将社会秩序称为服从或符合原则或规范的功能。这些规范最终根源必然是精神或上帝的意愿或人类的理性或获得公共认可的开明的利己心。

(《通过孔子而思》,第208页)

将西方的成文法与中国的"法"(或者说孔子的"刑")相提并论确实是有问题的。古典中国传统中,由于"法"也表示一种形式化的意义投注,因此它与"礼"有相合的部分。这就是说,"礼"和"法"拥有一个共同的出发点。另外,"法"也和"礼"一样意在组织规划社会。然而,"法"与"礼"显

of the exteriority of norms, is that transcendent laws, laws as external determining sources of order, are necessary to societies patterned by individualism in its stronger sense. This is the case because communal consensus is well-nigh impossible to achieve in a highly individualistic society. Under such circumstances, then, law must apply primarily to external behavior and must have a sanctioning power which guarantees conformity by threat of punishment.

(*Thinking Through Confucius,* p. 170)

The assurance of the latter type of order depends upon already existing patterns of relatedness which are in some very real sense independent of any particular instances. Here we can speak of social order as a function of obedience to, or conformity with, principles or norms. The ultimate source of these norms must be the mind or will of God, or human reason, or a commonly recognized sense of enlightened self-interest.

(*Thinking Through Confucius,* p. 171)

The association between the Western notion of positive law and Chinese *fa* 法 (or Confucius' *hsing* 刑) is certainly problematic. In the classical Chinese tradition, *fa* overlaps ritual action (*li*) in that it too represents a formalized investment of meaning. That is, *li* and *fa* share a common starting point. Furthermore, like ritual action, *fa* is directed at organizing and ordering society. *Fa* differs

然不同，因为，它既不是主体间性地融为一体也不是个体性的。"法"的实施不需要被施于者的主动参与。正因此，"法"所致力的社会秩序不能像"礼"那样表现同等长久的特殊性或偶然性。

（《通过孔子而思》，第 210 页）

只有在那些无法借助"礼"实现和谐的情况下才会吁求于"法"。"法"可被合理地描述为衍生于"礼"，却没有能保证适当的"宜"的当事者的有意义参与。

（《通过孔子而思》，第 210 页）

法（standards, norms, laws），既指涉服从的客体，也指涉"效仿"秩序的这些典范，暗示"境"（situation）对"行"（action）特定作用的优先性。（这也可看到佛教"法"的用法，"法"是"dharma"的翻译，既是事物又是事物秩序。）由于此自然宇宙论始于个体独特性，"典范"效仿替代了原则法规遵从所做的很多工作。模仿典范（身教）需要特定个人在其生活的种种状态以及他们所要效仿的特定典范之间某种适当的相类投射。例如，孔子

significantly from ritual action, however, in that it is neither intersubjectively integrating nor personal. The enforcement of *fa* in a given situation does not require the active participation of the object of enforcement. For this reason, in its project of bringing order to society, it is not able to register the same degree of insistent particularity or contingency as ritual action (*li*).

(*Thinking Through Confucius,* pp. 172-173)

The need to invoke *fa* presupposes the failure of those concerned to achieve the harmony possible by recourse to ritual action. *Fa* can be fairly described as being derived from *li* but lacking the meaningful participation of those involved which can insure optimum appropriateness.

(*Thinking Through Confucius,* p. 173)

"Standards, norms, laws." *Fa* refers to both the objects of compliance and also "to emulate" such models of order, suggesting the priority of situation over the specific agency of action. (This anticipates the Buddhist usage of *fa* as a translation of *dharma*: both things and the order of things.) Since this natural cosmology begins from the uniqueness of particulars, emulating "models" does much of the work of obeying principles and laws. To emulate a model requires an appropriate analogical projection between particular persons in their lived situations and the particular models they would emulate. Confucius, for example, does

并不提供正当行为的范畴戒律,也不诉诸某些道德律令作为规范理想。他毋宁作为一个秩序的特殊典范立在那里,赞美那些通过世世代代延续为典范的人,以至于他们生活之点滴言谈举止行为轶事都总是可创造性地适用到新的情况中。

(《生民之本:〈孝经〉的哲学诠释及英译》,第 88 页)

not provide categorical imperatives for right conduct, nor does he appeal to some moral law as a regulative ideal. Rather, he stands as a particular model of order and celebrates others who can be emulated by succeeding generations to the extent that the remembered pronouncements and chronicled events of their lives can be applied productively to always novel situations.

(*The Chinese Classic of Family Reverence: A Philosophical Translation of the Xiaojing*, p. 69)

势

Shih

显而易见,那些后来被称为"兵家"的早期思想家(至少是生活在公元前 6 世纪的孙武及其同时代人),他们就已经把"势"用作表示某种军事情势的术语。以后,法家思想家又发展了这个词语,并将其原有的军事含义扩大到政治方面。不过其用法在许多地方仍类似于早期兵家的用法。最后,具有儒家倾向的著作如《荀子》等亦同法家一样,把"势"这个概念当作政治术语来用,并使它适合于自己的政治哲学。

(《中国古代的统治艺术:〈淮

It would appear that at a relatively early period—at least by the time of Sun Wu in the sixth century B.C.—thinkers who were later to be classified as "Militarists" had already appropriated the character *shih* to represent a specific military situation. Having acquired military connotations, this same character at yet another stage in its development was taken over by Legalist theorists and given a political dimension in many ways analogous to its earlier military application. Finally, in response to the Legalist use of *shih* as a special political term, Confucian-oriented texts such as the *Hsün Tzu* appropriated this concept and shaped it to fit their own political philosophies.

(*Art of Rulership: A Study of Ancient*

南子·主术〉研究》,第111—112页)

"势"概念在《孙子》中至少有三层含义:(1)条件或情势;(2)与兵力部署相关之形势;(3)占据利地以获得潜在的利势。就这一方面而言,"势"这个概念无论是对集团作战抑或是对单兵作战,都指的是利地、它的利势和对此利势之控制。

像《孙子》这样一部薄薄的著作里,"势"概念得以频繁地运用和强调,无疑说明,它是这部著作中的一个核心概念。"势"概念以后一直成为兵家思想中的一个重要内容,这由它在《孙膑兵法》《商君书·兵守》和《管子》等中所处的地位,可以得到充分证明。

(《中国古代的统治艺术:〈淮南子·主术〉研究》,第115页)

"势"作为法家的特定术语,可以被解释为"政治地位"(political purchase)。我们何以选择"purchase"(身份或地位)这个词来对应"势"这个概念,这一点可以通过一个简单的类比来加以说明。虽然君主作为个人其规范他人行为之能力是有限的,然而他却可以凭借王位所带

Chinese Political Thought, p. 65)

In the Sun Tzu, then, the term *shih* has at least three dimensions of meaning: (1) "circumstances" or "conditions"; (2) "physical disposition" in connection with the deployment of troops; and (3) occupation of a superior position and access to the potential advantages it confers. In this respect the word can refer either collectively or individually to the superior position, the advantage inherent in the position, and the manipulation of this advantage.

In a work as short as the *Sun Tzu*, the frequency of *shih* and the emphasis placed upon it make it without question one of the central concepts of the text. That this concept continued to be an important aspect of Militarist thought is evidenced by its role in the *Sun Pin Art of Warfare* (*Sun Pin ping-fa*) and the military chapters of *The Book of Lord Shang* (*Shang-chün shu*) and *Kuan Tzu*.

(*Art of Rulership: A Study of Ancient Chinese Political Thought,* p. 68)

As a special Legalist term, *shih* can be rendered "political purchase." The choice of the word "purchase" as an occasional equivalent for *shih* may be clarified with a simple analogy. Whereas the ruler as *individual* is limited in his capacity to regulate the conduct of others, from the strategically advantageous position of the throne he can use his political status as *ruler* to amplify his influence over others. It

来的权势，运用他君主的政治地位去扩大对他人的影响。君主的政治地位及其作用，是增强其影响和维持其（权）"势"的重要手段（值得注意的是，法家引用了挥斧和张弩等类似的手段来比喻势）。因此，"势"概念所表达的政治作用，揭示了君主的地位与其他阶层之间的关系，这一关系可以用政治之差异或"势"来形容。

（《中国古代的统治艺术：〈淮南子·主术〉研究》，第120页）

《管子》中"势"的最重要的用法，是说明事物本质发展的趋势。如它用于说明社会关系："在子期年，子虽不孝，父不能服也。"（第十六《法法》）但是更多和更重要的，则是用来说明与之相关的政治地位和利益。

（《中国古代的统治艺术：〈淮南子·主术〉研究》，第126页）

尽管在《管子》中，"势"这一概念仍保留了许多它本来的兵学含义，然而其使用范围则确切无疑地已从军事领域扩大到了政治领域。

（《中国古代的统治艺术：〈淮

is this political status and its application as a fulcrum for increasing the ruler's capacity to influence others that constitute his *shih*. (It is significant that the Militarists cite fulcrum-like devices such as the axe handle and crossbow as metaphors for this purchase.) The concept of *shih* thus expressed in its political application indicates the relationship between the position of ruler and other elements of the state, a relationship which can be described in terms of political differentials or "purchase."

(*Art of Rulership: A Study of Ancient Chinese Political Thought*, p. 72)

The most significant use of *shih* in the *Kuan Tzu*, however, signifies the purchase available to a thing in consequence of its attributes and status. This use applies to social positions: "If the purchase lies with the son for the duration of a year, even though he proves to be unfilial, the father will be unable to make him obedient." More frequently and more importantly, though, it applies to political status and the advantage associated with it.

(*Art of Rulership: A Study of Ancient Chinese Political Thought*, p. 77)

While *shih* tends to retain many of its basic Militarist connotations, the area of its application has definitely been extended from the military to the political battleground.

(*Art of Rulership: A Study of Ancient Chinese Political Thought*, p. 80)

南子·主术〉研究》，第 130 页）

《荀子》中"势"的用法包括了所有兵家和法家著作中这个词用法的全部含义。另外，"势"最常用的是如法家思想家所发展的专门概念那样，用来表示政治地位和伴随而来的权势之含义。尽管《荀子》采用了"势"的兵家与法家的特殊含义，但这并不等于说，他接受他们所提出的这一概念，相反，《荀子》用"势"是反对他们的观点的。

（《中国古代的统治艺术：〈淮南子·主术〉研究》，第 134 页）

除了不赞同法家对于用兵之"势"的重要性予以过分强调外，《荀子》在论述中还反对法家在其治国思想中将"势"置于首要地位的做法。正如我们所了解的，法家的政治哲学排斥儒家仁德忠义的教化，主张恃势与苛政，因而不赞同儒家"选贤任能"的基本主张。尽管儒家寄希望于君主转变成为圣人，但法家则强调其位势的客观性。

（《中国古代的统治艺术：〈淮南子·主术〉研究》，第 135 页）

The usage of *shih* in the *Hsün Tzu* covers the full range of meanings found in the Militarist and Legalist texts. Again *shih* is most frequently used as the special term developed by the Legalist thinkers to connote political status and its attendant advantage. While the *Hsün Tzu* does make use of *shih* with its special Militarist and Legalist implications, this is not to say that it accepts the concept as it is propounded in these traditions. On the contrary, the *Hsün Tzu* employs *shih* to contest their assertions.

(*Art of Rulership: A Study of Ancient Chinese Political Thought*, p. 84)

In addition to setting aside the Militarist emphasis on the primacy of *shih* in the use of arms, the *Hsün Tzu* also argues against the primacy given *shih* in the Legalist conception of effective government. Legalist political philosophy, as we have seen, rejects the Confucian reliance upon moral suasion and loyalty in favor of the manipulation of *shih* and rule by intimidation—thereby repudiating the fundamental Confucian precept exalting persons of superior qualities and employing the able (*tsun hsien shih neng*). Where the Confucians placed their faith in the transforming influence of the ruler as a consummate *person*, the Legalists stressed the objective conditions of his *position*.

(*Art of Rulership: A Study of Ancient Chinese Political Thought*, p. 85)

荀子在某种程度上接受了法家任势而治的主张，在实际中，他也称赞古代圣人的任势而治，承认它对社会秩序的巩固作出了贡献。

（《中国古代的统治艺术：〈淮南子·主术〉研究》，第136页）

荀子谴责了法家要求君主倚势制其下臣的做法，认为这是强迫其下臣服从的非常拙劣的办法："非劫之以形势，非振之以诛杀，则无以有其下，夫是之谓暴察之威。"（《强国》）

荀子的思想与法家"势"的观念的主要分歧在于：法家把"势"看作是治国的一个充要条件；而荀子则确信，没有民众的拥护，"势"犹如一条沉船，是浮不起来的。"势"的获得与保持，只是赢得民众的一个结果。

（《中国古代的统治艺术：〈淮南子·主术〉研究》，第137页）

To a certain extent Hsün Tzu does accept the Legalist insistence on the importance of *shih* in maintaining political control. In fact, he even credits the enlightened sages of antiquity with the innovation of political purchase, accepting its contribution to the fabric of order in society.

(*Art of Rulership: A Study of Ancient Chinese Political Thought,* p. 85)

Hsün Tzu condemns the Legalist injunction that the ruler control his minister by exercising the purchase available to him as ruler as a decidedly inferior method of exacting obedience from subordinates: "Not being able to hold subordinates except by intimidating them with political purchase and terrorizing them with punishments and executions is what is called 'awe inspired by harsh scrutiny.'"

Hsün Tzu's primary objection to the Legalist conception of *shih* is that where the Legalists regard the *shih* itself to be a sufficient condition for political control, Hsün Tzu is convinced that *shih* without popular support is a sinking ship and ultimately untenable. The acquisition and retention of *shih* are a consequence of winning over the people.

(*Art of Rulership：A Study of Ancient Chinese Political Thought,* p. 86)

修养论

小人

对孔子来说,君子是一个质的术语,表明一个不断致力于个人发展的人,其成长过程是通过修身和社会政治领导能力展现的。既然"君子不器"(《论语·为政》),即不可根据特定技巧或专门技术来描述君子,那么,一个人之所以成为君子,就靠的是他对人类秩序贡献的"质",而非他所做具体工作的"量"。孔子反复在君子和他所谓的"小人"之间做出对比,用以作为强调君子这一素质根基的手段。君子能够与整体合而为一且展现自我,"小人"则迟钝、分裂,故步自封。"小人"对社会和谐完全没有质的贡献,反而会使之减损。即便其行为尚可容忍,他所贡献的也不过是简单的"同"而非质的增加——"和"。

(《通过孔子而思》,第228页)

Small Person

For Confucius, then, the exemplary person (*chun tzu*) is a qualitative term denoting someone who has an ongoing commitment to personal growth as expressed through the activities of self-cultivation and sociopolitical leadership. In that "the exemplary person (*chun tzu*) is not a functionary"(2.12) describable in terms of specific skills or expertise, a person qualifies as *chun tzu* by virtue of the quality of his contribution to the fabric of human order, not by what he specially does. As a device for underscoring this qualitative basis for identifying the exemplary person (*chun tzu*), Confucius repeatedly draws a contrast between the integrative and self-disclosing characteristics of the exemplary person (*chun tzu*), and the disintegrative and retarding characteristic of what he terms "the small person" (*hsiao jen* 小人)." That is "small person", far from making a qualitative contribution, detracts from social harmony. Even when his conduct is tolerable, it contributes nothing more than simple conformity (*tung* 同) rather than qualitative enhancement (*ho* 和).

(*Thinking Through Confucius,* pp. 188-189)

对于孔子来说，君子是个定性的词，用以指称这样一些人，他们坚持不懈地致力于人格成长，这是通过政治领导加以培育和表现的。"君子不器"意味着这种成长不能从特别的技术或才能的方面来加以描绘，它是道德品质和与他人交往能力提高的程度。孔子反复地将承担广泛的社会责任的君子，与使群体人心涣散、妨碍他人、他称之为小人的那些人加以对比，以此作为一种手段来强调君子这种称呼主要指品格的性质。这种"小人"不是对社会或在政治上作出贡献，而是为自私自利的动机所支配，破坏社群中富有成效的协作。君子和而不同，小人同而不和。品质上有所成的人，其鲜明特征表现于他们的创造性、想象力和影响力，使社群与众不同，而且更好。在全部经典之中，圣人经常与创新的活动（"作"）联系在一起。当孔子讲自己"述而不作"时，实际上他是在谦虚，是在说"我非圣人也"。

（《汉哲学思维的文化探源》，第166页）

For Confucius, the *junzi* is a qualitative term denoting someone who has an ongoing commitment to personal growth as it is cultivated and expressed through political leadership. "The *junzi* is not a functionary (君子不器)"means that such growth is not describable in terms of specific skills or expertise, but rather is a measure of character, and of the quality of one's interactions with others. As a device for underscoring the qualitative nature of this designation, Confucius repeatedly draws a contrast between the socially expansive and inclusive *junzi*, and the disintegrative and retarding characteristics of what he terms "the small person (*xiaoren* 小人)." This "small person," far from making a social or political contribution, is motivated by selfishness, and thus detracts from the effective coordination of community. Where the conduct of the small person is least obstructive, it simply reduplicates what is already there (*tong* 同) rather than contributing any qualitative enhancement to the situation (*he* 和).The signature of the qualitatively achieved person is found in the creativity, imagination, and influence to make community not only different, but better. Throughout the classical corpus, the sage (*shengren* 聖人) is frequently associated with innovative activity (*zuo* 作). When Confucius says of himself, "Following the proper way, I do not forge new paths(述而不作),"he is in fact with modesty saving, "I am not a sage."

(*Thinking from the Han,* p.160)

修 养 论

君子

常论孔子之前文献,"君子"是"君"的小称,即"君的孩子",表示出身、血统、地位等的高贵,却没有看到对品格高贵的敬意。而在孔子那里,此政治语词就被确然用来表达政治责任和个人尤其是伦理和精神成长的相关关系。也就是说,修身必然需主动参与到家庭和社会政治秩序中,这不只是为他人服务,而是使这种参与成为展现个人修养精进的关怀之平台。换句话说,一个人并不是首先成为君子,然后进入政治生活舞台;毋宁是,我们只能通过回应公共生活中的社会和政治责任而变成君子。的确,"君子"一词还有"君主"的意思,有时也得这样翻译。

《论语》中,君子几乎总被援引为可供弟子们学益的行为典范。他们行道良多,处处得体,惠及多人,亦受惠于如他们一样的人。尽管在遇到不义不公之事时,君子也会生气,但其外表平和。他们知晓礼乐,行礼弄乐通达娴熟优雅从容且怡然自乐。他们虽现在常怀"天下"却

Exemplary Person

It is often suggested that in the literature prior to Confucius, the expression *junzi*, a diminutive form of *jun* meaning "child of *jun*," denoted nobility of birth, blood, and rank, with no discernable reference to nobility of conduct. It is demonstrably the case that, with Confucius, this political category was appropriated and used to express the correlative relationship between political responsibility and personal, particularly ethical and spiritual, growth. That is, the cultivation of one's person necessarily entails active participation both in the family and in the sociopolitical order, not simply in service to others, but as the forum in which the compassion and concern that lead to one's own personal refinement are expressed. Said another way, one does not first become a *junzi* and then enter the arena of political life; rather, one can only become a *junzi* through responsiveness to the social and political obligations that emerge in communal living. Indeed, the term *junzi* can also mean "ruler," and must be so translated at times.

In the *Analects*, *junzi* are almost always invoked as a model of conduct, presumably for the benefit of the disciples. They have traveled a goodly distance along the way, and live a goodly number of roles. Benefactors

269

仍对父母长辈鞠躬尽孝。尽管君子的其他行为也确会时有差失，但他们在履行其角色时却绝对得体，不是被迫如此，而是无费吹灰之力的自发创造行为。总之，他们生活中有某种强烈的审美伦理尺度；他们对礼的重组同时也正是对人类之道的创造者们的尊重。

君子常跟小人形成鲜明对比。"小人"字面的意思是"small persons"，也即"petty and mean persons"。这一对比表明君子之行乃是不断阐发和扩充的结果。事实上，有成之人有时被说成是"大人"（great persons），他们的画像或其他表现形式都比真人大。

《孝经》里君子的责任既是积极意义上的典范又是消极意义上的监督。也就是说，转化教育要在家庭和社群中发挥作用，既要通过由这些典范形象所激励的效仿，亦需要个人进步所需的永不懈怠的内省。这同样双向共生的原动力亦作用于君子与其君主的关系中：他们至高无上的忠要求他们主动促发提升君主值得褒奖的行为，与此同时，亦设法通过诤谏针砭那些不可姑息的行为。

to many, they are still beneficiaries of others like themselves. While they are still capable of anger in the presence of inappropriateness and concomitant injustice, in their persons they are tranquil. They know many rituals and much music, and perform all of their functions not only with skill but also with grace, dignity, and beauty, and they take delight in the performances. They are still filial toward their parents and elders, but now take "all under the heavens" as their dwelling. While real enough to be still capable of the occasional lapse in their otherwise exemplary conduct, they are resolutely proper in the conduct of their roles— conduct that is not forced, but rather effortless, spontaneous, creative. There is, in sum, a very strong aesthetic and ethical dimension to their lives; they have reauthorized the *li*, and are therefore respected authors of the *dao* of humankind.

Junzi are frequently contrasted with *xiaoren* 小人—literally "small" and thus "petty and mean" persons. This contrast would suggest that becoming exemplary in one's personal conduct is the result of continuing articulation and extension. In fact, achieved persons are on occasion referred to as *daren* 大人—"great persons," and are depicted in paintings and other representations as larger than life.

In the *Xiaojing*, the *junzi* have responsibilities both as positive models and as negative censors. That is, transformative

修养论

（《生民之本：〈孝经〉的哲学诠释及英译》，第93—94页）

我们将"君子"翻译为"exemplary person"。"君子"时常与"小人"相对。"小人"中"小"的字面意思是"small"，而"小人"在英文中意思是"petty and mean persons"。这种对照意味着：在一个人的个体人格中成为君子，是一个不断表达和成长的结果。和"仁"（authoritative person）一样，"君子"这个词是一个在最早的文献中与孔子本人密切相关而被重新界定的范畴。

在《说文》中，"君"与"尊"在发音上同韵，其含义首先意味着"具有高位"，引申的含义则是"使荣耀"或"得到尊重"。在《说文》注释汇集的其他一些早期的来源中，"君"也由其同源字"群"来定义。"群"的意思是"聚合"。如此一来，就带来了这样一种含义，即"君子"是众人乐于趋向的人物。《说文》进而将"君"解释为一个"会意"字，将其两语源学的要素"尹"与"口"分别开来加以解释，前一个字意味着"管理、命令和调节"。因此，"君子"就是能够通过有效沟通带来

education is effected in families and community by the emulation that is inspired by these exemplary models, and by the unrelenting introspection needed for their own personal improvement. This same bidirectional and symbiotic dynamic is at work in the relationship between the *junzi* and their rulers, where their utmost loyalty (*zhong* 忠) requires that they actively promote what they find commendable in the conduct of their sovereign while at the same time taking steps to remedy what cannot be condoned through a process of vigilant remonstrance, *jian* 谏.

(*The Chinese Classic of Family Reverence: A Philosophical Translation of the Xiaojing,* pp. 74-75)

We render *junzi* as "exemplary person." *Junzi* are frequently contrasted with *xiaoren* 小人—literally "small," and thus "petty and mean" persons. This contrast would suggest that becoming exemplary in one's personal character is the result of continuing articulation and growth. This term *junzi*, like *ren* ("authoritative person"), is a category redefined and made popular in the earliest literature associated closely with Confucius himself.

The *Shuowen* lexicon defines *jun* 君 paronomastically with the rhyming *zun* 尊 meaning first "of high rank," and then derivatively "to honor" or "to hold in high

社会政治秩序的这样一种人。正是由于"君子"的品行常常被社会性地描述为一种他人仿效的典范，我们才将"君子"翻译为"exemplary person"（典范人物）。

通常为人所注意到的是，在孔子之前的文献中，"君子"这一表述是"君"的一个变小了的形式，意思是"君"的"孩子"。其蕴涵着由于出生、血缘和等级的高贵性，并没有明确可见的意思来指那种品德的高贵责任和个人道德增长之间的关系。这也就是说，一个人的修养必然包括了对于家庭和社会政治秩序两方面的积极参与。不仅仅是服务于他人，而且是作为一个场所，在那样一个场所中，导致一个人自身获得净化的同情与关怀得以表达。换言之，一个人不是首先成为一个君子，然后再进入政治生活的领域，毋宁说，只有通过对于公共生活中出现的社会和政治义务的回应，一个人才能够成为君子。

在《中庸》一书中，君子扮演着一个极其重要的角色。事实上，君子正是那些能够做到"中庸"的人。也就是说，君子就是那些能够"切中日用伦常"的人。君子们通晓

esteem." In other early sources collected in the *Shuowen* commentaries, *jun* is also defined by its cognate *qun* 群 meaning "to gather," with the implication that the *junzi* is the person to whom the crowd repairs. The *Shuowen* further identifies *jun* 君 as a "combined meaning (*huiyi* 會意)" graph, isolating the etymonic elements of *yin* 尹, "to manage, order, regulate," and *kou* 口, "the mouth." Thus the *junzi* is an agent that brings about sociopolitical order through effective communication. It is because the conduct of the *junzi* is most often described socially as a model for other persons to emulate that we translate the term "exemplary person."

It is often suggested that in the literature prior to Confucius, the expression *junzi*, a diminutive form of *jun* meaning "child of *jun*," denoted nobility of birth, blood, and rank, with no discernable reference to nobility of character. It is demonstrably the case that with Confucius, this political category was appropriated and used to express the correlative relationship between political responsibility and personal moral growth. That is, the cultivation of one's person necessarily entails active participation both in the family and in the scholia order, not simply in server to others, but as the locus in which the compassion and concern that leads to one's own personal refinement is expressed. Said another way, one does not first become a *junzi* and then enter the arena of political life; rather, one can become a

礼乐，其履行公共的功能不仅伴随着"善"，同时伴随着优雅、庄严和美丽。虽然君子们在家中仍然孝敬父母和尊长，但他们更是将"普天之下"作为其根源。在其各种角色和关系的行为中，君子们决然是得体的。尤有进者，君子们的行为不是被强制的，而是自然而然、自动自发以及富有创造性的。总之，君子们的生活和生命中具有一种很强的审美和伦理的向度。君子们是自身时空条件下的礼乐的新的作者，因此，君子们同时也是人道的令人尊敬的作者。

在《中庸》第十二章中，君子之道被描述为"费而隐"，这种表面上看起来自相矛盾的说法令人想起《道德经》。君子之道"费"，意思是说，君子之道始于常人的日常生活，即使对于那些最为鲁钝的人来说，君子之道也是显而易见的，所谓"夫妇之愚，可以与知焉"。另一方面，君子之道又是"隐"的，意思是说，就其微妙与复杂而言，君子之道又是如此的高深，其极致即使圣人也不能测度，所谓"及其至也，虽圣人亦有所不知焉"。因此，《中庸》指出：

junzi through responsiveness to the social and political obligations that emerge in communal living.

Junzi have a prominent role in the *Zhongyong* and are in fact defined as those who are able to "*zhongyong* 中庸"—that is, able "to focus the familiar affairs of the day." They know many rituals and much music, and perform all of their communal functions not only with felicity (*shan* 善), but also with grace, dignity, and beauty. Though they are still filial toward their parents and elders at home, they take "all under *tian*" as their provenance. They are resolutely proper in the conduct of their roles and relationships. Further, their conduct is not forced, but effortless, spontaneous, and creative. There is, in sum, a very strong aesthetic and ethical dimension to the lives of the *junzi*. They have re-authorized ritual propriety (*li* 禮) and music (*yue* 樂) for their own time and place, and are therefore the respected authors of the *dao* of humankind.

The way of the *junzi* is described in *Zhongyong* 12 as "both broad and hidden，" a correlative pairing of seemingly contradictory terms reminiscent of the *Daodejing*. This way is broad in the sense that, having its beginnings in the routine lives of ordinary people, there is much about it that is apparent to even the dullest of men and women. It is obvious and easy. On the other hand in its subtlety and complexity it

故君子语大，天下莫能载焉，语小，天下莫能破焉。

《中庸》第三十三章，也就是最后一部分，将其论述诉诸引自《诗经》的一系列段落，去解释在《中庸》开始部分看起来似乎自相矛盾的主张。开头部分的主张是这样的：

君子戒慎乎其所不睹，恐惧乎其所不闻。莫见乎隐，莫显乎微。

通过再次诉诸关联性的一对一的诗句，《诗经》将君子之道描述为既"近"且"远"，既"微"且"显"，既"敬"且"温"。正是在这个意义上，君子的典范，即"常"与"非常"之间的中道，预期并且蕴涵在个人修养的最高境界——圣人的出现之中。

（《切中伦常：〈中庸〉的新诠与新译》，第86—88页）

如果我们对上述篇章的解读无误的话，那么，为"士"的主要目标就是要成为表率之人，即"君子"。也就是说，"君子"所行远比

is so lofty and demanding that at its furthest limits even the sages cannot fathom it.

Thus, were exemplary persons to discourse on the profundity of their way, there is nothing in the empire that could take its weight; were they to discourse on its subtlety, there is nothing in the empire that could further refine it.

Zhongyong 33, the final section of the text, appeals to a series of passages taken from *the Book of Songs* in explanation of a seemingly paradoxical claim made in the opening passage of the *Zhongyong*:

...exemplary persons are so concerned about what is not seen and so anxious about what is not heard. There is nothing more present than what is imminent, and nothing more manifest than what is inchoate.

The Book of Songs, appealing again to correlative pairings, describes the way of exemplary persons as near yet distant, subtle yet conspicuous, awesome yet unintimidating. It is in this sense that the model of the *junzi*, the middle ground between the ordinary and the extraordinary, anticipates and is entailed in the emergence of the most exalted category of personal cultivation, the sage.

(*Focusing the Familiar: A Translation and*

"士"之所为的境界更高。《论语》总是在描述"君子"的所作（为弟子们），而不是在教导"君子"应该如何行事（这是因为其预设前提是"君子"不需要如此）。"君子"早已循道而行，并且成功地演绎了自己所承担的诸多社会角色。他既是众人的施恩者，又是与他自己相似的其他人的受益者。他既对失当与不公表示愤慨，也独享着内心的平静。他精通礼乐，并且以娴熟的技艺，优雅—高贵—美丽的内涵气度和欣喜的心态去完成自己在各种礼仪中的职责。他孝顺父母，敬爱兄长，但却在沉思冥想中掌有"天下"。尽管他身为"君子"而偶尔犯错（第十四篇第六章），却绝对忠实地履行着自己所负角色的义务。他的一切行为并非强迫所致，而是自发的独创。总而言之，"君子"的生命具有鲜明的美学和伦理学特质。他重新阐释了"礼"，并且成为一个可敬的人类之道的创始者。

对于我们大部分人来说，"君子"就是我们所能想象的最高奋斗目标。不过，儒家还有一个更为崇高的人生追求，那就是成为"圣人"。其实，即便是在《论语》中，

Philosophical Interpretation of the Zhongyong, pp.67-69)

If our reading of these passages is warranted, it will follow that major goal toward which the *shi* is striving is to become an exemplary person, or *junzi*. The *shi* does, while the *junzi* more nearly is. In the text, the *junzi* is almost always described (for the benefit of the disciples), not instructed (because presumably he doesn't need it). He has traveled a goodly distance along the way, and lives a goodly number of roles. A benefactor to many, he is still a beneficiary of others like himself. While he is still capable of anger in the presence of inappropriateness and concomitant injustice, he is in his person tranquil. He knows many rituals and much music, and performs all of his functions not only with skill, but with grace, dignity, and beauty, and he takes delight in the performances. He is still filial toward his parents and elders, but now takes "all under *tian*" as his dwelling. While real enough to be still capable of the occasional lapse in his otherwise exemplary conduct (14.6), he is resolutely proper in the conduct of his roles—conduct which is not forced, but rather effortless, spontaneous, creative. There is, in sum, a very strong aesthetic and ethical dimension to his life; he has reauthorized the *li*, and is therefore a respected author of the *dao* of humankind.

For most of us, the goal of *junzi* is the

"圣人"也是一个可望而不可即的目标。"圣人"与"君子"的共同之处就是超强的沟通能力。从字形来看,"君子"是一个通过有效的交流(口),监督团体活动的人(尹);"圣(聖)人"则堪称沟通大师,"耳"与"呈"不仅界定了人类的经验,而且还涵衍了和谐的意蕴。于是,我们不禁由孔子"正名"的观念(第十三篇第三章)想到,只有给事物取定了合适的名称,它才能顺理成章地发生、发展。

(《〈论语〉的哲学诠释》,第63—64页)

《说文》中"君"是由其同韵字"尊"(位尊)来定义的,生出"敬"(to honor)的意义。有意思的是,"君"和"尊"都各自有一个意思为"聚"(many together)的同源词——"群"和"僔"。而且,"尊"还有一个同音同源词"撙","撙"的意思是"适当、节制"。《说文》进一步分析了"君"的词根,认为,这是一个最初从"尹"(命令、治理、管理)派生的会意字,后来由于"治"民者乃发号施令者,所以它还从"口"。《系传通论》对《说文》做了

highest to which we can aspire. There is, however, an even loftier human goal, to become a "sage" or *shengren*; but in the *Analects* it is a distant goal indeed. What the *shengren* shares in common with the *junzi* is that both categories emerge out of effective communication. Etymologically, the *junzi* 君子 is one who "oversees (*yin* 尹)"community through effective "communication (*kou* 口)."The *shengren* (聖人) is a virtuoso of communication, "listening (*er* 耳)"and "presenting ideas (*cheng* 呈)"that not only come to define the human experience, but which further have cosmic implications. As we recall from Confucius' notion of "the proper use of names (*zhengming* 正名)"in 13.3, to name (*ming* 名) a world properly commands (*ming* 命) a proper world into being.

(*The Analects of Confucius: A Philosophical Translation*, pp. 62-63)

The *Shuo-wen* lexicon defines *chün* 君 with the rhyming *tsun* 尊, meaning "of high rank," and then derivatively, as "to honor." Interestingly, *chün* 君 and *tsun* 尊 both have cognates meaning "many together"(群 an 僔), and *tsun* 尊 has a homophonous cognate, 撙, meaning "to moderate, to regulate." The *Shuo-wen* further isolates the etymonic elements of *chün* 君, suggesting that it is a *hui-yi* 會意 character derived first from *yin* 尹 "to order, to manage, regular," and then, because the person who "orders" issues

这样的注解:

> 君者，尹也，正也。长民之通称也。天下之所取表正也。表正则影正，表曲则影曲。口以出令也……君，群下之所归往也。

"君"字中"尹"这个部首意义重大，《说文》将之释为"治"（to regulate, to direct, well-governed, in good order），并称"握事者也"。

总之，"君"的词源学信息提供了下面一些联想：（1）位尊；（2）表敬意；（3）秩序、文明、修养的典范，其个人品格吸引在下者的效仿和积极参与；（4）已之身"正"借政治责任和交流获得更大扩展。"君"在其所涉特定社会政治环境中是秩序的一个根源。该秩序不是预先指定的模式，由君子本人实证继而强加于他人；它根本产生于君子对社会政治环境的参与。

（《通过孔子而思》，第221页）

因此，对孔子来说，君子是一个质的术语，表明一个不断致力于个人发展的人，其成长过程是通过

commands, it is further constituted by *k'ou* 口, "mouth." The *Hsichuan t'ung lun* commentary on the *Shuo-wen* states:

> *Chün* 君 means "to regulate, to order," a generic name for leaders; one whom the empire can take as its model for uprightness and order. Where the model is upright, so is the shadow it casts; where it is bent, so is the shadow. His mouth is his means of issuing commands. ... The *chün* 君 is the one to whom the crowd below 群下 repairs.

The *yin* 尹 component in *chün* 君 is significant, defined in the *Shuo-wen* as *chih* 治 "to regulate, to direct, well-governed, in good order," and further, as "one who handles affairs."

To summarize, the etymological data on *chün* 君 provides the following associations: (1) noble rank, (2) a term of respect, (3) a model of order, cultivation, and refinement whose personal character attracts the emulation and participation of those below, and (4) one whose personal order is extended to a wider context through political responsibility and communication. *Chün* 君 is a source of order in a decidedly sociopolitical frame of reference. This order is not a preassigned pattern that the *chün* himself instances and then imposes on others, but is meant to be

修身和社会政治领导能力展现的。既然"君子不器"(《论语·为政》),即不可根据特定技巧或专门技术来描述君子,那么,一个人之所以成为君子,就靠的是他对人类秩序贡献的"质",而非他所做具体工作的"量"。孔子反复在君子和他所谓的"小人"之间做出对比,用以作为强调君子这一素质根基的手段。君子能够与整体合而为一且展现自我,"小人"则迟钝、分裂,故步自封。"小人"对社会和谐完全没有质的贡献,反而会使之减损。即便其行为尚可容忍,他所贡献的也不过是简单的"同"而非质的增加——"和"。

正是整个个人完善过程中君子要参照的这一社会政治框架,使得该范畴凸显出来且有理由将之译为"exemplary person"。而且,既然个人完善只能在社会经验和社会活动中实现,那么,君子交流和沟通的形式就成为吸引同情和参与到自然发生的秩序的重要促进因素。由于孔子认为言出必行,因而,他格外关心君子的"言责"。言行一致是个人完善、实现整体性的基础。而个人完整性("诚"[integrity])又是社会融合的基础。

an order that ultimately derives from his engagement with his sociopolitical context.
(*Thinking Through Confucius,* pp. 182-183)

For Confucius, then, the exemplary person (*chün tzu*) is a qualitative term denoting someone who has an ongoing commitment to personal growth as expressed through the activities of self-cultivation and sociopolitical leadership. In that "the exemplary person (*chün tzu*) is not a functionary" (2.12) describable in terms of specific skills or expertise, a person qualifies as *chün tzu* by virtue of the quality of his contribution to the fabric of human order, not by what he specially does. As a device for underscoring this qualitative basis for identifying the exemplary person (*chün tzu*), Confucius repeatedly draws a contrast between the integrative and self-disclosing characteristics of the exemplary person (*chün tzu*), and the disintegrative and retarding characteristic of what he terms "the small person" (*hsiao jen* 小人). Thus "small person," far from making a qualitative contribution, detracts from social harmony. Even when his conduct is tolerable, it contributes nothing more than simple conformity (*t'ung* 同) rather than qualitative enhancement (*ho* 和).

It is the sociopolitical frame of reference for this *chün tzu* aspect in the overall process of personal realization that makes this category distinctive and warrants its translation as

修养论

君子被当成社会政治秩序的第一动因。他依靠修身成为典范来履行这一功能。典范的作用对孔子来说如此重要,以至我们必须尽力使之获得透彻表达。

孔子顺着审美这条线来解释君子作为社会典范的作用。效仿典范是一种品质活动。对典范的反应根据个人独特的能力、环境和兴趣而定。通观《论语》,我们看到许多典范人物:尧、舜、文王、武王、管仲和颜回。孔子授课内容显然高度重视历史编年史和古代诗歌,它们都衍生于中国文化演进的特定历史事件。孔子借助历史典范和诗化的人物形象,说明他首先从理想行为的具体例证出发构织他的社会政治秩序。而且,即便孔子认为这些历史人物值得效仿,他同时也清楚表明,效仿不是被动重复某种确定行为。事实上,他要求学习者必须对榜样行为做出批判性评估,并加以改造以适应自己的情况。

(《通过孔子而思》,第228—229页)

君子是"义"的践行者,"礼"的具体化身,是个人和社会政治秩

"exemplary person." And since personal realization can only emerge in the process of social experience and activity, the exemplary person's (*chün tzu*) form of communication is an important stimulus for attracting sympathy with and participation in an emergent order. Hence, Confucius, believing that what is said is a prompting to act, is very much concerned about the exemplary person's (*chün tzu*) responsibility for his speech. Correspondence between what is said and what is done is the basis for one's integrity, one's capacity for "making whole." Thus, integrity is the ground for social integration.

The exemplary person (*chün tzu*) serves as the primary agent of sociopolitical ordering. He performs this function by virtue of his role as a model of cultivation. This modeling function is of such importance to the Confucian sensibility that we must take some pains to clarify it further.

For Confucius the exemplary person's (*chün tzu*) role as sociopolitical model is to be construed along aesthetic lines. Modeling is a qualitative activity. And the response to the model is qualified by the uniqueness of the respondent's resources, circumstances, and interests. Throughout the *Analects*, we are referred to particular examples of excellence: Yao and Shun, Wen and Wu, Kuan Chung and Yen Hui. Confucius' selection of curricular materials evidences a high regard for historical chronicles and classical songs that dramatize

序的典范。他既是传统的承续者，又是立基传统创造性产生的基础。他吸引社会成员参与到他所实现的秩序中，为他们提供榜样，提供展现他们个人修养和自我创造性的机遇。他的表率作用在各方面都发挥一种教育功能，因为他的影响力唤起他人参与社会并实现品格的转化。他的存在就是为了最充分展现对整体和谐秩序作出贡献的个体。就此，既展现了他个人的独特性和创新，也保证了他人独特性和创新的最充分表达。

君子既是"知"的榜样，也是"仁"的典范。他通过对传统和周围事件的独到认识，进而传播其最优秀的部分，而获得他的典范地位。正如我们讨论"思"时所谈到的，"知"并不是有意识地接纳所有的可选择性，即我们因"仁"而不"惑"。它的实现不是因为为思想和行动选出了一条最好的路，而是在可能之域中达致一个特定的关注点，从而不再有"惑"（two minds）。

（《通过孔子而思》，第232—233页）

如果我们把对"至大域境"之

specific events in the evolution of Chinese culture. Reliance upon historical examples and poeticized personal accounts suggests that the kind of sociopolitical order that Confucius envisions begins with specific instances of desirable conduct. And even while referring us to these historical exemplars worthy of emulation, Confucius makes it clear that modeling is more than a passive reiteration of some established behavior. The student is, in fact, required to evaluate the model's conduct critically and adapt it to his own conditions.

(*Thinking Through Confucius,* pp. 188-190)

The exemplary person (*chün tzu*), as a performer of *yi* 義 acts, as a concrete embodiment of ritual action, and as a model of personal and sociopolitical order, is both a source of continuity and a ground for creativity in the tradition. He is a model who engages the members of society in his achieved order, providing them the occasion for personal refinement and for creative self-disclosure. At all levels of engagement, he has an educative function in that his influence evokes the participation and qualitative transformation of others. His existence is in pursuit of the fullest disclosure of the concrete detail as a contribution to the harmonious order of the whole. As such, it reveals his uniqueness and novelty and serves as a warrant for the

内的"至刚聚焦视点"追求,翻译成一种人类社会语汇,我们可以说,"君子"是一种公共资源,是可资他人积极向上的榜样。君子之所以对他所在社会具有榜样效果,源于他们对自己的勤勉修养,修养使他们得以在林林总总的关系之中成长。人由于这种"至刚"及公认价值而受到赞颂,成为社会效仿的对象。同样,他们通过在平辈或上下辈之间形形色色的尊重之礼,扩散影响。《孟子》中的观点认为,作为影响深远之人,君子已是"至大",因影响广泛、长存、历久不衰,此是"至大";作为人们追求卓越人生的指路灯塔,也是"至刚"。

这样特殊榜样显示的是生生不息的社会之道,"道"需要模范人物引领人们去学习,这样,它就要求儒学哲学家发挥个人示范作用——如同一个先遣兵,为未来后辈探索并指明一条"道路"。这样类比地要求一些文化模范人物,在观念上是双向性的:既是给予,也是获取。人修养的本身就意味要向模范人物学习,将被尊为表率的人物视作自己所处世界的文化引领者。同时,向贤者学习而取得个人成长,也让

fullest expression of the uniqueness and novelty of others.

The exemplary person (*chün tzu*) is one who models both the activity of realizing (*chih* 知) and of personal articulation (*jen** 仁). He achieves his status as a model by a particular manner of focusing the events of his tradition and context so as to show and transmit what is excellent about them. As we suggested in our discussion of thinking, the act of realizing (*chih* 知) does not involve the conscious entertainment of alternatives; it is not grounded in hypothetical reflection. The modeling activity of the *chün tzu* depends upon the fact that personal articulation leads to a condition in which one is no longer troubled by doubts. This is not achieved by selecting the best from among a set of alternative paths for thought and action; it is realized by attaining a particular focus in the field of possibilities such that one is no longer of "two minds."

(*Thinking Through Confucius*, p. 192)

If we translate this pursuit of the most intensive focus within the most extensive field into the vocabulary of the human community, we might say that exemplary persons (*junzi* 君子) are communal resources that serve as an inspiration for others. What makes them "exemplary" for their community is the assiduous cultivation that has produced personal growth within their manifold of

个人产生一种对行为素质的追求志向。这种行为素质，久而久之，又将成为他所在家庭与人群的一种持久不断志向。最后，将这种志向充实到人类的文化宝库中去。

（《儒家角色伦理学》，第81—82页）

relations. By virtue of this personal intensity and its acknowledged worth, they are celebrated as objects of emulation within the community, thereby extending their influence through patterns of deference both within their own generational boundaries, and for generations yet to come. In the words of the *Mencius*, they have become "most vast"(*zhida* 至大) as persons of extensive and enduring influence, and "most firm" (*zhigang* 至剛) as resolute beacons that guide others toward human excellence.

Such particular exemplars provide the "heading" (*dao* 道) for the continuing community. This need for models to emulate, then, has required the Confucian philosopher to be a paradigmatic individual—a scout to reconnoiter and recommend a "way" for future generations. This analogical appeal to models is ideally bi-directional: a getting and a giving back. Personal cultivation entails the education of worthy exemplars available as cultural leaders within one's own world. At the same time, the personal growth made possible by such emulation allows one to aspire personally to a quality of conduct that will, in the fullness of time, make one a continuing inspiration for one's own family and community members, and that will ultimately add to the aggregating quantum of human culture.

(*Confucian Role Ethics: A Vocabulary*, p. 69)

圣 / 圣人

"圣人"(the sage)是《中庸》所尊奉的自我圆成(self-consummation)的过程的最高体现,"圣"(sagacity)则是圣人的首要的品质。作为一种品行的典范,"圣"是宇宙创造性的根本表达,那种宇宙创造性则是《中庸》的一个核心主题。

《中庸》第三十一章将"至圣"(the utmost sagacity)提升到可以和天相配("配天")的高度。所谓:

> 唯天下至圣,为能聪明睿知,足以有临也。宽裕温柔,足以有容也。发强刚毅,足以有执也。齐庄中正,足以有敬也。文理密察,足以有别也。溥博渊泉,而时出之。溥博如天,渊泉如渊。见而民莫不敬,言而民莫不信,行而民莫不说。是以声名洋溢乎中国,施及蛮貊。舟车所至,人力所通,天之所覆,地之所载,日月所照,霜露所队,凡有血气者,莫不尊亲。故曰配天。

Sage/Sagacity

The sage (*shengren* 聖人) is the highest exemplification of the process of self-consummation celebrated in the *Zhongyong*, and sagacity (*sheng* 聖) is the primary quality of the sage. As a mode of conduct, sagacity is the principal expression of that cosmic creativity that serves as the central theme of the *Zhongyong*.

Zhongyong 31 elevates those of the utmost sagacity to being the counterparts of *tian* 天:

> Only the most sagacious in the world. ...So broad, expansive, and profoundly deep, in a timely way they express these virtues. So broad and expansive like the heavens themselves; so profoundly deep like a bottomless abyss: They appear and all defer to them; they speak and all have confidence in what they say; they act and all find pleasure in what they do.
>
> It is for this reason that their fame spreads out over the Central states, extending to the Man and Mo barbarians in the south and north. Everywhere that boats and carriages ply, everywhere that human strength penetrates, everywhere that is sheltered by the heavens and is

"圣"和"诚"几乎是同义的。"诚"或许是"圣"字最为准确的理解。它是一种即使在其与"天"的互动中也行之有效的品行的典范。因此，正是作为"天成"的"圣人"，最能够符合"天"的表面上的无情。

"圣"是"溥博渊泉"，因此，它是最为广阔的文化蕴涵的最强的焦点。进而言之，通过"时出"的方式来表达其德行，"圣"就始终能够构成那些无所不包的各种场域的焦点。

（《切中伦常：〈中庸〉的新诠与新译》，第94—95页）

对孔子来说，圣人不仅是"礼仪大师"，他更是一个"制曲者"（a composer）（使各个部分获得组合）和"调解者"（compositor）（一个调节和解决纷争的人：仲裁者，调解人）。这就是说，圣人通过沟通和交流的种种模式推动和培养着协调性的"和"——获得一致性的同时保存着多样性，既显示稳定性同时也支持亲善的噪乱。圣人就是这一交响曲的指挥，他指导着所有的独特性同奏协和。

borne up by the earth, everywhere that is illumined by the sun and moon, everywhere that the frosts and dew settle—all creatures that have breath and blood revere and love them. Thus it is said that they are the complement of *tian* 天.

Sagacity is well-nigh synonymous with *cheng* 诚, which might well be the most precise rendering of that term. It is a mode of conduct that is efficacious even in its interactions with *tian*. Thus, it is the sagacious person, as "complement of *tian*," who qualifies most dramatically the apparent inexorability of *tian*.

The sagacious are "broad, expansive, and profoundly deep"—and are thus the most intensive foci of the most extensive fields of cultural significance. Further, by expressing their virtues "in a timely way," they always constitute appropriate foci of those inclusive fields.

(*Focusing the Familiar: A Translation and Philosophical Interpretation of the Zhongyong*, pp. 76-77)

For Confucius, the sage is not only the "master of ceremony," he is further a "composer" (one who makes up by putting together parts) and a "compositor" (one who composes or settles disputes: an umpire, arbiter, peacemaker). That is, the sage

(《通过孔子而思》，第342页)

圣人听先言后。听而后言对圣人来说同"从之"而后"和之"、"纯如"的行为是一样的。只有首先倾听，置身于潜在和谐得以发生的情境中，然后为使之"成"而调整可获最佳化和谐的成分，这样，协调（顺）才会产生。这种先参与既定环境，然后致力于建立秩序以实现和谐的方法，也就是"恕"（deference）的方法。

(《通过孔子而思》，第349页)

圣人先听，而后言而和之、歌而和之。"听"对无"倾听之耳"的人来说几乎毫无价值。"耳顺"是对种种沟通模式——言、礼和乐的把握。

(《通过孔子而思》，第368页)

圣人作为一个范畴，与政治影响以及人格价值紧密相连。圣人人格的与众不同之处就在于，其成就的品格成为意义、价值和目的的源泉，以至于成为像神那样的人，一个与天地一样伟大、参与宇宙的化育的人。圣人的观念具有深刻的宗

through the various media of communication and communion facilitates and fosters the negotiated harmony that at once achieves unity while preserving diversity, that evidences constancy while sponsoring a friendly chaos. In this symphony, the sage is the conductor who conduces to a collaboration of unique contributions.

(*Thinking Through Confucius,* pp. 277-278)

The sage must first listen and only then begin to speak. Speaking after listening is for the sage the same activity as harmonizing or improvising after playing or singing in unison with others. Attunement occurs when one first listens and places oneself into a position of potential harmony, then brings what is given to completion (*ch'eng** 成) by adding those elements to the situation which maximize harmony. The method of realizing harmony by first entertaining the given circumstances and only then addressing oneself to that given in such way as to communicate order is the method of *shu* 恕, deference.

(*Thinking Through Confucius,* p. 283)

The sage first listens, then he speaks or sings in harmony. Listening is of little value to one who lacks "ears to hear." The attunement of one's ear constitutes a mastery of the modes of communication—language, ritual action, and music.

(*Thinking Through Confucius,* p. 300)

教层面。恰如孟子所说：

> 可欲之谓善，有诸己之谓信，充实之谓美，充实而有光辉之谓大，大而化之之谓圣，圣而不可知之之谓神。（《孟子·尽心下》）

《孟子》中这段话从善于或擅长于建立关系这一认识开始。从某人自己的视角来看，建立这样的关系使他成为可以信赖。从别人的视角来看，这使他变得"美好"，将这种善于建立关系的能力加以扩大，这就使他依次成为一个伟大的人，一个圣人，最终成为神。神是文化上的超群绝伦，被当作行为完美的典范加以崇拜，并且由于赢得了其传统的服从，而成为所有的人的共同榜样。

（《汉哲学思维的文化探源》，第 165—166 页）

圣人（sage）跟君子的共同之处在于这两个行为范畴都体现有效沟通。对古典儒家来说，昌盛的社群就是一个沟通的社群，圣人是最佳沟通者。该字字形表明，圣（聖）

Sagehood as a category is strongly associated with political influence as well as personal worth. What is distinctive about sagehood is that the quality of one's achievement is a source of meaning, value, and purpose to the extent that one becomes godlike, a person of cosmic proportions and influence. The notion of sage has a profoundly religious dimension. As Mencius observes:

> That which is desirable is called being adept (*shan* 善); having it in oneself is called being trustworthy (*xin* 信); and manifesting it fully is allied elegance (*mei* 美). Manifesting it fully and being radiant with it is called being great (*da* 大); being great and being transformed by this greatness is called sageliness (*sheng* 聖); being sagely and going beyond the understanding of others, is called being godly (*shen* 神).

This passage in the *Mencius* begins from the idea of being adept or good at forging relationships. Viewed from one's own perspective, forging such relationships makes one trustworthy. Viewed from the perspective of others, it makes one "elegant." The extension of this adeptness at forging relationships makes one in turn a great person, a sage, and ultimately, a god. Gods are cultural heroes and ancestors, revered as models of desirable conduct, who become corporate by

人有"耳",听所当听,并基此沟通或"呈"其所当是。圣人的效能是靠成功凝聚百姓,实现人之所以为人的共同目标来衡量的。圣人这个艺术大师吟唱的是蛊惑世界的歌。圣人高于君子,君子"畏圣人之言"(《论语·季氏》)。

儒家的圣人不是英雄式地表演超人行为。他们毋宁是那些能够以某种非凡的方式做普通事的人,能够赋予日常生活以灵感的人。如果说儒家宇宙论中的人是由关系建构的,圣人暗含的就是一个谐和奏出的更高世界。

圣人除了拥有君子所有品格外,似乎还能整体性地看待感受、风俗、礼仪、传统,将之视为对人类社群的宽泛界定与整合,亦是对过去与未来社群的界定与整合。圣人此观感可被描述为某种给予我们能够超越自身所处特定时空的意识,使我们不仅可以跟我们的时代紧密相合,而且亦跟过去与未来连贯一致。

圣人的象征都是宇宙且神话的。此罕有之人身上集中的文化将人类经验提升到深远的审美和宗教精修高度,使人类成为天地的可贵

attracting the deference of their tradition.
(*Thinking from the Han,* pp. 159-160)

What the *shengren*, or "sage," shares in common with the exemplary person (*junzi* 君子) is that both categories of conduct entail effective communication. For classical Confucianism, the flourishing community is a communicating community, and the *shengren* are consummate communicators. The graph suggests that the sages have the "ears" (*er* 耳) to hear what is valuable to hear, and on that basis communicate or "manifest"(*cheng* 呈) their vision of what will be. Their effectiveness is measured by their success in drawing the hands and hearts of the people together to realize a shared project that shapes what it means to be human. The sage as virtuoso sings the songs that enchant the world. *Shengren* have risen above the level of *junzi*, who themselves stand in awe of the words of the *shengren* (see *Analects* 16.8).

The sage is not portrayed as heroic, performing superhuman deeds. Rather, sages are persons who are able to do the ordinary in an extraordinary way, who are able to inspire the everyday. Also, given that in this cosmology persons are constituted by their relationships, implicated within the sages are the worlds that they have orchestrated to a higher level.

In addition to possessing all of the qualities of the *junzi*, the *shengren* appear to see and feel custom, rituals, and traditions holistically, as

同伴。圣人的榜样光耀世代且穿越地缘边界，不仅是稳定保全人类世界之光，亦是人类文化繁荣昌盛之源。圣人将人道（the way of becoming human）带入其更确定的未来。

尽管圣人行为是宇宙意义的，但曾子在《孝经》中问得很清楚："敢问圣人之德，无以加于孝乎？"孔子的回答亦很简单：

> 天地之性，人为贵。人之行，莫大于孝。（《圣治章》）

这就是孝的重要性。

（《生民之本：〈孝经〉的哲学诠释及英译》，第103—104页）

"圣人"和"君子"所同者，就是二者都蕴涵着有效的沟通。对于古典儒学来说，繁荣的社群（flourishing community）就是一个沟通的社群（communicative community）。正如以上指出的，"君子"就是通过有效的沟通（"口"）来指导（"尹"）社群的人。而"圣人"则更是有效沟通的大师。"圣（聖）"这个字意味着"圣人""听"（"耳"）值得听的东西，进而在此基

defining and integrating the human community broadly, and as defining and integrating as well the communities of the past and of the future. This seeing and feeling of the *shengren* can be described as an awareness that gives one the capacity to go beyond the particular time and place in which we live, effecting a continuity not only with our contemporaries, but with those who have preceded us, and with those who will follow after.

The metaphors used to describe the *shengren* are cosmic and celestial, and the culture that finds its focus in this rare person elevates the human experience to heights of profound aesthetic and religious refinement, making the human being a worthy partner with the heavens and the earth. The model of the *shengren* shines across generations and across geographical boundaries as a light that not only stabilizes and secures the human world but also serves humankind as a source of cultural nourishment and inspiration. It is the *shengren* who leads the way of becoming human (*rendao* 人道) into its more certain future.

Although the conduct of the sages is of cosmic consequence, when in the *Classic of Family Reverence* Master Zeng asks Confucius explicitly "if there is anything in the excellence (*de*) of the sages that surpasses family reverence," Confucius' answer is simple:

Of all the creatures in the world,

础上与他人交流或提出（"呈"）他们有关将会发生什么的看法。"圣人"的成功在于将人们的心愿和力量集合在一起，以便实现大家共同的计划，这种共同的计划提升净化着人之所以为人的东西。通过这一点，"圣人"的有效性得以衡量。作为大师，"圣人"吟唱着令世界陶醉的歌曲。《论语》第十六篇《季氏》第八章有云："君子有三畏：畏天命，畏大人，畏圣人之言。"如果说"君子"敬畏"圣人"之言的话，那么，"圣人"则处在比"君子"更高的层次。

在提升人类经验的过程中，有效沟通和交流的关键是孔子有关"正名"的学说。这一学说断言，赋予事物恰当的名称（"名"），就会使（"命"）一个恰当的世界得以形成。

《论语》中经常提到"圣人"，从中，我们可以学到很多东西。在《述而》第三十四章中，孔子不敢以"圣人"自居，所谓"若圣与仁，则吾岂敢"。在《述而》第二十六章中，孔子也感叹他从未遇到过"圣人"，所谓"圣人，吾不得而见之矣"。诚然，根据《中庸》第二十九章，"圣人"是百代才一遇的，所谓"百世以俟圣人"。不过，"圣人"的

the human being is the most noble. In human conduct there is nothing more important than family reverence.

Such is the importance of *xiao*.

(*The Chinese Classic of Family Reverence*, pp. 84-85)

What the category of *shengren*, or "sage," shares with the exemplary person (*junzi* 君子) is that both entail effective communication. For classical Confucianism, the flourishing community is a communicating community. As noted above, the *junzi* 君子 is one who "oversees (*yin* 尹)" community through effective "communication (*kou* 口)." The *shengren*, then, is a virtuoso of communication. The graph suggests that the sages "hear (*er* 耳)" what is valuable to hear, and on that basis communicate or "present (*cheng* 呈)" their vision of what will be. Their effectiveness is measured by their success in drawing the hands and hearts of the people together to realize a shared project that refines what it means to be human. The sage as virtuoso sings the songs that enchant the world. *Shengren* have risen above the level of *junzi* who stand in awe of the words of the *shengren* (see *Analects* 16.8).

The centrality of effective communication in elevating the human experience is captured in the Confucian doctrine of "the proper use of names (*zhengming* 正名)" that asserts

典范却是在那里的。

　　孟子曾经用孔子来定义"圣人"意味着什么。在《论语》中,最谦虚的孔子曾经对子贡将他与"圣人"相提并论表示不敢。子贡称孔子为"天纵之圣"且"多能",孔子则谦称自己只有"多能",所谓:"吾少也贱,故多能鄙事。君子多乎哉?不多也。"将孔子的地位提高到"圣人"的地步,并不是只有这一处明确的表示。《论语》最后五篇有很多诸如此类的记载。其中,孔子常被视为具有神圣的地位。譬如,《论语》第十九篇《子张》第二十四章有这样一段记载:

> 叔孙武叔毁仲尼。子贡曰:"无以为也,仲尼不可毁也。他人之贤者,丘陵也,犹可逾也。仲尼,日月也,无得而逾焉。人虽欲自绝,其何伤于日月乎?多见其不知量也。"

　　在《论语》诸如此类的记载中,这段话很有代表性,它称颂一般意义上的"圣人"和特定意义上的圣人孔子的宇宙形象(cosmic stature)。在《中庸》第三十章中,

that "naming (*ming* 名)" things properly "commands (*ming* 命)" a proper world into being.

Much is to be learned from the frequent references to *shengren* in the *Analects*. In one passage Confucius dares not rank himself a *shengren* (7.34) and in another laments that he never has, and probably never will, meet one (7.26). Indeed, according to *Zhongyong* 29, the sage appears only once in a hundred generations. Yet the model is there.

In using Confucius to define what it means to be a sage, Mencius is picking up on a tradition that begins earlier in the *Analects* when the ever modest Confucius gently chastises Zigong for likening him to a *shengren* (9.6). It is not only this explicit use of *shengren* to describe Confucius that celebrates his status as a sage. In the last five books of the *Analects* that primarily record the observations of his now mature protégées, the metaphors used to celebrate Confucius are positively celestial. For example, *Analects* 19.24:

> Shusun Wushu spoke disparagingly of Confucius. Zigong responded, "Do not do this! Confucius cannot be disparaged. The superior character of other people is like a mound or a hill, which can still be scaled, but Confucius is the sun and moon, which none can climb beyond. When people cut themselves off from the

也正是孔子被挑选出来并被称颂为对宇宙的意义作出了持续不断的贡献的人。所谓：

> 仲尼祖述尧舜，宪章文武，上律天时，下袭水土。辟如天地之无不持载，无不覆帱；辟如四时之错行，如日月之代明。

除了拥有"君子"所有的品质之外，"圣人"会在历史的意义上去看、去感受习俗、礼仪和传统，将其视为当前人类社群以及过去和将来的各种人类社群的聚焦与整合。"圣人"的这种"看"和"感受"可以被描述为一种觉悟，这种觉悟给予人以能力去超越我们所居于其中的特定的时空，产生一种连续性，这种连续性不仅仅是与其同时代人之间的，也是与其先人和后继者之间的。

用来描述"圣人"的比喻是宇宙性和神圣的。在这种罕见的人格之中发现其聚焦的文化，将人类经验提升到深刻的审美和宗教净化的高度，使得人类成为天地的有价值的同伴。"圣人"的典范跨越时代与地理的疆界，成为稳定和护持人类

sun and moon, what damage would this do to the sun and moon? It would only demonstrate that such people do not know their own limits."

This passage is representative of a number to be found in the *Analects* that pay tribute to the cosmic stature of the sage in general, and Confucius in particular. In *Zhongyong* 30 it is the person of Confucius who is singled out in an unqualified celebration of the continuing human contribution to cosmic meaning:

> Zhongni (Confucius) revered Yao and Shun as his ancestors and carried on their ways; he emulated and made illustrious the ways of Kings Wen and Wu. He modeled himself above on the rhythm of the turning seasons, and below he was attuned to the patterns of water and earth. He is comparable to the heavens and the earth, sheltering and supporting everything that is. He is comparable to the progress of the four seasons, and the alternating brightnesses of the sun and moon.

In addition to possessing all of the qualities of the *junzi*, the *shengren* appear to see and feel custom, rituals, and traditions holistically, as focusing and integrating the present human community, as well as the communities of the past and future. This seeing and feeling of the

世界的一种手段，同时也成为一种文化滋养和灵感的持久的源泉。

（《切中伦常：〈中庸〉的新诠与新译》，第95—97页）

"圣（聖）人"则堪称沟通大师，"耳"与"呈"不仅界定了人类的经验，而且还涵衍了和谐的意蕴。于是，我们不禁由孔子"正名"的观念（第十三篇第三章）想到，只有给事物取定了合适的名称，它才能顺理成章地发生、发展。

"圣人"一词在《论语》中出现了八次。在第七篇第三十四章中，孔子自述不敢忝列于圣人之侧。在另一处，孔子哀叹自己从来没有，可能永远也不会见到圣人（第七篇第二十六章）。而在第九篇第六章中，当子贡以"圣"赞誉孔子的时候，孔子婉转地表达了批评。即便是提出"人皆可以为尧、舜（即圣人）"的孟子，也明确指出，这个目标超出了大多数人的能力。

不过，"圣人"确实存在，而且其境界远远高于"君子"。在第十六篇第八章中，孔子指出，"君子"畏"圣人"之言。而在第六篇第三十章的问答中，孔子认为，"博施于民而

shengren can be described as an awareness that gives one the capacity to go beyond the particular time and place in which we live, effecting a continuity not only with our contemporaries, but with those who have preceded us and who will follow behind.

The metaphors used to describe the *shengren* are cosmic and celestial. The culture that finds its focus in this rare person elevates the human experience to heights of profound aesthetic and religious refinement, making the human being a worthy partner with the heavens and the earth. The model of the *shengren* extends across generations and geographical boundaries serving as a means of stabilizing and securing the human world, and as a continual source of cultural nourishment and inspiration.

(*Focusing the Familiar: A Translation and Philosophical Interpretation of the Zhongyong*, pp.77-79)

The *shengren*（圣人）is a virtuoso of communication, "listening (*er* 耳)" and "presenting ideas (*cheng* 呈)" that not only come to define the human experience, but which further have cosmic implications. As we recall from Confucius' notion of "the proper use of names (*zhengming* 正名)" in 13.3, to name (*ming* 名) a world properly commands (*ming* 命) a proper world into being.

There are eight references to *shengren* in the text. In one passage Confucius dares not

能济众"者就是"圣人"。

　　子夏则认为,只有"圣人"才能够有始有终地成就大道(第十九篇第十二章)——这颇有几分《论语》中罕见的神秘意味。如果这种看法可以被归作神秘主义的话,它也应该是一种非同寻常的神秘主义——它出现在一个卓越人物的鼎盛时期,并且产生于社会、政治生活之中;它从了解身边的知识入手而最终通达天理(第十四篇第三十五章)。假如我们把孔子看作"圣人"的话,"有始有终"则是对其生平的最好概括——孔子在晚年已经达到了"从心所欲不逾矩"的最高境界(第二篇第四章)。

　　下面,我们对"士""君子""圣人"的性质特点和相互关系略作概括:所有"圣人"都是"君子";一切"君子"全为"士",反之则不然。如果由低到高按修身境界来排列的话,"士"最低,"君子"胜之,"圣人"最高。就数量而言,"士"的人数相对较多,"君子"则大大减少,"圣人"因"任重而道远"(第八篇第七章)成为凤毛麟角之属。

　　"士"是百折不挠的求道者。

rank himself a *shengren* (7.34), in another he laments that he never has, and probably never will, meet one (7.26), and in still another he gently chastises Zigong when the latter likens him to a *shengren* (9.6). And later, even though Mencius allows that the man in the street who acts like a Yao or a Shun (that is, a *shengren*) is a sage, he, too, suggests strongly that this goal is beyond the reach of most mortals.

　　Yet it is there. There are *shengren*. They have risen beyond the level of *junzi*, because 16.8 describes *junzi* as those who stand in awe of the words of the *shengren*. From 6.30 we learn that one who confers benefits on, and assists everyone, is a *shengren*.

　　And finally, Zixia allows that it is not even the *junzi*, but the *shengren* alone "who walks this path every step from start to finish"(19.12). There is a slight hint of the mystical here that is not common in the *Analects*. But if mysticism it is, it is a mysticism of an unusual sort, coming as it does as the culmination of an active and engaged social and political life, beginning with what was near, and getting to what was distant (14.35). If the career of Confucius is one example of sagehood, perhaps walking the path from start to finish reports on Confucius who, at the end of his life, could give his "heart-and-mind free rein without overstepping the boundaries"(2.4).

　　To summarize this brief reading of the qualities of, and relations between, the *shi*, the *junzi*, and the *shengren*: all *shengren* are

"道"则集中体现于"礼"之中。"礼"影响着决定了"士"的各种身份角色的人际关系。"士"在为学践履的道路上深入前进,就会达到"君子"之境。"君子"精通"礼"。所以,即便是在没有先例的情况下,"君子"也能清楚地阐述自己的思想。他们得心应手地扮演着各自的角色,而且从优雅高贵的气度、张弛相宜的状态和旺盛的创造力(此即"君子"与他人——无论是陌生人还是家族血亲,相处交往的方式)中获得了极大的满足。也正是出类拔萃的"君子",以其在各自社会政治角色中的出色表现,为我们树立了一个行为典范。

"圣人"达到了寻道者的最高境界。除了具有"君子"的所有特质之外,"圣人"在广泛划分整合人类社会(包括过去的和将来的)的同时,也在探究风俗礼仪和传统。"圣人"的感知力是一种赋予人超越现在特定时空能力的意识;它塑造了一个始自前代先人,经由我们自身,并延及后世子孙的绵长系列。

《论语》描述"圣人"的比喻颇具宇宙意义上的神圣意味:"仲尼,日月也,无得而逾焉。"(第十九篇

junzi, and all *junzi* were formerly *shi*, but the converse does not hold. These are, in other words, ranked types of persons, and the ranking is based on a progression from scholarly apprenticeship to sagehood. *Shi* are, relatively speaking, fairly numerous, *junzi* are more scarce, and *shengren* are very few and far between, owing to the heaviness of the burden, and the distance of the journey (8.7).

The *shi* are resolute in following the *dao* as it is embodied in ritual propriety (*li*) that governs the interpersonal relations definitive of the *shi*'s several roles. Much farther along this journey of learning and doing we have the *junzi*, who know the *li* thoroughly enough to express their spirit even in the absence of precedent; they perform their roles masterfully, and derive a deep satisfaction from the grace, dignity, effortlessness, and creativity with which they have come to conduct themselves with others, strangers no less than kin. And it is the *junzi* who ascend in the midst of many to provide a bearing for exemplary conduct through effective service in roles of social and political responsibility.

At the upper end of this continuum, then, are the *shengren*. In addition to possessing all of the qualities of the *junzi*, the *shengren* appear to see and feel custom, rituals, and traditions holistically, as defining and integrating the human community broadly, and as defining and integrating as well the communities of the past, and of the future.

第二十四章）关注孔子这个特别人物的中国文化，将人类经验提升到意蕴深远的美学的和宗教的高度，从而使人类能够与天地相提并论。"圣人"光耀万代，泽被四海。他的存在不仅有效地维护了社会安定，而且也成为推动文化发展的动力。正是"圣人"引导人类走向更加确定的未来。

我们在探讨"士""君子"和"圣人"三者关系的时候，将之看作三个渐进的层次。必须强调的一点是，这种垂直分层并不纯粹是我们的想象，而是一种先验的认定。我们致力于发掘"道"的丰富意象，而"圣人"却早已循"道"而行，远远超越了"士"和"君子"，并且成为后二者跋涉中的指路明灯和光辉榜样。大儒荀子曾在《礼论》篇末简洁地概括了"圣人""君子"和"士"的关系：

> 苟非圣人，莫之能知也。圣人明知之，士君子安行之，官人以为守，百姓以成俗。其在君子以为人道也，其在百姓以为鬼事也。

This seeing and feeling of the *shengren* can be described as an awareness which gives one the capacity to go beyond the particular time and place in which we live, effecting a continuity not only with our contemporaries, but with those who have preceded us, and with those who will follow behind.

The metaphors used to describe the *shengren* are cosmic and celestial: "Confucius is the sun and moon which no one can climb beyond" (19.24). The culture that finds its focus in this rare person elevates the human experience to heights of profound aesthetic and religious refinement, making the human being a worthy partner with the heavens and the earth. The model of the *shengren* shines across generations and across geographical boundaries as a light that not only stabilizes and secures the human world, but that also serves humankind as a source of cultural nourishment and inspiration. It is the *shengren* who leads the way of the human being (*rendao* 人道) into its more certain future.

In reading the relationship between the *shi*, *junzi*, and *shengren* hierarchically, we must emphasize that the hierarchy should not just be imagined vertically, concluding in a transcendent we-know-not-what. Rather do we want to maintain the rich path imagery of *dao*: the *shengren* have traveled, appropriated, and enlarged a longer stretch of the road than the *shi* and *junzi*, and they are providing signposts and a bearing for the latter as well. The later

以上就是我们对《论语》的文化语境、相关人物以及存在于其社会历史背景之中并且重构其思想世界的语言的扼要诠释。我们希望借此帮助西方读者理解中、西方文化的差异。莎翁笔下的哈姆雷特曾言："天地之间的事物远远多于我们的想象。"而中国的哈姆雷特则会喟叹道："感悟天地的道的数量远远超出了世人的想象。"

（《〈论语〉的哲学诠释》，第64—66页）

Confucian Xunzi has succinctly described this relationship at the close of his masterful essay on ritual, the *li*:

> Only the *shengren* is able to understand the observance of ritual propriety. The *shengren* understands this observance with clarity; the *shi* and *junzi* perform it with ease; the officials maintain it, and the common people use it to create their own customs. In the hands of the *junzi*, it becomes the way of humanity; in the hands of the common people, it becomes the business of ghosts and spirits.

This, then, in all too brief a compass is our interpretation of the eventful world of the *Analects*, the relational people who experience it, and the language which per-, in-, and re-forms that world and those people. We hope it will enable the Western reader of this text to appreciate how a Chinese Hamlet may have spoken somewhat differently had he read it. Rather than "There are *more things* in heaven and earth than are dreamed of in your philosophy," he may well have said, "There are *more ways of experiencing the heavens and the earth* than are dreamed of in your philosophy."

(*The Analects of Confucius*, pp. 62-65)

学

"学"作为"learning",是一个直接关涉"觉"(becoming aware)的过程,而非关于客观世界之概念意义上的间接知识,这一点意义重大。"学"字本身是"斅"的简写。"斅"的意思是"教"(to teach)和"觉"。在先秦,"觉"的意思是,当时力求学有所成的学者在教和学的双向过程中获得深刻认知。只是到后来,有可能随着文化传统更实际的发展,"学"的意义才侧重于"学习"。

"学"的第二个含义涉及文化传承问题。通过"闻"(to hear)与"学"的关联以及"学习"过程的字面含义可明显看出:"学"作为通过"闻"(教与学的相互作用和交流)而拥有和体现文化传统(文)的意思。

治"学"的对象是传承"文"(human culture)。"文"的本源意义是"刻画"或"纹饰",常常与陶器上装饰的整体性主题相连。它是人类对世界存在的精心组织和殚精竭虑的表述,是人类运用象征符号所清晰表达的人类价值和意义,进

Learning

It is significant that *hsüeh* 學 as "learning" refers to an unmediated process of becoming aware rather than a conceptually mediated knowledge of a world of objective fact. In fact, the character, *hsüeh* 學, is itself an abbreviated form of *hsiao* 教, meaning "to teach," "to become aware." During the pre-Ch'in period, this "becoming aware" denoted the heightening awareness of the scholar engaged in both studying and teaching as he pursued the goal of becoming a learned person. It was only later in the tradition, perhaps with the accumulation of a more substantive cultural tradition, that the focus of *hsüeh* came to rest on studying.

A second implication of *hsüeh* is that it involves the project of transmitting one's cultural legacy. In the association of the character *wen* 聞, "to hear," with *hsüeh*, and in the verbal nature of the learning process, there is a clear sense of *hsüeh* as the appropriation and embodiment of the cultural tradition (*wen** 文) through pedagogical interaction and exchange (*wen* 聞).

The objective of the exercise of *hsüeh* is the transmission of human culture (*wen** 文). The root meaning of *wen** is "lines" or "design," often associated with systematic themes in the decoration of pottery. It is the human organization and elaboration of the stuff of existence, the articulation of human values

而使之代代承传。文化在这种累积和传承的过程中逐渐提炼精髓:"周监于二代,郁郁乎文哉!吾从周。"(《论语·八佾》)孔子认识到自己处身于一个有传统的社会语境中,他把体现和传承自己的文化精粹视作个人的使命。

文化传承有许多模式和框架,但或许最明显的是体现在书面语言上。历史上的孔子实际上或多或少都担负了对归于他名下的各种古代经典的编纂和整理工作。显然,他相当强调熟知(如果不是死记)历史文献和文化典籍。这并不是说,书是仅有的承载文化意义的知识库。许多传统智慧是经由口头传承或存于社会制度、礼仪和音乐中的。尽管孔子将古代典籍视为必修之学是毋庸置疑的,但"学"是一项个体必须从精神到肉体、从认知到经验全身心投入的事业。从孔子为其弟子设立修习的根本学科"六艺"(礼、乐、射、御、书、数)中也可看出,"学"是一项人的全面发展的事业,书本知识仅是学者生涯中的一个(尽管很重要的)部分。

(《通过孔子而思》,第47—48页)

and meaning captured in symbol and then transmitted from generation to generation. In this process of accumulation and transmission culture undergoes gradual refinement (3.14): "The Chou surveys the two preceding dynasties. How resplendent is the culture! My choice is with the Chou." Confucius, perceiving himself from within the context of a traditional society, took the embodiment and transmission of his own cultural legacy as a personal mission.

There are many modes and structures for the transmission of culture, perhaps the most obvious being the written word. To whatever extent the historical Confucius was actually responsible for compiling and editing the various classics attributed to him, it is clear that he placed considerable emphasis on a familiarity with, if not a rote memorization of, historical and cultural documents. This is not to say that books were regarded as the only repository of significances. Much of the traditional wisdom was transmitted orally or captured in social institutions, rituals and music. Although Confucius' commitment to a literary corpus as a basic curriculum is beyond question, learning was perceived as an enterprise which engaged a person both mentally and physically, both cognitively and experientially. From the "six arts" (*liu-i* 六藝) established by Confucius as the curriculum for his followers—ritual (*li* 禮), music (*yüeh* 樂), archery (*she* 射), charioteering (*yü* 御), writing (*shu* 書), and calculations (*shu* 數)—it is clear that learning was a project requiring a commitment on the part of the entire person, and that written documents were only one, albeit important, element in the scholar's career.

(*Thinking Through Confucius,* pp. 44-45)

中 / 中庸

在《中庸》中,"中"字频繁出现,一直被译为"focus"和"equilibrium"。譬如,在《中庸》第一章中,便解释了"和"的不断协调与"中"所提供的这种和谐的稳定之间的关系。所谓:

> 喜怒哀乐之未发谓之中,发而皆中节谓之和。中也者,天下之大本也;和也者,天下之达道也。致中和,天地位焉,万物育焉。

在使世界成为富有意义的"中"的过程中,有人的参与;在保持这种"中"的过程中,有人的贡献,正是由于这一点,才使得人成为塑造自然、社会以及文化环境的其他各种力量的伙伴。由于"聚焦"("中")和"平衡"("中")的状态

Centering / Equilibrium / Focus / Balance

Zhong appears frequently in the *Zhongyong*, and has been translated as both "focus" and "equilibrium." *Zhongyong* 1, for example, explains the relationship between the ongoing negotiation of a productive harmony (*he*), and the anchoring of this harmony that focus (*zhong*) provides:

> The moment at which joy and anger, grief and pleasure, have yet to arise is called a nascent equilibrium (*zhong*); once the emotions have arisen, that they are all brought into proper focus (*zhong*) is called harmony (*he*). This notion of equilibrium and focus (*zhong*) is the great root of the world; harmony then is the advancing of the proper way in the world. When equilibrium and focus are sustained and harmony is fully realized, the heavens and earth maintain their proper places and all things flourish in the world.

排除了强制,对于将在构成任何特定环境的关系的模式中的各种创造性的可能性加以最大化来说,"中"就是一个至关重要的条件。并且,作为一种决定性的因素,真正的更新(novelty)在潜在的意义上是去稳定化的(destabilizing)。因此,创造性本身的质量有赖于圣人最佳效果地安顿世界和谐并根据变化的环境来随时调整它的能力。《中庸》第二十章用如下的术语解释了这种创造性:

> 诚者,天之道也;诚之者,人之道也。诚者不勉而中,不思而得,从容中道,圣人也。诚之者,择善而固执之者也。

(《切中伦常:〈中庸〉的新诠与新译》,第104—105页)

"中庸"这一表述意味着,获得和谐与平衡的关键在于"庸"。"庸"即"日用伦常"之意。使人类经验礼仪化,使那些普通的、例行的、具体的、当下的东西变得富有魅力,这一工作要求一种不懈的关注,去

It is the human participation in bringing the world into meaningful focus and the human contribution to sustaining this equilibrium that establishes the human being as a full partner with the other forces shaping the natural, social, and cultural environments. Because a state of equilibrium and balance (*zhong*) precludes coercion, it is an essential condition for maximizing the creative possibilities in the pattern of relationships that constitute any particular situation. And real novelty as an indeterminate element is potentially destabilizing. Thus, the quality of creativity itself is dependent upon the capacity of the sage to orchestrate harmony in the world, and to modulate it in accordance with changing circumstances. *Zhongyong* 20 explains creativity in these terms:

> Creativity is the way of *tian*; creating is the proper way of becoming human. Creativity is achieving equilibrium and focus without coercion; it is succeeding without reflection. Freely and easily traveling the center of the way—this is the sage. Creating is selecting what is efficacious and holding on to it firmly.

(*Focusing the Familiar: A Translation and Philosophical Interpretation of the Zhongyong,* p. 86)

The expression, *zhongyong*, suggests that the locus for achieving harmony and equilibrium is *yong*—the ordinary business of the day. This

富有成果地训练和运用那些在我们日常经验中涌现的自发的新生事物。将人类经验礼仪化既要求一种对于持久生活形式的欣赏，更要求我们充分运用想象力，为了我们自己的时空去创造它。

（《切中伦常：〈中庸〉的新诠与新译》，第105—106页）

儒家"角色伦理"在面对更为抽象层次的秩序上，并不是没有能力的。我们发现，儒家文本除了有时也诉诸抽象理念语言外，它还借用社会与审美意识的艺术术语。"中""和"是最常用的这等词语，用来表达较为概括性、聚合性的意义，表达人创立的功德，"功德"出自强穿透力的价值观。"和"指和谐、和谐状态、和谐性（harmonizing, harmony）；"中"指居中、平衡、聚焦点和保持平衡（centering, equilibrium, focus, balance）。"和"这个观念是一种实现的"和"状态，不是简单地凭借削弱分歧而有的"相异性"互相容忍；而更重要的，是一个创造性与丰富性结果——差异性被协调制造出一种最佳状态。其实，"和"的原

project of ritualizing the human experience and of enchanting the common, the routine, the concrete and immediate, requires an unremitting attentiveness to disciplining and exploiting productively what is spontaneously novel as it emerges in our everyday experience. Ritualizing the human experience requires both an appreciation of our ordinary and persistent life forms, and the full exercise of our imagination in reauthorizing them for our own time and place.

(*Focusing the Familiar: A Translation and Philosophical Interpretation of the Zhongyong*, pp. 86-87)

This is not to say that Confucian role ethics is without assets to deal with order at a more abstract level. But here again, in addition to sometimes appealing to the language of abstracted norms, we also find the Confucian texts invoking socially and aesthetically determined terms of art. The vocabulary that is most frequently used to express the more general, aggregated sense of human flourishing orchestrated out of these interpenetrating values are "harmonizing, harmony" (*he* 和) and "centering, equilibrium, focus, balance" (*zhong* 中). The kind of achieved "harmony" referenced by the term *he* 和 is not simply the mutual accommodation of difference that attenuates discord, but more importantly, the creative and productive outcome when such differences are coordinated to optimum effect. Indeed, the original character for "harmony" suggests that the desired outcome is to achieve

始字形，指的是一种理想效果，是达到和保持人与自然的"音乐性"。甲骨文中的"和"字，出现比较早且复杂，字形是"🅰"；青铜器铭文中是"🅱"。这个早期的"龢"字形含"龠"，是一种芦苇制作的管乐器，呈现一种奏乐之中的气氛，比喻之中使人体会到和谐之感。

意为"居中、平衡"的"中"，甲骨文中的字形是"🅲"和"🅳"，出现在青铜器铭文中是"🅴"。它们所指的含义，恐怕是再普通不过的召集军、民的两种警示，一是作为视觉信号的旌旗，一是作为听觉信号的建鼓。"中"象征旗杆上的旗帜随风飘扬，立于广场中心，以召集民众。"中"字中的"口"，其实像鼓形，以木立鼓，称为建鼓。中，和也，从口、丨，上下通。另，与"龢"字中龠乐器一样，"中"字的鼓形也暗示着音乐与和声。

《中庸》直接喻意"和"与"中"，此二字的重合意义表示儒家追求的远大抱负——人道与天地感应相参。《中庸》首章即明示"天地位、万物育"与人情感的"中和、未发"之联系：

and sustain a human and a cosmic "musicality." The composition of the earlier, more complex character for "harmony" (*he* 和) found on the oracle bones is 🅰 and on the bronzes is 🅱. This earlier graph 龢 is composed of a *yue* 龠 wind instrument constructed out of reed pipes, making the playing of music available as metaphor for understanding this sense of harmony.

The character *zhong* 中 meaning "centering, equilibrium" appears on the oracle bones as 🅲 and 🅳, and on the bronzes as 🅴. These graphs reference perhaps the two most common ways of assembling the people and of rallying the troops: The first way is by sight and the second is by sound. The *zhong* character depicts a banner or standard that would be hoisted in the market place as a visual signal for the people or for the troops to gather together. Another way of calling assembly for the people or the military implicated within the graph would be to sound a drum. The mouth of the drum 口 suspended on a stand is thus visually represented with the graph for *zhong* 中. As with "harmony" (*he* 龢) constructed with the *yue* wind instrument, *zhong* 中 in including a visual reference to the drum also has an immediate musical association.

The *Zhongyong* appeals directly to "harmony" and "equilibrium" in its own iteration of the holistic and aspirational Confucian project of coordinating human relations with immediate repercussions for the natural world. The opening passage of this text traces cosmic flourishing back to the achieved harmony of human feelings:

> 喜怒哀乐之未发，谓之中；发而皆中节，谓之和。中也者，天下之大本也；和也者，天下之达道也。致中和，天地位焉，万物育焉。

简而言之，人喜怒哀乐之未发，为天下道德之大本，得以中节而致中和；如此，儒家至善人生观和盘托出——万物育焉。此处强调，这种儒家的至善观点，通过家庭"角色"与关系进行教养才是真诚的。家庭才是在人一切"身份角色"与关系中所实现的"礼"的本源和必不可少的基础。如《论语·学而》所言：

> 礼之用，和为贵。先王之道斯为美，小大由之。有所不行，知和而和，不以礼节之，亦不可行也。

根据这样的道德是非观，优良行为可以加深、加强我们的关系并使之持久。不受关系与角色调停的行为、行动，皆毫无意义。那便是说，纯为维持秩序而贯彻的外来、强制性和谐（如通过法律、命令、

The condition when the feelings of joy and anger, grief and pleasure have yet to arise is called a nascent equilibrium (*zhong* 中); having arisen, that these feelings are then coordinated and brought into proper measure is called harmony (*he* 和). This notion of equilibrium is the great root of the world; harmony then is the advancing of the proper way (*dadao* 達道) in the world. When equilibrium and focus are sustained and harmony is fully realized, the heavens and the earth maintain their proper places and all things flourish in the world.

Stated more simply, when the expression of human feelings as the ultimate resource for achieving moral competence is orchestrated into a productive harmony, the Confucian vision of the consummate life is advanced, and all things in the world flourish. What needs to be emphasized here is the Confucian assumption that such human flourishing must be mediated through familial roles and relations for it to be genuine. It is the family that is the ultimate source and indispensable ground of an achieved propriety (*li*) in all of our roles and relations. As it states in the *Analects*:

> Achieving harmony (*he*) is the most valuable function of observing propriety in our roles and relations (*li*). In the ways of the Former Kings, this achievement of harmony by observing propriety in our

原则、规则等），便完全失去了人性，因为缺乏人的参与和配合。譬如说，有一些性情特征很容易流于冷漠、怯懦、粗暴与蒙昧之弊，而一经过适宜关系的调停，便升华而转变为礼让、谨慎、勇敢与坦率的品质：

> 子曰："恭而无礼则劳，慎而无礼则葸，勇而无礼则乱，直而无礼则绞。君子笃于亲，则民兴于仁；故旧不遗，则民不偷。"（《论语·泰伯》）

这样通过家庭角色、关系对行为进行的恰当教养以及如此君子行为而激发的担当心，结晶为恭、慎、勇、直的品质，具有为社会承认的意义与价值。

（《儒家角色伦理学：一套特色伦理学词汇》，第 187—189 页）

roles and relations made them elegant, and was a guiding standard in all things large and small. But when things are not going well, to realize harmony just for its own sake without regulating the situation through observing propriety in our roles and relations will not work.

Morality so understood describes that quality of conduct that makes relations stronger and thicker and more enduring. Without being properly situated within these roles and relations, actions are meaningless or worse. That is, a "harmony" that is affected by simply imposing external constraints as a means of enforcing order—the application of laws, edicts, principles, or rules—is dehumanizing to the degree that it precludes personal participation and confirmation. For example, thin dispositions that would otherwise be quite properly deemed lethargy, timidity, rowdiness, or rudeness by mediating them through appropriate relations can be elevated and transformed to express the important social values of deference, caution, bravery, and candor:

> The Master said, "Deference unmediated by observing propriety in our roles and relations (*li*) is lethargy; caution unmediated by observing propriety in our roles and relations is timidity; bravery unmediated by observing propriety in our roles and relations is rowdiness; candor unmediated by observing propriety in

our roles and relations is rudeness. Where exemplary persons are earnestly committed to their parents, the people will aspire to consummate conduct; where they do not neglect their old friends, the people will not be indifferent to each other."

It is the proper mediation of conduct through the roles and relations of family and through the responsiveness such exemplary behavior inspires that invests these actions—deference, caution, bravery, and candor—with their socially redeeming significance and value.

(*Confucian Role Ethics: A Vocabulary*, pp.168-171)

和

"和"习惯被翻译为"harmony"。我们也沿用这种译法。"和"这个术语的语源是和烹饪有关的。它是一种将两种或两种以上的食品添加并混合在一起的一种艺术,为的是那些食品能够互相补充强化,同时又不丧失它们各自本来独特的风味。在早期中国的各种文献中,"和"的这种意义随处可见,就是用来说明那种优雅的和谐之意。如此理解的"和"所蕴涵的意思,既意味着特定构成要素彼此之间的有机完整性,

Harmony

He is conventionally translated "harmony," and we follow that rendering. The etymology of the term is culinary. Harmony is the art of combining and blending two or more foodstuffs so that they mutually enhance one another without losing their distinctive flavors. Throughout the early corpus, the preparation of food is appealed to as a gloss on this sense of elegant harmony. Harmony so considered entails both the integrity of the particular ingredient and its ease of integration into some larger whole. Signatory of this harmony is the endurance of the particular

同时也意味着其有机完整性进入一个更大整体的从容自在。这种"和"的联署（Signatory）是特定各个成分以及"和"的审美属性的持久。这种"和"是一种优雅的秩序，它来自内在相关的各种细节之间的协作，为的是使每一个细节对整个秩序的贡献都能得到润色。

在《论语》一书中，这种"和"的意思被奉为最高的文化成就。其中，"和"与"同"是完全不一样的两个概念。后者完全抹杀了每一个体对于其存在脉络的个性，前者则在由每一个体共同构成的有机整体脉络中同时肯定个体自身的意义。家庭的比喻渗透于整个《论语》的文本，它是受到这样一种直觉的鼓舞，即：家庭是这样一种体制，在其中，通过礼义在不同境况下所主导的彼此之间的互动，所有家庭成员最为充分和毫无保留地将自己托付给这一团体的纽带。这种对于家庭的信托要求个体正直和真诚的充分表达，因此，它就构成一种脉络，在这种脉络之中，一个人能够最为有效地追求其个人的实现。

在《中庸》一书中，随着"中"

ingredients and the aesthetic nature of the harmony. Such harmony is an elegant order that emerges out of the collaboration of intrinsically related details to embellish the contribution of each one.

In the *Analects*, this sense of harmony is celebrated as the highest cultural achievement. Here, harmony is distinguished from mere agreement by defining it in terms of eliciting the optimum contribution of each particular to its context. The family metaphor pervades this text, encouraged by the intuition that this is the institution in which the members give themselves most fully and unreservedly to the group nexus, through interactions that are governed by those observances (*li*) most appropriate (*yi*) to the occasion. Such a commitment to family requires the full expression of personal integrity and thus becomes the context in which one can most effectively pursue personal realization.

In the *Zhongyong*, this Confucian sense of harmony (*he*) is further stipulated with the introduction of "focus" or "equilibrium" (*zhong* 中) as in "focusing (*zhong*) the familiar in the affairs of the day (*yong* 庸)." When Zilu asks Confucius about strength in *Zhongyong* 10, for example, a distinction is made between the tolerance and flexibility of the southerners, and the indefatigable tenacity of the northerners. It is bringing these two different senses of strength into

和"庸"这两个概念的引入——所谓"中庸"即意味着在日用常行("庸")中切中伦常("中"),这种儒家"和"的意义得到了进一步的说明。例如,在《中庸》第十章中,当子路问孔子什么是"强"时,孔子区分了两种不同的"强",即"宽柔以教,不报无道"的"南方之强",以及"衽金革,死而不厌"的"北方之强"。正是使这两种不同的"强"达到"和"和"中",所谓"和而不流","中立而不倚",才界定了君子的品格并使之与小人区别开来。

(《切中伦常:〈中庸〉的新诠与新译》,第84—85页)

harmony (*he*) and then sustaining this focus (*zhong*) that defines the conduct of exemplary persons and distinguishes them from the mean and petty.

(*Focusing the Familiar: A Translation and Philosophical Interpretation of the Zhongyong,* pp. 65-66)

无欲

与道家的感悟方式相联系的欲望,就是无对象的。无须规定、拥有或控制一个人乐的时刻,与无欲相联系的乐也是可能的。

因此,是无欲,而不是靠拥有和实现以中止欲望,才显示达到了顺应的欲望。以"无知"(a mirroring understanding,意为映照式的认识)

Objectless Desire

The desiring associated with the Daoist sensibility is objectless. The enjoyments associated with *wuyu* are possible without the need to define, possess, or control the occasion of one's enjoyment.

Thus, *wuyu*, rather than involving the cessation of desire through possession and consummation, represents the achievement of *deferential desire*. Desire, based upon

和"无为"(nonassertive relationship, 意为不自专的关系)为基础的欲望,并非由于需要拥有、控制和实现而形成,它只不过是肯定和欣赏。之所以想要那些部分地合意的事物,是因为它们仍然为人们所需要。但是那些仍然为人们所需要的事物其本身是依从的,意思是它们不可能要求人们想要它们。因为要求人们想要,就是寻求对想要的人有一种诱惑性的控制。在一个充满事件和过程的世界中,区别是习以为常的,并被看作是暂时、无常的,在这样的世界中,欲望是以"听其自然"和"洒脱"的能力为基础的。正是从这一意义上说,无欲是一种不加分析、无对象的欲望。

道家的问题框架关心的,不是想要什么,而是欲望的方式。无对象的欲望总是能使人听其自然和洒脱。对于道家来说,乐趣的获得是由于某一事实,而不是不顾这个事实,因为这样一个人可能会失去想要的东西。世界是一个极其复杂的转化过程,从不停息。物化(the transformation of things)意味着一个人永远不能声称,他力图保持的东西能永远维持其现状。

a mirroring understanding (*wuzhi*) and a nonassertive relationship (*wuwei*) is not shaped by the need to own, control, or consume, but simply to celebrate and to enjoy. Desire is for those things desirable in part because they *stand to be desired*. But those things that stand to be desired must themselves be deferential, which means that they cannot demand to be desired. For to demand to be desired is to seek a kind of seductive control over the desirer. In a world of events and processes in which discriminations are recognized as conventional and transient, desire is predicated upon the abilities to "let be" and "let go." It is in this sense that *wuyu* is a non-construing, objectless, desire.

The Daoist problematic does not concern *what* is desired but the manner of the desiring. Objectless desire always allows for letting be and letting go. Enjoyment for the Daoist is realized not *in spite of* the fact that one might lose what is desired, but *because of* this fact. The world is a complex set of processes of transformation, never at rest. *Wuhua* 物化, "the transformation of things," means that one can never pretend that what we seek to hold onto, has any permanent status.

In Plato, the desire for knowledge is the only thing that can define both embodied and disembodied existence; it is the only desire that can be permanent, eternal. In Daoism,

根据柏拉图，对知识的欲望是唯一能规定有形的和无形的存在的东西；只有这种欲望才是常住的、永恒的。而根据道家，暂时的欲望是唯一听任事物自然变化的欲望，它不以一种特定的方式剖析世界，不企图给万化之流安装一个制动装置。

理解无的诸形式的关键就在于将"客体"（按：也可译为对象）与"客观性"加以对比。以西方认识论的眼光来看，不论是《庄子》还是《道德经》，都预先规定了我们西方称之为唯实论的观点。在由语言、由我们自己的歪曲的概念和有倾向性的归类所引起的混乱的背后，存在着一个真实的世界。我们的任务就是尽可能客观地认识这个世界。

我们以为客观世界是一个充满客体的世界，它充满了具体的、不会变化的事物，它们与我们相对并存，问题就肇始了；事物向我们宣布："我反对！"对于道家来说，客观世界不可能是这种意义上的客观。这是由无数的事件和过程构成的万物之流，它使各种各样的区分归于无效，那些区分可能诱使人们编造世界构成物的最后清单。

transient desire is the only desire that lets things be, that does not construe the world in a certain manner, that does not seek to apply the brakes on a world of changing things.

The key to understanding the *wu* forms lies in the contrast between "objects" and "objectivity." From a Western epistemological perspective, both the *Zhuangzi* and the *Daodejing* presuppose what we in the west would term a realist perspective. Beyond the confusions introduced by language, and by our own distorted perceptions and tendentious categorizations, there is a real world. Our task is to entertain that world as objectively as possible.

The problem begins when we believe that the objective world is a world of objects, of concrete, unchangeable things which we encounter as over against us; things that announce themselves to us by saying "I object!" For the Daoist, the objective world cannot be objective in this sense. It is a constantly transforming set of events or processes that belie the sorts of discriminations that would permit a final inventory of the furniture of the world.

Maoqiang and Lady Li were beauties for human beings, but fish upon seeing them would seek the deeps, birds on seeing them would fly high, and deer upon seeing them

> 毛嫱、西施，人之所美也；鱼见之深入，鸟见之高飞，麋鹿见之决骤，四者孰知天下之正色哉？（《庄子·齐物论》）

我们在轻视对于丽姬（或曰西施）的其他几种看法的时候，也就确立了排他的标准，将大量的意义从我们对于美的认识中排除出去了，这种标准所决定的不仅是真正的美，而且还有难以忍受的丑。此外，这些标准，不论是关于美，还是善，或正义，都是一种手段，用以创造一个充满固定的客体的世界。

似非而是，对于道家来说，真实的世界是无客体的。圣人想象的是一个万化之流的世界，不论是什么原因，他可能决定暂时地将区分的方式固定下来，然而当他以慧眼看去，他能看出这种区分背后的东西。

> 物无非彼，物无非是。自彼则不见，自是则知之。故曰：彼出于是，是亦因彼。彼是方生之说也。虽然，方生方死，方死方生；方可方不可，方不可方可；因是因非，因非

would dash off. Which of these four understands what is really handsome in this world!

The moment we begin to discount these other views of Lady Li, we have drained a great deal of significance from our understanding of beauty by setting up exclusive standards that determine not only the truly beautiful but the unacceptably ugly. Further, these fixed standards, whether of beauty or goodness or justice, are the means of creating a world of fixed objects.

Paradoxically, for the Daoist, the real world is objectless. The sage envisions a world of transforming events that she *may*, for whatever reason, choose to freeze momentarily into a pattern of discrimination, but that she recognizes, when she sees clearly, as beyond such distinctions.

> There is nothing which is not a "that," and nothing which is not a "this." Because we cannot see from a "that" perspective but can only know from our own perspective, it is said that "that" arises out of "this" and "this" further accommodates "that." This is the notion that "this" and "that" are born simultaneously. And even though this is so, being born is simultaneously dying and vice versa; being acceptable is

因是。是以圣人不由而照之于天，亦因是也。是亦彼也，彼亦是也。彼亦一是非，此亦一是非，果且有彼是乎哉？果且无彼是乎哉？彼是莫得其偶，谓之道枢。枢始得其环中，以应无穷。(《庄子·齐物论》)

环（hinge，也可译为枢纽）的功用不是超越两方面，而是转动于这两者之间。这一隐喻使人联想到天门的开关和从《易经》到《鬼谷子》的文献中到处可见的阴阳消长。在变化进行的过程中，枢纽是位于外表的、有节奏的方面与环境的潜在方面的交叉处。正是这一有利的地位使得充分地了解某人情境本来具有的发展前途成为可能。

所有的无的形式都提供了欣赏、顺应一个无客体的世界的方式。因此，圣人关心的是那种不依赖于客体的认知、行为和欲望。这一点是道家关于自我的认识的关键。因为在当代西方世界可以看到的那一种区别开来的自我就是在与其他事物相遇中出现的，这些事物实际上是站在对面，"反对"在成长中的自我。自我不可能离开其他存在。在

simultaneously being unacceptable and vice versa; accommodating right is accommodating wrong and vice versa. It is for this reason that the sage, illuminating this situation with the way things really are rather than going along with discriminations, is also a case of accommodating what is right and what is "this." But "this" is also "that" and vice versa. And a "theses" "that" further has one set of right and wrong while "this" has another. In truth, is there really such a thing as "this" and "that" or not? Where neither "this" nor "that" has an opposite is called the hinge of *dao*. And as soon as the hinge is fitted to its socket, it can respond endlessly.

The function of a hinge is not to rise above the two sides, but to swing back and forth between them. It is a metaphor that recalls the opening and closing of the "heavenly gate" (*tianmen* 天門) and the moving back and forth between *yin* 陰 and *yang* 陽 that pervades the literature, from *Yijing* 易經 to *Guiguzi* 鬼谷子. In the ongoing process of change, the hinge is at the intersection between the formal, rhythmic aspect and the propensity of circumstances. It is the vantage point that allows full access to the possibilities inherent in one's situation.

The *wu*-forms all provide a way of

道家哲学中,自我被遗忘到这样的程度:区别开来的客体不再构成自我的环境。

　　眼光如此转变过后造成的一个后果是,认知、行为和欲望不再以剖析(construal)为基础。原理和固定的标准引导我们依靠这些原理去剖析我们认识的对象(按:即客体)。一个系列就成为一个种类,或一种为达到一个目的手段。感觉到我们同客体化了的其他人或物处于紧张之中,这引导我们以侵犯的或防备的姿态去行动,以实现我们的意愿。由对象勾引起的欲望引导我们力图拥有想要的东西,只是在它满足我们的需要时赋予它以意义。陶醉于对象的自我,缩小了、简化了、模糊了世界,就像常常发生的那样。另一方面,无知(unprincipled knowing)、无为(nonassertive action)和无欲(objectless desire)在以下这一点上是共同的:就其良好的后果而言,它们让过程按其自身的逻辑展开,从而丰富了世界,然而与此同时,它们也将自己完全地贡献给了这一过程。我们可以说,无的诸形式的实现使我们对世界听其自然。不过,这样说有个条件,即我们认

entertaining, of deferring to, an objectless world. Thus the sage is concerned with that sort of knowing, acting, and desiring that does not depend upon objects. This point is crucial to the Daoist understanding of the self. For the discriminated self of the sort recognized in the contemporary Western world comes into being through encountering other things that effectively stand over against, "objecting" to the burgeoning self. Selves cannot exist without others. In Daoism the self is forgotten to the extent that discriminated objects no longer constitute the environs of the self.

The consequence of this transformed vision is that knowing, acting, and desiring are no longer based upon construal. Principles and fixed standards lead us to construe the object of our knowledge by recourse to such principles. An item becomes one of a kind, or an instrument for the achievement of an end. Feeling ourselves in tension with objectified others leads us to act in an aggressive or defensive manner to affect our will. Desire motivated by an object leads us to seek possession of that which is desired, allowing it significance only insofar as it meets our needs. A self intoxicated by objects narrows, truncates, and obfuscates the world as it is. On the other hand, unprincipled knowing, nonassertive action, and objectless desire have this in common: To the extent they are successful, they enrich

识到,这种语境中的"世界"意指无数的自发的事情,它们的特征是以新的方式顺应已确认的卓越。

如果说道家圣人让世界听其自然,这是因为从某种意义上说他失去了创立客体的自我,而获得了顺应的自我。在《庄子》一书中,这两种自我之间的区别是以文字标明的。原有的内在的自我是"吾"。那种已习惯于将世界和他自己客体化的自我,是"我"。这就是说,剖析的自我(the construing self)是"我",顺应的自我是"吾"。

"我"作为一种知道其区别的后果的自我,它可能要努力取得"吾"的地位,后者不仅知道任何一种区别都是暂时的适当,而且有时能够达到"焦点模糊"(soft focus),这种状态使它能如实地反映世界。这个真实的世界是无限复杂的,各种条理相互重叠,它可以从无数的角度加以思索,每一个角度都以一个德(particular focus)为其特征,这种德要求在"吾"这种自我与构成这些德(foci)的物、事、过程之间有一种顺应关系。

南郭子綦隐机而坐,仰天

the world by allowing the process to unfold spontaneously on its own terms, while at the same time, contributing themselves fully to it. We may say that implementation of the *wu*-forms allows us to leave the world as it is. But we may say this only if we recognize that "world" in this context means myriad spontaneous transactions characterized by emerging patterns of deference to recognized excellences.

If the Daoist sage leaves the world as it is, it is because he has in some sense lost an objectifying self and found the deferential self. In the *Zhuangzi*, the distinction between these two selves is marked linguistically. The original embedded self is *wu* 吾. The self that has fallen into the habit of objectifying its world, as well as itself, is *wo* 我. That is, the construing self is *wo*; the deferential self is *wu*.

Wo, as the self unaware of the effect of its discriminations, may strive to achieve the status of *wu*, a self not only aware of the transitory relevance of any sort of discriminations, but capable at times of attaining that "soft focus" that allows her to mirror the world as it is. This real world is an indefinite complex of overlapping orders, which may be entertained from an indefinite number of perspectives, each perspective characterized by a particular focus that calls for a deferential relation between the *wu*-self and the things, events, or processes

而嘘，荅焉似丧其耦。颜成子游立侍乎前，曰："何居乎？形固可使如槁木，而心固可使如死灰乎？今之隐机者，非昔之隐机者也。"子綦曰："偃，不亦善乎而问之也！今者吾丧我，汝知之乎？汝闻人籁而未闻地籁，汝闻地籁而未闻天籁夫！"（《庄子·齐物论》）

丧失了的是剖析的自我——"我"。隐机而坐的那个人现在是一个顺应的自我——"吾"，他显然超越了日常的、区别的人类语言，倾听"吹万不同，而使其自己也，咸其自取"的天籁。

（《汉哲学思维的文化探源》，第57—60页）

"无欲"就不是停止欲望或没有欲望，而展现的是谦恭的欲望（deferential desire）的成就。欲望，当它是基于同这个世界的非强制性关系（无为），和对这个世界的反映性认知（无知），那么，它就不是靠占有、控制或毁灭定形的欲望，而纯粹是由赞美和欣赏塑造的，它是敬意。由那些理想的东西引发的欲

constituting these foci.

Ziqi of the southern suburb sat in a meditative posture leaning on an armrest. He breathed deeply with his head raised toward the sky, and achieving a trance-like state, seemed to have lost his sense of "other." Yancheng Ziyou, standing in attendance before him, said, "Where are you? Can you really make the body like rotting wood and the heart-and-mind like dead ashes? The person meditating now is not the same one who was meditating a time ago."

Ziqi replied, "Yan, marvelous that you should ask such a question! Were you aware that just now 'me' left 'I' behind? You have heard of the piping of humankind and yet not that of the earth. Or perhaps you have heard of the earth's piping and yet not that of *tian*?"

It is the construing *wo*-self that is lost. The person leaning on the armrest is now a deferential *wu*-self who, apparently has moved beyond the conventional, discriminating, language of humankind, and has listened to the piping of *tian* which consists of "blowing out a myriad different

望是因为它们值得欲求。但是那些值得欲求的东西本身也必须是谦恭的,即它们不能要求被期望,要求被期望就是在运用某种类似催眠术的东西控制欲求者。在一个充满过程和现象的世界里,事物间的区分都只不过是约定和暂时的,欲望的预测根据的是个体在任何既定时刻都可以"放开"的能力。正是在这个意义上,我们说"无欲"是一种非分解、非客体化的欲望。

道家关于欲望的问题,不是关涉所欲望的东西,而是关涉欲望的方式。对于道家来说,愉悦的实现,不是要无视我们可能失去我们所欲望的东西这样一个事实,而是产生于这一事实。这个世界是各种转化过程的复杂组合,这一组合过程永无止息。"物化",种种事物的"变异"(不要与"无"形式相混淆),说明我们从来就不要妄想,我们想要固守的东西会保住某种恒久的状态。在道家看来,只有暂时的欲望才是不给事物以任何干扰的欲望,不以任何确定方式解析这个世界,不试图去阻挠这个千变万化的世界。

理解"无欲"的关键——确

things, causing each of them to be itself, and all of them to take what they want."
(*Thinking from the Han,* pp. 54-58)

Wuyu, rather than involving the cessation and absence of desire, represents the achievement of deferential desire. Desire, based upon a noncoercive relationship (*wuwei*) with the world and a "mirroring" understanding (*wuzhi*) of it, is shaped not by the desire to own, to control, or to consume, but by the desire simply to celebrate and to enjoy. It is deference. Desire is directed at those things desirable because they *stand to be desired*. But those things which stand to be desired must themselves be deferential, which means that they cannot *demand* to be desired. For to demand to be desired is to exercise a kind of mesmerizing control over the desirer. In a world of events and processes in which discriminations are recognized as conventional and transient, desire is predicated upon one's ability at any given moment to "let go." It is in this sense that *wuyu* is a nonconstruing, objectless, desire.

The Daoist problem with desire does not concern what is desired, but rather the manner of the desiring. Enjoyment for the Daoist is realized not in spite of the fact that one might lose what is desired, but because of this fact. The world is a complex set of transtormative processes, never at rest.

实也是理解构成道家思想特质的所有"无"形式的关键——就在于"客体"(objects)与"客观性"(objectivity)的对比中。运用西方认识论的术语,《庄子》和《道德经》关于这个世界的认识,表现了或许可以称作某种唯实论的视角。如果排除语言、层层我们自己歪曲的概念,以及带有倾向性的分类的间接纷扰,让我们给道家作个适当评定,无疑它展示一个客观的现实世界。我们的任务就是尽量客观地去体验这一世界。

从道家的观点来看,当我们认定"客观世界"(objective world)是个由"客体"(object)(即我们所遭遇的与我们相对且独立于我们的具体、不可改变的各种事物,那些通过断然宣称"我客体!"向我们通告其自身的各种事物)构成的世界时,问题就出现了。对于道家来说,客观世界在这种意义上不可能是客观的,因为迥然有异于可给这个世界财产开一张最后清单的种种区分,它是各种现象和过程始终不断转换的恒动之流。

矛盾的是,对于道家来说,客观世界又是"无客体的"(objectless)。

Wuhua 物化, the metamorphosis of things (and not to be confused with the *wu*-forms), means that we can never pretend that what we seek to hold on to has any permanent status. In Daoism, transient desire is the only desire that lets things be, that does not construe the world in a certain manner, that does not seek to apply the brakes on a world of changing things.

The key to an understanding of *wuyu*—indeed of all these *wu*-forms that comprise the Daoist disposition—lies in the contrast between "objects" and "objectivity." Using Western epistemological terms, the thoughts about the world expressed in both the *Zhuangzi* and the *Daodejing* represent what we might call a realist perspective. Beyond the mediating confusions introduced by language, and by layers of our own distorted perceptions and tendentious categorizations, there is nevertheless, with properly Daoist qualifications, an "objectively" real world. Our task is to experience that world as "objectively" as possible.

From the Daoist perspective, the problem begins when we insist that the "objective world" is a world made up of objects—namely, concrete, unchangeable things that we encounter as over against and independent of us; things which announce themselves to us by asserting "I object!" For the Daoist, the objective world cannot be objective in this sense because it is a constantly transforming

不管出于什么原因,圣人们构想了一个充满了不断变化的现象的世界。在这个世界里,他们可以选择暂时地凝定于一个差别鲜明的范式里,但当他们看得更清晰一些,他们允许对这些差异的超越。

在道家看来,这一变换视角带来的结果就是,这个世界上的知识、行动、欲望不再基于"可分析性"。在与各种客体化的他者之间的紧张关系中感受自身,容易导致以一种侵略或防范性的方式来使我们的意愿生效。原理和确定的标准容易使我们借助这些标准来解析我们知识的客体。在这种解析中,某一物件成为"某类中的一个"(one of a *kind*)(而非"某类之一"*one-of-a-kind*),或者成为实现某种目的的手段(与以自身为目的相对)。为某种对客体的欲望所引发的欲望会使我们企图占有我们所欲之物,只有满足了我们的欲求,它才具有意义。一个被客体欲望所支配的自我,限制、缩短且蒙蔽了这个世界本身。

相反,非强制性行为、非理性知识,以及非客体化欲望,拥有下面这一共同点:由这些术语界定的品格一旦发生作用,它将会通过认

flow of events or processes that belie the sorts of discriminations that would permit a final inventory of the furniture of the world.

Paradoxically, for the Daoist the objective world is objectless. Sages envision a world of changing events that they can, for whatever reason, choose to freeze momentarily into a distinct pattern of discrimination, but that they recognize, when they see clearly, as beings beyond such distinctions.

For the Daoist, the consequence of this transformed vision is that knowing, acting, and desiring in the world are no longer based upon construal. Feeling ourselves in tension with objectified others can lead us to act in an aggressive or defensive manner in order to affect our will. Principles and fixed standards can lead us to construe the object of our knowledge by recourse to such principles. In this way, an item becomes one of a *kind* (rather than *one-of-a-kind*) or an instrument for the achievement of an end (as opposed to an end in itself). Desire motivated by an object of desire leads us to seek possession of that which is desired, allowing it significance only insofar as it meets our needs. A self that is consumed by objects of desire narrows, truncates, and obfuscates the world as it is.

On the other hand, noncoercive action, unprincipled knowing, and objectless desire have the following in common: To the extent that a disposition defined in

可事物据其自身条件自动展开发展过程,而同时又能够全身心地参与到这个世界中,来使世界变得丰富多彩。我们或许会说,践行"无"形式会允许我们脱离现在的世界。但是我们的说法只有在这样的前提下才能成立:也就是说,该背景下的"世界"是一个无数次自然交流的结果,这种交流以对我们已确认美德之敬意模式的不断出现为特征。在道家哲学里,自我在某种程度上会被遗忘,那就是那些被区分的客体不会再来建构自我的世界。

(《道不远人:比较哲学视域中的〈老子〉》,第51—53页)

物化

《庄子》中存在过程常被表达为"物化"。由于道家的"真人"修己以与其周围环境的自然倾向融合,因此,他就成为越来越有影响力的万物的"转化者"。从一个不同的焦点来说,他不是化己而是化他者;从其漫入整个语境的角度看,他又成为自我转化过程中一个更大的中心。就其更大存在为创造和创新提

these terms is efficacious, it enriches the world by allowing the process to unfold spontaneously on its own terms, while at the same time participating fully in it. We may say that the implementation of the *wu*-forms allows us to leave the world as it is. But we may make this claim only if we recognize that "world" in this context means a myriad of spontaneous transactions that are characterized by emerging patterns of deference to acknowledged excellences. In Daoism the self is forgotten to the extent that discriminated objects no longer constitute the environs of the self.

(*Daodejing*: "Making This Life Significant", pp. 42-44)

Transformation of Things
(*Wu Hua*)

In the *Chung Tzu*, the process of existence is frequently referred to as the "transformation of things" (*wu hua* 物化). As the Taoist *chen jen* extends himself to become coextensive with the natural direction of his context, he becomes an increasingly influential "transformer" of things. Viewed as a discriminated focus, he is transforming something other than himself; from the perspective of his

供可能性来说,他确实如此。就其将全体之德涵容个体独特性而言,他也同样成功。他与"他者"的融合实际是合于"德",即他推动和诠释着所有与之适逢的自然表达:他的手表达泥土,泥土也表达了他的手。

(《通过孔子而思》,第 276 页)

在《庄子》中,存在本身的过程被称为"物化"。道家的真人在将其自身扩展到与他的自然环境为一体之时,他也就越来越顺应物化。当他将其全体之德包含于其特殊性之中时,他就会在其所做的任何一件事上完美无缺,造成神奇效果。他得心应手,挥洒自如。

(《汉哲学思维的文化探源》,第 68 页)

道家哲学避免相对主义的办法是,为同等确定一个基础,即与庄子的物化相联系的万物一体论。道是生成变化的总过程,它构成了事物之道。这些事物构成了世界,而这个世界可以按照这个总过程中每一个类目的眼光加以描绘。假定以所有事物的独特性作为出发点,在

diffusion throughout his context, he has become a larger focus of what it is that is self-transforming. To the extent that his broad presencing has possibilities for creativity and novelty, so too does he. To the extent that he embraces the *te* of the whole within his particularity, he is integrated and efficacious at whatever he does. What might be perceived as his interface with "other" is in fact coincident *te* such that he facilitates and interprets the natural expression of whatever he encounters: his hands express the clay, and the clay expresses his hands.

(*Thinking Through Confucius,* p. 225)

In the *Zhuangzi*, the process of existence itself is referred to as the "transformation of things" (*wuhua* 物化). As the Daoist *zhenren* extends himself to become one with his natural environment, he becomes increasingly deferential to the transformation of things. To the extent that he embraces the *de* of his totality within his particularity, he is integrated and efficacious at whatever he does. His hands express the clay, and the clay expresses his hands.

(*Thinking from the Han,* pp. 64-65)

Philosophical Daoism avoids relativism by asserting a ground for parity by virtue of the continuity among

任何一个特定的问题上,特殊事物必定处于一种层级系统的关系中。这是顺应的基础。所有的事物都要以这种或那种方式顺应所有别的事物,相互关联的阴阳范畴通常总是能够表达各种关系,就是这个缘故。我们说"通常"是因为特殊的事物和事件有一种难以捉摸的性质,以及由此带来的模糊性,因此有时阴阳的语言就不起作用了。"阴阳不测之谓神。"

万物之转化涵衍了两个重要的结论:第一,总是有无数可以替代的心境,它们对一个人目前的心态(configuration)的终结性构成了挑战;第二,经验的连续性保证一个人能够实际地经历无数这样的心态。以哲人的姿态承认这一事实是道家最高明的幽默的源泉。

由于道家哲学,特别是庄子那一种,相对主义问题通常被视为无意义的。虽然我们关于庄子是现实主义者的论断肯定会遭到许多学者的质疑,他们坚持认为,庄子是怀疑论的相对主义的极其高明的辩护者,庄子的物化理论似乎使他相信,世界是作为变换中的一系列存在方式、作为无数系列的重叠的世

things, associated with Zhuangzi's "transformation of things (*wuhua* 物化)." *Dao* is the total process of becoming that constitutes the ways of things. These things form worlds characterizable from the perspective of each and every item in the total process. Given the uniqueness of all things as a starting point, particulars must, with reference to any given issue, stand in hierarchical relationships. This is the ground of deference. All things defer, in this way or that, to all other things. This is why a correlative *yin-yang* vocabulary usually works to articulate relationships. We say "usually," because, given the porous nature and attendant vagueness of particular things and events, there are occasions on which the *yin-yang* language is not functional: "What *yin-yang* does not fathom is called inscrutable (*shen* 神)."

The transformation of all things entails two important consequences: First, there are always myriad alternative postures that challenge the ultimacy of one's present configuration. Secondly, the processional nature of experience guarantees that one will in fact actually proceed through an indefinite number of such configurations. The sagely recognition of this fact is the source of Daoist humor at its best.

With Daoism, specifically the

界、作为充满诸此（thises）或诸彼（thats）的混沌、作为秩序的各种各样的聚集而实际存在着。被理解为所有秩序的总和的混沌，指称事物之道。此外，庄子似乎相信，这种多元论有一些非常重要的、直接的实际后果。通过无的各种形态表现出来的顺应的自我，自然地致力于映照反应，这种反应非常重视顺应的自我所遇到的事物或事件的德。

因此，"理论"层面的庄子的"相对主义"（这是一个会造成错误的提法）在实际的层面大大地减弱了，因为顺应所涵衍的，既有一体性，又有投入参与。因此映照事物之道的巨大的、无偏向的复杂系统，有一些直接的实际后果，这种映照能使人将所有的事物视为可供顺应的反应进行选择。

（《汉哲学思维的文化探源》，第 75—76 页）

物化是不能加以干预的，而要对它顺应。就这一点而言，〔道家〕哲人赞同浮士德对〔恶魔〕靡菲斯特说的话："假使我在这一时刻说：'你真美呀，请停留一下！'那末你就拥有我的灵魂了。"把道家哲人的

Zhuangzian variety, the issue of relativism is usually seen to be irrelevant. Though our assumption that Zhuangzi is a realist would doubtless be challenged by many scholars who would insist that he is an extremely subtle proponent of a kind of skeptical relativism, Zhuangzi's transformation of things seems to commit him to the belief that the world actually exists as a shifting set of ways of being, a myriad set of overlapping worlds, a chaos of thises and thats, a multifarious congeries of orders. Chaos, *hundun* 渾沌, understood as the totality of all orders, names the way of things. Moreover, Zhuangzi seems to believe that there are crucial and direct practical consequences of such pluralism. The deferential self, expressed through the modalities of the *wu*-forms, spontaneously engages in mirroring responses that take into account the *de* of the items or events it encounters.

Thus, Zhuangzi's "relativism" (a misleading description) at the level of "theory" is seriously moderated at the level of practice, since deference entails both *continuity* and *commitment*. There are, therefore, direct practical consequences of mirroring the vast indifferent complex of the ways of things in a manner that allows one to see all things as viable candidates for deferential response.

(*Thinking from the Han*, pp. 71-72)

生活与浮士德追求快乐的生活区分开来的是，侵犯性的欲望与无欲之间的差别。对浮士德来说，每一时刻都有新的东西引诱他，供他享用，或欣赏，然后放弃。

> 告诉我水果在哪里，在它们腐烂之前，一遍又一遍地去树上采集。
>
> 还有那一次又一次重新茂盛的树林。

道家既不为了永远获得新的东西而要求不停息的转化，也不想刹车，让一个时刻停留下来，阻止转化。顺应的自我不勉强地顺从时刻。

（《汉哲学思维的文化探源》，第77页）

莱布尼茨认为，之所以说这个世界是最好的，是因为任何一种别的可能的世界都会受害于更多的恶。他相信这一点是由于他以为，一个完美的世界必定会包含"不可合成的"（incompossible）东西，即那些在逻辑上不能并存的事物。这种最好的单一世界，由合乎条理的行为和事件间的预定和谐而格式化。与

The transformative processes (*wuhua* 物化) are not to be interfered with, but are to be met with *deference*. To this extent, the sage is in agreement with Faust who proclaims to Mephistopheles: "If I ever say to the moment, 'Hold! Thou art so fair!,' then thou canst require my soul of me." What distinguishes the life of the Daoist sage from that of the pleasure-seeking Faust lies in the difference between aggressive desiring and *wuyu* 無欲. For Faust each moment brings a new object of desire to be seduced, consumed, or otherwise enjoyed, and then abandoned.

**Show me fruits which rot ere ever gathered from the tree.
And trees that ever bloom anew.**

The Daoist neither demands constant transformation for the sake of the ever new, nor does she object to transformation, attempting to apply the brakes and hold onto the moment. The deferential self yields to the moment, without constraint.

(*Thinking from the Han,* p. 73)

Leibniz held that this world is best because any other possible world would suffer from a greater amount of evil. He believed this because he held that a perfect world would perforce contain "incompossible" items, things

此不同，庄子的观点似乎是，没有一个人，或一个东西，也不是"大块"、"天"或"道"，在无数的世界中决定哪一个将被允许存在。由于物化，一切可能有的世界都将出现。每一个世界对于任何一个别的世界成为现在的样子，以及将要成为未来的样子都是必需的，从这个意义上说，任何一个世界都不高于另一个世界。不仅如此，"不可合成性"的逻辑概念（庄子几乎肯定决不考虑这个概念）化解于"不协调性"（incongruity）这一更加宽泛的概念中了，后者产生于事物的多样性，认为每一个事物都具有其特殊的焦点，每一个都行其顺应之道。

（《汉哲学思维的文化探源》，第78页）

在庄子的道家哲学中，物化的理论阻碍了悲剧意识的发展。这样一种意识是以失为依据的。物化保证了没有最终的失；只存在转化的过程，它使我们能够成为我们尚未变成的那种存在。此外，道家幽默的轻松绝不是产生于这样一种企图：为了回避钉十字架而集中注意仙人跳舞。

（《汉哲学思维的文化探源》，

that could not logically coexist. This single best world then is patterned by a preestablished harmony of ordering actions and events. Zhuangzi's view, on the other hand, seems to be that there is no one or no thing, neither the Great Clod 大块, nor *tian* 天, nor *dao* 道, which has decided which among an indefinite number of worlds will be allowed existence. All possible worlds will obtain by virtue of the transformation of things. No world is privileged over any other in the sense that all are required for any other to be what it is, and what it will be. Furthermore, the logical notion of "incompossibility" (which Zhuangzi almost certainly never entertained) is dissolved into a broader notion of "incongruity" that results from the diversity of things, each possessing its particular focus, each owning its claim to deference.

(*Thinking from the Han,* p. 74)

In Zhuangzi's Daoism, the doctrine of the transformation of things precludes the development of a tragic sense. Such a sense is predicated upon *loss*. The transformation of things guarantees that there is no final loss; there are only processes of transformation that allow us to become what we have not yet become. Further, the lightness of Daoist humor is by no means a

第 80 页）

庄子的道家哲学清除了最终的特权（按：指裁决理论的是非得失和"主宰时刻"的特权）的缺陷，表现了显示真正的幽默的无忧品性。因为道家思想家不会为"仙人跳舞而基督被钉死于十字架"的事实而迷惑。他们知道我们每一个人都要轮到跳舞和上十字架。靠浑沌帝无边的无差别之境和他的领地万象福地之福，我们将要抵达这两种境界。一切事物都要转化，这里没有任何悲剧性的事物。因此不需要一个喜剧的伪装用以隐藏。有的是无忧无虑、轻松自如，它们产生了幽默。这是真正的幽默。笑话，就像常见的那样，总是我们喜欢讲的。

（《汉哲学思维的文化探源》，第 80—81 页）

在对其称之为"物化"(transforming events）的探讨中，《庄子》也许包含了对这一过程的最为彻底的表述。在"物化"的过程中，往昔事物消融入各种彼此融合、互相渗透的过程之流中。对庄子而言，在这一经验之流中，人类并没有特权的位置。

consequence of focusing upon the fairies' dance in order to avoid the vision of the crucifixion.

(*Thinking from the Han,* p. 76)

Zhuangzi's Daoism, purged of any taint of ultimate privilege, expresses the sort of lightheartedness that manifests true humor. For the Daoist thinker would not be undone by the fact that "the fairies dance and Christ is nailed to the cross." He or she knows that we shall each have our turn at the dance, and on the cross. There, by the grace of the Vast Indifference of Lord Hundun and the Blessed Multifariousness of His Realm, we *shall* go. This is the transformation of all things. There is nothing tragic here. No need, therefore, for a comic mask behind which to hide. There is lightheartedness and lightmindedness, and the humor it engenders. This is true humor. And the joke, as always (if we would but recognize it), is on us.

(*Thinking from the Han,* p. 76)

The *Zhuangzi* contains perhaps the most radical statement of this process in its discussions of what it terms "transforming events (*wuhua* 物化)," in which erstwhile things dissolve into the flux as porous, interpenetrating processes. For *Zhuangzi*, in this flux of experience, the human being has no place of privilege.

同其他事物一样，人类的形式也同样是过程性的。并且，人类必须谦卑地屈从于那无时不在又必然发生的大化之流。

（《切中伦常：〈中庸〉的新诠与新译》，第45页）

《庄子》设想，在更大的转化过程之中，"人"有可能是一种武断的、并非特别受欢迎甚至容易招致混乱之物的存在形式。人人可能怀有对于死亡的疑惧，对此，庄子的反应是，一种状态的事物会不断地需要经历转变为其他的事物，我们应该顺应这种转换，认识到这一点会使我们获得一种真正的安慰，甚至的确是一种宗教性的敬畏。并且，通过中断和完满这一始终进行的过程，死亡以这样一种方式来认可每个人的独特存在，以便产生许多独特的密切关联的事件，这些事件是根据我们与他人的独特关系来界定的。这种对连续性和亲密性的推崇，很可能会激发出对于和我们处在同一个世界中的其他生物的同情和关爱。

（《切中伦常：〈中庸〉的新诠与新译》，第46—47页）

Like everything else, the human form is processive, and must yield deferentially to the ongoing, ineluctable propensity of transformation.

(*Focusing the Familiar: A Translation and Philosophical Interpretation of the Zhongyong*, p. 22)

The *Zhuangzi* envisions the possibility of assuming a human form as an arbitrary and not especially welcome perturbation within the larger processes of transformation. Zhuangzi's response to the misgivings one might have about death is that there is real comfort and indeed even a religious awe in the recognition that assuming the form of one kind of thing gives way to the ceaseless adventure of becoming other things. Also, death celebrates the uniqueness of each person by punctuating and consummating the ongoing process in such a way as to produce distinct intimate events defined in terms of our unique relations with someone else. Such a recognition of continuity and intimacy presumably stimulates empathetic feelings for other creatures in a shared environment.

(*Focusing the Familiar: A Translation and Philosophical Interpretation of the Zhongyong*, p. 23)

Zhuangzi's expression *wuhua* 物

庄子"物化"（transforming of processes and events）的表述提示着，当一个"事物"转化为另一个时，各种过程的所有形式之间的相互性和彼此渗透。

（《切中伦常：〈中庸〉的新诠与新译》，第 99 页）

化 —"the transforming of processes and events"—suggests the mutuality and interpenetration of all forms of process as one "thing" transforms to become another.

(*Focusing the Familiar: A Translation and Philosophical Interpretation of the Zhongyong*, p. 81)

真人

Chen Jen

道家的自然化的生成观念把生成着的事物视为最终的实在，尽管在其行进状态中它们不是客观的、独立的，或任何意义上永恒的真实。事实上，真通常译作 real，这个字显然表述了一种对于真实性的过程的理解。作为自成的道指称转化的混沌母体，这种转化只能按照其中的特殊的、具体的差异加以表述。任何试图通过世界的所是（beings）使是（Being）在场都必定会遭到拒绝。庄子坚持认为："天下诱然皆生而不知其所以生。"

（《期望中国：对中西文化的哲学思考》，第 286—287 页）

道家传统中充满德性之人被称为

The Daoist naturalized sense of becoming makes of the things that become, the final realities, though in their processive state they are not objectively, substantively, or in any sense *permanently* real. In fact, the character conventionally translated "real," *zhen* 真, explicitly entails a processional understanding of reality. *Dao* as becoming-itself names the chaotic matrix of transformations which may be spoken of only in terms of their particular, concrete differences. Any attempt to make Being present through the beings of the world must perforce be rejected. Zhuangzi insists that "each thing comes into being from its own inner reflection and none can tell how it comes to be so."

(*Anticipating China: Thinking through the Narratives of Chinese and Western Culture*, p. 237)

"真人"。"真"的意思是"true"或"real",由它的词根"化"(transform)标志。《庄子》中存在过程常被表达为"物化"。由于道家的"真人"修己以与其周围环境的自然倾向融合,因此,他就成为越来越有影响力的万物的"转化者"。从一个不同的焦点来说,他不是化己而是化他者;从其漫入整个语境的角度看,他又成为自我转化过程中一个更大的中心。就其更大存在为创造和创新提供可能性来说,他确实如此。就其将全体之德涵容个体独特性而言,他也同样成功。他与"他者"的融合实际是合于"德",即他推动和诠释着所有与之适逢的自然表达:他的手表达泥土,泥土也表达了他的手。

"真人"既包含他的社会环境之德也包括自然之德。例如,庖丁的合牛之德,充德之人以其对牛之自然肌理的表达和诠解而成为一个出神入化的屠夫;而与黏土合德之人,也通过表达和诠释土的自然机理成为鬼斧神工的能工巧匠。因为他不是一个"否定—整合"的自我,因此能够向整个自然环境之德打开,使得环境有助于他变得更富生命力

The person of pervasive *te* in the Taoist tradition is called *chen jen* 真人. The character *chen*, meaning "true" or "real," is classified under the radical *hua* 化, meaning "to transform." In the *Chung Tzu*, the process of existence is frequently referred to as the 'transformation of things" (*wu hua* 物化). As the Taoist *chen jen* extends himself to become coextensive with the natural direction of his context, he becomes an increasingly influential 'transformer' of things. Viewed as a discriminated focus, he is transforming something other than himself; from the perspective of his diffusion throughout his context, he has become a larger focus of what it is that is self-transforming. To the extent that his broad presencing has possibilities for creativity and novelty, so too does he. To the extent that he embraces the *te* of the whole within his particularity, he is integrated and efficacious at whatever he does. What might be perceived as his interface with "other" is in fact coincident *te* such that he facilitates and interprets the natural expression of whatever he encounters: his hands express the clay, and the clay expresses his hands.

The *chen jen* embraces the *te* of his natural as well as his human environment. By becoming coextensive with the *te* of the ox, for example, the person of pervasive *te* is able to express and interpret the natural impetus of the ox in such a manner as to become an efficacious butcher; by becoming coextensive with the *te* of the clay, he is able to express and interpret the natural impetus of the clay to become an efficacious craftsman. The absence

和价值，而他为环境所作的贡献，则巩固、加强和诠释了其自然取向。他的存在因合整体之德，因而发扬光大，最终惠及所有的存在。

（《通过孔子而思》，第 276—277 页）

在道家传统中，描绘一个人扩充德的语汇，与儒家文献相比，更具有普遍性。与儒家传统一样，这种人有时成为人类秩序的体现者和维护者，新文化的设计者和新意义的源泉。然而道家超越了这一范围，进入自然的世界。道家的完美人格——真人所具备的德，既有人类环境中的，又有自然环境中的。例如，由于游心于牛之德，庖丁解牛时能够物我皆忘地刺入自然的结节和窍隙，因此能够成为一个技艺高的屠夫；由于游心于木之德，梓庆对其木料之质与潜在用处有一种特别敏锐的感觉，工作时物我皆忘，因此能够成为一个技艺高的工匠。由于没有一个"分裂的"、分离的自我，这就使这些典范的自然环境的德在他们面前暴露无遗，结果是环境对他们作出贡献，使他们富有创造力和多产，他们对其环境的贡献

of a "disintegrating" ego-self makes him open to the *te* of his whole natural environment, so that the environment contributes to him, making him potent and productive, and he contributes to his environment, strengthening, enhancing, and interpreting its natural direction. His presence in the world is coincident with the *te* of his whole environment, extending out to ultimately focus all of existence.

(*Thinking Through Confucius,* p. 225)

In the Daoist tradition, the extension of one's *de* is described in more pervasive terms than in the Confucian literature. As in the Confucian tradition, at times such a person becomes the embodiment and protector of the human order, a styler of new culture and a source of new meaning. But the Daoists take it beyond this into the natural world. The *zhenren* 真人, the Daoist version of the consummating person, embraces the *de* of the natural as well as the human environment. By becoming coextensive with the *de* of the ox, for example, Cook Ding in butchering its carcass is able to penetrate its natural lineaments and interstices without distraction, and hence is able to become an efficacious butcher; by becoming coextensive with the *de* of the wood, Carpenter Ching is sensitive to the quality and potential of his materials without distraction, and hence is able to become an efficacious craftsman. The absence of a "disintegrating" discrete self makes these exemplars open to the *de* of their

修养论

是,对组成他们的世界的那些事物的种种可能性加以说明,并且使这些可能性增加到最大的限度。

在规定道家传统的语汇中,扩充一个人的德的过程的能动性被加以强调。例如,那些具有持久的、富有成果的德的人被称为"真人"(the authentic person)。"真"这个字意为"真实的"或"真正的",它可分解出词根"匕"("真"字繁写印刷体为"眞"),意为化。在《庄子》中,存在本身的过程被称为"物化"。道家的真人在将其自身扩展到与他的自然环境为一体之时,他也就越来越顺应物化。当他将其全体之德包含于其特殊性之中时,他就会在其所作的任何一件事上完美无缺,造成神奇效果。他得心应手,挥洒自如。

(《汉哲学思维的文化探源》,第67—68页)

道家及其真人的观念,主张在一个不断地变化的世界中,为了成为一个总是独特的人,要致力于完全融入环境(full contextualization)。至少从表面上看,无论是儒家还是道家,其哲学的奠基者似乎表达了

natural environments, so that the environment contributes to them, making them potent and productive, and they contribute to their environments, interpreting and maximizing the possibilities of those things which constitute their world.

The dynamic nature of this process of extending one's *de* is underscored in the vocabulary that defines the Daoist tradition. The person of insistent and productive *de*, for example, is called *zhenren* 真人, "the authentic person." The character, *zhen* 真, meaning "authentic" or "genuine," is classified under the radical *bi* 匕, which means *hua* 化, "to transform." In the *Zhuangzi*, the process of existence itself is referred to as the "transformation of things" (*wuhua* 物化). As the Daoist *zhenren* extends himself to become one with his natural environment, he becomes increasingly deferential to the transformation of things. To the extent that he embraces the *de* of his totality within his particularity, he is integrated and efficacious at whatever he does. His hands express the clay, and the clay expresses his hands.

(*Thinking from the Han,* pp. 64-65)

Daoism and its notion of the "authentic person"(*zhenren* 真人) is a celebration of the pursuit of full contextualization for the always unique person within an ever changing world. On the surface at least, it would seem that the patriarchs of both Confucian and Daoist

那种被描绘为女性的意见的思想。鉴于儒道两家思想在中国哲学形成时期广泛流行,可以公正地说,中国文化的发展染上了强烈的女性性别特征的色彩。

(《汉哲学思维的文化探源》,第88页)

真的东西是作为一种自然的表达而产生的,它是与被流俗支配的状况完全相反的。构造人们的世界并赋予其意义的,是人们自己的意义和价值的展现,是制度和礼的人格化。

"真"是人格的、社会的和政治的整合的基础,这种整合使人们与他们的自然的和文化的环境融为一体。制度和习俗不过是一种人为的结构,它们是由人类所创立,用作表达适、乐以及和的手段,构成了统一的人类经验的经纬。争论的矛头不是指向习俗本身,它应有其存身之地。准确地说,所疑虑的是压倒一切地过分关心、迷恋于这些习俗,以至于不致力于展示人们自己的独特的真实,即人们的自然性(self-so-ness)。这里的争辩是针对错位的具体性。

philosophy expressed themselves in what is being described as a feminine voice, and given the pervasiveness of Confucianism and Daoism in the formative period of Chinese philosophy, it can be fairly argued that the development of Chinese culture has been strongly colored by feminine gender characteristics.

(*Thinking from the Han*, p. 85)

What is genuine (*zhen*) arises as a natural expression as opposed to being dictated by convention. It is the disclosure of one's own significance and value, personalizing the institutions and rituals that structure one's world and rendering them meaningful.

Zhen is the ground of personal, social, and political integration that makes one continuous with one's natural and cultural environments. Institutions and conventions are nothing more than artificial structures established by the human being as an apparatus for giving expression to the accommodation, enjoyment, and harmony, that constitute the fabric of an integrated human existence. The quarrel is not with the conventions *per se*; which have their place. Rather, there is suspicion of an overriding concern for and attachment to these conventions at the expense of the disclosure of one's own distinct genuineness, one's self-soness. The argument here is against misplaced concreteness.

(*Thinking from the Han*, p. 165)

（《汉哲学思维的文化探源》，第 170 页）

在对真人作这样的描绘中，我们不禁想起本书第一篇中讨论的《道德经》的"无的诸形式"。在早期道家的全部著作中，对一系列的整合过程作了相当充分的讨论，它们有"无为"——非自专的活动；无知——未理则化的认知；无欲——无对象的欲望。这种活动在《庄子》中被比喻为"堕肢体"，因而消除了自我与他人的对立，从而"同于大通"。

这种整合产生的后果是，它使真人在其生存的性质上不同于他人。真人的活动被描绘为具有灵活性，有功效，不争，与社会的和自然的环境协同作用，相互展示。

与万化同流之人，与存在的整个过程有一种不可分割的联系，他又是寂然不动的，这源于不迷恋。真人超越了太多的二元分裂，如自我与他人、造物主与创造物、本质与现象、生与死，他获得了某种不朽——不是靠遁入某种更加纯洁的境地，而是通过在具体的、持续不断的此时此地的自我实现。

In this characterization of the genuine person, we cannot but recall the "*wu*-forms" of the *Daodejing* discussed in part I. Throughout the early Daoist literature, there is considerable discussion of a series of integrative processes: *Wuwei* 無為 is nonassertive activity; *wuzhi* 無知 is unprincipled knowing; *wuyu* 無欲 is objectless desiring. Such activities are described figuratively in *Zhuangzi* as "breaking up one's body (*duo zhi ti* 墮肢體)" and thus dissolving the dichotomy of self and other to integrate fully into the continuity of existence (*tong yu da tong* 同於大通).

This integration has the effect of making the genuine person different from others in the quality of his existence. The activity of the genuine person is characterized by flexibility, efficacy, and noncontention, collaborating with the social and natural environments in mutual disclosure, and serving as frictionless ground for their "self-so-ing," and they for his own.

The transforming person has an uninterrupted continuity with the whole process of existence, and a calmness and imperturbability that comes with nonattachment. Existing beyond the plethora of disintegrative dualisms of self and other, creator and creature, reality and appearance, life and death, the genuine person achieves a kind of immortality—not by escaping to some purer realm, but by realizing himself in the concrete and persistent here and now.

The choice of the word "genuine" to translate *zhen* is calculated. The root, *gen*-, meaning "to

选择"genuine"（意为真正的）这个词来翻译"真"是有所考虑的。它的词根"gen-"意为"产生、出产"，因而捕获了这样一种意义，即特殊的个人的创造性贡献具有头等重要性。这种贡献被当作最根本的真实，这里说的真实其意义是与周围环境谐动，是"正好如此"，"完全如此"，"正中目标"。

真正的人（*auth*entic person）的"作"、真人（authorship）（*gen*uine person）的自生的性质是很重要的，由此可以理解：

　　且有真人而后有真知。

这里《庄子》拒绝了任何一种表象论的或符合论的知识理论，这种理论要求有一种固定的实在，一种思想能够与这种实在相符：

　　夫知有所待而后当，其所待者特未定也。

认知者不是去认识一个先在的实在，而是按照自我展示（self-disclosure）的方式积极地参与世界的实现。认知确实涵衍了认识

beget, produce," captures the primacy given to the creative contribution of the particular person. It further registers this contribution as what is most fundamentally true in the sense of being consonant with its environing conditions, being "just so," "exactly," "on the mark."

The importance of the "authorship" of the *auth*entic person, the self-*gen*erating character of the *gen*uine person, is precisely why

> there must be the genuine person (*zhenren* 真人) before there can be genuine knowledge (*zhenzhi* 真知).

Here the *Zhuangzi* rejects any representational or correspondence theory of knowledge that demands a fixed reality to which an idea can correspond:

> Knowledge depends on something to which it can correspond, but what it depends upon is never fixed.

The knower does not cognize a preexisting reality, but participates actively in the realization of the world through self-disclosure. Knowing certainly entails cognition, but it is also profoundly experiential and performative, involving the making of one's own world. The genuine person must "realize" the world in order to "know" it. This integration of *zhen* cancels the familiar dichotomies of knower and known, and knowledge and experience. *Zhen* is *how* the world (cognition),但也是深刻的体验和履行,它创造着一个人自己的世界。真人为了"认识"(know)世界,必须"体认、实现"(realize)世界。"真"的这种整合取消了认知者与被认知者、知识与经验的分野。"真"作为世界被体验的方式,只是派生出这样的意义:世界是什么。"真"描绘了一个人所作出的、对其周围社群的真正的适应。"真"的同根词"慎"表示人们在其态度中所显示的谨慎和敏感。"真"的另外一些同根词,如"缜",意为"稠密、密集、紧密"。还有另外一些同根词,如"填",意为"塞住、堵住"。宽泛地讲,〔这些字的〕内含的意思似乎是充实、丰富,既不能增添,也不能减少,这种充实、丰富本身就是充裕的。

然而,仍然需要进一步加工。当我们说"自然"(意思是"自己的样子"或"自我展示")时,我们必须记住,自我在语境中总是一个能动的存在区域中的特殊的焦点,而这种焦点与存在的全部后果相联系,并且最终在其自身中反映了这全部后果。就像处于持续流淌过程中的一股特殊流体那样,真人与他周围

is experienced, and only derivitively *what* the world is. *Zhen* describes the *true* accommodation one makes to one's environing community. A cognate of *zhen* 真 that suggests care and sensitivity in the posture one strikes is *shen* 慎 "to be cautious and circumspect." Other cognates of *zhen* such as 缜 mean "dense, compact." Yet others such as *tian* 填 mean "to stop up, to plug." Broadly, the underlying idea would seem to suggest a kind of fullness that can neither be added to nor diminished, a fullness that in itself is ample.

However, there is need for even further refinement. When we say *ziran* 自然, meaning "self-so-ing" or "self-disclosing," we must bear in mind that self is always in context, a particular focus in a dynamic field of existence that is continuous with and ultimately reflects in itself the full consequence of existence. As a particular current in an ongoing fluid process, the genuine person has a synergistic interdependence with all of his environing conditions. Disclosure for self and context is mutually entailing.

Full disclosure of a particular person in coordination with his environing others is the ground for optimum creativity. This creativity can be compromised, however, by attempting to express one's individuality in disintegrative ways. One must not fail to accommodate the interdependence of things. This limitation on creativity can emerge either by forcing one's environment into fixed conceptual structures, thereby impoverishing context in service

的整个环境处于一种相互协同促进、相互依赖的关系之中。自我与环境的展示是相互涵衍的。

一个特定的个人在与其周围的人们的协作中充分地展示，是最大程度发挥创造力的基础。然而，由于企图以分裂的方式表达一个人的个体性，这种创造力就可能受到损害，人们决不能不适应事物的相互依赖的关系。对创造力的这种损害可能会出现于以下两种情况之下：或者是由于强使人们的环境变为固定的概念结构，而使环境在服务于自我时变得贫乏；或者是由于完全让环境塑造自己，而不贡献自己的独特性，因而在自我服务于环境时变得贫乏。为了能够被充分地整合，人们必须对正在出现的存在秩序亲身地、创造性地作出贡献，以培育与其环境的最密切的血肉联系。在一个人保持其作为一贯的特性的诚时，任何分立、分离的意识都需要加以克服。

就像我们在前面所看到的，在中国古典传统中，我们可以将那种规定成圣事业之不同方面的一系列术语析离出来，所有这些术语用以表示某人的自我向外扩展的不同阶

to self, or by allowing oneself to be shaped wholly by context without contributing one's own uniqueness, thereby impoverishing self in service to context. In order to be fully integrative, one must cultivate an optimum continuity with one's context by contributing personally and creatively to the emerging order of existence. While maintaining one's full integrity as an insistent particular, any sense of discreteness or disjunction needs to be overcome.

As we have seen above, in the classical Confucian tradition, we can isolate a range of terms that identify different dimensions in the project of becoming a sage, all of which refer to different aspects of extending oneself outward from the "small person (*xiaoren* 小人)" to the "interpersonally achieved person (*renzhe* 仁者)" to the "sociopolitically exemplary person (*junzi* 君子)," and ultimately to the "cosmically sagacious person (*shengren* 聖人)." A comparable situation obtains in the Daoist texts, where the genuine person (*zhenren* 真人) is alternatively described as "the superlative person (*zhiren* 至人)," "the spiritual person (*shenren* 神人)," "the great person (*daren* 大人)," or "the intact person (*quanren* 全人)." As with the Confucian terminology, we find that these Daoist expressions converge in the meaning of "extension" and "integration." Such integration is effected largely through modes of communication such as language and ritual for the Confucian, and natural communion for the Daoist.

段,从"小人"到"仁者",再到"君子",最后到"圣人"。在道家经典中也有类似的情况,其中的"真人"又分别被描绘为"至人"、"神人"、"大人"或"全人"。就像儒家术语那样,我们发现,这些道家的语词会聚于"扩展"和"整合"的意义之中。这些整合对于儒家来说,主要是通过诸如语言和礼这样的交往方式实现的,而对于道家来说,则主要是通过自然的契合(natural communion)。

(《汉哲学思维的文化探源》,第171—173页)

道家并不拒绝社会。准确地说,他们拒绝的思想是:认为人类社会存在于真空之中,存在的全部过程能够归结为人的价值和目的。他们拒绝人类中心主义,他们以为这种人类中心主义隐含于儒家的宗教——人文主义之中。他们之所以拒绝它,是因为它赋予人在这个世界上的特殊地位,这种地位最终将使人类经验脱离作为一个整体的自然这样的环境。《庄子》将儒家的圣人有虞氏(即传说中的舜)与道家的泰氏("泰"部族的族长)加以对比:前者全神贯注

(*Thinking from the Han,* pp. 167-169)

The Daoists do not reject society. Rather they reject the notion that human society exists in a vacuum, and that the whole process of existence can be reduced to human values and purposes. They reject the authropocentrism they take to be implicit in Confucian religio-humanism because it gives the human being special status in the world, a status that ultimately decontextualizes the human experience from nature as a whole. The *Zhuangzi* contrasts the Confucian sage, Youyu (the legendary Shun), who is preoccupied with the human world, and the Daoist Tai (the patriarch of the "Ultimate" clan), who roams freely throughout the natural world unfettered by the limitations of purely human values and concerns:

> The House of Youyu is no match for the House of Tai. As for Youyu, he is still hangs onto his "humanity (*ren* 仁)" in order to intercept others, and he does indeed win them over, but he has never begun to venture out into what is not-human (*feiren* 非仁).As for Tai, he sleeps deeply and contentedly, and wakes up vacant, this time taking himself as a horse, and another taking himself as an ox. His awareness is sensitive and credible, and his potency (*de* 德) is utterly genuine (*zhen* 真). And he has never begun to entertain the

于人类世界，而后者自由自在地漫游于自然界之中，不受纯粹的人类的价值和关切的束缚：

> 有虞氏不及泰氏。有虞氏其犹藏仁以要人，亦得人矣，而未始出于非人。泰氏其卧徐徐，其觉于于。一以己为马，一以己为牛。其知情信，其德甚真，而未始入于非人。（《庄子·应帝王》）

在这一段文字中，儒家圣人没有出于非人，因为他一心一意、心无旁骛地投身于人的世界。对于道家来说，如果人们将其关心的焦点限于纯粹的人的事情，那么，存在就贫乏了。道家的族长（按：指泰氏）自由自在地遍游整个世界，没有人与非人的分野。如果一个人目光短浅地将"常道"当成"人道"，那么他必定要在说明预设观念的忙乱中体验世界。如《庄子》所劝诫：

> 古之真人，不知说生，不知恶死。其出不䜣，其入不距。翛然而往，翛然而来而已矣。不忘其所始，不求其所

idea of "the non-human."

In this passage, the Confucian sage does not venture out into what is non-human because of his exclusive commitment to the human world. For the Daoist, existence is impoverished when one limits the focus of one's concerns to purely human matters. The Daoist patriarch moves freely throughout a world without such human and nonhuman boundaries. If one reads "constant *dao*" (*changdao* 常道) myopically as "the human *dao*" (*rendao* 人道), one is bound to experience the world through a welter of delimiting presuppositions. As the *Zhuangzi* enjoins,

> The genuine persons(*zhenren* 真人) of antiquity did not know to be pleased at being alive nor to dislike the prospect of dying. They embarked on life without rejoicing, and passed on without resistance. In a flash they came, in a flash they went, and that was all. They did not forget where it began nor seek after where it would end. On receiving life they were glad; forgetting about it, they gave it back. This is what is meant by: "Neither harm *dao* with the heart-and-mind nor help nature (*tian* 天) with what is human."

On the basis of this passage and others like it, one might want to argue that the Daoist

修养论

终。受而喜之，忘而复之，是之谓不以心损（捐）道，不以人助天。是之谓真人。（《庄子·大宗师》）

根据这一段话以及与之相似的别的文字，人们可能会提出，道家确实在事实上主张人与非人的区分，推崇自然的方面，排斥人的方面。就像荀子对庄子的批判："蔽于天而不知人。"这似乎是《庄子·秋水》表达的旨意：

> 天在内，人在外，德在乎天。知乎人之行，本乎天，位乎得……无以人灭天，无以故灭命，无以得殉名。谨守而勿失，是谓反其真。

然而如果我们想要给《庄子》下一个最后的论断，我们就必须说，这本著作确认了"人与非人"之别的问题框架〔在庄子思想中〕的地位，我们还要说，其恢复自然的地位这一弥补性的努力，不应被看作是以舍弃人的方面为代价来主张自然的方面。

（《汉哲学思维的文化探源》，第 178—179 页）

does in fact allow for the distinction between the human and the nonhuman by siding with the natural against the human. This is certainly Xunzi's criticism of Zhuangzi: "Being blinded by nature (*tian*), he does not know the human experience." This would also seem to be the message in the "Autumn Floods" chapter of *Zhuangzi*:

> The natural (*tian*) resides within, the human resides without, and potency (*de* 德) resides in what is natural. Being aware of the workings of nature and the human, root yourself in the natural and take up a place with potency.... Don't destroy the natural with the human; don't destroy possibilities (*ming* 命) with preconceived ideas; don't chase after fame with your potency. Guarding it carefully, don't lose it—this is what is meant by "returning to the genuine (*zhen* 真)."

But if we want to give the *Zhuangzi* its best argument, we have to allow that the text acknowledges the problematic status of this "human/nonhuman" distinction, and that its compensatory efforts to reinstate the natural should not be read as an advocacy of the natural at the expense of the human.

(*Thinking from the Han,* pp. 174-176)

参考书目

1. 《通过孔子而思》,[美]郝大维、安乐哲著,何金俐译,北京:北京大学出版社,2005年。

   Thinking Through Confucius. David L. Hall and Roger T. Ames. Albany: State University of New York Press, 1987.

2. 《孙子兵法:汉英对照》,[春秋]孙武著,李零今译,[美]安乐哲英译,北京:中华书局,2012年。

   SUN-TZU: The Art of Warfare. Translated, with an introduction and commentary, by Roger T. Ames. New York: Ballantine Books, 1993.

3. 《中国古代的统治艺术:〈淮南子·主术〉研究》,[美]安乐哲著,滕复译,南京:江苏凤凰文艺出版社,2018年。

   The Art of Rulership: A Study of Ancient Chinese Political Thought. Roger T. Ames. Albany:State University of New York Press, 1994.

4. 《期望中国:对中西文化的哲学思考》,[美]郝大维、安乐哲著,施忠连等译,上海:学林出版社,2005年。

   Anticipating China: Thinking through the Narratives of Chinese and Western Culture. David L. Hall and Roger T. Ames. Albany: State University of New York Press, 1995.

5. 《汉哲学思维的文化探源》,[美]郝大维、安乐哲著,施忠连译,南京:江苏人民出版社,1999年。

   Thinking from the Han: Self, Truth, and Transcendence in Chinese and Western

Culture. David L. Hall and Roger T. Ames. Albany: State University of New York Press, 1998.

6. 《〈论语〉的哲学诠释：比较哲学的视域》，[美]安乐哲、罗思文著，余瑾译，北京：中国社会科学出版社，2003年。

 The Analects of Confucius: A Philosophical Translation. Roger T. Ames and Henry Rosemont, Jr. New York: Ballantine Books, 1998.

7. 《切中伦常：〈中庸〉的新诠与新译》，[美]安乐哲、郝大维著，彭国翔译，北京：中国社会科学出版社，2011年。

 Focusing the Familiar: A Translation and Philosophical Interpretation of the Zhongyong. Roger T. Ames and David L. Hall. Honolulu:University of Hawaii Press, 2001.

8. 《道不远人：比较哲学视域中的〈老子〉》，[美]安乐哲、郝大维著，何金俐译，北京：学苑出版社，2004年。

 Daodejing: "Making This Life Significant": A Philosophical Translation. Roger T. Ames and David L.Hall. New York:Ballantine Books, 2003.

9. 《生民之本：〈孝经〉的哲学诠释及英译》，[美]罗思文、安乐哲著，何金俐译，北京：北京大学出版社，2010年。

 The Chinese Classic of Family Reverence: A Philosophical Translation of the Xiaojing. Henry Rosemont, Jr., and Roger T. Ames. Honolulu: University of Hawaii Press, 2009.

10. 《儒家角色伦理学：一套特色伦理学词汇》，[美]安乐哲著，[美]孟巍隆译，济南：山东人民出版社，2017年。

 Confucian Role Ethics: A Vocabulary. Roger T. Ames. Hong Kong: The Chinese University Press & Honolulu: University of Hawaii Press, 2011.